Dynamics of Contention

Dissatisfied with the compartmentalization of studies concerning strikes, wars, revolutions, social movements, and other forms of political struggle, McAdam, Tarrow, and Tilly identify causal mechanisms and processes that recur across a wide range of contentious politics. Critical of the static, single-actor models (including their own) that have prevailed in the field, they shift the focus of analysis to dynamic interaction. Doubtful that large, complex series of events such as revolutions and social movements conform to general laws, they break events into smaller episodes, then identify recurrent mechanisms and processes within them. *Dynamics of Contention* examines and compares eighteen contentious episodes drawn from many different parts of the world since the French Revolution, probing them for consequential and widely applicable mechanisms, for example, brokerage, category formation, and elite defection. The episodes range from nineteenth-century nationalist movements to contemporary Muslim–Hindu conflict to the Tiananmen crisis of 1989 to disintegration of the Soviet Union. The authors spell out the implications of their approach for explanation of revolutions, nationalism, and democratization, then lay out a more general program for study of contentious episodes wherever and whenever they occur.

Doug McAdam is Professor of Sociology at Stanford University and Director Designate of the Center for Advanced Study in the Behavioral Sciences. His previous books include *Political Process and the Development of Black Insurgency, 1930–1970* (1982, 1999) and *Freedom Summer* (1988), which shared the 1990 C. Wright Mills Award and for which he received a Guggenheim Fellowship to support research.

Sidney Tarrow received his Ph.D. at the University of California at Berkeley in 1965, where he studied comparative politics and did the research for his first book, *Peasant Communism in Southern Italy* (1967). He taught at Yale and Cornell before becoming Maxwell Upson Professor of Government (and then also of Sociology) at Cornell. He specializes in European politics and social movements and recently (with Doug Imig) has completed a collective volume entitled *Contentious Europeans*.

Charles Tilly (Ph.D. in Social Relations, Harvard, 1958) is Joseph L. Buttenwieser Professor of Social Science at Columbia University. His recent books include *European Revolutions* (1993), *Popular Contention in Great Britain* (1995), and *Durable Inequality* (1998), for which he received the 2000 Distinguished Scholarly Publication Award from the American Sociological Association.

Cambridge Studies in Contentious Politics

Ronald Aminzade et al., *Silence and Voice in the Study of Contentious Politics*
Doug McAdam, Sidney Tarrow, and Charles Tilly, *Dynamics of Contention*

Dynamics of Contention

DOUG MCADAM

Stanford University

SIDNEY TARROW

Cornell University

CHARLES TILLY

Columbia University

CAMBRIDGE
UNIVERSITY PRESS

CAMBRIDGE UNIVERSITY PRESS
Cambridge, New York, Melbourne, Madrid, Cape Town, Singapore,
São Paulo, Delhi, Dubai, Tokyo

Cambridge University Press
32 Avenue of the Americas, New York, NY 10013-2473, USA

www.cambridge.org
Information on this title: www.cambridge.org/9780521011877

First published 2001
Reprinted 2003, 2004, 2007, 2008

A catalog record for this publication is available from the British Library

Library of Congress Cataloging in Publication data

McAdam, Doug.
Dynamics of contention / Doug McAdam, Sidney Tarrow, Charles Tilly.
p. cm.
Includes bibliographical references and index.
ISBN 0-521-80588-0 – ISBN 0-521-011887-6 (pb.)
1. Collective behavior. 2. Social movements. 3. Revolutions. 4. Democratization.
I. Tarrow, Sidney G. II. Tilly, Charles. III. Title.
HM866.M23 2001
303.48'4 – dc21 2001016172

ISBN 978-0-521-80588-9 Hardback
ISBN 978-0-521-01187-7 Paperback

Transferred to digital printing 2010

To the CASBS staff,
for their unique combination of wisdom,
tolerance, and effectiveness.

Contents

List of Figures and Tables

Preface and Acknowledgments

Our enterprise began with a failed coup. In 1995, friends, students, and collaborators of Chuck Tilly organized a gathering in Amsterdam that was supposed to ease Tilly into retirement. He failed to get the message. As second best, McAdam and Tarrow decided to divert Tilly temporarily from his other projects into one that would minimize the evils he might otherwise inflict on the world. This book is the result.

Uncertain of their ability to coerce Tilly into compliance with their schemes, the two conspirators plotted to expand their cabal. Wouldn't it be great, they mused, if scholars from the related fields of social movements, revolutions, nationalism, and democratization could find a venue in which to explore the possibilities for synthesis across these nominally distinct subfields? That conversation led to a proposal to the Center for Advanced Study in the Behavioral Sciences for a one-year Special Project to be devoted to the kind of exploration and synthesis they had in mind. After enlisting Tilly as co-conspirator, a proposal was drafted, ably vetted by Phil Converse and Bob Scott (then Director and Associate Director of the Center), and approved by both the Center's Advisory Committee on Special Projects and its Board of Trustees. The plot had thickened!

Once the Special Project began, our broader enterprise took a fateful turn. Realizing faster than we did how excessive were our aims, Bob Scott encouraged us to seek support that would allow us to stretch the project over a longer time frame. At his suggestion, we made application in 1995 to the Mellon Foundation's Sawyer Seminar Series, seeking support for a three-year seminar series organized around the broad topic of Contentious Politics. To our delight and surprise, Mellon granted our request. Our thanks go to Harriet Zuckerman for the vision – and the patience – to have encouraged this unusual variation on the Sawyer Seminar format and to

Neil Smelser (Phil's successor as Center Director) and Bob for agreeing to host it at the Center. We also thank the Center staff for their patience and good humor as they faced the onslaughts of the "contentious crowd" over the years of our association.

But we now faced a new challenge: finding the right core faculty around whom to build that conversation. We were fortunate to attract four colleagues who joined us in founding what came to be called the "Invisible College of Contentious Politics". With Ron Aminzade, Jack Goldstone, Liz Perry, and Bill Sewell, we worked as a team for three years to fashion a more interactive approach to contentious politics. One fruit of that effort appears in a companion volume to this one, *Silence and Voice in the Study of Contentious Politics*. Others, we hope, will soon join the first two volumes. Our own book profited tremendously from interaction with these friends and colleagues and we thank them warmly.

Our debts go beyond the core faculty of the Contentious Politics group. Though neither the Center nor our Mellon sponsors required us to do so, the seven of us agreed immediately to involve graduate students – and not just our own – in the project. Who better to offer fresh perspectives on important topics than promising young scholars not wedded to disciplinary boundaries or subfield conventions? To the five voices of that first graduate cohort in 1996–1997 – Lissa Bell, Pamela Burke, Robyn Eckhardt, John Glenn, and Joseph Luders – were added nine others over the next two years: Jorge Cadena-Roa, David Cunningham, Manali Desai, Debbie Gould, Hyojoung Kim, Heidi Swarts, Nella Van Dyke, Heather Williams, and Kim Williams. They not only helped to enrich the larger project but also made more contributions to *Dynamics of Contention* than they can know. We thank them warmly and hope that their association with us was as rewarding for them as it has been to us.

Still others helped. In each of the Mellon project's three years the seven core faculty members and their junior associates organized three small conferences, each focused on a specific topic relevant to a general understanding of contention. Among the topics explored were religion and contention, emotion and contention, the globalization of contention, identity and networks in contention. Each of these conferences featured participation by two or three invited experts. We owe thanks to Mark Beissinger, Craig Calhoun, Bill Gamson, Jeff Goodwin, Roger Gould, Susan Harding, Michael Hechter, Lynn Hunt, Jane Jenson, Arthur Kleinman, Hanspeter Kriesi, Marc Lichbach, John Meyer, Ann Mische, Aldon Morris, Maryjane Osa, Gay Seidman, Kathryn Sikkink, Verta

Taylor, Mark Traugott, Paul Wapner, and Tim Wickham-Crowley for their collaboration.

Our debts go even further. During year three of the project, while we were in residence at the Center, our colleague Ron Aminzade joined us in organizing a general seminar on the topic of contentious politics for interested Center Fellows. We were lucky to enjoy the participation in this seminar of an unusually large and talented group of our fellow Fellows. These included: Jerry Davis, Jane Mansbridge, Rob Sampson, Carol Swain, Ed Tiryakian, and Katherine Verdery. We thank them for their willingness to take part in our sometimes contentious conversations.

Away from the Center, we had to defend what we had learned to the many experts who helped us on our paths to some knowledge of their areas. They will have to judge whether we have expanded their knowledge as well as our own. We received precious advice, criticism, information, and technical assistance from Paloma Aguilar Fernández, Benedict Anderson, Ron Aminzade, Ramón Adell Argilés, Mark Beissinger, Richard Bensel, Valerie Bunce, Jorge Cadena-Roa, Lars-Erik Cederman, Ruth Collier, Maria Cook, Donatella della Porta, Rita di Leo, Rafael Durán Muñoz, Neil Fligstein, Jonathan Fox, Carmenza Gallo, Miriam Golden, Jack Goldstone, Roger Gould, Davydd Greenwood, Ernst Haas, Judy Hellman, Steven Kaplan, Peter Katzenstein, Mark Kesselman, Bert Klandermans, Gerry van Klinken, Ruud Koopmans, Hanspeter Kriesi, Hyeok Kwon, David Laitin, Peter Lange, Vina Lanzona, Marc Lerner, Mark Lichbach, James Mahoney, David S. Meyer, Jose Ramón Montero, Reynaldo Yunuen Ortega Ortiz, Elizabeth Perry, Hayagreeva Rao, William Roy, Hector Schamis, Cathy Schneider, Jane Schneider, Peter Schneider, William H. Sewell Jr., Vivienne Shue, Jack Snyder, Bö Strath, Yang Su, Andrew Walder, Elisabeth Wood, Barry Weingast, Thomas Weskopp, Viviana Zelizer, and members of the Columbia University Workshop on Contentious Politics.

As our project drew to a close, the Center for Advanced Study in the Behavioral Sciences offered still another opportunity to refine our work. A Summer Institute with twenty lively young scholars pitted their own intellectual steeds against our manuscript in the summer of 2000, with McAdam and Tilly in the saddle and Tarrow briefly running alongside. Enthusiastic thanks to Kenneth Andrews, Joe Bandy, Neal Carter, David Cunningham, Christian Davenport, Bob Edwards, Gautam Ghosh, John Guidry, Frederick Harris, Peter Houtzager, Jason Kaufman, Deborah

Martin, Byron Miller, S. Mara Pérez-Godoy, Kurt Schock, Paul Silverstein, Jackie Smith, David Stone, and Deborah Yashar for thoughtful, probing comments on our book.

All books are learning experiences as well as attempts to communicate knowledge to others. Writing this one – perhaps more than most – was an intense learning experience. This was the case for three reasons. First, our program called for analysis of many episodes that lay outside our previous areas of geographical and historical expertise. Second, the program demanded constant learning in the course of assembling our materials. For if – as we will maintain in what follows – the same processes and mechanisms of contention recur across wide bands of territory and different forms of contention, what we learned from one episode could not be neatly partitioned off from the others. Each foray into new territory caused a return to familiar terrain for new interrogation of once-comfortable understandings. Third, because no single one of us possessed sufficient authority to exercise a veto power over the others ("Just let him try!"), discussions over content and interpretation were vigorous – often contentious. Our working sessions proceeded like rotating seminars, with roles of teacher, student, and kibbitzer revolving dizzily around the table.

Where does the resulting book fit into the rapidly expanding field of contentious politics and into social science as a whole? Like other scholars and teachers, in our book we work through incessant dialogue with previous ideas and findings, including our own. Hardly a paragraph has taken shape without reflection or debate on the relation between what the paragraph says and earlier work: This confirms X, that contradicts Y, Z made the same point somewhat differently, and so on. The book's first two chapters identify scholarly literatures on which we have drawn extensively, but they do not pinpoint the book's location with respect to other writings. Earlier versions included much more painstaking specifications of origins for particular ideas, disagreements with competing accounts, and identifications of work that paralleled our own. Spurred by complaints from readers of those earlier drafts, we recognized that such references to relevant work were obscuring our arguments while producing a lengthy, ponderous tome.

In rewriting, we eliminated almost all detailed discussions of previous work. In general, we restricted explicit mentions of other authors to distinctive ideas and findings on which our arguments directly depend. Specialists in the various fields the book traverses may sometimes feel that we have given insufficient credit to relevant work by others or insufficient attention to contrary views. On balance, nevertheless, we think that most readers will gain from considering our analyses without being distracted by ostentatious finger-pointing toward adjacent literatures.

We hope that the resulting sparseness of references to other people's analyses will not suggest disdain for the ideas and efforts of our respected colleagues. We have not hesitated to relate our arguments to other work on contentious politics in separate publications, both joint and individual (see e.g., McAdam, Tarrow, and Tilly 1997; McAdam 1999; Tarrow 1998; Tilly 2001). It will soon become clear, in any case, how much this book depends on dialogue and respectful engagement with recent investigations of contentious politics.

Students of contentious politics may want to decide where we stand on current controversies among structuralists, culturalists, and rationalists. If they look for evidence of the kind of paradigm warfare that often rages across the pages of learned journals, they will be disappointed. If our frankly syncretic view has a label, it would have to be "relational." While acknowledging the crucial contributions of rationalists, culturalists, and structuralists, we think the area of contentious politics will profit most from systematic attention to interaction among actors, institutions, and streams of contentious politics. Our program starts from this perspective to explore a variety of areas of contention using the comparative analysis of mechanisms and processes to do so.

How should students of contentious politics who find the book's program attractive proceed? Plenty of previous analyses actually identify robust causal mechanisms and use them to explain salient features of contentious episodes. Such analyses should continue to provide practical models for future work. Many of the questions, and some of the answers, posed by analysts in what we distinguish roughly as structuralist, culturalist, and rationalist approaches remain important guides for the next round of inquiry. Instead of burning their manuals and junking their toolboxes, we hope that skilled users of existing intellectual tools will invent new ways of wielding them. We hope they will attempt seriously to refute, challenge, modify, extend – now and then, even verify – our book's arguments.

Ithaca, New York
September 23, 2000

Abbreviations

ANC	African National Congress
BANAMERICA	Bank of America (*Banco de América*)
BANDILA	The Nation United in Spirit and Mission (*Bayan Nakiisa so Diwa at Layunin*)
BANIC	Nicaraguan Bank (*Banco Nicaragüense*)
BAYAN	The New Nationalist Alliance (*Bagong Alyansa Makabayan*)
BC	Black Consciousness
BCCs	Basic Christian Communities
BISIG	The Federation for the Advancement of Socialist Thought and Praxis (*Bukluraan para sa Ikauunlad ng Sosyalistang Isip at Gawa*)
BJP	Bharatiya Janata Party
CBCP	Catholic Bishop's Conference of the Philippines
CC.OO	Workers' Commissions (*Comisones Obreras*)
CCP	Chinese Communist Party
CCTV	Chinese Central Television
CEOE	Confederation of Spanish Employers' Organizations (*Confederación Español de Organizaciones Empresariales*)
COSATU	Congress of South African Trade Unions
COSIP	(Later COSEP) Higher Council of Private Enterprise (*Consejo Superior de Iniciativa Privada*)
CORE	Congress of Racial Equality
CPP	Communist Party of the Philippines
CSCE	Commission on Security and Cooperation in Europe
EATUC	East Africa Trades Union Congress

ETA	Basque Homeland and Freedom (*Euzkadi Ta Azkatasuna*)
FAT	Autonomous Workers' Federation (*Federación Autonoma de Trabajo*)
FRAP	Anti-fascist Revolutionary Patriotic Front (*Frente Revolucionario Antifascista Patriótico*)
FSLN	Sandinista National Liberation Front (*Frente Sandinista de Liberación Nacional*)
IMF	International Monetary Fund
INDE	Nicaraguan Development Institute (*Instituto Nicaraguense de Desarrollo*)
INMECAFÉ	Mexican Coffee Institute (*Instituto Mexicano de Café*)
JAJA	Justice for Aquino, Justice for All
JOC	Young Catholic Workers (*Juventudes Obreras Católicas*)
KASAMA	The Federation of People's Organizations (*Kalipunan ng mga Samaban ng Mamamayan*)
KAU	Kenyan African Union
KCA	Kikuyu Central Association
MIA	Montgomery Improvement Association
MIL	Iberian Liberation Movement (*Movimiento Ibérico de Liberación*)
NAACP	National Association for the Advancement of Colored People
NAFTA	North American Free Trade Agreement
NAMFREL	National Movement for Free Elections
NPA	New People's Army
OAS	Organization of American States
PAN	National Action Party (*Partido de Acción Nacional*)
PBSP	Philippine Business for Social Progress
PCE	Spanish Communist Party (*Partido Comunista Español*)
PCI	Italian Communist Party (*Partito Comunista Italiano*)
PKI	Indonesian Communist Party (*Partai Komunis Indonesia*)
PLN	National Liberation Party (*Partido de Liberación Nacional*)
PRC	People's Republic of China
PRI	Institutional Revolutionary Party (*Partido Revolucionario Institucional*)

PRD	Party of the Democratic Revolution (*Partido de la Revolución Democrática*)
PRONASOL	National Solidarity Program (*Programa Nacional de Solidaridad*)
PSOE	Spanish Socialist Workers' Party (*Partido Socialista Obrero Español*)
SCLC	Southern Christian Leadership Conference
SNCC	Student Non-violent Coordinating Committee
UCD	Union of the Democratic Center (*Unión de Centro Democrático*)
UDEL	Union of Democratic Liberation (*Unión Democrática de Liberación*)
UDF	United Democratic Front
UGT	General Workers' Union (*Unión General de Trabajadores*)
UMALUN	Alliance of the Urban Poor (*Ugnayan ng mg Maralita taga Lunsod*)
USSR	Union of Soviet Socialist Republics
VHP	World Hindu Council (*Vishwa Hindu Parishad*)

PART ONE

What's the Problem?

1

What Are They Shouting About?

"On thinking of the events that have happened since the beginning of the week," confided Parisian bookseller Siméon-Prosper Hardy to his journal on July 17, 1789, "it is hard to recover from one's astonishment" (BN Fr 6687 [Bibliothèque Nationale, Paris, Fonds Français, no. 6687]). It had, indeed, been quite a week in Paris; that week's pages of Hardy's neatly penned journal contain extraordinarily vivid portraits of contentious politics. No such tumults had shaken Paris since the Fronde of 1648–1653. From the time when the Third Estate's representatives to the Estates General in Versailles declared themselves a national assembly on June 17, detachments of royal troops had been gathering around the Paris region. On several occasions, however, whole companies had refused to use their arms against civilians or had even joined in popular attacks on troops that remained loyal to the king. By early July, signs of great division were appearing within the regime.

When the king dismissed popular finance minister Jacques Necker on July 11, mass marches and gatherings began to overflow Parisian streets. That night people sacked tollgates on the city's perimeter, then danced around the ruins. During the next few days, electoral assemblies, their provisional committees, and their hastily formed militias began running much of Paris. Meanwhile, bands of Parisians broke into prisons and other public buildings, freeing prisoners, seizing arms, and taking away provender stored within.

On the 14th of July, searches for weapons continued. According to Hardy's account:

> People went to the castle of the Bastille to call the governor, the marquis Delaunay, to hand over the weapons and ammunition he had; on his refusal, workers of

> the faubourg St. Antoine tried to besiege the castle. First the governor had his men fire on the people all along the rue St. Antoine, while making a white flag first appear and then disappear, as if he meant to give in, but increasing the fire of his cannon. On the side of the two drawbridges that open onto the first courtyard, having pretended to accept the call for arms, he had the gate of the small drawbridge opened and let in a number of the people who were there. But when the gate was closed and the drawbridge raised, he had everyone in the courtyard shot, including three of the city's electors . . . who had come to bargain with him. Then the civic militia, indignant over such barbarous treatment of fellow citizens, and backed by grenadiers of the French guard . . . accomplished the capture of the castle in less than three hours. [BN Fr 6687; for a more detailed and accurate account, see Godechot 1965]

During that day Parisians killed not only the Bastille's governor but also the Arsenal's powder-keeper, two veterans of the Invalides who had fired on invaders there, and the chairman of the city's Permanent Committee. Over the next few days, delegations from many parts of the region, including members of the National Assembly and dissident royal troops, ceremoniously committed themselves to the Parisian cause. On the sixteenth and seventeenth, the king himself recalled Necker, withdrew troops from the region, and, on foot amid deputies and militiamen, made a symbolically charged pilgrimage to the Parisian Hôtel de Ville. The threatened king had another thirty-odd months to live, most of them as nominal head of state. Yet by July 16, 1789, France entered a long and tortuous period of contentious politics.

Contentious Politics

To call the events of 1789 "contentious politics" may seem to demean a great revolution. This book aims to demonstrate that the label "contentious politics" not only makes sense but also helps explain what happened in Paris and the rest of France during that turbulent summer. The book before you also examines the relations between two variants of contention – contained and transgressive – as they intersect in major episodes of struggle. Further, it shows how different forms of contention – social movements, revolutions, strike waves, nationalism, democratization, and more – result from similar mechanisms and processes. It wagers that we can learn more about all of them by comparing their dynamics than by looking at each on its own. Finally, it explores several combinations of mechanisms and processes with the aim of discovering recurring causal sequences of contentious politics.

What Are They Shouting About?

By contentious politics we mean:

> episodic, public, collective interaction among makers of claims and their objects when (a) at least one government is a claimant, an object of claims, or a party to the claims and (b) the claims would, if realized, affect the interests of at least one of the claimants.

Roughly translated, the definition refers to collective political struggle.

Of course, each term in such a definition cries out for further stipulations. The term "episodic," for example, excludes regularly scheduled events such as votes, parliamentary elections, and associational meetings – although any such event can become a springboard for contentious politics. Again, we take "public" to exclude claim making that occurs entirely within well-bounded organizations, including churches and firms. Despite obvious parallels between some struggles occurring inside and outside these boundaries, we concentrate here on those having manifestly political ramifications.

Nevertheless, we can hear the objections: Doesn't this definition demarcate an impossibly broad field of study? And what of politics within institutions that break out of the boundaries of their rules or make claims that challenge existing norms and expectations? Let us take up these objections in turn.

Is all of politics contentious? According to a strict reading of our definition, certainly not. Much of politics – the majority, we would guess – consists of ceremony, consultation, bureaucratic process, collection of information, registration of events, and the like. Reporting for military service, registering to vote, paying taxes, attending associational meetings, implementing policies, enforcing laws, performing administrative work, reading newspapers, asking officials for favors, and similar actions constitute the bulk of political life; they usually involve little if any collective contention. Much of politics takes place in the internal social relations of a party, bureau, faction, union, community, or interest group and involves no collective public struggle whatsoever. The *contentious* politics that concerns us is episodic rather than continuous, occurs in public, involves interaction between makers of claims and others, is recognized by those others as bearing on their interests, and brings in government as mediator, target, or claimant.

What about definitional breadth and contention within institutions? Is this subset of politics still too sprawling and amorphous to constitute a coherent field of inquiry? We are betting against that supposition. Let us put the matter starkly. The official inquiry and later impeachment proceedings against Richard Nixon belong within the same definitional universe as the so-called Mau Mau rebellion of Kenya in the 1950s. Both qualify, in our terms, as *episodes of contention*. Such episodes constitute the terrain of our investigations.

We do not claim that these episodes are identical, nor that they conform to a single general model. They obviously differ in a host of consequential ways. Yet we group them under the same definition for two reasons. First, the study of political contention has grown too narrow, spawning a host of distinct topical literatures – revolutions, social movements, industrial conflict, war, interest group politics, nationalism, democratization – dealing with similar phenomena by means of different vocabularies, techniques, and models. This book deliberately breaches such boundaries in a search for parallels across nominally different forms of contention. It searches for similar causal mechanisms and processes in a wide variety of struggles.

Second, we challenge the boundary between institutionalized and noninstitutionalized politics. The Nixon impeachment inquiry operated almost exclusively within legally prescribed, officially recognized processes for adjudicating such conflicts. Mau Mau did not. We recognize this difference. We will, indeed, soon use it to distinguish two broad categories of contention – contained and transgressive. But even as we employ the distinction, we insist that the study of politics has too long reified the boundary between official, prescribed politics and politics by other means. As an unfortunate consequence, analysts have neglected or misunderstood both the parallels and the interactions between the two.

Reification reached its peak in American social science during the 1950s and 1960s by creating a sharp disciplinary and conceptual distinction between conventional and unconventional politics. Political science claimed "normal" prescribed politics as its bailiwick, leaving social movements (in William Gamson's ironic phrase) to "the social psychologist whose intellectual tools prepare him to better understand the irrational" (Gamson 1990: 133). Sociologists claimed movements as their chosen terrain, frequently ignoring their complex relations to institutional politics. Over the past thirty years, this neat disciplinary division of labor has largely dissolved. Yet we are left with a language and a set of categories (revolution, social movement, interest groups, electoral politics, and so on) reproducing the original duality.

Boundaries between institutionalized and non-institutionalized politics are hard to draw with precision. More important, the two sorts of politics interact incessantly and involve similar causal processes. Coalitions, strategic interaction, and identity struggles occur widely in the politics of established institutions as well as in the disruptions of rebellions, strikes, and social movements. The underground war waged by Richard Nixon that resulted in the botched Watergate break-in and the resulting impeachment inquiry stemmed, in large part, from Nixon's hostility to the antiwar movement and other movements of the New Left. Similarly, Mau Mau had its origins, not in some spasm of anticolonial violence, but in a circumscribed conflict involving a set of four legally constituted political actors: Kenya's colonial authorities, British officials, Kenyan nationalists, and Kenya's white settler community. Virtually all broad social movements, revolutions, and similar phenomena grow from roots in less visible episodes of institutional contention. Excavating those roots is one of this book's central goals.

Contained and Transgressive Contention

We begin by dividing contentious politics into two broad subcategories: *contained* and *transgressive*. (We prefer this distinction to the more familiar one between "institutional" and "unconventional" politics because it allows us to emphasize transgression within institutions as well as the many routine activities of external challengers.)

Contained contention refers to those cases of contention in which all parties are previously established actors employing well established means of claim making. It consists of episodic, public, collective interaction among makers of claims and their objects when (a) at least one government is a claimant, an object of claims, or a party to the claims, (b) the claims would, if realized, affect the interests of at least one of the claimants, and (c) all parties to the conflict were previously established as constituted political actors.

Transgressive contention consists of episodic, public, collective interaction among makers of claims and their objects when (a) at least one government is a claimant, an object of claims, or a party to the claims, (b) the claims would, if realized, affect the interests of at least one of the claimants, (c) at least some parties to the conflict are newly self-identified political actors, and/or (d) at least some parties employ innovative collective action. (Action qualifies as innovative if it incorporates claims, selects objects of claims, includes collective self-representations, and/or adopts means that are either unprecedented or forbidden within the regime in question.)

This book's cases fall overwhelmingly on the transgressive side of the line: They usually involve either formation of new political actors, innovation with respect to new political means, or both. We deploy the distinction contained/transgressive for two reasons. First, many instances of transgressive contention grow out of existing episodes of contained contention; that interaction between the established and the new deserves explicit attention. Second, substantial short-term political and social change more often emerges from transgressive than from contained contention, which tends more often to reproduce existing regimes. Or so we argue.

For the sake of clarity, this book concentrates its attention on contentious episodes involving transgressive contention. We stress sorts of contention that are sporadic rather than continuous, bring new actors into play, and/or involve innovative claim making. For further simplification, our sustained examples come chiefly from episodes in which national states were direct participants or significant parties to the claims being made. This focus on national, as opposed to local or regional, contention springs primarily from practical concerns. Episodes of national contention more often produce the requisite volume of scholarly materials than do localized events. This does not mean, however, that our alternative analytic program applies only to periods of broad national contention. Suitably modified, it also applies to local, sectoral, international, and transnational contention.

Our strategy is to examine comparatively the causal processes discernible in fifteen major episodes of contention, and component mechanisms of those processes. We illustrate our approach to mechanisms and processes in this and the next chapter with respect to three such episodes – the French Revolution, American civil rights, and the Italian protest cycle – returning to them later in the book for the sake of their relative familiarity. In Chapter 3, we describe our strategy of paired comparison more fully. For now, suffice it to say that the strategy rests on detailed analyses of multiple episodes whose primary requirements were that (a) they involved substantially different varieties of contention within significantly different sorts of regimes, (b) they lent themselves to analytically valuable comparisons, and (c) there exist sufficient scholarly materials to make sense of the events in question.

Let us return to the distinction between continuous and episodic processes. Public politics can involve conflicting claims but proceed within incremental processes. The controversies over slavery we examine in Chapter 6, for example, were fought out largely within congressional debates through most of their forty-year history. Conversely, well-institutionalized forms of politics are often episodic, as when the Swiss doubled their electorate in 1971 by admitting women to the vote. The combination of conflicting claims and episodic action attracts most of our attention.

We emphasize that combination not because it is the only site worthy of interest but because it often:

- creates uncertainty, hence rethinking and the search for new working identities
- reveals fault lines, hence possible realignments in the body politic
- threatens and encourages challengers to take further contentious action
- forces elites to reconsider their commitments and allegiances, and
- leaves a residue of change in repertoires of contention, institutional practices and political identities in the name of which future generations will make their claims.

What's News?

This book identifies similarities and differences, pathways and trajectories across a wide range of contentious politics – not only revolutions, but also strike waves, wars, social movements, ethnic mobilizations, democratization, and nationalism. In recent years, specialized scholars have made substantial advances in describing and explaining each of these important contentious forms. On the whole, they have paid little attention to each other's discoveries. Students of strikes, for example, rarely draw on the burgeoning literature about ethnic mobilization. Students of ethnic mobilization return the compliment by ignoring analyses of strikes. Yet strong, if partial, parallels exist between strikes and ethnic mobilization, for example in the ways that actions of third parties affect their success or failure and in the impact of previously existing interpersonal networks on their patterns of recruitment.

Again, students of social movements, ethnic mobilization, religious conflict, worker-capitalist struggles, and nationalism have independently discovered the political salience of rituals in which adherents to one side or another publicly display symbols, numbers, commitment, and claims to disputed space. Yet these specialists hardly ever notice their neighbors' work, much less undertake systematic comparisons of rituals in different settings. A historian knowledgeably locates attacks on Muslims and Jews in the social structure of fourteenth century Aragon, for example, but draws no guidance whatsoever from anthropologists' and political scientists' contemporary studies of similar categorical violence (Nirenberg 1996; for missed parallels see, e.g., Brass 1996, Connor 1994, Daniel 1996, Roy 1994). Again, an anthropologist's richly documented study of parades and visual displays by Ulster activists draws extensively on anthropological and rhetorical theory, but quite ignores analogous performances elsewhere in the British Isles and Western Europe perceptively treated by geographers, political scientists, sociologists, and historians (Jarman 1997; for relevant studies see, e.g., Baer 1992; Brewer 1979–1980; Butsch 1995, 2000; Davis 1975; della Porta 1998; Fillieule 1997; Lindenberger 1995; Plotz 2000; Steinberg 1999).

Like many of its European counterparts, the Ulster study identifies a phenomenon that cuts across nominally different forms of politics. Observers tend to associate public displays of uniforms and other explicitly political symbols with government-prescribed politics, because of their frequent use by authorities to advertise state power. But similar displays of uniforms and symbols sometimes form crucial features of hotly fought contention. Indeed, parody of official ceremonies in forms such as hanging in effigy or coronation rituals often provides readily recognizable drama for dissidents. Under repressive regimes, authorized public ceremonies and holiday celebrations frequently provide occasions for making of claims, however fleeting, whose statement elsewhere would put the claimants at high risk to detection and punishment. Similarly protected times and spaces attract claim making over a wide variety of contention (Polletta 1999). Much of this book's effort goes into the identification of such parallels, connections, and variations.

From Polity Model to Dynamics of Contention

But that happens in later chapters. For now, we must ask how to identify actors in contentious politics, their claims, the objects of those claims, and responses to claim making. Of the many names in which people sometimes make claims, why do only a few typically prevail as public bases of contentious interaction in any given time and place? What governs the course and outcome of that interaction? Why and how do people move collectively between action and inaction? We adopt two initial simplifications in order to clarify connections between our analyses of contentious politics and studies of political life in general.

Our first simplification is to start from a static conception of political settings before moving to dynamic analyses. Figure 1.1 presents a simple static model of political settings in which contention occurs. Regimes, as schematized there, consist of governments and their relations to populations falling under their claimed jurisdictions (Finer 1997). Singling out constituted collective political actors (those that have names, internal organization, and repeated interactions with each other in the realm of public politics), we distinguish:

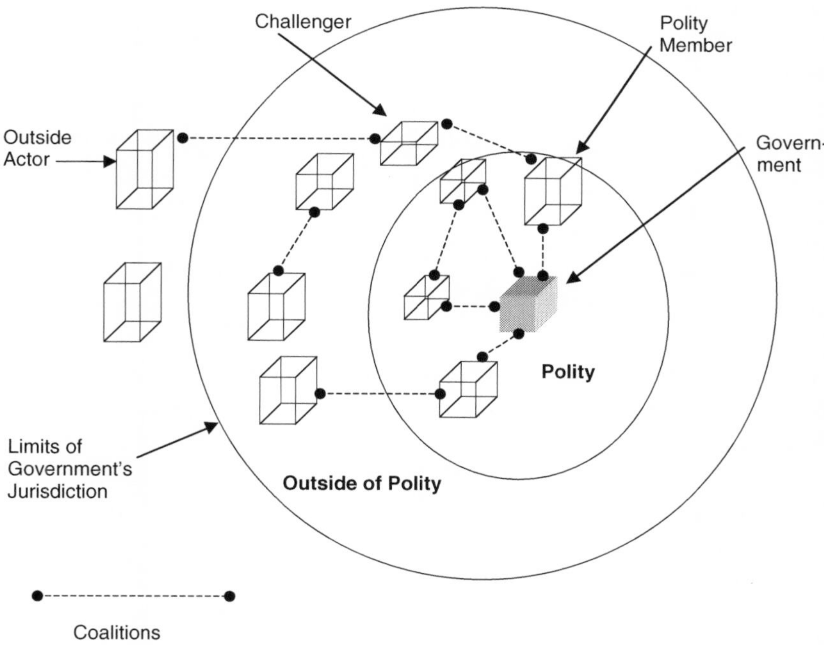

Figure 1.1. The Simple Polity Model

agents of government
polity members (constituted political actors enjoying routine access to government agents and resources)
challengers (constituted political actors lacking that routine access)
subjects (persons and groups not currently organized into constituted political actors), and
outside political actors, including other governments.

Public politics consists of claim making interactions among agents, polity members, challengers, and outside political actors. *Contentious* politics consists of that (large) subset in which the claims are collective and would, if realized, affect their objects' interests. *Transgressive* contention is present when at least some parties employ innovative collective action and/or at least some of them are newly self-identified political actors. To make such a model represent dynamic political processes effectively, we must put each of the actors into motion; allow for multiple governments and segments of government; show coalitions as subject to growth, decline, and incessant renegotiation; and represent construction, destruction, or transformation of political actors explicitly.

Our second simplification concerns political actors. We will soon discover that movements, identities, governments, revolutions, classes, and similar collective nouns do not represent hard, fixed, sharply bounded objects, but observers' abstractions from continuously negotiated interactions among persons and sets of persons. Since every person only displays a small portion of her wide-ranging physiological states, cognitive conditions, behaviors, and social connections in any particular situation, even persons are much less fixed and bounded than ordinary language suggests. Moreover, any particular person often plays parts within more than one political actor, sometimes participating as a worker, sometimes as member of a religious congregation, and so on. To get our analysis started, nevertheless, we assume that political actors consist of sets of persons and relations among persons whose internal organization and connections with other political actors maintain substantial continuity in time and space. Later we relax that confining assumption, examining ways that boundaries blur, organization changes, and political position shifts. Our serious effort in that direction begins in Part II.

How, then, shall we move from static to dynamic analysis? We must battle on two fronts at once: with respect to what we explain and to how we explain it. Social *processes*, in our view, consist of sequences and combinations of causal *mechanisms*. To explain contentious politics is to identify its recurrent causal mechanisms, the ways they combine, in what sequences they recur, and why different combinations and sequences, starting from different initial conditions, produce varying effects on the large scale. We begin in the next chapter with the familiar process of mobilization and its component mechanisms. We will quickly discover that mobilization is not an isolated process: It intersects with other mechanisms and processes – such as creation and transformation of actors, their certification or decertification, repression, radicalization, and the diffusion of contention to new sites and actors in complex trajectories of contention. Our book takes as its principal objects of explanation a range of dynamic processes. Instead of seeking to identify necessary and sufficient conditions for mobilization, action, or certain trajectories, we search out recurrent causal mechanisms and regularities in their concatenation.

This program is demanding. It obliges us to adopt some economizing devices:

First, we do not claim that we have information on all the world's politics. Instead, we sample from a reduced grid of regime characteristics derived from our mapping in Chapter 3.

Second, we do not give equal attention to all the reified forms of contention that are potentially comparable, concentrating instead on social movements, nationalism, revolutions, and democratization.

Third, we will consider ourselves successful if we are able to identify – instead of merely asserting – some specific mechanisms and processes that recur across contentious politics' many forms;

Fourth, we hope to start the process of explaining these specificities with respect to several partial sequences; but we will not complete it in this volume.

Covering Laws and Recurrent Causes

Our emphasis on recurring mechanisms and processes does not mean that we intend to pour all forms of contention into the same great mold, subjecting them to universal laws of contention and flattening them into a single two-dimensional caricature. On the contrary, we examine partial parallels in order to find widely operating explanatory mechanisms that combine differently and therefore produce different outcomes in one setting or another. To discover that third parties influence both strikes and ethnic mobilization by no means amounts to showing that the origins, trajectories, and outcomes of strikes and ethnic mobilization are the same, any more than identifying similarities in memory processes of mice and men proves mice and men to be identical in all regards. To discover mechanisms of competition and radicalization in both the French Revolution and in the South African freedom movement is not to say that the Jacobins and the African National Congress are the same. We pursue partial parallels in search of mechanisms that drive contention in different directions. Only then, and in Part III, do we examine how mechanisms combine in robust political processes.

We proceed through a series of paired comparisons. We call attention, for example, to similarities between the Mau Mau rebellion in Kenya and the Philippine Yellow revolution of 1986; in the mechanisms that drove Hindu–Muslim conflict in South Asia and South Africa's democratization in the 1990s; between the breakdown of the antebellum American polity in 1860 and the collapse of Franco's regime in Spain. We compare the unfolding of revolutionary situations with the expansion of social movements, episodes of democratization, and strike waves. At the same time, we identify historically specific features in different kinds of contentious politics, for example how the previous history of social movements in a given country shapes that country's next round of contention, and how its routine institutional processes intersect with sequences of contentious, episodic politics. Though we aim to go beyond that agenda and challenge it, we start from the bedrock of findings and approaches that developed out of the movements of the 1960s in Western Europe and the United States.

The Classic Social Movement Agenda

During the 1960s and 1970s, much of the best North American and European work concerning these questions concentrated on social movements, then assimilated other forms of contention to prevailing explanations of social movements. Attention focused on four key concepts: *political opportunities*, sometimes crystallized as static opportunity structures, sometimes as changing political environments; *mobilizing structures*, both formal movement organizations and the social networks of everyday life; *collective action frames*, both the cultural constants that orient participants and those they themselves construct; established *repertoires of contention*, and how these repertoires evolve in response to changes in capitalism, state building, and other, less monumental processes.

This line of thought grew from a quadruple critique of prior research traditions. First, social historians were launching what many of them called "history from below" as an intellectual rebellion against the emphasis on elites and high politics that prevailed in earlier historical writing. With their social science allies, many social historians sought to reconstruct political experiences of ordinary people, ground those experiences in routine social life, and challenge the dismissal of popular politics as irrational reactions to stress or temporary hardship. Second, in a similar vein many social scientists rejected the prevailing conception of mass movements and similar phenomena as collective behavior, as a confusion of common sense by fads, delusions, demagogues, and crowd influence. Third, the historians and social scientists in question combated official interpretations of civil rights activism, student movements, worker mobilization, and other popular politics of the 1960s as impulsive, irresponsible outbursts of self-indulgence. Fourth (and in partial reaction to the first three lines of thought), Mancur Olson (1965) and other rational action theorists countered simple assertions of rationality on the part of protesters. They made two telling observations about analysts of popular protest. Those analysts (a) had ignored the fact that many, perhaps most, sets of people who share a grievance or interest fail to act on it and (b) lacked a plausible theory of the conditions or process under which people who do share an interest organize and act on it.

One major form of these critiques soon took the name "resource mobilization," a term epitomized and publicized by the work of John McCarthy and Mayer Zald on American social movements and their organizations. Resource mobilization models emphasized the significance of organizational bases, resource accumulation, and collective coordination for popular political actors. They stressed similarities and convergences between social movements and interest group politics. Read twenty or thirty years later, early resource mobilization models exaggerate the centrality of deliberate strategic decisions to social movements. They downplay the contingency, emotionality, plasticity, and interactive character of movement politics. But at least they draw attention to the significance of organizational processes in popular politics.

Drawing precisely this element from resource mobilization thinking, a second current soon emerged within this stream of thought. "Political process" analysts moved away from their confreres by stressing dynamism, strategic interaction, and response to the political environment. (At different stages, all three authors of this book played parts in the development of political process thinking, as well as in the criticism of the simpler resource mobilization model.) Historical work on the political process produced investigations of the forms of claim making that people use in real-life situations – what has come to be called "the repertoire of contention." For political-process theorists, repertoires represent the culturally encoded ways in which people interact in contentious politics. They are invariably narrower than all of the hypothetical forms they might use or those that others in different circumstances or periods of history employ. More recently, scholars reacting to the structuralism of these earlier studies have drawn on social-psychological and cultural perspectives, adding a fourth component to studies of social movements: how social actors frame their claims, their opponents and their identities. They have argued cogently that framing is not simply an expression of preexisting group claims but an active, creative, constitutive process.

In an academic version of the identity politics this book analyzes extensively in later chapters, analysts sometimes drew boundaries among themselves, observers sometimes detected separate schools of thought, while still other observers attended only to the boundary separating these related lines of thought from rational action and collective behavior. It would do no good to exaggerate the distinctions among enthusiasts for resource mobilization, political process, repertoires of contention, and framing. In fact, by the 1980s most North American students of social movements had adopted a common social movement agenda, and differed chiefly in their relative emphasis on different components of that agenda.

Figure 1.2 sketches the classic agenda in that vein. With varying degrees of emphasis on different elements and connections, investigators – ourselves included – regularly asked:

1. How, and how much, does social change (however defined) affect: (a) opportunity bearing on potential actors, (b) mobilizing structures that promote communication, coordination, and commitment within and among potential actors, (c) framing processes that produce shared definitions of what is happening? Example: under what conditions, how, and why does the expansion of capitalist property relations in an agrarian population expose different segments of

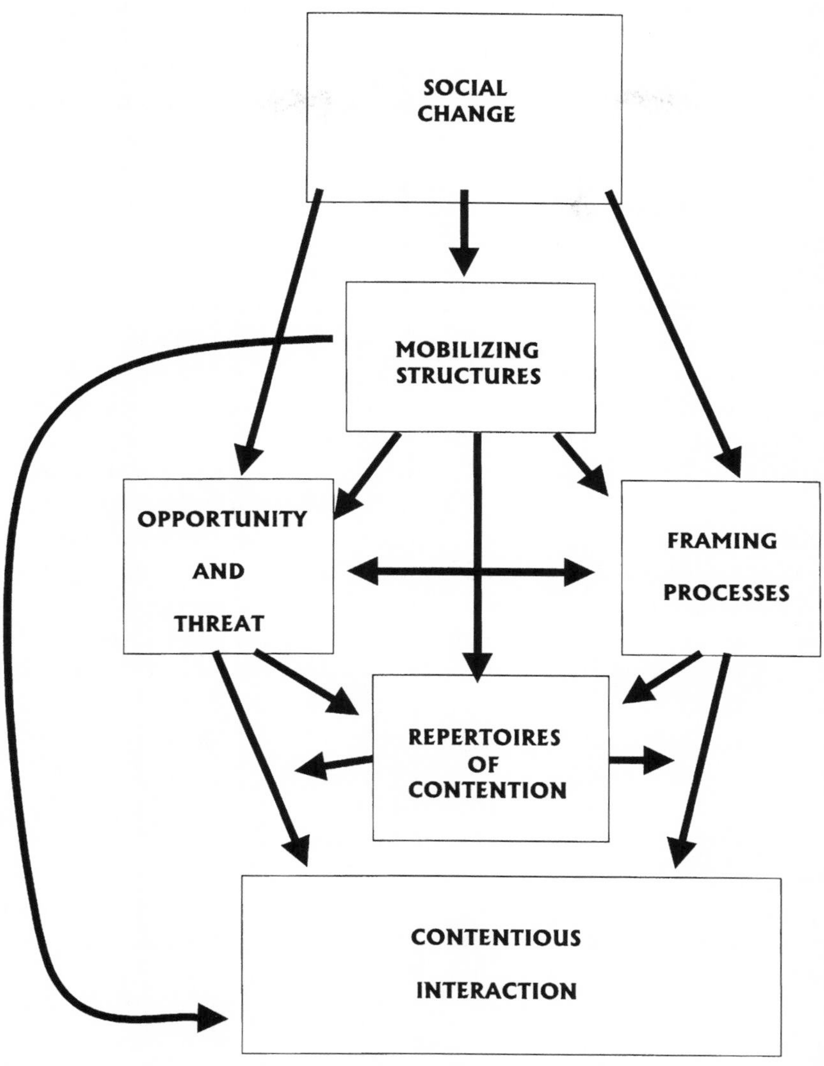

Figure 1.2. The Classic Social Movement Agenda for Explaining Contentious Politics

that population to new opportunities, transform politically potent connections among people affected by the changes, and alter available definitions of what is happening?

2. How much and how do mobilizing structures shape opportunity, framing processes, and contentious interaction? Example: Does the creation of new markets for commodities and labor alter the opportunities to which participants in those markets are exposed as well as the way that shared definitions of what is possible or probable emerge?
3. How much and how do opportunity, mobilizing structures, and framing processes determine repertoires of contention – the array of means by which participants in contentious politics make collective claims? Example: To what extent, and how, do attacks of capitalists on communal property, formation of extensive markets, and emergence of shared ideas concerning exploitation promote the creation of new forms of popular politics such as machine-breaking?
4. How much and how do existing repertoires mediate relations between opportunity and contentious interaction, on one side, between framing processes and contentious interaction, on the other? Example: Does the fact that a given population has a long tradition of public shaming ceremonies for reprobates affect the sorts of opportunities, and the available interpretations of those opportunities, to which members of that population respond collectively?

In the next chapter, we return to this agenda as a source of ideas for explaining the process of mobilization. For now, it is enough to say that it served the field of social movement studies well by stimulating much empirical work, but also by providing a reasonable, if overly structural and static, baseline model of social movements. It worked best as a story about single unified actors in democratic polities; it worked much less well when it came to complex episodes of contention, both there and especially in nondemocratic states. Furthermore, by packing more of its cause-and-effect relations into its underspecified arrows than in its labeled boxes, it provided still photographs of contentious moments rather than dynamic, interactive sequences. Both because it is a static, cause-free single-actor model and because it contains built-in affinities with relatively democratic social movements politics, it serves poorly as a guide to the wide variety of forms of contentious politics outside the world of democratic western polities. Even in the United States, the model proved partial, overly focused on a limited range of activities.

Consider the American Civil Rights movement, as seen in Greenwood, Mississippi, during the early 1960s. A base of white supremacists, Greenwood lay in the Mississippi Delta's plantation country. During a year that began in the spring of 1962, Greenwood went from intermittent assertion of black rights to swelling (and ultimately quite effective) mobilization. Although many members of Greenwood's black community gave tacit and material support, during that first year, as Charles Payne reports, "the viability of the movement hinged largely on the ability of young organizers to win the confidence of yardmen and maids, cab drivers, beauticians and barbers, custodians and field hands" (Payne 1995: 133). Civil rights activists from elsewhere worked closely with local people, gradually building up networks of mutual trust as they organized around voter registration but faced harassment from local authorities on every front.

It was intense, dangerous work. An idea of the intensity and danger comes from a field report by Joyce Ladner, who later became a major analyst of race, politics, and family life in the United States. Ladner spent the last week of March 1963 in Greenwood during the spring break from her studies at Tougaloo College:

Sunday, March 24: In the evening, someone torched the Council of Federated Organizations office, where she had worked all day.

Monday, March 25: She salvaged office records left by the fire, then prepared for an evening mass meeting.

Tuesday, March 26: Ladner spent the day doing general office work; that evening, the home of Dewey Greene, Sr., (long-time NAACP member with children active in civil rights) was shotgunned.

Wednesday, March 27: Protest march against the shooting, confrontation with mayor, civil rights workers attacked by police dogs and arrested, another mass meeting.

Beside excitement and danger, it also involved boring routine and institutional processes:

Thursday, March 28: Moving temporary headquarters, taking people to register for the vote, teaching citizenship class, group of marchers attacked by police with dogs, then a mass meeting with well-known local and national leaders.

Friday, March 29: citizenship class, voter registration, confrontation with police (one arrest), and mass meeting.

Saturday, March 30: office work and canvassing for registration (Payne 1995: 168–170).

"In concentrated form," remarks Payne, "Ladner's report captures both the mundane and the dramatic sides of the movement at that point. In the course of one week, she had met three national officers of civil rights groups, had met organizers from across the South, had been exposed to one burning, one shooting, and numberless acts of police violence and intimidation, in-between typing a lot of stencils and stuffing a lot of envelopes. She was also seeing a Black community responding to more repression with more activism – with more mass meetings, with daily marches" (Payne 1995: 170). What analysts often lump together as a single civil rights movement consisted of numberless acts, including not only police violence and confrontation, but also day-by-day creation and transformation of connections among people as well as routine political interactions within and around institutions.

If a single week of 1963 in Greenwood, Mississippi, displays such complexity, compressing the entire civil rights movement into the boxes in Figure 1.2 may provide a convenient checklist of questions to ask, but it cannot yield compelling explanations. What happened inside those boxes? What causal processes do the arrows represent? In order to answer those questions, we have to first call upon other intellectual resources.

Intellectual Resources

If we step back from narrow concentration on the classic social movement agenda and look around, we find other intellectual resources as well as an obstacle to their use. The new resources consist of four overlapping but competing lines of explanation for contention. The obstacles were the significant incompatibilities in the ways followers of those various lines have gathered evidence and assembled explanations. Although the names themselves generate controversy, we can call the four main traditions structural, rationalist, phenomenological, and cultural.

Structural analyses in their purest form, impute interests and capacities to whole collectivities – communities, classes, sometimes even those vague collectivities people call societies. They then explain the behavior of individuals and groups primarily through their relation to the collectivities in question. Methodologically, structuralists commonly concentrate on demonstrating that participation and action within episodes of contention conform to divisions of social organization to which the theories of structure and change at hand assign distinctive interests and capacities.

Rationalist analyses sometimes impute direction to collectivities such as firms and states, but mostly focus on deliberate choices made by individuals in the light of previously defined interests, resources, and situational constraints. Since the 1960s, rationalists have pursued a program of explanation that competes directly, and often self-consciously, with the structural program. Within such fields of contention as industrial conflict and electoral politics, rationalists have often predominated. In practice, rationalists often focus on evidence that individuals, or collectivities considered as if they were decision-making individuals, make crucial choices (e.g., whether to join a collective action or abstain from it) conforming to their imputed interests, resources, and situational constraints.

Phenomenological approaches likewise concentrate on individuals (although sometimes individuals writ large), plumbing their states of awareness for explanations of involvement in contentious politics. Many phenomenological analysts emphasize identity questions, answers to the interrogations "Who am I?", "Who are we?", "Who are you?", or "Who are they?" In carrying out their research, phenomenological analysts typically scrutinize utterances and texts (sometimes including symbols, objects, and practices considered as texts) for their implications concerning consciousness. Students of ethnic mobilization, nationalism, religious conflict, and identity-affirming social movements have frequently made phenomenology the fulcrum of their explanations.

Cultural approaches overlap with phenomenology as they often lodge culture in individual minds. In their pure form, however, such approaches attribute causal power to norms, values, beliefs and symbols that individuals experience and absorb from outside themselves. Cultural analysts have given special attention to two sets of circumstances: explicit organization of contentious action on behalf of ideologies or other well articulated belief systems and action based on membership in culturally distinctive communities. Like phenomenologists, cultural analysts often engage in hermeneutic treatment of texts. They also sometimes interpret structures such as kinship and trade networks in the style of ethnographers who are more concerned with the meaning than with the topology of those structures.

The labels structural, rational, phenomenological, and cultural, to be sure, designate tendencies rather than neatly segregated camps. Most actual analyses of contentious politics locate themselves in one or two of these categories, but employ some ideas from the others (Goodwin, et al. 1999; McAdam, Tarrow, Tilly 1997). The best rational action analysis, for example, focuses on the structural properties and effects of markets, firms, or states as it closes in on how individuals make decisions within them. The line of analysis called "collective behavior" concentrates on phenomenological changes that occur within aggregates of people, but in its most compelling versions incorporates structural and cultural constraints on the likelihood that such phenomenological changes will occur. Many structural analysts draw on rational choice or phenomenology when trying to explain how critical shifts in contentious interaction occur. In recent years, however, a number of analysts coming from different perspectives have begun to adopt what we call a "relational" perspective.

The Relational Persuasion

We come from a structuralist tradition. But in the course of our work on a wide variety of contentious politics in Europe and North America, we discovered the necessity of taking strategic interaction, consciousness, and historically accumulated culture into account. We treat social interaction, social ties, communication, and conversation not merely as expressions of structure, rationality, consciousness, or culture but as active sites of creation and change. We have come to think of interpersonal networks, interpersonal communication, and various forms of continuous negotiation – including the negotiation of identities – as figuring centrally in the dynamics of contention.

Something similar has happened to rational action analysts, who increasingly conceive of principal-agent problems, relations to third parties, multiparty games, and similar relational phenomena as strongly affecting initiation, processes, and outcomes of contentious politics. As a consequence, ironically, both confrontations and collaborations between structural and rational analysts are becoming more frequent (see Lichbach 1998; Lichbach and Zuckerman 1997). The "analytic narratives" proposed by Robert Bates and colleagues (Bates, et al. 1998), for example, generally start from a rationalist perspective, but incorporate multiple relations among political actors. As that study shows, nevertheless, three large gaps continue to separate relational approaches from most rational analysts.

The first gap is ontological. It entails a choice between (a) considering individual minds as the basic, or even the unique, sites of social reality and action and (b) claiming that social transactions have an efficacious reality that is irreducible to individual mental events. The methodological individualism of choice (a) focuses explanation on crucial decisions and their rationales, while the relational realism of choice (b) focuses explanation on webs of interaction among social sites. This book gives ample attention to individual action, but assigns great causal efficacy to relational processes.

The second gap is epistemological and logical, the choice between (c) construing explanation to consist of subsuming low-level empirical generalizations under higher-level empirical generalizations, which at the summit cumulate to covering laws and (d) recognizing as explanation the identification of causal chains consisting of mechanisms that reappear in a wide variety of settings but in different sequences and combinations, hence with different collective outcomes.

In the first view, general accounts of contentious politics would show that all instances of contention conform to laws embodied in recurrent situations, structures, and sequences. Here we would find similarities between analyses of contention and physical mechanics. In the second view, no truly general accounts are practically attainable, but strong if selective recurrent mechanisms and processes appear across ostensibly different varieties of contention. Here we would find resemblances between analyses of contention and molecular biology. This book bets on the second view.

The third gap is historical and cultural. The choice runs between (e) assigning no importance to history and its accumulation into the shared understandings and practices we call culture except insofar as they translate into specifiable interests, resources, and constraints on decision making and (f) supposing that the historical and cultural setting in which contention occurs significantly affects its mobilization, actors, trajectories, outcomes, and concatenations of causal mechanisms. As contrasted with a pure rationalist view in this regard, we think of contentious processes as sufficiently embedded in history that within concrete social settings the vast majority of actors, actions, identities, mobilization processes, trajectories, and outcomes that are logically possible – or have even happened in broadly similar settings elsewhere in history and culture – do not materialize. Common properties across historically and culturally distinct settings do not consist of similar large structures and sequences but of recurrent causal mechanisms concatenating into causal processes. These are what we hope to reveal through the interactions we observe in the episodes of contention this book takes up.

Causal Mechanisms, Causal Processes, Contentious Episodes

Our book shifts the search away from general models like rational choice that purport to summarize whole categories of contention and moves toward the analysis of smaller-scale causal mechanisms that recur in different combinations with different aggregate consequences in varying historical settings. Let us draw rough distinctions among social mechanisms, processes, and episodes:

Mechanisms are a delimited class of events that alter relations among specified sets of elements in identical or closely similar ways over a variety of situations.

Processes are regular sequences of such mechanisms that produce similar (generally more complex and contingent) transformations of those elements.

Episodes are continuous streams of contention including collective claims making that bears on other parties' interests.

Let us turn first to our conception of mechanisms, which draws on a distinguished, but long-dormant tradition in sociology, and then to processes and episodes.

Merton's Mechanisms

Our interest in social mechanisms goes back to Robert Merton, who defined them as "social processes having designated consequences for designated parts of the social structure" and thought the main task of sociology was to identify such mechanisms (1968: 43–44). While political scientists have always paid attention to institutional mechanisms, rather statically conceived, few sociologists or political scientists took up Merton's challenge to look at dynamic *social* mechanisms until the 1990s, when Jon Elster (1989) and Arthur Stinchcombe (1991) turned to the theme.

Elster focused on the internal "social cogs and wheels" that specify the relations between variables or events (1989: 3). "Mechanisms," wrote Stinchcombe, are "bits of theory about entities at a different level (e.g., individuals) than the main entities being theorized about (e.g., groups) which serve to make the higher-level theory more supple, more accurate, or more general" (1991: 367). Both the Stinchcombe and the Elster view differed from the classical "covering law" model advocated by Hempel and his followers. Following Elster and Stinchcombe, Hedström and Swedberg then chose to specify mechanisms linking variables to one another rather than to focus on the strength of correlations between them that has become the stock in trade of quantitative social science and causal modeling (Hedström and Swedberg 1998: 8–9).

We follow Hedström and Swedberg in this persuasion. We see mechanisms as delimited sorts of events that change relations among specified sets of elements in identical or closely similar ways over a variety of situations. Yet, we part company from them when they conclude that the core idea of the mechanism approach is and must be "methodological individualism" – albeit its weaker and less holistic version (Hedström and Swedberg 1998: 12–13). Their conclusion leads to a focus only on mechanisms that operate at the individual level – such as the "self-fulfilling prophecy" – or on the "network effects" and "bandwagon effects" that derive from it. With such individual-level processes, scholars like James Coleman and Mark Granovetter have made great progress; but they severely limit our ability to interpret collective processes like the ones involved in contentious politics.

Within contentious politics, we can impose a rough distinction among environmental, cognitive, and relational mechanisms.

Environmental mechanisms mean externally generated influences on conditions affecting social life. Such mechanisms can operate directly: For example, resource depletion or enhancement affects people's capacity to engage in contentious politics (McCarthy and Zald, ed. 1987).

Cognitive mechanisms operate through alterations of individual and collective perception; words like recognize, understand, reinterpret, and classify characterize such mechanisms. Our vignettes from Paris and Greenwood show people shifting in awareness of what could happen through collective action; when we look more closely, we will observe multiple cognitive mechanisms at work, individual by individual. For example, commitment is a widely recurrent individual mechanism in which persons who individually would prefer not to take the risks of collective action find themselves unable to withdraw without hurting others whose solidarity they value – sometimes at the cost of suffering serious loss.

Relational mechanisms alter connections among people, groups, and interpersonal networks. Brokerage, a mechanism that recurs throughout Parts II and III of the book, we define as the linking of two or more previously unconnected social sites by a unit that mediates their relations with one another and/or with yet other sites. Most analysts see brokerage as a mechanism relating groups and individuals to one another in stable sites, but it can also become a relational mechanism for mobilization during periods of contentious politics, as new groups are thrown together by increased interaction and uncertainty, thus discovering their common interests.

Environmental, cognitive, and relational mechanisms combine. In Chapter 6, for example, we will see how the onset of the American Civil War occurred against the background of an *environmental* mechanism (the massive antebellum shift of population and voters to the West); through a *cognitive* mechanism (the widespread interpretation of southern vs. northern westward expansion as a zero-sum game); and a *relational* mechanism (brokerage of a coalition between free-soil-seeking Westerners and antislavery Northerners). We give some attention to environmental mechanisms such as population growth and shift, proletarianization and urbanization, but pay more attention in our narratives to cognitive and relational mechanisms.

How will we recognize a relevant social mechanism when we see one? In general terms, when a mechanism is at work, we see interactions among the elements in question altering the established connections among them. Consider the familiar mechanism in contentious politics that we call "signaling." In a risky situation, participants often scan each other for signs of readiness to incur costs without defecting, modulating their behavior according to estimates of the likelihood that others will flee. As would-be marchers mill before a demonstration, for example, exchanges of words and gestures signal their degrees of determination, self-possession, and fear. Veteran demonstrators and skilled organizers project confidence to less experienced participants. In most circumstances, that form of signaling reduces the likelihood that the inexperienced will run away. If, however, demonstration veterans recognize the lineup of glowering troops as dangerous and show their fear, signaling actually promotes defection. The mechanism is essentially the same, the outcome significantly different.

Mechanisms and Processes

Mechanisms seldom operate on their own. They typically concatenate with other mechanisms into broader processes (Gambetta 1998: 105). Processes are frequently recurring causal chains, sequences, and combinations of mechanisms. Processes worth singling out here involve recurrent combinations and sequences of mechanisms that operate identically or with great similarity across a variety of situations. Part III takes up the analysis more systematically than the book's earlier sections. Starting from the well-known macro-processes of revolution, democratization, and nationalism, Part III examines the concatenation of mechanisms into narrower processes such as actor constitution, polarization, and scale shift. We will find such robust processes recurring in wide varieties of contentious episodes.

Mechanisms and processes form a continuum. It is arbitrary, for example, whether we call brokerage a mechanism, a family of mechanisms, or a process. In this book, we generally call it a mechanism to emphasize its recurring features. At one end of the continuum, a mechanism such as "identity shift" – alteration during contentious claim making of public answers to the question: "Who are you?" – qualifies as a narrow-end mechanism. At the continuum's other end, democratization cannot possibly qualify as a single mechanism. It clearly involves multiple mechanisms that combine differently in various concrete experiences. Chapter 9 sketches a process theory of democratization involving combinations or sequences of mechanisms producing moves toward (as well as away from) democracy.

A preview of the mechanisms and processes appearing in Chapter 2 will illustrate what we have in mind:

- mobilization, a familiar process we elaborate first in Chapter 2, concatenates a number of interacting mechanisms, starting from the environmental ones that have been broadly labeled "social change processes" passing through mechanisms such as attribution of opportunity and threat, social appropriation, framing of the dispute, and arraying of innovative forms of collective action. Using the civil rights movement as our benchmark here, we will explore how concerted attention to these mechanisms can put mobilization into motion
- another family of mechanisms is what we call "political identity formation." As in the case of mobilization, some of these mechanisms are cognitive and some relational. The establishment of political identities involves changes in the awareness within the persons involved as well as within other parties to those identities, but it also involves alterations in connections among the affected persons and groups. Later chapters track regularities in the process of political identity formation, observing how different combinations and sequences of the same small set of mechanisms produce significantly different variants on that process, hence significantly different outcomes, in revolutions, nationalist mobilizations, democratization and social movements. Chapter 2 moves from mobilization to illustrate the mechanism of identity shift from our benchmark case of the French Revolution
- both sets of processes come together in the trajectories of contention, alongside a family of mechanisms typically associated with protest cycles, revolutions, and other forms of contention. We complete Chapter 2 by using our third benchmark case, Italian contention, to illuminate how the mechanisms of repression, diffusion, and radicalization operate within complex episodes of contention

Episodes

We seek to get causal mechanisms and processes right by locating them within episodes of contention. Episodes are not merely complicated processes. They always involve two or more processes. However narrowly we delimit the episode called the Parisian revolution of July 1789, we always discover some combination of mobilization, identity shift, and polarization, three very general but distinct processes and mechanisms in contentious politics. The explanatory agenda becomes clear. It consists of

- identifying contentious episodes or families of contentious episodes having some problematic feature
- locating the processes within them that constitute or produce the problematic feature
- searching out the crucial causal mechanisms within those processes

Thus we can examine a set of episodes in which people respond to increased repression by striking back at their enemies instead of fleeing or subsiding into passivity. In such episodes we frequently find the processes of mobilization and polarization occurring together. Within those processes we will find such mechanisms as collective attribution of threat and reinforcement of commitment producing crucial effects. In this way, we can begin to fashion a causal account of resistance to massive threat.

To treat an entire stream of confrontations as a single episode allows us to think through similarities and differences with conflict streams that have occurred elsewhere or in the same system in different historical moments. France's having had revolutions in 1830, 1848, and 1871 that resembled in some ways the one in 1789 does not make all French revolutions identical, but it does make their comparison interesting. That France, Germany, Italy, and the United States had peaks of contention in 1968 does not make them part of One Grand Movement, but it raises the issue of whether similar mechanisms and processes were activated in each – not to mention drawing attention to the relations among them.

Regarding an entire stream of confrontations as a single episode poses enormous problems. Many scholars have thought of revolutions, wars, social movements, massacres, demonstrations, tax rebellions, food riots, and other such episodes as self-contained entities, while others have proposed generalizations concerning their typical sequences, forms, origins or outcomes. Our idea goes beyond those approaches in four related ways:

- First, we treat the idea of recurrent uniformities in whole episodes as a dubious hypothesis to be tested with care, rather than assumed at the outset. In our work, we have detected variable sequences and combinations of mechanisms and processes.
- Second, we see episodes not as natural entities but as observers' lenses, bounded and observed according to conventions established by participants, witnesses, commentators, and analysts of past episodes. We insist on self-conscious creation of comparability in

delineating episodes, as well as the recognition that the principles of that delineation – long or short, in small areas or large, through a top-down or bottom-up vision – significantly affect which mechanisms and processes become visible.

- Third, we consider the naming and labeling of episodes to be consequential political acts in their own right, part of what we must eventually explain. For participants or their successors to decide that an episode qualifies as a revolution or as a huge riot makes a difference to the identities activated, allies gained or lost, governmental measures the episode triggers, and readiness of other citizens to commit themselves in the course of later political action.
- Fourth, we see such episodes not as linear sequences of contention in which the same actors go through the repeated motions of expressing preestablished claims in lock-step, but as iterative sites of interaction in which different streams of mobilization and demobilization intersect, identities form and evolve, and new forms of action are invented, honed, and rejected as actors interact with one another and with opponents and third parties.

We employ mechanisms and processes as our workhorses of explanation, episodes as our workhorses of description. We therefore make a bet on how the social world works: that big structures and sequences never repeat themselves, but result from differing combinations and sequences of mechanisms with very general scope. Even within a single episode, we will find multiform, changing, and self-constructing actors, identities, forms of action and interaction, as a glimpse at our third benchmark case reveals.

By the early 1960s, Italy's postwar economic "miracle" was coming down to earth. As the supply of cheap labor from the South began to dry up, Cold War tensions eased, secularization eroded Catholic political dominance, and the contradictions built into its growth model began to sharpen. A spurt of industrial conflict in the early 1960s warned that changes had to be made. A brief reprieve occurred as Socialists entered the government, leaving their Communist allies isolated in opposition (Ginsborg 1989: ch. 8). Reforms followed, but each attempted reform either triggered a right-wing backlash (as did the nationalization of electricity), or opened the floodgates to broader contention (as did the passage of a modern industrial relations law).

When the explosion came in the late 1960s, a surprise was in store for those who had feared a Communist-led working class onslaught. The

1967–1968 wave of protest began with a social actor outside the PCI's traditional subculture: the middle-class student population. It was significant of the new identities emerging in the student population that the earliest outbreaks of insurgency took place in both the secular Universities of Turin and Pisa and Catholic centers of learning in Milan and Trento. Indicative of the remaining potency of Italy's Marxist subculture, the insurgents framed their demands in workerist terms. But their links to the industrial working class were weak. The main force of university-based rebellion subsided by 1969 (Tarrow 1989).

A second wave of contention began even before the first one was spent. From the start, Italy's 1968 was marked by violent clashes between extreme left and right – and by both against the forces of order which, however, appeared to the leftists to be soft on the rightists. A major turning point in the new cycle of violence was the bombing of the Bank of Agriculture in Piazza Fontana in Milan, followed by "the accidental death of an anarchist" in police custody and the assassination of the police official thought responsible for his death. Fed by both new recruits from the high schools and by police repressive tactics, this new wave evolved into the terrorist attacks on industrialists, state officials, and journalists in the early-to-mid-1970s (della Porta 1990).

The year 1969 also saw the rise of a third, and largely autonomous wave of contention. Stimulated by the students' example, by the new industrial relations law then under discussion, and the external factor of the Vietnam-era inflation, contention spread to the factories (Franzosi 1995). The "Hot Autumn" was at first limited to the large factories of the North, but it was especially violent among the new wave of semi-skilled "mass" workers who had entered the workforce in the "miracle" years of the 1950s. Skilled workers and white-collar workers who had enjoyed higher wages responded to the successes of the mass workers by demanding the preservation of wage differentials. Unions, anxious not to be outflanked, quickly took hold of working class insurgency and moved sharply to the left in their demands and their ideology.

These streams of mobilization interacted in different ways with public politics. For all three sets of actors, splits in the elite exacerbated conflict and created opportunities for contention. But the University students' movement was dealt with through a combination of dispersed repression and pallid educational reform. The industrial workers gained new rights of participation and major wage increases, and the terrorist threat was met by concerted repression. Eventually, the political class closed ranks in a coalition of national solidarity that included the parties of the Left to restore economic growth and defend the state from its enemies.

How we see this episode will differ according to whether we focus on the students of 1968 – in which case Italy does not look very different from any of the other countries that experienced student rebellions in that year; on the industrial workers' movement – which described a much longer parabola and was far more contained than the student movement; or on the violent end of the period, whose actors were different and whose forms of action far more transgressive. Not only that: we will find different mechanisms and processes at work according to which sector of contention we focus on or which period of the cycle we examine. That we will see clearly in the next chapter.

Our Agenda

In this study, a search for explanatory mechanisms and processes takes the place occupied by the checklist of variables – opportunity, threat, mobilizing structures, repertoires, framing – we saw in the classic social movement agenda. Although we helped promote the agenda displayed in Figure 1.2, we mean this book to go well beyond it. The problems posed by each box and arrow in the diagram recur throughout the chapters to come. But we seek more adequate ways of dealing with such phenomena as formation of political identities, mobilization of different actors, fragmentation or coalescence of collective action, and mutation of the paths taken by ongoing struggles. We seek, for example, to lodge interpretive processes firmly in the give-and-take of social interaction rather than treating them as autonomous causal forces. Because of the urge to get causal connections right, we reject the effort to build general models of all contention or even of its varieties. Instead, within each major aspect of contention we search for robust, widely applicable causal mechanisms that explain crucial – but not all – features of contention.

Seen as wholes, the French Revolution, the American civil rights movement, and Italian contention look quite different from each other; the first toppled a national regime and reordered relations among all its political actors, the second introduced into a surviving national regime a bit more political equality and a powerful set of precedents for political claim making, while the third – despite its high level of violence – led to little palpable change in political practice. Yet when we take apart the three histories, we find a number of common mechanisms that moved the conflicts along and transformed them: creation of new actors and identities through the very process of contention; brokerage by activists who connected previously insulated local clumps of aggrieved people; competition among contenders that led to factional divisions and re-alignments, and much more. These mechanisms concatenated into more complex processes such as radicalization and polarization of conflict; formation of new balances of power; and re-alignments of the polity along new lines.

Those are the sorts of connections we seek in this book. Our project is not to identify wholesale repetitions of large structures and sequences, but to single out significant recurrent mechanisms and processes as well as principles of variation. Our general strategy is the following:

- recognize that in principle contention ranges among wars, revolutions, social movements, industrial conflict, and a number of other forms of interaction that analysts have ordinarily conceived of as *sui generis*
- elaborate concepts calling attention to these similarities; call upon the major concepts developed out of the study of social movements in western democracies since the 1960s to make a start
- improve on those concepts by critique and autocritique, then by applying the product of critique and autocritique to other settings and periods of history
- across these settings and periods, look for recurrences not among whole phenomena but among mechanisms revealed within these phenomena – for example, parallels between the mechanisms of brokerage in social movement cycles and revolutionary situations
- examine how these causal mechanisms combine into longer chains of political processes, for example how identity shift and brokerage combine in episodes of nationalism. From identification of such processes, create not general theories of contention but partial theories corresponding to these robust causal similarities
- establish scope conditions with regard to time, space, and social setting under which such partial theories hold and those in which they do not. Ask, for example, whether transnational mobilization mirrors the same international mechanisms as mobilization at the national or local levels

- treat discontinuities in those scope conditions – for instance, the discovery that explanations built into social movement theories coming from liberal democracies apply badly outside such regimes – not as cultural roadblocks but as challenges to undertake new theories and comparisons

The present book is no research monograph. Despite its innumerable examples and its sustained presentation of cases, it works with its evidence primarily to advance and illustrate new ways of thinking about contentious politics. For this reason, it often features schematic summaries of episodes rather than deep explorations of their foundations. Never, never do we claim to have provided comprehensive explanations of the contentious events the book examines. We seek to establish illuminating partial parallels and use them to identify recurring causal processes. We hope thereby to inspire new ways of studying contentious politics.

Mobilization, Actors, Trajectories

We group these problems provisionally under three broad headings: mobilization, actors, and trajectories, categories which will guide our efforts in the next chapter and in Part II:

- With respect to *mobilization* we must explain how people who at a given point in time are not making contentious claims start doing so – and, for that matter, how people who are making claims stop doing so. (We can call that reverse process *de*mobilization.)
- With regard to *actors* we need to explain what sorts of actors engage in contention, what identities they assume, and what forms of interaction they produce. Fortified by these contributions, we elaborate an approach to actors as contingent constructions as well as an approach to contentious interaction in terms of repertoires that vary as a function of actors' political connections.
- When it comes to *trajectories*, we face the problem of explaining the course and transformation of contention, including its impact on life outside of the immediate interactions of contentious politics.

Relations among mobilization/demobilization, actors, and trajectories will preoccupy us throughout the book. To what extent, for example, do certain political actors display distinctive mobilization patterns that produce standard trajectories? When provisional committees and militias formed all over France in the summer of 1789, to what extent and why did mobilization, struggle, and transformation in one locality resemble their counterparts in Paris or in other localities? How regular were the patterns by which black southerners got involved in civil rights, and how much did those patterns determine the course and outcome of civil rights struggles? And for all their inventiveness, did Italian workers of the 1960s move from inaction to action or back in ways so predictable that the trajectory of one struggle usually resembled that of the last?

In Part II of the study we move from our three touchstone cases to a broader set of paired comparisons designed to force the analysis toward connecting mobilization, actors, and trajectories. In the course of those comparisons we single out recurrent causal mechanisms and processes affecting mobilization, action, trajectories, and their interaction in a wide variety of settings and types of contention.

Eventually that effort will require us to abandon the distinctions among mobilization, actors, and trajectories that organize the book's first part. Questions about who acts, how they move between action and inaction, or what trajectories their actions follow turn out to be just that: good questions. Their answers dissolve the questions in two ways. First, we discover that the same array of causal mechanisms and processes operates in the three ostensibly separate spheres. Then we find that each is simply a different way of looking at the same phenomena. Mobilization questions become trajectory questions once we stop assuming a sharp discontinuity between contention and all other politics, trajectory questions become questions about actors, identities, and actions once we start examining how interactions among sites change as contention proceeds. Thus, as we move into Part III, we take down the scaffolding within which we built Parts I and II.

Parts II and III use their comparisons differently. Part II searches for causal mechanisms and processes that produce similar effects in a wide variety of contentious politics. It does so by matching obviously different sorts of episodes, then showing that identical mechanisms and processes play significant parts in those episodes. Chapter 3 explains that strategy in greater detail. Holding provisionally to a division among mobilization–demobilization (Chapter 4), actors (Chapter 5), and trajectories (Chapter 6), the analyses in Part II yield an inventory of nine wide-ranging mechanisms.

Part III adopts a different strategy. Abandoning distinctions among mobilization, action, and trajectories, it turns to three varieties of contentious episodes for which conventional names and separate literatures exist: revolution, nationalism, and democratization. The aim is threefold: first, to show that the sorts of mechanisms and processes identified in Part II actually help explain salient differences between contrasting episodes within such categories as revolution, nationalism, and democratization, then to establish that similar mechanisms and processes actually recur across such broad types of contention, and, finally, to examine whether recurring processes are regularly composed of the mechanisms we identify them with in our cases. Examined in detail, revolutions, nationalism, and democratization result from similar causes in different settings, sequences, and concatenations.

Here, then, is how our book works. The following chapter (Chapter 2) sets the book's explanatory problems. It uses our three touchstone cases to examine mobilization, actors, and trajectories. Chapter 3 concludes Part I by laying out the map of our comparisons and the logic behind them. Chapter 4 begins Part II with the mobilization process in the Mau Mau rebellion and the Philippine Yellow revolution. Chapter 5 compares the construction and politicization of Hindu–Muslim conflict and its implications for mobilization and trajectories with similar mechanisms and processes in South Africa. In Chapter 6, we trace the trajectories of American antislavery and Spanish democratization to explicate how identities were transformed and mobilization formed in those episodes. We then sum up our conclusions concerning intersections of mobilization, actors, and trajectories before dissolving those distinctions.

Part III of the study takes up three distinct literatures regarding contention – revolution, nationalism, and democratization – in view of the paths our quest has followed. The goal of that concluding section is to emphasize the commonalities as well as the differences in those forms of contention through an examination of the explanatory mechanisms and political processes we have uncovered in Parts I and II. To do that, we make two integrative leaps, moving (a) outward from the classical social movement agenda that has dominated research on contentious politics in the United States during recent years and (b) across a variety of methods. We accomplish those leaps chiefly by showing how the same sorts of causal mechanisms we identified in Part II reappear in the course of revolutionary processes, nationalist claim making, and democratization.

In terms of the classic social movement agenda, we offer new answers to old questions. Before concerted contention begins, whose opportunity, threat, mobilizing structures, repertoires, and framing processes matter, and how? Of the many names in which people sometimes make claims, why do only a few typically prevail as public bases of contentious interaction? What governs the course and outcome of that interaction? How does participation in contention itself alter opportunities, threats, mobilizing structures, repertoires, and framing processes? Questions of this sort make clear that the classic approach to social movements concentrates on mobilization and demobilization; it provides relatively weak guides to explanation of action, actors, identities, trajectories, or outcomes. Even within the zone of mobilization, it works best when one or a few previously constituted political actors move into public contention. To understand broader and less structured processes of contention, we must develop an expanded research agenda.

Let us insist: Our aim is not to construct general models of revolution, democratization, or social movements, much less of all political contention whenever and wherever it occurs. On the contrary, we aim to identify crucial causal mechanisms that recur in a wide variety of contention, but produce different aggregate outcomes depending on the initial conditions, combinations, and sequences in which they occur. We start with what we know best, or think we know: three episodes of modern western contention in France, the United States, and Italy. We move from there to systematic comparison of cases we know less well. In the book's final section, we take up revolution, nationalism, ethnic mobilization, and democratization to identify interactions and parallels among them. If we have succeeded, readers will leave this book with refreshed understanding of familiar processes and a new program for research on contentious politics in all its varieties.

2

Lineaments of Contention

Under what conditions will normally apathetic, frightened, or disorganized people explode into the streets, put down their tools, or mount the barricades? How do different actors and identities appear and transform in episodes of contention? Finally, what kinds of trajectories do these processes follow? As the last chapter makes clear, our ultimate interest lies not in the recruitment of static, unchanging actors into single movements, but in the dynamic processes through which new political actors, identities, and forms of action emerge, interact, coalesce and evolve during complex episodes of contention. Since the road to those processes is long and arduous, we approach it through a series of incremental steps.

In this chapter we move first, to the mobilization of people into movements; from there to the formation of collective actors and identities; and from there to the trajectories of contention in which these processes occur, deploying evidence from our three touchstone cases in the United States, France, and Italy. We first depart from the classical social movement agenda to propose a more dynamic model of the mobilization process. We then interrogate that model by showing how mechanisms attached to actors, identities, and actions intersect with mobilization. We finally examine some mechanisms associated with trajectories of contention to suggest how both mobilization and actors, identities and actions can transform in the course of episodes of contention.

Mobilization in Montgomery

In the years following World War II, the onset of the Cold War renationalized the issue of race in the United States. Over a decade of contained contention involving various federal officials, southern politicians, and established civil rights groups preceded the transgressive phase of the civil rights struggle (McAdam 1999). That early postwar phase provided court cases, splits in the Democratic party, activists and experiences that combined in the mid-1950s to produce the major episode of contention that history identifies as the Civil Rights movement. We begin with the incident that touched off that transgressive phase.

Montgomery, Alabama, December 1955

The Civil Rights movement's critically important phase began in this medium-size southern city. On December 1, 1955, forty-two-year-old seamstress and longtime civil rights activist Rosa Parks was arrested for violating the city's ordinance regulating racial seating on city buses. Her actual offense was not failing to sit in the back of the bus, but something more complicated and illustrative of the pettily degrading quality of Jim Crow segregation. Montgomery's buses were divided into three sections: one at the front reserved for whites; a smaller one at the back reserved for blacks; and one in the middle that members of either race could occupy, provided that no black sat in front of any white. On boarding the crowded bus, Parks conformed to this convention, but with the bus now full, a second mandated requirement came into play. If a bus became full, black riders were obliged by law to yield their seats in the middle section to any white who boarded after them. This Parks refused to do. What followed was what history remembers as the Montgomery bus boycott. Said Parks later:

> From the time of the arrest on Thursday night [December 1, 1955] and Friday and Saturday and Sunday, word had gotten around over Montgomery of my arrest. . . . And people just began to decide that they wouldn't ride the bus on the day of the trial, which was Monday, December 5th. And Monday morning, when the buses were out on their regular run, they remained empty. People were walking, getting rides in cars of people who would pick them up as best they could. On Monday night the mass meeting at the Holt Street Baptist Church had been called and there were many thousand people there. They kept coming, and some people never did get in the church, there were so many. The first day of remaining off the bus had been so successful it was organized, and that we wouldn't ride the bus until our request had been granted. [Quoted in Burns 1997: 85]

Parks later said that she simply "had been pushed as far as I could stand to be pushed . . . I had decided that I would have to know once and for all what rights I had as a human being and a citizen." [Quoted in Raines 1983: 44.]

Parks's arrest was hardly the first of its kind under Montgomery's bus seating ordinance. Indeed, mistreatment on city buses was so common it had "emerged as the most . . . acute black community problem" in Montgomery in the early 1950s (Burns 1997: 7). So why did Rosa Parks's decision provoke the broader community reaction it did in 1955? Part of the answer probably lies in Ms. Parks's strong ties to both Montgomery's civil rights and middle-class black church communities – the two organizational arenas that would form the nucleus of the subsequent boycott (Morris 1984: 51–53). But part of the reason also emerged from the dynamics of the incident itself, from how both the black and the white communities perceived it, and from how it was framed by the media and the political establishment.

Whatever the answer to the question, Montgomery's black community *did* respond to Parks's arrest in dramatic and unprecedented fashion. On the morning of December 5, an estimated 90 to 95 percent of the city's black bus patrons stayed off the buses, taking Montgomery's white establishment – and ordinary citizens – totally by surprise. Buoyed by the success of what had been planned as a one-day symbolic protest, black leaders decided to put the boycott on a more permanent footing. At a meeting held that afternoon in Dexter Avenue Baptist Church, boycott organizers formed the Montgomery Improvement Association (MIA) electing as its first President, twenty-six-year-old Martin Luther King, Jr., who was also chosen to lead the boycott. This he did for nearly thirteen tumultuous months, until the successful conclusion of the campaign and desegregation of the city's buses on December 21, 1956.

More important than the desegregation itself were the broader effects of the campaign. The boycott drew favorable attention from the national press, thereby generating much broader public awareness of the issue. The campaign then spawned similar boycotts in at least six other southern cities. More significantly, it led to the creation of the first exclusively southern civil rights organization. That organization, eventually named the Southern Christian Leadership Conference (SCLC) and also headed by King, was to serve as a key driving wedge of the mainstream movement throughout the 1950s and 1960s. The rest, as they say, is history.

But we are getting ahead of ourselves. Our real interest here is not with the subsequent movement but with the events in Montgomery. We begin with a question: What led normally accepting accepting African-Americans both in Montgomery and throughout the South to risk their livelihoods and their lives in support of civil rights? Recall from Chapter

1 that in the "classical social movement agenda" the following factors come into play:

- *Social change processes* initiate a process of change and trigger changes in the political, cultural, and economic environments.
- *Political opportunities and constraints* confront a given challenger. Though challengers habitually face resource deficits and are excluded from routine decision making, the political environment at any time is not immutable; the political opportunities for a challenger to engage in successful collective action vary over time. These variations shape the ebb and flow of a movement's activity.
- *Forms of organization* (informal as well as formal) offer insurgents sites for initial mobilization at the time opportunities present themselves and condition their capacity to exploit their new resources. Despite some evidence to the contrary (Piven and Cloward 1977), a large body of evidence finds organizational strength correlated with challengers' ability to gain access and win concessions (Gamson 1990).
- *Framing*, a collective process of interpretation, attribution, and social construction, mediates between opportunity and action. At a minimum, people must both feel aggrieved at some aspect of their lives and optimistic that acting collectively can redress the problem (Snow, et al. 1986; Snow and Benford 1988). Movements frame specific grievances within general collective action frames which dignify claims, connect them to others, and help to produce a collective identity among claimants.
- *Repertoires of contention* offer the means by which people engage in contentious collective action. These forms are not neutral, continuous, or universally accessible; they constitute a resource that actors can use on behalf of their claims (Traugott, et al. 1995). The use of transgressive forms offers the advantages of surprise, uncertainty, and novelty, but contained forms of contention have the advantage of being accepted, familiar, and relatively easy to employ by claimants without special resources or willingness to incur costs and take great risks.

That classical agenda made three enduring contributions to the study of social movements. First, it made strong claims regarding the close connection between routine and contentious politics, helping to reframe the study of social movements as the proper province of both sociology and political science. Second, calling attention to the role of "mobilizing structures," it represented a powerful challenge to the stress on social disorganization and breakdown in the older collective behavior paradigm. Third, it produced a credible picture of mobilization into social movements that was supported by a good deal of empirical evidence correlating the factors outlined above with increases in mobilization.

We have not abandoned the central questions that motivated the formulation of that model. But it has four major defects as a tool for the analysis of contentious politics: (1) It focuses on static, rather than dynamic relationships. (2) It works best when centered on individual social movements and less well for broader episodes of contention. (3) Its genesis in the relatively open politics of the American "sixties" led to more emphasis on opportunities than on threats, more confidence in the expansion of organizational resources than on the organizational deficits that many challengers suffer. (4) It focused inordinately on the *origins* of contention rather than on its later phases (for a more detailed critique see McAdam 1999).

Perhaps no case is more closely associated with the classic social movement account of the origins of mobilization than the U.S. Civil Rights struggle (McAdam 1982; Morris 1984). The prevailing account of that movement mirrors the model sketched above, first, in holding that it developed in response to a series of cumulative societal and political changes between 1930 and 1955. Those changes, runs the argument, gradually undermined the system of racial politics that had prevailed in the United States since Reconstruction ended in 1876 (McAdam 1982, ch. 5). The key environmental mechanisms that destabilized the system were the decline in the southern cotton economy and the twin migratory flows – south to north and rural to urban – that the collapse of King Cotton set in motion.

All four of the constitutive "boxes" in the classical social movement agenda then go to work:

- By transforming the previously nonexistent "black vote" into an increasingly important electoral resource in presidential politics, the northern exodus reshaped the *political opportunities* available to African-Americans.
- At the same time as northern migration was reshaping the political landscape, the urbanization of the South was keying the development of the specific *mobilizing structures* – black churches, black colleges, and NAACP chapters – within which the mass movement of the 1950s was to develop.

- These changes loosened the cultural hold of Jim Crow, thus enabling civil rights forces to *frame grievances* in new and more contentious ways.
- It also gave them the capacity to embrace a broader *repertoire of contention* through marches, sit-ins, and other transgressions of white power.

Students of civil rights have offered plenty of evidence in support of this account. But the account was static rather than dynamic, focused on a single movement rather than on the broader episode of contention of which it was a part, underspecified the historical and cultural construction of the dispute, and featured the period of transgressive contention, leaving out many of the more contained transactions that preceded and accompanied it. Morover, it offered a structurally determined account of what must be explained: the creation of the organizational, the institutional, and the behavioral bases for mobilization. We begin our quest with a reformulation of that agenda for mobilization.

Toward a Dynamic Mobilization Model

Where the classic social movement agenda assigned central weight to social change, political opportunities, mobilizing structures, frames, and transgressive forms of action, we try to identify the dynamic mechanisms that bring these variables into relation with one another and with other significant actors. Our perspective puts each of the constituent parts of the classical agenda – opportunities, mobilizing structures, framing, and repertoires – into motion.

- Rather than look upon "opportunities and threats" as objective structural factors, we see them as subject to attribution. No opportunity, however objectively open, will invite mobilization unless it is a) visible to potential challengers and b) perceived as an opportunity. The same holds for threats, an underemphasized corollary of the model (but see Aminzade et al. forthcoming, ch. 2). While the threat of repression is more palpable than the opportunity to participate, numerous movements arose because their participants either failed to perceive them or refused to recognize them as a menace. Attribution of opportunity or threat is an activating mechanism responsible in part for the mobilization of previously inert populations.

- Instead of pointing to pre-existing mobilizing structures, we call attention to the active appropriation of sites for mobilization. The original resource mobilization theorists built their theory on a trend they correctly observed in the United States in the 1960s and 1970s: expansion of organizational opportunities for collective action (McCarthy and Zald 1973, 1977). But that emphasis does not ring true in much of the world, where challengers are more likely to possess organizational deficits than resources. Even in the United States, challengers, rather than creating new organizations, appropriated existing ones and turned them into vehicles of mobilization. Social appropriation is a second mechanism that permits oppressed or resource-poor populations sometimes to overcome their organizational deficits.
- Rather than limit "framing" to a strategic tool of movement leaders, we expand our view of framing to involve the interactive construction of disputes among challengers, their opponents, elements of the state, third parties, and the media. The political context in which a movement is mounted helps to frame its demands; the media and other sources of communication inadvertently frame a movement for its participants as well as for others; and cultural resources constrain and shape the deliberate framing efforts of movement leaders.
- Instead of limiting our purview to the action repertoires of challenging groups, we focus on innovative collective action by challengers and their member opponents.
- Finally, rather than focus on the origins of an episode of contention in which previously intert people mobilize into action, we focus on the mobilization process in general, leaving the question of the origins of contention to be specified as an empirical variant of the general process.

Putting Mobilization in Motion

The transformations from a static agenda to a set of interactive mechanisms are summarized in our revised mobilization model in Figure 2.1. The figure provides a tentative, dynamic, and interactive framework for analyzing the origins of contentious politics. It depicts the onset of contention as a highly contingent outcome of an interactive sequence

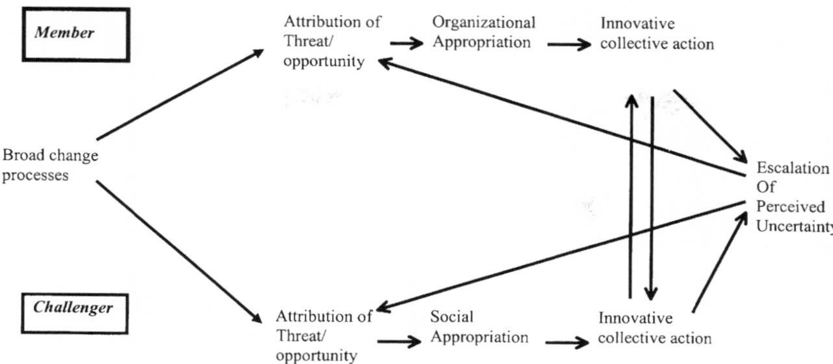

Figure 2.1. A Dynamic, Interactive Framework for Analyzing Mobilization in Contentious Politics

involving at least one set of state actors and one insurgent group. To summarize:

- Opportunities and threats are not objective categories, but depend on the kind of collective attribution that the classical agenda limited to framing of movement goals. They also involve other actors than formal movement organizations: members of the polity and subjects as well as other challengers.
- Mobilizing structures can be preexisting or created in the course of contention but in any case need to be appropriated as vehicles of struggle.
- Entire episodes, their actors, and their actions are interactively framed by participants, their opponents, the press, and important third parties.
- Innovative action gains attention, introduces new perturbations into an interactive field, and typically results in a ratcheting up of shared uncertainty among all parties to an emergent conflict.
- Mobilization occurs throughout an episode of contention. The interaction among the mechanisms in the model is both continual and recursive, and mobilization can be understood, in part, as a function of their interaction. But before turning to their interaction, let us say something more about the activation of each of these components using the example of American civil rights to illustrate our perspective.

From Opportunity Structure to Attribution of Threat and Opportunity

"Threats" and "opportunities" cannot be automatically read from the kinds of objective changes on which analysts have typically relied. Let us return to Rosa Parks. This was no demure southern lady who automatically took advantage of an objective structure of opportunities. She had a history of civil rights activism which led her and her Montgomery supporters to attribute an opportunity, not only to the injustice of bus segregation but to the potential economic clout of the city's black population. It was not just urbanization – an environmental mechanism – that led to the bus boycott, but the perception that the city's economy depended on black workers and black consumers and that this resource, if it could be mobilized effectively, would give the movement the opportunity to put pressure on the city fathers.

Nor were opportunities and threats only interpreted by movement actors. The Civil Rights movement emerged in response to grudging reform efforts by federal officials, which granted black insurgents more leverage with which to press their claims. But for all this attention to facilitation, analysts have generally limited their attention to the transgressive phase of the movement. This both exaggerates the distinctiveness of the mass phase of the conflict and impedes a clear understanding of the unfolding of the episode as a whole. Rather than conceiving of only insurgents as interpreters of environmental stimuli, we see challengers, members, and subjects as simultaneously responding to change processes and to each others' actions as they seek to make sense of their situations and to fashion lines of action based on their interpretations of reality.

In the Civil Rights movement, not only established civil rights groups, but federal officials (especially in the executive and judiciary) and southern segregationists attributed threat and opportunity to an evolving and uncertain situation and acted according to these calculations. The first break with tradition came as early as 1946, when President Truman appointed a Civil Rights Committee and charged it with investigating "current remedies of civil rights in the country and recommending appropriate legislative remedies for deficiencies uncovered." Action by civil rights groups escalated in the face of such federal efforts, as did membership in the NAACP and other organizations (Lawson 1976; McAdam 1982; Meier and Rudwick 1973). For their part, southern segregationists grew more restive too, faced by the double threat of federal legislation and growing black activism. During the Truman administration, white southerners began to defect from the solid southern traditions of the Democratic Party. This "Dixiecrat rebellion" was magnified in the Eisenhower years by the judicial activism of the Warren Supreme Court.

Responding both to increased protest and to the growing disintegration of the Solid South, the Kennedy administration, with its razor-thin congressional majority, came to see securing the votes of African-Americans as an opportunity. But this too was no automatic opening of an objective opportunity structure; it had to be perceived, constructed, and carefully balanced against the threat of white southern defection and the absence of northern working class enthusiasm for civil rights. It was only after much hesitation that the administration came to attribute to civil rights the status of an opportunity to be seized despite the political risks it entailed.

Notice how far we have come from Montgomery. Rather than the start of the movement, the bus boycott there emerges as a transgressive local episode in a national conflict whose onset preceded Montgomery by many years and involved the interactive attribution of threat and opportunity by constituted actors.

From Mobilizing Structures to Social Appropriation

It is a challenger's capacity to appropriate sufficient organization and numbers to provide a social/organizational base – and not that organization itself – which makes mobilization possible. Would-be activists (members no less than challengers and subjects) must either create an organizational vehicle or utilize an existing one and transform it into an instrument of contention. In the case of civil rights, it was local networks rooted for the most part in black churches. But until the rise of the mass movement, the black church was a generally conservative institution with a decided emphasis, not on the "social gospel in action," but on the realization of rewards in the next life (Johnson 1941; Marx 1971; Mays and Nicholson 1969). To turn even some black congregations into vehicles of collective protest, early movement leaders had to engage in creative cultural/organizational work, by which the aims of the church and its animating collective identity were redefined to accord with the goals of the emerging struggle.

Just like opportunity and threat attribution, the process of social appropriation applies to all parties in an emerging contentious episode.

Members and challengers, no less than subjects, confront the problem of mobilizing organizational resources. All of these actors are likely to have to contend with established organizational leaders who do not share their interpretation of recent events as posing a significant threat to, or opportunity for, the realization of group interests. Members and challengers possess one clear advantage over subjects when it comes to social appropriation. For members and challengers, most of the ongoing interpretation of environmental conditions takes place within formal organizations geared to the defense or advocacy of well established interests and organized around stable collective identities explicitly tied to these aims.

From Strategic Framing to Social Construction

For all of their importance, the framing efforts of mature movements depend on earlier and far more contingent interpretive "moments" in the life of a given contentious episode. The preceding two sections highlight such moments. Long before Martin Luther King's consummate framing abilities became evident, it was the collective interpretation and attribution of new threats and opportunities by established political actors that set the Cold War era civil rights struggle in motion. Later it was interpretive efforts in Montgomery that transformed the black church into a legitimate vehicle of mobilization, thereby triggering the transgressive phase of the episode.

Thus, in contrast to the classical agenda portrayed in Figure 1.2, we do not see framing as a distinct "box" or variable in the onset of contentious politics; for us, framing and interpretation go well beyond how a movement's goals are strategically formed to a much broader set of interpretive processes. Among the most important are those that result in attribution of new threats and opportunities by one or more parties to an emerging conflict and the reimagining of the legitimate purposes attached to established social sites and/or identities. In short, like all of social life, mobilization is suffused throughout with collective efforts at interpretation and social construction.

From Transgressive Repertoires to Innovative Collective Action

Finally we put the static concept of repertoire in motion, highlighting innovative shifts in the locus, forms, and meaning of collective action that typically occur at the onset of a contentious episode.

Lineaments of Contention

On the whole, shared prior knowledge, connections among key individuals, and on-the-spot direction guide the flow of collective action. Claimants generally interact strategically with objects of their claims, significant audiences, and representatives of public authorities. Often they must contend with rivals or enemies as well. Those interactions proceed from prior connections and accumulated experience. For that reason we can think of the repertoire as performances – as scripted interactions in the improvisatory manner of jazz or street theater rather than the more repetitious routines of art songs or religious rituals. Such performances group into repertoires, arrays of known possible interactions that characterize a particular set of actors.

Performances innovate around inherited repertoires and often incorporate ritual forms of collective action. Innovative contention is action that incorporates claims, selects objects of claims, includes collective self-representations, and/or adopts means that are either unprecedented or forbidden within the regime in question (see Chapter 1). In the Civil Rights movement, each new phase of innovation and each new site of contention chosen were in part responses to the response of authorities to the previous phase (McAdam 1983). Repertoires evolve as a result of improvisation and struggle. But at any given time, they limit the forms of interaction that are feasible and intelligible to the parties in question.

Innovation is not limited to challengers. In the case of the civil rights struggle, the adoption of a new and far more uncertain view of the postwar world led a wide array of groups – members, challengers, and subjects – to engage in innovative action on the "Negro question." Angered and frightened by this rejection of the status quo, segregationists reacted in a host of novel ways, from the staging of the Dixiecrat revolt in 1948, to the founding of the White Citizens Councils, to the "massive resistance" campaign of the mid to late 1950s. Obsessed with the threat of Communism, certain federal officials broke with the state's longstanding "hands off" policy with respect to race in favor of a campaign of significant civil rights reform. Buoyed by this transparent shift in federal policy, new civil rights groups joined old in a sustained campaign of innovative insurgency (McAdam 1983).

Rarely, however, were the innovative forms of action adopted by these parties to the conflict truly new. Rather they were creative modifications or extensions of familiar routines. Justice Department attorneys, for example, were not strangers to the filing of *amicus curiae* briefs, but they had never before filed them on behalf of civil rights litigants. Similarly, white southerners had engaged in violence against African Americans since Africans came to the continent; but it was the civil rights campaign that led them to use bombings, beatings, and murders in new and concerted ways. Finally, the black congregations that spearheaded the transgressive phase of the struggle merely adapted familiar church routines to the demands of the movement. The habitual practices of the church service became the behavioral script for the "mass meeting." With only slight alterations of lyrics, traditional gospel hymns became "freedom songs." And, as Martin Luther King himself put it:

> The invitational periods at the mass meetings, when we asked for volunteers, were much like those invitational periods that occur every Sunday morning in Negro churches, when the pastor projects the call to those present to join the church. By twenties and thirties and forties, people came forward to join our army." [King 1963: 59]

How Far Have We Come?

We see three principal virtues to the perspective on mobilization sketched above. These correspond to various "objections" raised earlier with respect to the classic social movement agenda.

- First, comparing the classical social movement agenda sketched in Figure 1.2 with the framework proposed in Figure 2.1 shows a clear move away from static variables to dynamic mechanisms. Verbs have replaced nouns. In place of an objective accounting of the opportunities, the organizational capacity, the available frames and repertoires of a given "mobilizing structure," we substitute a dynamic analysis of the internal debates and interactive processes through which social groups seek to define and act on a shared sense of collective purpose and identity.
- Our new perspective also allows us to transcend the single-actor framework embodied in the classic social movement agenda. To be sure, the figure even understates the typical extent of this interaction, by representing it as involving only two parties. But even restricting ourselves to just two actors, the general point should be clear. All politics – transgressive as well as contained – operates though interaction involving members, challengers, and subjects.
- The third implication of Figure 2.1 concerns the relation between the temporally limited concept of "origins" and the more general

process of mobilization. Although we have illustrated this discussion with the origins of a movement, we believe that mobilization takes place throughout episodes of contention. We go further: The framework can help us to initiate the analysis of *de*mobilization as well as mobilization; indeed, we will ultimately argue that it is as relevant to an understanding of routine as to contentious politics.

- The most important implication of our agenda is to stress development of contention through social interaction and to place social construction at the center of our analysis.

We have illustrated these points in the case of a well-known social movement, but we think the mechanisms we have deduced also combine in other forms of contention too. The start of a strike wave, a declaration of war, a nationalist episode, or the onset of democratization also involve the interactive attribution of opportunity and threat, appropriation of existing institutions and organizations, the framing or reframing of allies and enemies, goods and bads, and a combination of innovative and contained forms of collective action. As we will see below, the Parisian revolution of 1789 provides plenty of instances in which royal forces took the initiative and provoked defensive responses; much Italian contention was triggered by the actions of police, political parties, or third parties. As we will see in later chapters, similar mobilization processes can be observed in anticolonial movements such as the Mau Mau rebellion in Kenya, in democratization episodes such as the so-called "Yellow Revolution" in the Philippines, and in episodes of nationalism and national disintegration. Once we turn from the static components of the classical social movement agenda to a dynamic model based on the mechanisms of mobilization, that model applies to a variety of forms of contention.

Yet we must not claim too much too soon. More theoretical and empirical work needs to be done before we can put these ideas into motion. For one thing, we have so far dealt with only one form of contention – a social movement. Later chapters will examine how well the framework fits mobilization in other forms of contention. Second, contention does not consist only of mobilization; that process intersects with environmental constraints and with other processes and mechanisms. For example, we have so far paid little attention to the formation and transformation of actors, their actions, and identities. Nor have we analyzed the features of sustained trajectories of contention such as the diffusion of mobilization, the effect upon it of repression, the impact of radicalization or moderation, and the relations between different challengers. To illustrate the workings of these mechanisms and processes and their interactions with mobilization, we first return to another of our benchmark cases – the onset during the French Revolution of 1789 – and then turn to Italian contention during the 1960s and 1970s.

Insurgent Parisians

Burdened by his state's incapacity to pay its war-generated debts, baffled in his attempts to bulldoze regional *parlements* into authorizing new revenues, frustrated in his efforts to establish new revenue-yielding authorities in regions where those intermediary bodies lacked jurisdiction, and too dependent on future creditors and guarantors for a straightforward default of governmental debt, Louis XVI reluctantly called the French Estates General to assemble in Versailles at the start of May 1789. After a country-wide campaign of preparatory assemblies, elections, pamphlets, debates, and drafting of *cahiers de doléances* – statements of an assembly's complaints and proposals – national delegates of the three estates (clergy, nobility, and commoners) streamed to Versailles for separate deliberations.

Royal hopes for crisp resolution of the fiscal crisis soon foundered. The Third Estate's delegation, joined by some members of the separately convened clergy and nobility, declared itself the authentic national assembly on June 17, 1789.

> "What is the Third Estate," rhetorically asked the Abbe Sieyès in the first deliberate attempt to reshape identity in this identity-shaping revolution. "Everything," he answered rhetorically.
>
> "What has it been until now in the political order?" "Nothing," he answered himself.
>
> "What does it want to be? Something," he concluded. [Quoted in Sewell 1994: 41]

On July 7, the new assembly dominated by members of the Third Estate named a committee to draft a constitution.

The Third Estate was not alone in emerging as a political identity in those early days. In nearby Paris, orators were advocating radical reform in free spaces, such as the Palais Royal, members of military units were declaring their unwillingness to act against the populace, electors of Paris were debating drastic measures at the Hôtel de Ville, while groups of Parisians were meeting and marching to voice their support for representatives of what they increasingly called the Nation. After the king dismissed and exiled popular finance minister Jacques Necker on July 11, on Sunday the 12th, people who had gathered at the Palais Royal removed busts of Necker and of the duke of Orléans (the king's reputedly liberal nephew) from Curtius's waxworks and formed a parade of 5,000 people through Paris streets beneath black flags of mourning. Marchers battled royal troops in the Place Vendôme and the Tuileries, where members of the (equally royal) French Guards joined the crowd's attack on a German regiment that was trying to clear the palace grounds.

During the day, determined groups liberated the prisoners held in La Force and the Conciergerie. That evening, organized marauders wrecked tollhouses all around the Parisian perimeter, sacked the Saint-Lazare monastery, and broke into gunshops throughout the city. By that time, the King's French Guards units were either refusing to act or actively participating in attacks on prisons and other bastions of tyranny. On the following day (July 13) the Paris assembly of electors met at the Hôtel de Ville to establish a city – wide militia (a *milice bourgeoise*) and a Permanent Committee to administer it. The committee's members promised their electors that they would not cede control of the city hall so long as current troubles continued. In the name of the Parisian people they openly defied royal authority to govern Paris.

These steps amounted to revolution, for within France's very center they established an autonomous power disposing of its own military force. Agents of parish assemblies beat a drum or sounded the tocsin (the rapid ringing of a single church bell that signaled collective crisis) and held emergency sessions in churches throughout the city. Many of the local assemblies created militias, then sent them off to demonstrate support for the Committee. "While assemblies deliberated," reported Siméon-Prosper Hardy,

> one saw in the streets nothing but people armed every which way, many of them ragged; they were carrying rifles, bayonets, swords, sabers, pistols, staves with metal points, et cetera. Almost everyone was shouting Long Live the Third Estate, which for the moment seemed to have become the rallying cry. [BN Fr 6687]

The Third Estate, which had entered the episode as an abstract social category invited to Versailles to vote the King new taxes, had been transmuted into a political identity. Others – triggered by the diffusion of contention to Paris – were soon to move into action. At the city hall, militiamen were to meet Third Estate deputies who were proceeding from Versailles to Paris. Around 8:00 P.M. Hardy saw:

> seven or eight horsemen of the Third Estate, followed by about three hundred soldiers of the French Guard, the grenadiers, and other units, armed and marching to a drumbeat, led by sergeants and without officers, followed by a considerable multitude of insurgents armed in many different ways and dressed in a great variety of uniforms; they, too, had drums. They were going, people said, to the Place de Grève, to greet the eighty deputies from Versailles when they arrived at the Hôtel de Ville. [BN Fr 6687]

When the tocsin sounded once more on July 14, citizens again assembled in their parishes. Perhaps 7,000 people went to the Invalides, where they demanded and received weapons – a dozen cannon and thirty to forty thousand rifles – from the semi-retired veterans (*invalides*) who lodged there.

The next stop was across town, at the Bastille, where crowds had begun to gather on the evening of the 13th. To the venerable prison and fortress, city authorities had hastily moved a good deal of the city's gunpowder under protection of the Bastille's governor, the marquis de Launey. When the governor refused to surrender his gunpowder or the fortress, members of the growing crowd broke into the outer courtyard, where his small detachment of troops fired on them. Civilians and members of disaffected royal regiments rushed to the Bastille, began an assault complete with artillery, and forced capitulation of the fortress after about three hours of siege in which one defender and some hundred attackers died. Vindictively victorious Parisians released the Bastille's seven prisoners, massacred six of its defenders, killed de Launey, and paraded his head through the streets. They likewise decapitated Jacques de Flesselles, chair of the Permanent Committee, whom they accused of betraying the cause by refusing guns, powder, and bullets to would-be attackers of the Bastille.

These actions moved well into the range of transgressive politics, indeed into the realms of lèse-majesté and revolution. Although the Bastille itself had little strategic value and yielded only seven bedraggled prisoners, a force of defecting royal troops, popular militias, and ordinary citizens seized a notorious prison-citadel and executed its governor. Such acts revealed the regime's vulnerability far more dramatically than did days of debate in the National Assembly. By July 16, the king was calling Necker back from his native Switzerland and ordering the troops that had encircled Paris and Versailles back to their regular quarters. A day later, flanked by two hundred horsemen of the Parisian militia and a hundred members of the National Assembly, the king himself came in procession to the Hôtel de Ville, thereby symbolizing his acceptance of the new regime. No popular rising had forced so great a royal reversal since the Fronde of 1648–1653.

Yet the dramas of July 12–14, 1789 also drew on familiar scripts. When authorized by appropriate officials, calling of parish and city assemblies, formation of militias, and processions with banners all belonged to established old-regime responses to crises. Decapitation and display of a severed head formed parts of a rare but notorious punishment reserved by the royal executioner for nobles who had committed treason. By performing these deeds without royal sanction and in the company of armed attacks, Parisians were innovating, taking the law into their own hands, edging into revolution. But they were also borrowing heavily from old-regime precedents.

Who's Who?

The greater novelty of these events lay in who acted and in whose name – in the activation, creation, and transformation of collective identities that were occurring in Versailles and in revolutionary Paris. As members of the Third Estate, as citizens attached not to the monarchy but to the Nation, as participants in self-constituted militias, and as identifiable enemies of constituted authorities, Parisians were forming new identities. They were also on their way to constructing paired identities as revolutionary or counterrevolutionary, patriot or aristocrat, citizen or subject. None of these identities rested simply on stable attributes of individuals. None of them ever became the sole marker for any individual. All of them coexisted with other identities, such as carpenter, parishioner, or spouse. All of them had fatefully contested boundaries. All of them changed continuously as a function of interaction with other parties. Yet most of the time, participants and observers in the revolution's contentious politics talked and behaved as if such identities as Patriot or Republican were coherent, real, solid, and compelling. In these regards, identities that emerged in revolutionary Paris resembled political identities wherever they operate.

The formation of political identities matters, not so much because it affects communication and disputation among scholars but for two much more profound reasons: first, because they become matters of intense dispute among participants; second, because the answer to the question of identity affects the very explanation of contentious political processes in general. We advance, and attempt to reconcile, six distinct claims about creation, appropriation, activation, transformation, and suppression of political identities:

1. participants in contentious politics constantly manipulate, strategize, modify, and reinterpret the identities of parties to their contention, including themselves
2. in a wide variety of contentious politics mobilization of identities constitutes a major part of claim making
3. while new identities emerge during contentious episodes, most individuals initially join the fray through interactive appeals to, and successful appropriation of, existing identities
4. the form, content, and effectiveness of identity mobilization strongly affect both collective action and its outcomes
5. creation, transformation, and extinction of actors, identities, and forms of action in the course of contention alter the array of actors, identities, and actions that appear in routine politics and further contention once the particular episode of contention has ended
6. when it comes to explaining contentious politics, the crucial arena for causal mechanisms lies not in individual minds but in social interaction

The six claims point toward a thoroughgoing dynamic and relational analysis of actor formation and transformation in contentious politics that interacts with the mobilization process and indeed affects its course and outcomes.

Why do we combine an analysis of action with actors and identities? This follows from our interactive view of contentious politics. Actors, in our view, are not neatly bounded, self-propelling entities with fixed attributes, but socially embedded and constituted beings who interact incessantly with other such beings and undergo modifications of their boundaries and attributes as they interact. Actions consist not of self-deliberated emissions of individual energy, but of interactions among such sites. Identities do not inhere in fixed attributes of such sites, much less in states of consciousness at those sites, but in connections between those sites and the interactions in which they are involved. Within ostensibly unitary actors, the work of coordination, negotiation, and modification goes on unceasingly. Contentious politics does not simply activate preexisting actors but engages actors in a series of interactive performances – our repertoires – that proceed through incessant improvisation within broadly defined scripts and organizational constraints. Contention alters parties, relationships, and forms of action as it goes.

Our relational view of actors, identities, and actions can be usefully confronted with two currently popular approaches that have been applied to the study of contentious politics – rationalism and culturalism.

- *Rationalism:* In taking interests and capacities as given and individually based, in treating trajectories from decision-making to action to consequences as either given or unproblematic, and in treating collective decision making as nothing but individual decision-making writ large, rational action theorists condemn themselves to trouble in explaining how social interaction – including outright struggle – and its outcomes alter actors, actions, and identities. When we ask rationalists to explain Parisian struggles of July 11–14, 1789, they can tell us what was at stake for the king, Necker, or Flesselles, but they stumble when it comes to explaining the emergence of the Third Estate as a political category and a mobilizing symbol or the emergence of militias and committees as major actors on the Parisian scene. In fact, just such difficulties have drawn rational actor analysts recently into closer study of contexts, trust, third-party relationships, and games with multiple players (e.g., Bates, et al. 1998; Burt and Knez 1995; Gambetta 1988, 1993; Greif 1994; Greif, Milgrom and Weingast 1994; Landa 1994; Lichbach and Zuckerman 1997).
- *Culturalism:* Our approach also distinguishes itself from recent cultural explanations of contentious politics. These approaches are more concerned than their rationalist rivals with the construction of identities, but in their accounts, construction and interpretation take place within people's heads. Actions result from phenomenological states, and identities constitute one of the most important aspects of phenomenological states. To become an activist, therefore, consists of adopting a certain state of mind – by "imagining" oneself a member of a nation, in one popular version (Anderson 1991). But by digging so deeply into phenomenology, culturalists deprive themselves of the opportunity to describe, much less explain, how collective representations change, how collective states of consciousness produce their effects on contentious interaction, and to examine contentious interaction as a constitutive site in the formation of actors and identities.

> Culturalists have, for example, created no plausible causal account of the process that checked Louis XVI's determined attempt to regain military and political control over the city in July 1789.

As a consequence of the large effort that has flowed into these issues recently, members of both rationalist and culturalist schools are beginning to understand that contentious politics always involves the social construction of politically relevant categories, such as indigenous peoples or feminists; always adopt forms of interaction with allies, supporters, or targets of claims that innovate within strong limits set by previously known forms of claim making; and never mobilize without some significant grounding in ties created by previous contention and/or routine social life. Our relational approach goes further in this direction by explicitly focussing on social interaction as the site in which identities form, coalesce, split, and transform and intersect with other processes – such as mobilization. In what follows, we illustrate how identity formation interacted with the four mobilization mechanisms we sketched in the first section of this chapter.

Creating Republicans

From the traveling hagiography of the assault on the Bastille after July 14, to the choreography of revolutionary festivals, to the conflicts over how revolutionary monuments should look, to the design of republican costumes and secular religion, we know much about how the men who struggled to transform France into a Republic tried to reshape French identities (Hunt 1984; Ozouf 1988; Schama 1989). But because many of these writers focused statically on cultural objects and were at pains to distance themselves from political history, their work lacks an explicit link between identity formation and political mobilization. Later chapters give explicit attention to the mechanisms of identity formation in a variety of cases, most deliberately in South Asian and South African contention (Chapter 5), in democratizing Spain and antebellum America (Chapter 6) and in nationalizing Italy and the disintegrating Soviet Union (Chapter 8). For now, let us illustrate the intersection of actor and identity shift with the mobilization mechanisms we isolated for attention in Figure 2.1.

First, returning to the *environmental mechanisms* that trigger the start of the process, in France, identity construction built on social change processes. Although the Third Estate emerged as a political category only in 1789, it had its basis in the nonnoble and nonclerical accumulation of wealth over the decades prior to the revolution. Sieyès' famous essay would have fallen on deaf ears had there not been among the delegates of the Estates General objective correlates for the claim of universalism and preeminence that he made for the Third Estate. Moreover, French identity construction did not occur in a national vacuum. The very term "patriot" that became a mark of Republican identity was taken bodily from the American and Dutch revolutions of the previous decade (Schama 1989: ch. 7).

Second, with respect to the *attribution of opportunity and threat*, the new identities that emerged from the early phase of the revolution were rapidly deployed to bring together new combinations of actors against constructed enemies and villains. The crowds that mobilized on the various *journées* in Paris were animated by paired identities – revolutionary or counterrevolutionary, patriot or aristocrat, citizen or subject – that emerged out of the first phase of contention. Although many of the Revolution's early leaders came from the aristocracy (think of Lafayette and Mirabeau), attacks on opponents increased in ferocity as they were branded aristocats or antipatriots and as the attackers came to see themselves as Patriots or Republicans. Key mobilization episodes frequently turned on the array and transmutation of such mobilized identities. For example, when the king was brought forcefully to the Hôtel de Ville, his subservience to the Republic was literally crowned when a revolutionary bonnet was unceremoniously thrust upon his head.

Third, with respect to the *social appropriation of existing organizations*, the so-called "municipal revolutions" that followed the assault on the Bastille mobilized new identities in contentious action: In the name of the Revolution, groups of local republicans appropriated local administrations as tools of provincial revolution, laying the groundwork for both the future Napoleonic state and for the federalist movement that, in parts of France, would eventually mount regional revolts against Parisian power. With respect to the Church, the Civil Constitution of the clergy had similarly polarizing effects: Where it succeeded, the secularization process turned religion to the purposes of statebuilding. Where it failed, it produced a savage civil war between Republicans and a coalition of legitimists, clericals, and peasants (Tilly 1964).

Fourth, with respect to *framing*, the entire revolutionary decade constitutes a study in the framing and reframing of identities, meanings, and rituals. Mona Ozouf's work on revolutionary festivals (1988) and Lynn

Hunt's work on revolutionary monuments and dress (1984) and on the denigration of the royal family (1992) show how symbols of identity were manipulated to produce a republican identity and decertify the monarchy. These campaigns mobilized French men and women in the names of new or transformed identities and stripped their targets of legitimacy – to the point at which revolutionary officials sometimes had to brake enthusiastic attacks on imagined aristocrats and spies by citizens whose ardor was enhanced by sharply etched identity polarities (Hunt 1984: 52).

Finally, *innovative collective action* turned on and helped to shape the changing definitions of members, challengers, and subjects. Governments both prescribe, tolerate, or forbid different claims-making performances and respond differently to various political actors. They recognize some (e.g., royal troops in July 1789) as *agents* of the regime, others (e.g., assemblies of electors) as established *members* of the polity, some (e.g., militias) as constituted but illegitimate *challengers* and some (e.g., people on the street by the Bastille) as *subjects* with no capacity to act. In a situation of relative certainty, where it is fairly clear what will happen next, subjects and some constituted challengers remain inactive. With increasing uncertainty, both types of actors move toward tolerated and forbidden forms of action. Even polity members resort to forbidden performances when uncertainty reaches its peak. Most of the time, however, the more established the political actor, the greater the likelihood that an actor's claim making will go on within the channels of prescribed or tolerated public politics.

The Parisian uprising increased uncertainty throughout France, which stimulated excluded actors (including oppressed peasants) to mount both tolerated and forbidden forms of claim making. Even polity members responded to the uncertainties of summer 1789 by moving away from prescribed toward tolerated and, occasionally, forbidden forms of contention. Because contentious interaction involved authorities and brought new authorities into being, the struggles in question started to redefine the boundaries among forbidden, tolerated, and prescribed performances for the polity as a whole. Over the next year, for example, militia assemblies went from being forbidden or barely tolerated to being standard features of French political life. The Parisian crowds that recurrently erupted into the National Assembly or the Convention did so with the assurance that they represented the People, and had a right to insert their claims upon their representatives.

Let us refine the strategic situation of contentious actors. Consider a situation in which a socially constructed actor – say a Parisian militia company on July 13, 1789 – finds itself at a given instant during the course of contention. From the perspective of a single actor in stop time, a number of possible interactions are available. Each interaction has a distribution of possible outcomes, a distribution our hypothetical actor estimates from previous interactions with similar supporters, allies, objects of claims, authorities who are not objects of claims but have the power to intervene, and bystanders. Members of our hypothetical actor reason in both directions: from actions to outcomes (If we do X, what will happen?) and from outcomes to actions (If we want outcome Y, what interactions might produce it, with what probabilities?). A significant part of organization, deliberation, and negotiation within collective actors consists of creating provisional agreements concerning the contents of such grids, as well as forming choices of paths through them. But contentious claim making and its actual outcomes modify the grids, hence available forms and choices of interactions, continuously. Imagine the scene we have just constructed, then, as a single frame from a very long movie.

In the bloody encounter at the Bastille on July 14, 1789, we see just such a movie unfolding: Military forces inside the fortress fashion a reading of their situation, multiple clusters of soldiers and civilians gather outside, and action proceeds from delegations to armed combat to ritual execution. In retrospective accounts, furthermore, the outsiders become a heroic unitary actor: the determined People that conquered a bastion of tyranny. Thus social construction of action occurs and changes as a consequence of continuous interaction – both among socially constructed actors and within them. In summary, the neat four-mechanism schema of mobilization presented in Figure 2.1 needs to be intersected with the formation of new actors and identities, and with how they interact with others through the performances of contentious politics.

How might we proceed? Take five steps:

Step one: Recognize the contingent, collective, constructed character of actors, actions, and identities in contentious politics. That recognition would place high on our explanatory agenda accounting for variation in the sorts of identities that participants in contention actually mobilize, experience, and deploy. In the case of Paris in 1789, examine how Parisians were creating, transforming, and representing categorical social relations as revolutionaries, as citizens, as members of militia units, and as the Third Estate.

Step two: Specify relations between routine noncontentious actors, actions, and identities, on one side, and identities figuring prominently in contention, on the other. To what extent and under what conditions are they similar or different? In Paris of 1789, map previously existing social ties and practices corresponding to such pairs as noble-commoner, priest-parishioner, or master-worker into those of the new pairs patriot-aristocrat, citizen-elected official, and soldier-militiaman.

Step three: Specify connections between (a) construction and appropriation of actors, actions, and identities and (b) relations of the relevant actors, actions, and identities to changing structures of power in the actors' environments. In revolutionary Paris, explain the process by which the militias' Permanent Committee became the center of a collective seizure of power in the nation's name through means of action no one dared employ a month or two earlier.

Step four: Analyze how contention itself transforms collective identities, then how such transformations alter the character and effects of contention. In the Parisian situation, show how and why the Bastille's seizure redefined who were the major actors on the national scene and how they connected with each other.

Step five: Examine how creation, transformation, and extinction of actors, identities, and forms of action in the course of contention alter both transgressive and routine politics after a particular episode of contention ends. In the French case, trace the impact of July 1789's turbulent contentious processes on the nature of Parisian and national politics during the following months, for example, by examining how the pathways of diffusion, the pressures of repression, and the strains of radicalization produced an increasingly polarized polity.

This takes us to the general issue of the trajectories of contention, which is not so much a process as a field on which various processes, such as mobilization, actor constitution and polarization, proceed in tandem. Let us turn to our third benchmark case to illustrate one such pattern of interaction, drawing on a family of mechanisms that are typically associated with dynamic processes. We will observe those dynamic mechanisms at work in the Italian protest movements of the late 1960s and early 1970s.

Contentious Italians

In the 1967–1968 academic year, long-delayed parliamentary debates began in Rome over the reform of Italy's antiquated educational system. As a side-product of the economic miracle of the 1950s, thousands of new students poured into universities whose structures were ill-equipped to receive them and whose professors yearned for the elitist system they had inherited from fascism. But as in the case of civil rights and the French Third Estate, environmental changes start our story but by no means explain it: As a coalition of Socialists, Christian Democrats and minor parties of the center left began their noisy deliberations over university reform, the official student groups – most of them either corporatist or dependent on the major political parties – sought to influence the parliamentary debate. In this, they would fail, but radical minorities within them appropriated these structures and seized the opportunity of the educational debate for their own purposes, framing the issue not as one of the technical reform of an overloaded system but as one of the "autonomy" of the students from their universities. Around this theme, they developed a contentious repertoire of actions aimed at establishing their autonomy both from their organizations' leaders and from the parties that until then had controlled them.

The episode is noteworthy, first, because it began in an episode of contained contention and, second, because it illustrates our checklist of mobilization mechanisms (Tarrow 1989: ch. 6). But most important was that it was the crucible in which a new student identity was formed and new actors emerged. Coming variously from Marxist, liberal, and Catholic backgrounds, student activists merged their claims around the theme of autonomy from both the authoritarian structures of the universities and from the heavy hand of the political-party-led student groups. That construction took place partly in people's heads – for example, there was a run on books by Italian Marxist theorist Antonio Gramsci – but mainly through interaction within the students' chosen instrument of contention, the faculty building occupation.

Occupations were not just a new transgressive form of innovative collective action. They were interactive encounters in which different groups of students met, debated earnestly, engaged in lively study groups, planned future activities, fought off outside opponents, and – especially for young women – experienced a sense of personal liberation from cloistered family lives. An atmosphere of permanent fair fostered a sense of solidarity and created bonds that, for many, would last for a generation (Lumley 1990).

Out of these student occupations and identity shifts came a new panoply of left-wing organizations and little journals, leading older organizations and journals to scramble to keep up with the rapid pace of ideological and programmatic change (Tarrow 1989: ch. 6). Analyzing their documents we see an iterative process of radicalization of their themes and in the expansion of their subject matter. The first of the new groups were loosely structured and prided themselves on their internal democracy and spontaneity. Foreign models – Maoism, Situationism, the Berkeley student revolt – blended with domestic traditions such as workerism and anarchism to produce an alphabet-soup jumble of *gruppuscoli*. They were unified only by a strong opposition to authority and by the desire for autonomy from political party sponsors, who were increasingly condemned as revisionist, Leninist, or both. The French May, which followed hard on these developments, crystallized them in an antiauthoritarian mold and allowed the students to identify their movement with an imagined worldwide wave of revolution that would be led by the students.

But this phase of enthusiastic university occupations soon lost both its unity and its spontaneity. Though old divisions between Marxists and left-wing Catholics had disappeared, new ones appeared among sympathizers with one or another tendency or leader. These groups began by meeting separately to design resolutions and stage manage debates within the student assemblies. Disillusioned by this renascent Leninism, bored by the endless drone of debate the organized groups fostered, and intimidated by increasingly brutal evacuations by the police and attacks by fascist groups, the mass of the students began to drift away, leaving a committed core of activists to lick their wounds and look outside the universities for new opportunities for contention. A process of polarization followed the 1968 "moment of madness" (Zolberg 1972), leading some activists into the dangerous terrain of terrorism while others began a long march through the institutions (Tarrow 1989: ch. 11).

Two Partial Models

How can we capture the dynamic of the Italian university student movement? Two classical models have been appropriated by students of trajectories: the "movement career" and the "protest cycle":

The movement career model emerged from the core tradition of Weberian-Michelsian sociology (Alberoni 1968). It posited spontaneous noninstitutional origins for movement organizations, a linear trend toward deradicalization and bureaucracy, and a shift from charismatic leaders calling for radical change to organizational specialists more intent on defending their positions (Michels 1962). As a result, contention describes a rough parabola from movement to interest group, from a mood of *statu nascenti* to one of rational decision making, and from principled opposition to institutions to participation in pragmatic politics (Lowi 1971; Piven and Cloward 1977).

That model summarized aptly what had happened to central European Social Democracy in the early twentieth century. But that was a single movement, not a protracted episode of contention; and it had specificities that badly matched the situation of movements in the 1960s and beyond (Calhoun 1995). By that time the modal movement organization was decentralized and informal, activism was more likely to take the form of "transitory teams" than bureaucratic monoliths, and supporters were recruited on a campaign basis, rather than depending on the serried ranks of dues-paying members (McCarthy and Zald 1977; Rosenthal and Schwartz 1990).

Moreover, the Michelsian model – though dynamic – was linear and rigid. As our Italian example suggests, many of the movement organizations that emerged out of the 1960s belied the inexorable trend to deradicalization that Michels predicted. Most important, the movement career model privileged the internal dynamics of single-movement organizations, detaching them from the interactions that influence their goals, organization, and tactics (Oliver 1989). In Italy, these interactions produced new actors and identities, helped to radicalize some groups, institutionalize others, and move the episode along toward its ragged and contradictory close. Can these other actors and interactions be excluded from the evolution of movement organizations? Surely not. This takes us to a second and more ambitious approach to contentious trajectories.

The protest cycle model abandoned the idea of tracing episodes of contention through the careers of single-movement organizations and observed broader trajectories involving a variety of groups and actors (Tarrow 1989). It posited a phase of heightened conflict and intensity of interaction across the social system, a rapid diffusion of collective action from more mobilized to less mobilized sectors of society, a heightened pace of innovation in the forms of contention, the creation of new or transformed collective action frames, and a combination of organized and unorganized contention.

Cyclical theory is a perfect representation of the classical social movement agenda once it goes beyond movement origins. It combined the idea of expanding political opportunities, new and old organizational resources, the organization of collective action around "master frames," such as rights or autonomy, and an explosion of innovative collective action. It insisted on the role of uncertainty, which provides opportunities for claim making but also threatens established groups, leading to competition among claimants for political space (Eisinger 1973; Stinchcombe 1999). In some versions it emphasized the alteration in identities over the course of a cycle (Klandermans 1994). And in contrast to the movement career model, it saw both radicalization and institutionalization as important mechanisms in episodes of contention.

The strength of the theory was that it was interactive. Through publicly mounted contention, challengers' actions are communicated to, and produce political opportunities for, other groups. This leads states to devise broad strategies of repression and facilitation. Movements respond to these strategies either by radicalization or moderation. Cycles end through a combination of exhaustion, sectarianization, and cooptation. The theory's weakness was that it remained largely a *stage theory* based on a deductively posited phase of mobilization followed by a distinct phase of demobilization, failing to account for mobilizations that emerge at various stages of the cycle and leaving untheorized the relations between actors, their actions, and their identities. By positing a recurring parabolic shape to episodes of contention, cyclical theory begged the question of the internal composition of the cycle and whether there are episodes that take different forms altogether.

Our perspective leads us beyond both career and cyclical models of trajectories.

- Once we realized that single movements are embedded in different contexts of contention and interact with other actors in an iterative dance of mobilization and demobilization, identity formation and innovative collective action, we understood the limitations in the Michelsian model.
- Once we came to understand that trajectories of contention need not take a parabolic form, that they do not pass through invariant stages,

and that the driving force in their progression lies in the interaction of the actors, we came to see the cyclical model as one empirical form of trajectories and were free to turn directly to the mechanisms and processes that power them.

- By understanding which mechanisms and processes put an episode of contention in motion and where they take it, we can better understand why some episodes are brief while others are protracted, why some end in demobilization while others expand into revolution, and why some produce fundamental shifts in alignments and political culture while others leave behind nothing but a residue of bitter memories.

Note the implications of our discovery. It does not mean that no patterns exist, or even that all imaginable sequences actually occur. Instead, it means that regularities in trajectories lie elsewhere than in standard sequences, whether movement careers, protest cycles, or otherwise. Regularities lie in the mechanisms that bring in new actors, eliminate old ones, transform alliances, and shift the strategies of critical actors. These concatenate into processes we will identify later. For the moment, by way of illustration, let us simply outline some of the mechanisms observable in this episode of contention.

Mechanisms in Dynamic Processes of Contention

Nearly all protracted episodes of contention produce a mechanism of *competition for power*. All three of our touchstone episodes reveal these two mechanisms:

- Take our oldest episode: After the initial period that Crane Brinton called "the reign of the moderates" (1965: ch. 5), radical members of the revolutionary coalition competing for power turned on the moderates, using the tools of state repression and popular mobilization to liquidate them in a "reign of terror and virtue." First constitutional moderates were defeated by a coalition of Republicans; then the republican coalition split into competing groups and then into Girondins and Jacobins; and finally, the triumphant Jacobins defeated and elimimated their Girondin colleagues. Through a process of polarization, the French revolution "devoured its children."
- The dynamics of the American Civil Rights movement also illustrates internal competition, but with less disastrous results. As Martin

Luther King and the moderate branch of the movement became the darlings of the mainstream media, radical currents associated with SNCC and CORE contested his leadership and pushed toward a more radical interpretation of civil rights (Carson 1981; Meier and Rudwick 1973). And as the movement moved north, a new generation of ghetto activists condemned the leadership of groups such as the NAACP for their moderation and compromise with authorities.
- Finally, our Italian case shows clear evidence of competition too: first between more moderate and radical student groups; then as the more radical groups competed for support, between those who adopted armed struggle and those who moved toward a more institutional path; and finally between extreme left and extreme right, as they fought to extinguish the Republic from opposite extremes.

When specialists examine these episodes from close up, they, of course, find contextual and historical factors that help to explain competition in each case: the threat of foreign invasion that induced the Jacobins to accuse their opponents of collaborating with the enemy; the exhaustion of the moderate agenda of the Civil Rights movement after passage of the Voting Rights Act of 1964; the historical anomaly that Italy retained vestiges of both militant workerism and fascism. These factors are not so much wrong as specific expressions of the same mechanism.

The lessons from examination of competition can be generalized. Instead of digging deeper into context to provide evidence for the case-specific causes of the mechanisms we find, our project is to examine the specific contexts in which they arise and their connections with others in more general processes of contention. We look for mechanisms present in all three cases, not to flatten our episodes into one great mold but to explore whether the processes of contention are constituted of the same basic fabric wherever we find them.

Other mechanisms that we will find in many trajectories of contention are diffusion, repression, and radicalization.

Consider first *diffusion*, a mechanism that is virtually coterminous with protest cycles (Hedström, Sandell, and Stern 2000; McAdam 1995; McAdam and Rucht 1993; Myers 2000; Oliver and Myers 1999; Strang and Meyer 1993). At the most general level, diffusion includes any transfer of information across existing lines of communication. Here we concentrate on *transfer in the same or similar shape of forms and claims of contention across space or across sectors and ideological divides.* We see it in the

French Revolution in the spread of insurrection from Paris, in the contagion of the peasant "great fear" across the countryside, and in the "municipal revolutions" that permitted local Republicans to take control of cities in various parts of the country. We find it again in the Civil Rights movement in the spread of the form of the "sit-in" in various forms of public accommodation across the South and in the various "freedom marches" that different civil rights groups organized. We find it in Italy in the adoption of the "autonomy" frame from the student's movement in the industrial workers' movement and in a branch of the extraparliamentary groups who adopted *Autonomia* as their label.

Now consider *repression, efforts to suppress either contentious acts or groups and organizations responsible for them.* In one form or another, repression is a predictable response to contention, with relatively predictable effects – generally stiffening resistance on the part of threatened communities, encouraging evasion of surveillance and shifts of tactics by well organized actors, and discouraging mobilization or action by other parties. Repression may be selective, in which case it isolates more militant groups and closes off to them prescribed or tolerated means of contention. Or it can be generalized, in which case it throws moderates into the arms of the extremists.

We find repression and its effects in all three of our benchmark cases: Faced with the threat of being dragooned into Republican armies, young peasants in Western France flocked under the banners of clerical-legitimist resistance. Faced by rejection by the broader civil rights community and perceiving themselves threatened by the white police, ghetto militants formed tight urban groups such as the Black Panthers, who wore military-like uniforms, brandished guns, and alienated liberal white supporters of civil rights. Driven into clandestinity by repression, militant veterans of the Italian student movement turned to the only kinds of contention that were still open to them – violent attacks on their opponents or on the state.

Next consider *radicalization, the expansion of collective action frames to more extreme agendas and the adoption of more transgressive forms of contention.*

In an epochal move to radicalization, French Jacobins voted the execution of the King in 1791 to close the door on backsliding in their revolutionary project. Less tragically, the exhaustion of the equal opportunity agenda of the southern Civil Rights movement left younger activists in the movement searching for new themes and new forms of action that they could use to keep the movement vibrant and move it to the North. And as newly formed student groups struggled for recognition and support in

Italy, they outdid each other with more and more extreme programs and radical forms of action.

Diffusion, repression, and radicalization combined in the trajectories of all three of our touchstone cases, producing processes of polarization.

Let us step back: We do not maintain that all episodes of contention are based on the same mechanisms or describe the same trajectories. Many episodes, in fact, remain contained within their original sites, pose few threats to opponents, and close with relatively minor calibrations in the polity. There will also be additional factors to consider – how the history of contention in a particular country provides lessons for the present, how the presence of other mechanisms, such as "brokerage," can bridge ideological chasms and deter competition, or how "radical flank effects" drive opposing actors toward one another to oppose threats from the extremes. Our book examines a number of episodes in which such mechanisms come together in more or less explosive combinations, while in others, trajectories move toward relatively contained closure. What is important here is not to posit deductively linear trajectories and predictable outcomes but to identify the processes and their constituent mechanisms that constitute different dynamics of contention.

Conclusion and Premise

No general law has been proposed here for the study of contentious politics, nor will it be in our book. Thus far we have tried to illustrate where we want to go with a number of loosely connected mechanisms and processes:

- A mobilization process triggered by environmental changes and that consists of a combination of attribution of opportunities and threats, social appropriation, construction of frames, situations, identities, and innovative collective action.
- A family of mechanisms still to be elucidated around the processes of actor and identity constitution and the actions that constitute them.
- A set of mechanisms often found in trajectories of contention that recurs in protracted episodes of contention, competition, diffusion, repression, and radicalization.

In Parts II and III of our book we return to some of these mechanisms and processes, adding others that emerge from our investigations.

More generally, the challenge of substituting dynamic and interactive explanations of contention for the static, single-actor models that have prevailed over much of the field generates a whole series of new adventures. First, we must dig deeper into mobilization, action, and trajectories in order to detect the continuous negotiation that goes on within each of them. Second, we must examine the interplay among mobilization, actors, and trajectories rather than treating them as three independent phenomena. Eventually, indeed, we will dissolve these conventional distinctions in favor of seeing them as different abstractions from the same continuous streams of social interaction. Third, we must recast the analytic problem as the identification of robust, consequential mechanisms and processes that explain crucial features of contentious episodes. To these tasks we now turn.

3

Comparisons, Mechanisms, and Episodes

Parisian revolutionary struggles, American civil rights, Italian postwar conflicts: The three sequences sketched in Chapters 1 and 2 represent distinctive and well known varieties of contentious politics in the western tradition. Our treatment of them raised standard questions concerning mobilization, actors, and trajectories. In the course of contentious politics: (1) What processes move people into and out of public, collective claim making, and how? (2) Who's who and what do they do? (3) What governs the course and outcomes of contentious interaction? In each case, we found that the standard social movement agenda – social change, mobilizing structures, opportunity – provided a disciplined way of asking questions about the events, but pointed to unsatisfactory answers. The answers were unsatisfactory because they were static, because they provided accounts of single actors rather than relations among actors, and because at best they identified likely connections rather than causal sequences.

Chapters 1 and 2 explored both weaknesses of existing approaches and intellectual resources for repairing those weaknesses. When it comes to the origins and mobilization of contention, we discover that the very definition of the problem in those terms entails serious difficulties: Despite the urge to tell stories having well defined beginnings, middles, and ends, contentious episodes rarely start and stop crisply. Instead, mobilization of some actors, demobilization of others, and transformation of one form of action into another occurs frequently in most complex contention. We find many circumstances, for example, in which contained contention continues over a substantial period only to mutate into transgressive contention: contention in which previously unrecognized actors and/or forms of action figure prominently. Even the conventional separation of mobilizing structures from collective action turns out to pose difficulties, since contentious interaction actually transforms routine social relations within communities, churches, associations, firms, and other structures that analysts have commonly thought of as existing prior to action and shaping that action. Here again, the static, individualistic, and often reified character of previous analyses – including our own – bars the door to dynamic, interactive analyses of mobilization and demobilization.

In the case of contentious action, analysts of the subject clearly need new formulations that capture and help explain the fluid, strategic, and interactive operation of actors, identities, and forms of collective action. Structuralist, rationalist, and culturalist approaches do not provide sufficient means for the task at hand. In all of them, reification and individualization block the way to dynamic, interactive accounts of contentious action.

Similar difficulties beset available treatments of contentious trajectories. The ideas of movement career and protest cycle introduce some dynamism into treatments of contention, but at the cost, in the first case, of an excessive focus on isolated movement organizations and, in the second, of an image of relatively invariant sequences having well marked beginnings, middles, and ends. So far, available models give little guidance to what actually happens at critical junctures. How and why do relations among actors and predominant forms of interaction shift significantly in the course of contention?

We are not, to be sure, the first to notice weaknesses in existing models of contentious mobilization, action, or trajectories. Rationalists have repeatedly sought to introduce dynamism into their models by treating contentious episodes as iterated strategic games, culturalists and collective behavior theorists by plumbing alterations of consciousness, structuralists by specifying large scale processes of social change. None of these efforts has yielded the dynamic, interactive account of contention called for by such episodes as the Parisian revolution of 1789, American civil rights struggles, and postwar Italian conflicts. The political process version of the classic agenda for study of social movements (as its very name indicates) came into being as a way of thinking about dynamic aspects of contention. But it proceeded chiefly by promoting attention to changes in mobilizing structures, opportunities, threats, frames, and repertoires as causes of changes in action. It did not provide satisfactory theories of alterations in those individual elements or of their interdependence.

What is more, the standard social movement agenda handles interactions among actors, their targets, their opponents, and third parties awkwardly. To the extent that it enters at all, the state generally acts as a *diabolus ex machina*, producing opportunities, awaiting mobilization, landing heavily on some actors and facilitating others, but not participating directly in contention. As Chapter 2 (e.g., Figure 2.1) argues, states and challengers actually engage in continuous interaction. Each defines threats and opportunities, mobilizes existent and newly created resources, undertakes innovative collective action in response to other actors' maneuvers, and in some cases transforms the course of interaction.

To Broaden Explanation's Scope

We can broaden our explanatory scope by shifting the search away from general models that purport to summarize whole categories of contention and toward the analysis of smaller-scale causal mechanisms that recur in different combinations with different aggregate consequences in varying historical settings. We do not seek to isolate general laws of "collective action" covering social movements, ethnic conflict, interest group politics, or revolution. Instead, we search for mechanisms that appear variously combined in all these forms of contention and in others as well. A viable vision of contentious politics, we claim, begins with a search for causal analogies: identification of similar causes in ostensibly separate times, places, and forms of contention.

We began in Chapters 1 and 2 by concentrating on a small number of familiar and well documented episodes in France, the United States, and Italy. Now it is time to extend the range. In the remainder of the study, we reach out beyond our "home bases" for several reasons: to avoid mistaking historically specific features of western polities for general features of contention; to see how far it is possible to extend concepts and explanations across distinctively different political settings without bending those settings out of shape; to multiply opportunities for unexpected discoveries and unanticipated challenges to received ideas.

In Part II we examine a number of contentious phenomena from the period since 1800 that vary significantly with respect to period, place, scale, duration, unity, political regime, types of actors, and forms of contention. Here is the roster of six cases we will examine in Part II, laid out as matched pairs:

- anti–Marcos mobilization in the Philippines, 1983–1986 and the Mau Mau mobilization in Kenya, 1950–1960

- recent Hindu–Muslim conflict in South Asia and South African struggles over apartheid and its aftermath, 1980–1995
- antislavery mobilization in nineteenth century United States and the democratization of Spain in the 1970s

Clearly we have not assembled a random sample of the world's contentious episodes since 1800 for examination – whatever such a sample might contain. We have instead sought out instructive contrasting chunks of contentious politics for which substantial scholarly analyses already exist. We have then fashioned paired comparisons around them, comparisons aiming to isolate key mechanisms in the context of substantial differences.

Part II begins from the three now-familiar themes of the preceding chapters – mobilization versus demobilization, actors and their modes of action, and trajectories of contention. But it does so across a wider range of cases, with less concern with the existing canon, and with a first attempt to identify causal analogies across different forms of contention. Part III extends this logic through analysis of six more cases by addressing deliberately paired but even more widely varying episodes that are usually clustered within three normally distinct literatures:

Revolutions: Chapter 7 compares the mechanisms we find in Nicaragua's Sandinista revolution of 1979 and China's Tiananmen crisis of 1989.

Nationalism: Chapter 8 looks at nation-constructing and state-collapsing nationalist episodes, comparing Italian unification, 1848–1900, and Soviet decomposition after 1985.

Democratization: Chapter 9 compares mechanisms and processes in Swiss political conflict, 1830–1848 and in Mexico's protracted democratization since 1968.

Table 3.1 summarizes the range and variety of our cases – including those we covered in Part I – according to historical-geographical setting, regime type, and the kind of contention under which these cases are usually coded. Labels as "social movement," "revolution," and "democratization" do not, then, represent our own classifications of the episodes, but the rubrics other analysts have most commonly adopted when analyzing them.

Table 3.1. *Distribution of Episodes by Geography and Conventionally Assigned Forms of Contention*

Episodes	Geography					Forms of Contention			
	United States	Europe	Asia	Africa	Latin America	Social Movement	Revolution	Democratization	Nationalism
1. U.S. antislavery	+					+		+	
2. Contemporary Hindu–Muslim conflict			+			+			+
3. Italian unification		+						+	+
4. Mau Mau revolt				+			+		+
5. Tiananmen crisis 1989			+			+	+		
6. Anti–Marcos movement, Philippines			+			+	+	+	
7. Sandinista revolution					+		+	+	
8. South Africa 1980–1995				+		+	+	+	
9. Soviet decomposition		+				+	+	+	+
10. Spanish democratization		+						+	
11. Swiss unification		+						+	+
12. Mexican democratization					+	+	+	+	
13. U.S. civil rights		+				+		+	
14. Italian protest cycle, 1960s/1970s		+				+			
15. Parisian revolution, 1789		+					+		

As a glance at Table 3.1 will verify, this is no random sample. Although our cases include two Latin American cases, two Asian ones, and two from Africa, we have striven harder to increase cultural variation than to achieve geographical spread. Our two Asian instances, for example, differ enormously. The anti–Marcos revolution of the mid-1980s unfolded in a Philippines whose political, religious, and economic institutions bore strong marks of the region's two colonial masters: Spain and the United States. Contemporary Hindu–Muslim conflict in South Asia, while shaped in part by British colonialism, draws extensively on non-western religious and cultural cleavages.

Similarly, our two African cases – the Mau Mau rebellion of the 1950s and South African struggles over white supremacy since 1980 – spring from distinct patterns of European domination and embody quite different regional cultures. Our two Latin American cases – Mexico's protracted democratization and the Sandinista revolution – differ profoundly in their speed, dynamics, and outcomes. Even the relative cultural-geographic proximity of our United States and European episodes masks significant cultural and historical diversity: Swiss confederation, antebellum United States antislavery, Italian unification in the 1860s, Spanish democratization in the 1970s and Soviet decomposition in the 1990s hardly fit into a single category of events or political regimes.

As will soon become obvious, Table 3.1's classification of instances as "social movement," "revolution," "democratization," or "nationalism" provides only a rough first cut. It offers an invitation to unpack such grand terms into specific processes and mechanisms. It nevertheless illustrates that analysts have often treated six of our fifteen cases – United States antislavery and civil rights, Hindu–Muslim conflict, Italian postwar struggles, anti-Marcos mobilization, and Mexican democratization – in terms of the classic social movement agenda, while generally regarding the nine others as distinct species of contention. Our aim is not to attack that agenda but to point out that these various forms of contention both overlap with, and partially resemble one another in key particulars and that their outcomes result from different combinations of basically similar mechanisms in different historical settings.

For example, while many observers have seen South African struggles between 1980 and 1995 as a case of "democratization," one could just as plausibly code these struggles as social movements or revolutions, not to mention the war, industrial conflict, and ethnic mobilization that Table 3.1 omits from its headings. Similarly, American antislavery mobilization includes the militant social movement of abolitionism, a civil war, an attempt to found the Confederacy as a separate polity, and an important democratizing process, Reconstruction. About Soviet decomposition, we can easily ask: Of what general phenomena is it an instance? Nationalism? Yes, of course, but in the same episode we find social movements, industrial conflicts, and ethnic civil wars emerging and interacting in a composite process that any analyst should hesitate to pigeonhole. Optimists would also include democratization. Many other observers, furthermore, have treated Eastern Europe's crisis as a series of revolutions – or at least of revolutionary situations.

State Capacity and Democracy

In addition to their geographic and cultural spread, we have arrayed our cases over different regime types, as defined by two crucial dimensions: state capacity and extent of democracy.

By *state capacity* we mean the degree of control state agents exercise over persons, activities, and resources within their government's territorial jurisdiction. When state capacity increases, it does so through four often-complementary processes: the replacement of indirect by *direct rule*; the *penetration* by central states of geographic peripheries; the *standardization* of state practices and identities, and *instrumentation* – growth in the means of carrying out intended policies. States in question vary from the high (if already threatened) capacity of the South African state around 1980 to the spectacularly low capacity of the Swiss confederation as a whole (although not of its individual cantons) in 1830.

These four dimensions are logically and at times empirically distinct. For example, though the regimes that followed the French Revolution advanced direct rule, standardized identities, penetrated the periphery, and constructed new instruments to carry out intended policies, the post-revolutionary regime in America moved crookedly toward direct rule through a federal and sectional path and standardized identities only after a major civil war, even as penetration and instrumentation were proceeding apace. But historically, the various channels of evolution of state capacity tended to bleed into one another and to cluster temporally around major watersheds.

By *democracy*, we mean essentially regimes of protected consultation. In judging democracy or its absence we combine four dimensions, to be explicated further in Chapter 9. They are: *breadth* of polity membership;

equality of polity membership; strength of collective *consultation* among polity members with respect to governmental personnel, policy, and resources. We see this last as a multiple of (a) how binding that consultation is, and (b) how effectively that consultation controls the full range of governmental personnel, policy, and resources, and *protection* of polity members and persons belong to them from arbitrary action by governmental agents.

These four dimensions are also logically distinct; to some extent we can analyze variation within each dimension independently, for example by noting that authoritarian regimes often impose broad polity membership in the form of corporatist structures or mass parties while offering little or no protection to their citizens. Nevertheless, the four dimensions interact strongly enough that much of the logical space they imply is empirically empty. Broad polity membership, for instance, rarely accompanies sharply unequal polity membership. Over the period since 1800 correlations among the four dimensions have been high enough for us to lump whole regimes together as more or less democratic. If we were to rate breadth, equality, consultation, and protection for today's capitalist democracies, with 0 on each dimension representing the lowest value in history and 1 the highest ever observed anywhere at a national scale, likely scores would run between .65 and .85 on each of the four dimensions.

Figure 3.1 roughly estimates the location of each regime at our episode's beginning. It simplifies greatly by treating both capacity and democracy as high, medium, or low. In these terms, for example, postwar Italy would figure as medium in capacity and high in democracy, while Italy of the unification process (which involved, of course, consolidation of many states into one) qualifies as low in capacity but quite mixed in democracy. The fact that the regimes in question were composite, contested, and in transition provides a salutary reminder: Our taxonomy provides no more than a starting place. It serves mainly to signal that the contentious processes we are comparing began and ended in very different social settings.

The taxonomy also serves to underscore the effort we are making to transcend the relatively narrow range of most social movement studies. While most of these habitually reside in the upper-right-hand quadrant of Figure 3.1, most of our cases concentrate in the other three quadrants. If the classic social movement agenda from which we are departing is "Euramerican," we will quickly know it. An additional use of the taxonomy will be to help us examine the role of contentious politics in trajectories of polity shift. How and to what extent, we ask, are different forms and outcomes of contention necessary to transform polities from low

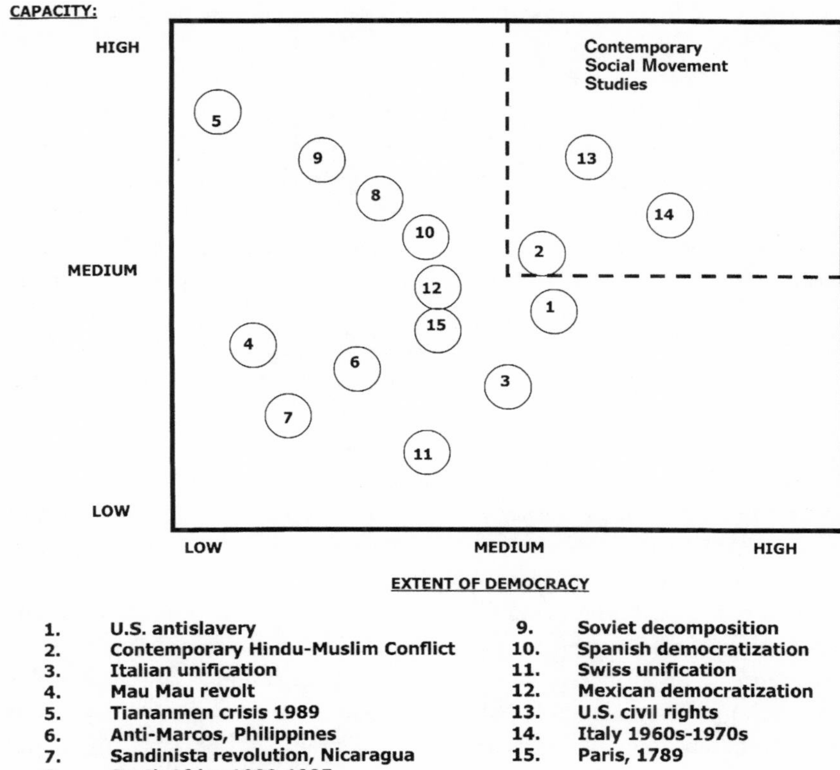

Figure 3.1 Location of Our Episodes in Regime Space

capacity to high capacity categories; from nondemocracy to democracy; and across these sets of categories? We use a strategy of paired comparison to help us to do so.

Strategies of Paired Comparison

In the field of comparative politics, two main kinds of comparison predominate:

Most different systems analyses: These are mainly quantitative analyses of multiple cases selected to represent variation across a whole universe:

all polities, all democracies, all OECD countries, all recent wars, all cases of democratization, or something of the sort.

Most similar systems analyses: Treatments of two, or few, cases are chosen narrowly to maximize comparability, employing configurative, historical, and qualitative methods. These comparative treatments range from anecdotal and ethnographic comparisons to systematic and rigorous ones.

Social scientists have much debated the extent to which the two methods do or should rely on the same logic. Some argue that the same logic of inference should underlie small–N qualitative comparison as informs large–N quantitative analyses (King, Keohane, and Verba 1994, 2000). Others maintain that attempts to apply the logic of statistical inference from large–N studies to small–N studies squander the rich contextual information provided by configurative and narrative analyses.

Advocates of small–N comparisons rest their analyses on solid bedrocks of cultural or institutional similarity and geographic proximity intended to control for variation, but their critics point out that their work both suffers from a "many variable/few cases" problem and habitually samples on the dependent variable (see APSR 1995). In the case of revolutions, this typically singles out "great revolutions" and ignores the less-great ones or the revolutions that failed to occur (Geddes 1990). Among qualitative researchers, only Charles Ragin (1987, 1994) and a few other brave souls have attempted to fit small numbers of cases into rigorously systematic analyses of key variables.

Advocates of large–N quantitative studies follow a contrary logic, hoping to exploit the potential for manipulating variations provided them by the large number of cases and significant variance in the populations of cases they study. Their critics point to their lack of intimate knowledge of individual countries and their histories, and to the significant reduction in specificity caused by the need to standardize variables across many different cases. In the study of contention, this takes the form of reducing to "conflict studies" a wide range of phenomena from microviolence to social revolutions, by way of riots, rebellions, and social movements.

Common and Uncommon Foundations

Like the students of most similar cases, we choose a logic of paired comparison between contextualized cases based on largely qualitative evidence. But we differ from most of these advocates of paired comparison. Most of these scholars choose cases for comparison in which the variations they observe are analyzed in the context of underlying common foundations, using the common features of their cases to close in on differences that make a difference. They bet on the hope that the similarities of their cases make it less likely that unseen variables are explaining the outcomes they wish to explain. For example, Barrington Moore, Jr., (1966) rests much of his analysis of the violent French path to democracy on a paired comparison with Britain. Peter Katzenstein (1984) compares Swiss and Austrian corporatist economic policies as two instances of small states' adaptation to international competition. Peter Hall (1986) views variations in political economic policy making in Britain and France in the light of the two countries' underlying commonalities as liberal states.

This "common foundations" approach has both strengths and pitfalls. We can illustrate both by recalling the collapse of democracy in Germany and Italy after World War I. When these two countries turned to authoritarianism after recent suffrage expansions that brought the working class into the polity, some observers concluded that "working-class authoritarianism" was the main cause of democracy's demise (Lipset 1960: ch. 4). But the "common foundations" approach obscured the profoundly different starting points of democratic collapse in the two countries: a Germany with a large but bureaucratized Social Democratic subculture situated largely in the working class and an Italy in which a reservoir of rural radicalism outweighed the importance of the industrial working class in the movements of the Left. That created a polarization in the Italian countryside that drove both landed proprietors and small-holding peasants into the hands of Mussolini. The Italian political process differed profoundly from the polarization that paralyzed the Weimar Republic. Focussing on these *un*common foundations would have helped Lipset and others locate the different mechanisms that led to the downfall of democracy in Italy and Germany.

How does our work in the following chapters differ? We depart from the "common foundations" tradition by using paired comparisons, not to maximize resemblance or even to pinpoint differences among whole countries, but to discover whether similar mechanisms and processes drive changes in substantially divergent periods, places, and regimes. Consider Valerie Bunce's research on policy innovation in state socialist and western democratic regimes (1981). In the early 1980s, Bunce observed that leadership succession in the Soviet Union coincided with major increases in budgetary expenditure. She did not retreat to the (then predominant) area studies treatment of Soviet politics, which might have highlighted internal struggles for power, bureaucratic features of the system, or personality characteristics of new leaders. Instead, Bunce turned to political succession in liberal capitalist regimes, where she discovered substantial similarities in the budgetary consequences of leadership change. Uncovering similar outcomes of leadership change in such unlike systems led her to look for the mechanisms that link succession to policy innovation in very different types of systems. Had Bunce stayed within the safe precincts of "Soviet Studies" her work would have been far less rich and theoretically suggestive.

The challenge of the paired comparison of uncommon cases is to unearth how similar mechanisms of change combine differently with varying environmental conditions in distinctive trajectories of historic change. Consider again mobilization: a familiar example is how social-democratic Marxism mutated as it diffused from West Central to Eastern Europe around the turn of the twentieth century. Marxists such as Plekhanov and Lenin were exposed to an essentially social-democratic model in the West, which mobilized its militants through loose and open electoral and trade union forms. But in the backward conditions of Tsarist Russia, mobilization had to take covert and controlled forms – exactly what Lenin prescribed in *What is To Be Done?* The historically unique episode of the Russian Revolution issued in part from a process of mobilization that in turn resulted from specific mechanisms of recruitment, control, and conflict.

Identifying causal mechanisms in widely different cases can also better explain outcomes that are seldom compared or are even contradictory. Consider nationalism: Most studies of the phenomenon either focus on nation-state construction or on state disintegration as the result of nationality. In contrast, in Chapter 8 we compare state-building nationalism in nineteenth century Italy with state disintegration in the late twentieth century Soviet Union, discovering similar mechanisms in these two ostensibly opposite cases. Similar mechanisms; radically different outcomes. Our comparisons not only highlight such mechanisms but also reveal how they intersect with each other and with contextual features of the individual cases. We also want them to show how different settings, sequences, and combinations of mechanisms produce contrasting political processes and outcomes.

An "uncommon foundations" strategy poses considerable risks. Apart from the fact that we are not – and do not aspire to be – experts in all the cases we will examine in Parts II and III, we risk ignoring the contextual factors that enrich the study of contentious politics. We have attempted to counter the first danger by consulting experts on our cases as an integral part of the writing process. As for the second danger, we would be more concerned if our goal were the identification of a general covering law of contentious politics.

What Sort of Program Is This?

Seeking explanation of contentious politics by identifying crucial mechanisms and processes within and across episodes requires a break with conventional ways of studying contention. On the negative side, the program implies:

1. abandoning efforts to repair the boxes and arrows of the classic social movement agenda by adding variables, reinterpreting its elements, or specifying new connections among them
2. eliminating analyses that consist essentially of matching episodes to the boxes – social change, mobilizing structures, political opportunities, framing processes, repertoires, and contentious action – posited by the agenda
3. using the divisions among mobilization, actors, and trajectories as organizing devices when useful, but turning away from them as explanations
4. employing case comparisons concentrating on necessary and sufficient conditions (e.g., strike or no strike, revolution or no revolution) only sparingly, and chiefly to specify what a more dynamic analysis must explain
5. similarly, employing analysis of covariation (e.g., through statistical correlations) chiefly to specify what features of contention are robust and therefore require explanation

The program also has a strong positive side. It encourages empirical analyses of contention that follow one or more of the following prescriptions:

6. single out relatively common processes (combinations and sequences of mechanisms) for closer study, comparing episodes and families of episodes to detect how those processes operate: later chapters of this book, for example, track similar processes of mobilization/demobi-

lization, identity shift, and polarization across a wide variety of episodes

7. identify particular mechanisms that figure in a variety of contentious episodes, and show how they produce their effects; repeatedly, for example, later chapters show us the mechanism of brokerage creating connections among previously less connected or unconnected social sites, and thus facilitating coordinated action among those sites
8. when dealing with whole episodes, (a) recognize that assignment of beginnings and endings entails establishment of observers' conventions, and look closely at the consequences of the conventions adopted; (b) specify what is distinctive about an episode or family of episodes, and therefore requires explanation; (c) solidify that specification by comparison with at least one other episode that differs with respect to the distinctive feature; (d) identify crucial mechanisms and robust processes that produce the distinctive features. Although this book gives relatively little attention to problems of observation, measurement, and formal comparison, the three paired comparisons of Part II illustrate what happens when we select episodes for comparison on the basis of salient processes occurring within them – respectively processes of mobilization and demobilization, identity- and action-transforming processes, and processes most directly affecting trajectories of mobilization and action
9. take families of episodes that share sites, actions, actors, trajectories, or outcomes, and repeat the program just laid out. Part III of this book pursues comparisons of logically comparable but highly disparate episodes involving revolutionary processes, processes of ethnic-nationalist mobilization, and processes of democratization

Parts II and III of this book present preliminary attempts to implement just such a program while searching for important mechanisms and processes.

Our Episodes

Mechanisms and the processes they produce compound into episodes: unique sequences of alterations in relations among connected elements. A recognizable commitment-performance spiral may well form part of a longer sequence in which participants in a country's democratization (for example, Italy's workers, students, landlords, labor unions, parties, regional nationalists, entrepreneurs, legislators, and Fascist holdovers during the 1960s) mobilize, demobilize, form coalitions, and struggle with each other. To explain that country's unique democratization after World War II means breaking it into coherent, recurrent, documented mechanisms and processes.

Chapters to come draw a relatively sharp line separating episodes on one side from the mechanisms and processes that comprise them on the other. They scan and compare different episodes in hopes of identifying (1) mechanisms and processes that figure significantly in those episodes and explain major features of their unfolding; (2) distinctive configurations of mechanisms that set episodes apart and account for major differences among them.

Under the heading of mobilization, for example, Chapter 4 compares the mechanisms of threat/opportunity attribution, social appropriation, and brokerage as they combine in Kenya's Mau Mau rebellion and the Philippine Yellow revolution of the mid-1980s. Chapter 5 analyzes some features of two complex contentious episodes: the development of politicized Hindu–Muslim conflict in South Asia and the toppling of apartheid in South Africa. In each case, we pinpoint the operation of four mechanisms – brokerage, category formation, object shift, and certification – that affect in whose names and on the basis of what sort of organization contentious actors mobilize and make claims. Under trajectories (Chapter 6), we find brokerage in both the construction of the American Republican Party before the Civil War and in Spanish democratization, and also encounter the mechanism of the "flanking effect," in which forceful action at the extremes of a political continuum drives actors who occupy the middle ground into closer alliances and more concerted claim making than they would otherwise pursue.

We also examine repertoire change in contentious interaction; those changes incorporate or result from the mechanisms of brokerage, category formation, object shift, and certification, but they also depend on other mechanisms that become more salient as we shift from actions, actors, and identities to our other two foci: mobilization-demobilization and trajectories. We mean our paired comparisons to uncover powerful but still partial recurrent mechanisms in differing episodes, thus identifying mechanisms of extensive scope.

As a practical matter, no one can ever explain a whole contentious trajectory in all its complexity, any more than a geologist can explain – or would bother trying to explain – every feature of a whole mountain range.

Comparisons, Mechanisms, and Episodes

Explanation consists of singling out problematic features of the phenomena at hand, then identifying recurrent mechanisms that produce those features. A challenging agenda awaits us. We must revisit contentious mobilization, action, and trajectories, now identifying causal mechanisms and processes that figure prominently in them. We must examine our contentious episodes in greater detail, sketching partial explanations of their problematic features. We must turn to whole classes of episodes – notably those involving nationalist mobilization, democratization, and revolution – in order to show how the discovery of salient mechanisms and the processes they produce recast explanations for those kinds of episodes.

Parts II and III take quite different approaches. In Part II, we examine contrasting episodes chiefly to establish two principles. First, similar causal mechanisms and processes appear in quite dissimilar varieties of contentious politics. Despite the temptation to think of industrial conflict, war, genocide, and other forms of contention as each conforming to separate sets of regularities, looked at closely their fine grain consists of similar causal chains. Second, similar mechanisms and processes appear in episodes producing massively different general outcomes. Although by definition robust mechanisms and processes generate the same immediate effects wherever they operate, their contexts and concatenations matter; initial conditions, combinations, and sequences significantly affect outcomes on the large scale. Even if the basic arrays of mechanisms and processes within two episodes were identical, then, we would not expect their trajectories and outcomes to be identical unless, fantastically, initial conditions, combinations, and sequences were also identical.

Part III switches direction. It builds on Part II by deliberately pairing episodes having these features:

- they belong to categories of contention for which analysts have often proposed general models of one sort or another
- their overall trajectories and outcomes differ dramatically
- their explanations nevertheless pose similar problems in principle
- we can identify certain features of them as problematic in the light of conventional understandings concerning the phenomena at hand – revolutions, nationalist mobilization, and democratization

Thus Part III bids up the analysis of Part II by showing that small, well-chosen sets of causal mechanisms and processes explain problematic features of dissimilar episodes. Indeed, that demonstration occurs twice: first within the paired comparisons, then, for certain mechanisms and processes that cross conventionally distinguished broad types of contention: revolutions, nationalism, and democratization.

For convenience, the chapters of Part II maintain distinctions among mobilization, action, and trajectories. By now it should be clear that the three labels serve chiefly as heuristic devices rather than identifying analytically distinct phenomena. Chapter 4, which concentrates on mobilization, does so by introducing mechanisms and processes involved in identity formation and trajectories as well. In Chapter 5, the discussion of actors, action, and identities takes up issues of mobilization and trajectories and in Chapter 6 the new analysis of trajectories capitalizes on its predecessors by incorporating observations on actors and their mobilization.

So we proceed. Chapters 4, 5, and 6 take up mobilization, actors, and trajectories in turn, concentrating on provocative pairs of episodes: Kenya's Mau Mau and the Philippines' ouster of Ferdinando Marcos (Chapter 4), Hindu-Muslim conflict in South Asia and South Africa's destruction of apartheid (Chapter 5), antislavery mobilization in the United States and the transition from authoritarianism to the first phases of Spain's postwar democratization (Chapter 6). We then move on to separate discussions of revolution (Chapter 7), nationalism (Chapter 8), and democratization (Chapter 9), before wrapping up the whole adventure (Chapter 10).

PART TWO

Tentative Solutions

4

Mobilization in Comparative Perspective

Where do we stand now? Chapter 2 identified difficulties in standard analyses of contentious origins. Chapter 3 then proposed remedies for those difficulties in the identification of widely applicable causal mechanisms and their compounding into recurrent processes of mobilization and demobilization, actors, and trajectories. In this chapter, we begin to show the applicability of that approach to the wide range of episodes included in Table 3.1 and Figure 3.1. We are not testing some general theory concerning the origins of contention. Instead, we seek to identify important mechanisms that play significant causal parts in a wide variety of mobilization and demobilization.

We highlight the Mau Mau revolt in Kenya in the 1950s and the Yellow revolution of the Philippines in the 1980s to raise important questions about mobilization – the process we first featured in Chapter 2. The episodes differed enormously from each other: Mau Mau featured high levels of violence; the movement in the Philippines was largely nonviolent. Mau Mau involved almost no formal organization; the Philippine Yellow Revolution depended on a rich array of established and emergent national organizations and institutions. Though long viewed as an anticolonial revolt, Mau Mau was simultaneously something of an internal Kikuyu civil war. Events in the Philippines were neither anticolonial revolt nor civil war, but came closer to a broad social-democratic movement uniting most of Manilan, if not Filipino society. Though more moderate in its rhetoric and overall texture than Mau Mau, from the perspective of outcomes, the Filipino episode would have to be counted as a revolution. After all, it produced a regime's overthrow. Meanwhile many people, despite much scholarship to the contrary, still regard Mau Mau as a cultist, atavistic insurrection.

Despite their differences, analysis of the two cases will reveal the operation of three causal mechanisms – *attribution of threat and opportunity*, *social appropriation*, and *brokerage* – that we find recurring in many instances of mobilization. This is not to say that other mechanisms are not at work, here or elsewhere. For example, both episodes will reveal the working of both certification and decertification, mechanisms to which we turn in detail in later chapters. Here and in the rest of Part II, we are not chiefly concerned with explaining the overall differences between our paired episodes. We want to show that identical causal mechanisms occurred in both of them and that all three mechanisms contributed centrally to mobilization. Sustained comparison of episodes in order to explain their salient differences will not become major business until we reach Part III, Chapters 7 through 9.

The Mau Mau Revolt

Mau Mau is the term normally used to describe the armed insurrection that took place in Kenya in the early to mid-1950s, pitting an irregular predominantly Kikuyu force of "freedom fighters" against both British troops and loyalist units of the Kikuyu Guard. The beginning and end dates of the revolt are difficult to pinpoint with precision. The key date in the escalation of the revolt, however, was October 20, 1952. On that day, the Colonial Administration declared a State of Emergency resulting in the arrest of nationalist leader Jomo Kenyatta and 145 other Kenyan political figures. The immediate precipitant of the declaration was the assassination of Senior Chief Waruhiu – a conservative tribal leader and nominal ally of the British – on October 7. But a more general increase in attacks on conservative African leaders and the occasional European settler in the two years leading up to the declaration prompted the government to act. Imagining a unified, centralized conspiracy, the government charged Kenyatta with "managing Mau Mau, a secret society sworn to force British rule and white farm settlement out of Kenya" (Lonsdale 2000: 197).

The declaration changed the conflict's nature in a profound and enduring way. Threatened by the government's action, thousands of Mau Mau loyalists took to the forest reserves to the north and west of Nairobi where they waged a largely defensive guerrilla campaign that persisted in more or less continuous form until the middle of 1956. But as Rosberg and Nottingham (1966: 277) have noted, the quasi-military phase of the revolt "derived from the conditions of the Emergency itself." In this sense, "the Emergency . . . was a pre-emptive attack carried out by the incumbent colonial authorities against a significant segment of the African political leadership of Kenya and its supporters" (Berman and Lonsdale 1992: 253). It was understood in this way both by colonial authorities and by the Kikuyu who believed "the intent of the white man was to eliminate the whole Kikuyu tribe" (Barnett and Njama 1966: 71). But the conflict should not be understood as simply an anticolonial revolt initiated and led by Kikuyu insurgents. In addition, as Lonsdale and Berman (1992: Ch. 12) are at pains to point out, the conflict was also a kind of Kikuyu civil war, born of a severe post-World War II land shortage and the corrosive effect it had on the traditional "moral economy" of Kikuyu society.

In the end, the revolt succumbed to superior military force and chronic shortages and lack of overall coordination on the part of the Mau Mau. But in the final irony of a conflict rife with ironies, the forces of colonial reaction wound up winning the war and losing the country. The political fallout from Mau Mau, which extended well beyond the period of active fighting and came to be embodied in the death and attempted cover-up of the incident of eleven "detainees" at the Hola "rehabilitation" camp in March of 1959, ultimately robbed the Colonial Administration of its support by the British Home Office and hastened the end of its rule. Writes Edgerton:

> Convinced by the events at Hola that the pace of change in Africa had to be speeded up, [British Prime Minister Harold] Macmillan made a decision that would change the course of Kenya's future. He replaced [Colonial Secretary] Alan Lennox-Boyd with Ian Macleod, a man who was profoundly offended by what had happened at Hola. [1989: 198]

Macleod, in turn, quickly engineered an agreement among the various parties – white settlers, African nationalists, colonial authorities – that called for the rapid transformation of Kenya into a parliamentary democracy based on universal suffrage. Final independence was granted on December 12, 1963, barely eleven years after the initial State of Emergency had been declared.

Historical Change Processes in the Origins of Mau Mau

The origins of the movement that came to be known as Mau Mau illustrate the importance of broad change processes as catalysts for contention.

Before taking up the specific changes that helped set the context for Mau Mau, it is worth underscoring a point first made in Chapter 2. We do not attach a different epistemological status to these "change processes" than to the various mechanisms we take up in the book. (Indeed, were we to focus our empirical lens on these change processes, we would see that they too combined relational, cognitive, and environmental mechanisms.) But to avoid infinite empirical regress, we treat them here more as necessary historical context than as objects of study in their own right.

The relevant changes in this case were of two types, those affecting the internal political economy of Kenya in the postwar period and the general trend toward decolonization following World War II (Cooper 1996; Mamdani 1996). The latter trend is well documented and is not peculiar to Kenya. The former set of changes requires more explanation.

The end of World War II marked the beginning of a period of unprecedented economic prosperity for Kenya and of high levels of immigration by white settlers into the country. The two trends were clearly related, with immigration increasing agricultural output and the generally rosy economy fueling additional in-migration. There was a downside to this otherwise salutary dynamic, however. White immigration in the post-war years resulted in a serious land shortage affecting Kenya's African population in general and the Kikuyu in particular. This land squeeze was further exacerbated by the mechanization of settler agriculture, rapid African population growth, and the imposition of specific agricultural policies by the Colonial Administration. These policies included the eviction of African – usually Kikuyu – squatters from Maasai land and settler districts, followed by their forced resettlement back onto Kikuyu reserves.

The effect of these various demographic and economic pressures was thoroughgoing disruption of the material and moral economy of Kikuyu life. As John Walton (1984: 111) puts it:

> Expandable landholdings were crucial to the system of family clans and village to regional governments. Having reached the age of majority and passed through circumcision rituals, with their first marriage young Kikuyu warriors were awarded an existing or new plot of family land. Possession of land confirmed the warrior and his wives as full citizens of the family clan and village. Propertied males later could become village elders in the councils that were organized in a decentralized democratic hierarchy reaching the regional and tribal levels. . . . When the colonialists began occupying Kikuyu land they simultaneously . . . began to destroy the foundations of that society.

The accelerated pace of white settler in-migration and resulting loss of formally Kikuyu land after World War II aggravated class, generational, and gender tensions among the Kikuyu. That aggravation helps account for the different factions that developed during the conflict. Older householders with dynastic control of land tended to be conservative and to refrain from involvement or to be actively loyalist in their sympathies and actions. Members of junior "age sets" who lacked land (or rights to land) were apt to be more militant and active in their support for the movement.

The land crisis confronting the Kikuyu – and specific communities in particular – played out against the backdrop of another destabilizing change process: the general postwar trend toward decolonization and the increase in contained political activity by Kenyan nationalists that the prospect of independence helped set in motion. This institutionalized political activity met total resistance by the colonial authorities, caught as they were between the increasingly liberal policies of the British Home Office and the intransigence of the white settlers. There was an ideological basis to the resistance of the colonial authorities as well. They genuinely believed that political activity would only exacerbate the strains of "modernization" and undermine the comforting (and apolitical) traditions of tribal life. Africans were seen as ill prepared culturally and psychologically for western-style politics and thus any favorable response to "native" political initiatives was viewed, by authorities, as an abrogation of their paternalistic responsibility to shelter their "charges" from the strains of modernization. These, then, were the relevant change processes affecting Kenya in the postwar period. But the origins of Mau Mau lie, not in the changes themselves, but in how the various parties to the conflict interpreted and sought to respond to these processes.

Attribution of Threat and Opportunity in Postwar Kenya

Collective attribution of threat or opportunity is a crucial mechanism in mobilization. It involves (a) invention or importation and (b) diffusion of a shared definition concerning alterations in the likely consequences of possible actions (or, for that matter, failures to act) undertaken by some political actor. Threat-opportunity attribution often emerges from competition among advocates of differing interpretations, one of which finally prevails. That sort of competition certainly occurred in the Mau Mau case. Parties to the unfolding Kenyan conflict interpreted major social changes as significant threats and opportunities. The postwar trend toward decolonization and the wave of nationalist movements it helped spawn was viewed as a serious threat by Kenya's sizable white settler population, and, to a lesser extent, by the colonial authorities. This sense of threat was heightened perceptibly by the onset in 1948–1949 of a vigorous pro-Communist rebellion in the British colony of Malaya (Kattenburg 1990). (Colonial authorities there responded in 1949 by declaring a State of Emergency, a model that would soon be borrowed by their counterparts in Kenya.)

For their part, Kenyan nationalists viewed these events as evidence that an unprecedented opportunity for independence lay at hand. The result was increased popular mobilization in Kenya as elsewhere in Africa. Indeed, even before the end of the war, increasing optimism about the shape of the postwar world had inspired an increase in contained political activity among Kenya's moderate nationalists. One organizational manifestation of this trend was the founding of the Kenyan African Union (KAU) in 1944.

Cessation of military hostilities did nothing to dampen the spirits of Kenyan nationalists. On the contrary, there followed in quick succession a series of events that clearly reinforced the prevailing sense of imminent change. First came the announcement from London of the British government's new policy of "multiracialism" with respect to its African colonies. Although vague, the announcement seemed to promise a radical departure from the prewar reality of white supremacy. Then there was the unfolding drama of Indian independence. The excitement that greeted the 1946 return from exile of Kenya's leading nationalist figure, Jomo Kenyatta provides a sense of the mood that prevailed among Kenya's nationalist community in the heady days following the war. Kenyatta's ascension to President of the Kenyan African Union in 1947 reinforced that mood. It ushered in a period of heightened political activity, not only by KAU, but also by other established political organizations as well. For example, the Nairobi based East Africa Trades Union Congress (EATUC) staged a general strike in Mombasa involving 15,000 workers that further reinforced the general sense of uncertainty and flux that prevailed in Kenya during the immediate postwar period.

If white settlers were concerned by the general postwar trend of decolonization, the increase in popular political activity among Kenya's African majority alarmed them all the more. Threatened by both developments, as well as by London's vague policy of "multiracialism," the settlers formulated and in 1949 made public their plan for South African style white supremacy. Titled *The Kenya Plan*, the manifesto was, in turn, widely publicized within African political circles and interpreted as a serious threat to native interests by Kenyan nationalists.

Episodes of contention typically grow out of and depend on a perception of significant environmental uncertainty on the part of state and nonstate elites and challengers alike. This shared perception insures that both sides continue to see the situation as one posing significant threats to and/or opportunities for the realization of group interests. The broad trend toward decolonization in the immediate postwar period served to create exactly this kind of generalized uncertainty with regard to the structuring of racial politics in Kenya. To quote Lonsdale:

> After the second world war . . . the discordant strands of Kenya's history were tied into the knotty question of future control. Was Kenya to become a minority white dominion, like South Africa; a multi-racial partnership, as mooted for Central Africa; or a black state? How long could colonial rule, on the wane around the world, keep the future unraveled? [Lonsdale 2000: 202]

In turn, the heightened sense of threat or opportunity associated with the uncertainty prompted all established parties to the conflict to monitor one another's actions closely and engage in reactive mobilization on an escalating basis. By 1950, the familiar pattern of iterative action that characterizes the mobilization of contention (see Figure 2.1) was clearly evident in Kenya. Indeed, that year saw a classic example of this iterative sequence, born of the widespread sense of uncertainty that permeated postwar Kenyan politics. The East African Trades Union Congress launched a campaign against Britain's seemingly innocuous and largely ceremonial plan to grant a Royal Charter to the city of Nairobi. The plan was interpreted by nationalists as an attempt of colonial authorities to grant political control of the surrounding Kikuyu districts to the white-controlled city government. During the ensuing campaign, the leader of the Congress, Fred Kubai, and other activists were arrested. There followed a general strike that lasted eighteen days before being put down by police and soldiers.

In the same year, Kenyatta and KAU initiated a petition campaign aimed at the restoration of lost (mostly) Kikuyu land. The campaign stretched into 1951 and resulted in the collection of some 67,000 signatures. Colonial authorities never dignified the petitions with a response. Kenyatta followed up the petition campaign with a direct appeal to James

Griffiths, Secretary of State for the Colonies, to add twelve elected African members to Kenya's Legislative Council. The appeal took place during Griffith's May 1951 visit to Kenya and resulted in, not twelve, but two new African Council seats and a promise to hold a "constitutional conference" on the general issue the following year. Because of the Emergency, the conference never took place.

From Contained to Transgressive Contention

In broad relief, these were the events that defined the increasingly active mobilization of contained contention in Kenya in the immediate postwar period. But, at the same time, there was a second, emergent stream of collective action that represented a more transgressive challenge, not only to Kenya's racial establishment, but also to traditional age, class, and gender relations within Kikuyu society. This second stream responded, not so much to the threat or promise of a decolonizing Kenya as to the postwar period's severe land crisis.

The beginnings of this second stream of insurgent activity are not entirely clear, but a good case can be made for the decisive importance of the grassroots resistance campaign that developed among some recently evicted Kikuyu "squatters" in a Maasai-land settlement known as Olenguruone. The so-called squatters had, in fact, been evicted in the early 1940s from the white highlands where they still held land rights, and then resettled on Maasai land at Olenguruone. The way of life that had developed among the highland squatters was thoroughly disrupted by the eviction and resettlement at Olenguruone. Adding fuel to the fire, the squatters were required, as part of the resettlement program, to take part in a labor-intensive and culturally demeaning program of land terracing aimed at soil conservation. Other onerous rules were applied as well.

This encounter between the colonial authorities and the networks of shared fate and trust that had developed among the Olenguruone squatters led to a generalized resistance campaign. A long struggle between Kikuyu refusal to obey these rules and official threat of eviction ensued.

To complicate things all the more, colonial authorities relied heavily on the coercive power of officially recognized Kikuyu "chiefs" and other traditional tribal elites to enforce compliance with the terms of the resettlement program. The conflict came to a head in 1946 when a large group of squatters marched 150 miles from Olenguruone to consult with

Senior Chief Koinange. They simultaneously appealed to Kenyatta for help as well.

The oldest African political association in Kenya, the Kikuyu Central Association (KCA), helped to organize 3,000 of the Olenguruone settlers into the Kikuyu Highlands Squatters Landlords Association. Notwithstanding this flurry of activity, all came to naught. Chief Koinange, Kenyatta and the other landed Kikuyu elites were less than aggressive in their support for the embattled squatters. Colonial authorities, determined to nip any "native uprising" in the bud, responded aggressively to quash the insurgency. The revolt collapsed by the middle of 1947, but not before it had: (1) deepened class, age, and dynastic divisions among the Kikuyu – in the end most chiefs opposed the revolt, and (2) hardened colonial authorities and white settlers to the threat of popular unrest, even as they remained blind to splits developing among the Kikuyu.

The revolt at Olenguruone shaped the developing conflict in an even more important way. The revolt started the "radical oathing" that came to be the hallmark of Mau Mau and its principal means of recruitment. The practice of building solidarity and reinforcing collective commitments via the administration of oaths had long been a staple of Kikuyu tribal life. But the practice had conventionally been restricted only to those Kikuyu (e.g., older householding, land tenured males) deemed worthy of the responsibilities conferred by the oath. What marked the oathing that took place in connection with the Olenguruone revolt as so significant – and so threatening to older Kikuyu householders – was its sharp break with traditional cultural practices. In the context of the revolt, oaths were used to recruit anyone – non-householding males, women and even children – who was willing to join the struggle and resist the terms of the resettlement program. In addition to their close ties to the colonial authorities, it was the stark political and cultural challenge posed by the radical oathing that soured the traditional Kikuyu elite on the squatters' campaign.

Significantly, radical oathing did not end with the collapse of the squatters' revolt. The postwar land shortage had created conditions similar to those at Olenguruone throughout the white highlands and Maasai-land. The Olenguruone oath spread rapidly among the affected squatters, as did a generalized commitment to resist the onerous components of the resettlement programs. Still, this second grassroots resistance campaign might well have remained diffuse and eventually petered out but for a short-lived alliance between a loose federation of young, landless Nairobi-based militants and older, moderate KCA veterans based in Kiambu, the rural district surrounding Nairobi. Motivations underlying the alliance are not entirely clear. Perhaps the spread of the oathing had convinced the KCA veterans that there was a younger, more radical constituency out there to be tapped. Or perhaps they were simply frustrated by the total intransigence of the colonial authorities and really did intend to create a grassroots alternative to the more traditional politics of petition and persuasion.

Whatever their aims, the KCA veterans quickly abandoned the alliance, probably out of the same general sense of threat and cultural revulsion that the chiefs had reserved for the Olenguruone squatters. For the abortive alliance spawned an even more radical oathing campaign than the one that had fueled the Olenguruone revolt. The campaign was more radical than its predecessor in two ways. First, while there was no standardized form for administering the oath, some of the variants were coercive and composed of culturally compromised (e.g., sexual and/or physically painful) practices. Second, the behavioral requirements of the oath came, for at least some initiates, to involve something more than the generally passive forms of resistance that had characterized the squatters' revolt. So with the onset of the campaign in 1950, we begin to see a low level of proactive violence directed against persons and property associated with colonial rule and Kikuyu complicity in that rule. One of the earliest instances of this violence exemplifies the general practice. Early in 1950 one of the sons of Senior Chief Koinange was killed for allegedly refusing to take the oath or on general suspicion of being a government informer.

Though based initially in Nairobi, the new oathing campaign quickly spread to other Kikuyu districts – especially Murang'a and Nyeri – as did the related attacks on those deemed responsible for the growing inequities within Kikuyu society. Not surprisingly, the attacks – especially when coupled with the institutionalized ferment of Kenyan politics – produced widespread alarm and fear among white settlers and colonial authorities. The violence was also responsible for a deepening crisis among the Kikuyu themselves. But, blind as they were to divisions within Kikuyu society, white Kenyans and the British read the sporadic attacks as a coordinated and generalized Kikuyu rebellion. Specifically, colonial authorities were convinced that the institutionalized or *contained politics* of Kenyatta and KAU were somehow linked to (and perhaps a cover for) the growing wave of violence.

The decisive moment in the escalating dynamic of action, interpretation, and reaction was declaration of a State of Emergency on October 20, 1952. The nominal justification for the declaration was the assassination of yet another traditional tribal leader and ally of the British. But the murder of Senior Chief Waruhiu – Chief Koinange's successor in the position – on October 7 was but a welcome excuse for the decisive preemptive strike that the white settlers had been urging on colonial authorities for some time. The authorities' actions on October 20 and in the immediate aftermath of the declaration betrayed their conviction that the attacks and stepped-up political activity by Kenyatta and other moderate Kikuyu politicians were but different aspects of a unified insurgency.

Immediately following the declaration, authorities swept through Nairobi and the surrounding Kikuyu reserves and arrested 146 political figures, most of whom were relatively moderate in their views. The prize catch from the sweep, however, was Kenyatta, who authorities remained convinced was the evil mastermind behind the rebellion. He was subsequently tried and, on the basis of clearly fabricated evidence, jailed for nearly ten years. Far from quelling African resistance, Kenyatta's trial at Kapenguria promoted widespread opposition to British colonial rule both inside Kenya and elsewhere. A confidential police report from December 1952 noted that:

> A spirit of nationalism has been born in Kenya and . . . it is the obvious intention of the intelligentsia to exploit this fully. The scene at Kapenguria, providing . . . clear evidence of the support which the Kenya African can expect from the West Coast, India and the Sudan, is having a far reaching effect on Africans who look upon it, not only as a trial of Kikuyu leaders, but also as a trial of strength between "nationalism" and "imperialism." This insidious external influence is most dangerous and, as is obviously its intention, will encourage the belief that the Kikuyu are fighting for a righteous cause. [Lonsdale 2000: 236]

Popular reaction to the mass arrests was swift among the most committed of the Mau Mau initiates. Over the next few months, as many as 20,000 mostly young, poor (read landless), male Kikuyu fled to the forest reserves to the north and west of Nairobi. The active military phase of the struggle had begun. It grew out of a complicated, but by now familiar pattern of conflictual interaction among various challengers and state and nonstate elites increasingly attuned to each others' actions and to the shared sense of uncertainty and threat embodied in the developing situation. In this sense, the declared Emergency and the Kikuyu retreat to the mountains were but two of the later and more dramatic iterative moves in the escalating conflict.

Social Appropriation and Brokerage in Mau Mau

What were the social structural and cultural bases of the contentious episode sketched above? When attributions of threat and opportunity lead to the kinds of innovative collective action that clearly took place in Kenya, particular actors frequently appropriate existing social space and collective identities in the service of these interpretations. We call that mechanism – which we first saw in the mobilizing role of the black churches by the American civil rights movement – *social appropriation*. Related to this, we see *brokerage* as a second key mechanism in the social production, aggregation, and transformation of contentious actors. Brokerage we defined in Chapter 1 as the linking of two or more previously unconnected social sites by a unit that mediates their relations with one another and/or with yet other sites. What did these two mechanisms look like in the case of the Kenyan conflict?

Many instances of contentious politics grow out of an initial sequence of innovative collective actions by established parties. But they only devolve into revolutions, peasant rebellions, nationalist risings, or mass movements *if* the conflict leads to mobilization by previously unorganized or apolitical segments of the population. The squatters' revolt at Olenguruone and the campaign of radical oathing and generalized resistance it set in motion served this function in the case of the developing conflict in postwar Kenya.

These grassroots events derived much of their significance from the generalized uncertainty regarding the future of colonial rule that characterized postwar Kenya. But in turn, they transformed the conflict from one of strategic interaction among established political forces (e.g., colonial authorities, KAU, white settlers organizations, etc.) into a true episode of transgressive contention. As in many such episodes, this transformation was keyed by the mobilization of the previously unmobilized – in particular, of the Olenguruone squatters, and later, of the early initiates in the second, Nairobi based, wave of radical oathing. What existing social structures and associational networks figured in the mobilization? What established identities were appropriated in the process? Who served as brokers in the spread of the radical oathing?

Since the grassroots phase of the struggle had two distinct geographic-temporal origins – Olenguruone in the mid-1940s and Nairobi around 1950 – we want to answer these questions separately for each "site." Alas, perhaps because of the closer temporal link between the Nairobi-based campaign, the Emergency, and the onset of the military phase of the conflict, more systematic scholarship exists on the Nairobi campaign than for the earlier events at Olenguruone. We will, in any case, treat the two sites separately.

Olenguruone

There exists very little systematic scholarship on the social origins and routine identities that informed the Olenguruone revolt. But given the broad-based nature of the revolt and its seeming acceptance throughout the settlement, we might surmise that it spread along the lines of established dynastic and generational lines of authority. The few sketchy accounts of events at Olenguruone that do exist (Buijtenhuijs 1982; Furedi 1974; Spencer 1977) are consistent with this surmise. For example, we know "that Samuel Koina, the leader of the Olenguruone settlement, 'brought the [radical] oath to Kiambaa and Githkunguri [two nearby Kikuyu settlements] . . . [where] it merged with the traditional oath and became an oath of unity'" (Spencer 1977: 238, quoting James Beauttah, a prominent Kiambu political figure and eyewitness to the above event).

If the "leader" of the settlement was himself actively involved in the spread of the new oath, we can safely assume that the campaign enjoyed widespread and semiofficial acceptance throughout the community. Given this, it may well be that the oath and the related resistance campaign developed within the settlement's established decision-making bodies and was fueled by nothing more than traditional appeals to village unity and the normal complement of dynastic, generational, and gender identities on which community life turned. But, plausible as this account may be, we reiterate that it is grounded in very limited and sketchy empirical materials.

We do, however, know a great deal more about the spread of the Olenguruone oath throughout the white highlands and the forms of *brokerage* that fueled the diffusion process. Systematic scholarship points to the role of three kinds of brokers in the spread of the Olenguruone oath and resistance campaign (Furedi 1974a, 1974b). Furedi identifies two of the groups involved in the diffusion process:

> The struggle at Olenguruone had a great impact on squatters in Nakaru district. A direct road connected Olenguruone to Molo and Elburgon . . . The Elburgon KCA activists were in constant contact with Olenguruone. In early 1946 a number of militants from Olenguruone left for the farms to obtain support for their struggle from the squatters. They administered the new oath of unity to a number of KCA activists in the Elburgon area and on the huge Soysambu estate . . . an important centre of KCA activity. [Furedi 1974a: 3]

Both "KCA activists" and "militants from Olenguruone" were active in the spread of the radical oath and the commitment to grass roots struggle it implied.

The role of the KCA activists is consistent with accounts of the spread of grass roots protest in the early days of a good many movements and revolutions. Sensing an opportunity to strengthen or revitalize their organization through the facilitation of grass roots activity, members of established organizations commonly serve as brokers for emergent movements. In the present case, motivations of the KCA veterans were probably very similar to this. Clearly, they supported the general aims of the Olenguruone campaign. In addition, they might well have hoped that, by tapping the grassroots energies mobilized by the campaign, they could revitalize an organization somewhat eclipsed by the founding of KAU and its association with charismatic Jomo Kenyatta.

But KCA activists were not the only ones spreading the "good news" of the Olenguruone struggle. Intent on mobilizing support for the campaign, leaders of the struggle were actively involved in carrying the oath and the broader aims and understandings of the movement to the farms of the White Highlands. For Furedi (1974a: 1); "the importance of Olenguruone [was] . . . not merely symbolic or exemplary but lies in the field of political organization. The Olenguruone settlers initiated a process of political mobilization that gave a direct organizational impetus to the growth of the Mau Mau movement in the White Highlands."

One final group was active in the spread of the initial squatters' revolt. These were itinerant traders whose daily routines required them to travel back and forth between their home reserve, Nairobi, and the farms of the White Highlands. Since links maintained by these trades already existed, they functioned less as brokers of new connections than as agents of diffusion. But they were no less important to spread of oaths for that distinction. The presence of these traders was itself partly a function of the postwar land squeeze. They were not wealthy merchants who had chosen their trade by the lure of profit, but marginal men forced by the scarcity of land and lack of adequate urban employment to scrape by through occasional tenant farming and opportunistic trade activities organized around the tripartite world of the postwar Kikuyu.

Humble though the traders' lives were, their regular movements from the urban environs of Nairobi through both the reserves and the White Highlands made them indispensable sources of information and communication. They knit Kikuyu society together. They were brokers whose brokerage long preceded the Mau Mau revolt. In their account of Olenguruone, Berman and Lonsdale (1992: 418) speak to the role of these commercial "weak ties" (Granovetter 1973) in the spread of the radical oath: "They swore solidarity farm to farm, encouraged by ex-squatter traders in touch with Olenguruone."

Nairobi

What of the later Nairobi based campaign? What existing social structures and established collective identities did it succeed in appropriating? Can we identify brokers who served the same function with respect to the urban movement that the KCA veterans, Olenguruone activists, and itinerant traders played in connection with the earlier squatters' revolt? Fortunately, far more systematic scholarship is available to answer these questions for Nairobi than for Olenguruone. What do these materials tell us?

The origins of this second, more radical, oathing campaign remain the subject of debate (cf., Buijtenhuijs 1982: 14). Yet the broad contours of the story are generally agreed upon. Spencer provides a representative account of the beginnings of the campaign:

> While some people who lived in Nairobi had taken the [Olenguruone] oath, it had been given mostly in the rural areas. To spread it into Nairobi, the "Mbari" [the term reserved for dynastic rights-holders within Kikuyu society and thus traditional tribal leadership] directed . . . [Chief] Koinange to contact two of the best known union leaders, Fred Kubai and J.M. Mungai (respectively the Secretary and the President of the Transport and Allied Workers Union) and see if they would join the movement. He approached them late in 1948, and they agreed to take the oath on two conditions, first that it cease being restricted to those who could pay . . . and who were KCA members or whom KCA members had approved and henceforth be given to any Kikuyu who were trustworthy and, second, that the oath become more militant. The "Mbari" hesitated but finally agreed, and Kubai and Mungai brought ten of their most trusted associates to Kiambaa (Chief Koinange's home) to be oathed. These men were to become known as the Action Group. Then, Kubai chose twenty-four trade union leaders,

and they took the oath at Kiambaa. After this, a group of carefully selected "criminals" (Kubai's words) were oathed and given the job of collecting arms – slowly and surely. Then the oath was taken by the Nairobi taxidrivers [*sic*], who would organize the transportation for much of the further mass oathing. [Spencer 1975: 9–10]

The early initiates of this second campaign appear to have been drawn from two principal solidarity communities. Far and away the most important of these was Nairobi's community of radical trade unionists. This community was implicated in the campaign, and thus to Mau Mau, in four principal ways. First, to the extent that one can speak of "leaders" in connection with the campaign, Kubai and Mungai could lay claim to the designation. Second, the all-important "Action Group" came disproportionately from the trade union movement. Third, twenty-four additional trade union leaders were "oathed" early in the campaign. Finally, the rank and file membership of one of the key affiliated unions – the taxi drivers – were among the earliest, and as we shall see, most important initiates of the campaign.

The second solidarity community that figures prominently in this and a number of other accounts (e.g., Furedi 1973) of the campaign is the Anake wa Forty, or so-called Forty Group, from whence came most of the "criminals" mentioned by Kubai. Termed the Forty Group to designate the approximate year when group members passed culturally into manhood, the Anake wa Forty was an ephemeral collection of young street toughs or petty criminals that the Action Group tapped for the all important job of collecting arms for the movement. Although the group ceased to exist in any organized way by 1949–1950, the associational network that formed the group's core continued to serve as an important point of entry into the burgeoning movement.

So much for the social structures and collective identities that keyed the campaign in Nairobi early on: What of the brokers who facilitated its spread? Three crucial kinds of figures emerge from Spencer's account and the literature more generally. Ironically, the first of these figures constituted a solidary community that quickly abandoned the movement as its aims grew more radical and violent. They constituted the loose network of KCA veterans/mbari rights-holders (including Kenyatta) who set the campaign in motion. But to the extent that this group did act to forge ties and thereby facilitate diffusion to the radical trade union community, they clearly served as critical brokers for the struggle.

The second key group of brokers was the so-called Action Group, which (for a short time anyway) mediated the oathing campaign's spread. It was, after all, the Action Group that selected the groups and communities (e.g., trade union leaders, the Forty Group, the taxi drivers) within which the first initiates were recruited. But, in many ways, the campaign's key brokers were the taxi drivers, for it was this group that served as the all important network of weak ties that linked elites (e.g., the mbari, trade union leaders) and masses and Nairobi with the surrounding rural areas. Indeed, it was precisely for this reason that the Action Group tapped them for service to the movement. It was an inspired, fateful choice. For as the taxis shuttled back and forth among Nairobi and the rural reserves and white highlands, they brought the oath to increasingly disparate groups who knew little of the Action Group and accorded them even less authority to direct their activities. Thus, the weak ties forged by the taxi drivers facilitated the spread of the movement, but not its centralized direction. The mass arrest of key leaders – including Kubai and Mungai – following the declared State of Emergency cut the movement adrift all the more.

The lack of centralized direction and the absence of formal organizational brokerage mark Mau Mau as dramatically different from the anti-Marcos movement that developed in the Philippines between 1983–1986. After describing this second case in some detail, we return to these issues in a concluding section. We thereby seek to refine our understanding, not only of the general relevance of our mechanisms, but also of how their specific combinations and sequences shape an unfolding contentious episode.

The Philippines Yellow Revolution

Our second case of contentious mobilization concerns the movement that developed in the Philippines in the period 1983–1986 and ultimately deposed Ferdinand Marcos after some seventeen years of autocratic rule. The movement came to be known as the Yellow revolution, for the yellow ribbons (yellow being Benigno Aquino's favorite color) that festooned marches and demonstrations during the climactic stage of the struggle. Though there had long been an active opposition to Marcos' rule, the main actors in that opposition – the Communist Party – stayed on the sidelines of the Yellow revolution. That struggle brought new, and mainly elite and middle-class groups against the regime, and was set in motion by the assassination of Marcos's longtime rival, Benigno Aquino, on his return from exile in the United States, to the Philippines on August 21, 1983. The assassination solidified and broadened opposition to the regime and set in motion a series of institutional challenges, which were aggravated and polarized by Marcos's reaction to the movement.

In the assassination's aftermath, Marcos sought to appease those outraged by the killing by appointing a panel to investigate the crime. But in stacking the panel with his longtime friends and cronies, Marcos only added fuel to the fire. Pressed by foreign and domestic opposition, Marcos eventually relented on this issue, appointing a new – more or less neutral – board to investigate the slaying, but he was to repeat this general pattern of open defiance and intransigence followed by grudging efforts to appease throughout the course of the struggle. The climactic instance came in February of 1986 with the staging of the "snap election" that he had announced on American television the previous fall. The election was designed to assuage Marcos' critics by demonstrating popular support for his regime. Despite the presence of both domestic and international election watch teams, however, the Marcos forces engaged in transparent electoral fraud and voter intimidation, delayed the announcement of results, and then proclaimed Marcos the winner by a wide margin.

Events came to a head on February 16, when Marcos' opponent in the election, Cory Aquino, called for a general strike to protest the results. Hundreds of thousands of demonstrators heeded Aquino's call and took to the streets. Six days later Defense Minister Juan Ponce Enrile and Lieutenant General Fidel Ramos – heretofore Marcos allies – seized control of the military headquarters at Camp Aguinaldo in Manila. Fearing military retaliation by Marcos, Archbishop Jaime Cardinal Sin called on citizens to surround the base to protect the military rebels. Hundreds of thousands of citizens again responded to the call, effectively barring a military response by Marcos. Denied the military option and with his political support – even that of the Reagan administration – gone, Marcos left the Philippines on February 25 and took up exile in Hawaii. Aquino was subsequently sworn in as the country's new president, initiating a period of intense mobilization by various parties to the conflict. Party struggle focused on the restructuring of Philippine politics. This later struggle ran through at least 1987. This chapter concentrates, however, on origins of the Yellow revolution itself. As in the Mau Mau insurgency, we begin with the broad historical change processes behind the episode.

Historical Change Processes in the Origins of the Yellow Revolution

The Yellow revolution is an interesting case because of its mix of longterm change processes and sudden transformative events (McAdam and Sewell 2001; Sewell 1996) that helped set it in motion. Among the latter, the Aquino assassination served as the episode's immediate catalyst. But to understand the event fully, especially the reaction of Manila's middle-class and elite elements to it, one must place the killing in its proper historical context. This will require recounting the Marcos regime's history up to the time of the Aquino slaying. That history comprises two distinct, yet clearly linked, story lines. One concerns the unfolding personal and political competition *cum* feud between Marcos and Aquino, the other, Marcos' initial conformity and then break with what Anderson (1998) has termed "cacique democracy in the Philippines." We begin with the latter.

The establishment of the Republic of the Philippines in 1946 did little to change the basic distribution of political and economic power in the country. The same small handful of powerful families who had dominated Filipino society before independence continued to constitute a recognizable oligarchy afterward. The only real change was establishment of a powerful presidential position – tamed only by a two-term limit – that promised (and, for a time, delivered) circulation of oligarchs as an institutional feature of Filipino politics. Marcos' ascension to the presidency in 1965 was entirely consistent with the existing normative-institutional framework. His declaration of martial law in 1972 (penultimate year of his second and final presidential term), however, marked a decisive break with cacique democracy's established conventions, and with the other oligarchs who had fashioned them. Anderson (1998: 214–215) explains:

> As far as the oligarchy was concerned, Marcos went straight for the jugular – the "rule of law." From the very earliest days, Marcos used his plenary martial-law powers to advise the oligarchs who dreamt of opposing or supplanting him that property was not power, since at the stroke of the martial pen it ceased to be property. The Lopez dynasty . . . was abruptly deprived of its mass-media empire and its control of Manila's main supplier of electricity. The 500-hectare Hacienda Osmenda was put up for "land reform" somewhat later. There was no recourse, since the judiciary was fully cowed and the legislature packed with allies and hangers-on. But Marcos had no interest in upsetting the established social order. Those oligarchs who bent with the wind and eschewed politics for the pursuit of gain were left mostly undisturbed.

But martial law held not simply because Marcos had coopted the other oligarchs. In addition, he mobilized a powerful, if amorphous, coalition of countervailing allies who initially gave the martial-law regime a patina of progressive legitimacy. Anderson (1998: 215) again supplies crucial insights:

> At its outset, the martial-law regime had a substantial . . . social base. Its anticommunist, "reformist," "modernizing," and "law and order" rhetoric attracted the support of frustrated would-be technocrats, much of the . . . urban middle-class, and even sectors of the peasantry and urban poor. . . . But as time passed, the greed and violence of the regime became ever more evident, much of the support dried up. By the later 1970s the technocrats were a spent force, and the urban middle class was increasingly aware of the decay of Manila, the devastation of the university system, the abject and ridiculous character of the monopolized mass media, and the country's economic decline.

To this list of estranged former allies we should add one other: the official hierarchy of the Catholic Church of the Philippines. By the end of the 1970s all of these sectors had soured on Marcos. Some were beginning to act on this discontent.

In light of subsequent events, activities of the anti–Marcos business community and the Church hierarchy merit special attention. Though relations between the regime and the Church deteriorated steadily throughout the 1970s, those at the top of the Church hierarchy did not want to "risk a breach with the government either by engaging in trenchant criticism or by defending those most active in the Church's social justice programs" (Youngblood 1982: 52). The regime's increasingly repressive response to left-progressive elements within the Church, however, made this kind of strategic silence impossible to maintain. Sparked in part by the papal visit of 1981, Church leaders began to challenge the regime more openly. "In January 1983, the CBCP [Catholic Bishops' conference of the Philippines] decided to withdraw from the Church–Military Liaison Committee in open acknowledgment of the increasingly acute conflict between military forces and Church activists" (Hedman 1998: 278). A month later, "the bishops issued a blistering pastoral letter accusing the regime of repression, corruption, and economic mismanagement" (Youngblood 1990: 197).

Though lagging behind the pace of oppositional activity in the Church, Manila's moderate business community followed much the same arc of initial support, then tacit tolerance, and finally public opposition to the regime. If groups such as the Philippine Business for Social Progress (PBSP) were already engaged in various sorts of political activities as early as Marcos's second term (1969–1973), most of the business community remained firmly behind the regime, regarding the declaration of martial law as a necessary stabilizer of political and economic life. But the increasingly compromised state of civil liberties in the mid to late 1970s, the growing threat of communist insurgency in the countryside, and the sharp decline of the economy as the decade wore on gradually eroded business support for the regime. Still, like the Church, the business community remained largely silent on these and other issues as the 1980s dawned. "This only began to change, observes Eva-Lotta Hedman (1998: 289–290):

> with the onset of a world recession in the early 1980s which sent shock waves through the Philippines and thus contributed to the unraveling of the political economy of "crony capitalism" . . . the cautiously non-political proclamations and projects associated with the PBSP slowly gave way to the renewed business activism of the 1980s which converged around the increasingly outspoken and powerful voice of the Makati Business Club, first introduced onto the scene of Philippine national politics in 1981.

Even more important than the Makati Business Club in mobilizing and expressing growing corporate opposition to the regime was the Philippine Businessmen's Conference. Originally founded in 1971, the group initially aligned itself with the regime. But, reflecting the general pattern sketched above, by the early 1980s, the Conference had become a hotbed of anti–Marcos sentiment and activity.

By the early 1980's, key institutional and ideological centers of Philippine society, once key Marcos allies, had grown openly hostile to the regime. In short, the Aquino assassination did not in any simple sense cause the movement. "If the assassination provided the catalyst that triggered prayer vigils and confetti rallies around the country's plazas and business districts, the swift and coordinated reactivation of Catholic and corporate associational networks in the mid-1980s thus also reflected" . . . [the] long-term social change networks reviewed here (Hedman: 266). Yet to say that key sectors of Philippine society were badly estranged from the regime by the early 1980s is not to discount the importance of the Aquino assassination, and the broader Marcos–Aquino feud, to the onset of the episode.

Attribution of Threat and Opportunity in the Yellow Revolution

The Philippine experience points up limits of the "big bang" imagery associated with the idea of a single precipitating event. For the catalytic event is often neither accidental nor the primordial starting point of the episode. In the case of the Philippines, Aquino's assassination merely culminated a longstanding political rivalry between Marcos and Aquino. Their feud dated to at least the early 1970s. Indeed, Marcos' declaration of martial law in 1972 was designed, in part, to avoid facing Aquino in the presidential election scheduled for 1973. Subsequently, Aquino was jailed by Marcos' regime for various "political crimes." While still in jail, however, Aquino led a slate of opposition candidates in the 1978 Interim Legislative Assembly elections. Though denied his assembly seat through election fraud, Aquino's star only grew brighter as a result of his courageous opposition to Marcos' regime.

Under pressure from the Carter administration, Aquino was eventually released and allowed to come to the U.S. to undergo heart surgery. He remained in exile in the United States, thereafter, voicing his opposition to Marcos at every opportunity. By all accounts, Aquino's return to the Philippines in 1983 was motivated, in large part, by reports that Marcos was in ill health and therefore not long for power. Indeed, Aquino thought it possible that he might be able to persuade Marcos "to arrange for a peaceful transfer of power to the opposition, or failing that, to assume leadership of that opposition himself" (Lande 1986: 115). In other words, it was Aquino's conviction that Marcos was newly receptive or vulnerable to challenge that prompted him to terminate his exile.

If Aquino's actions were motivated by a sense of "political opportunity," then the assassination represented an innovative – if ill advised – tactical response on the part of Marcos loyalists within the armed forces to the perceived threat of Aquino's return to the Philippines. In turn, the assassination helped to create the generalized sense of uncertainty and flux about the future of Philippine politics that we have argued is so critical to a sustained episode of contentious politics.

More precisely, this sense of generalized uncertainty was itself born of the reactions of various key parties to the conflict in the wake of the assassination. Specifically, it was the strong condemnation of the assassination and of the regime more generally by nominal Marcos allies or previously silent elites that fueled the emerging "crisis" definition of the situation. These new critics included elements within the Philippine business community, the mainstream Philippine news media, certain United States government officials, and Cardinal Jaime Sin and the official hierarchy of the

Philippine Catholic Church.[1] A case can be made that the last of these groups was the most important to the burgeoning movement.

Cardinal Sin and other high ranking Church officials had, for years, been under considerable pressure from leftist elements active in church-based organizing among the poor to come out foursquare against the regime. Until the assassination, however, Sin had generally refrained from openly criticizing Marcos or taking strong stands on political issues. This is not to say that Sin and the formal Church hierarchy, as embodied in the Catholic Bishop's Conference of the Philippines (CBCP), were strong allies of Marcos's. On the contrary, relations between the Church and regime had been strained since the mid-1970s and had been further weakened, in the early 1980s, by the government's increasingly strident campaign against "communist infiltration" in Church ranks (Youngblood 1987: 352). Still, the rift was largely invisible, thus preserving the public perception of tacit Church support for the regime.

With the assassination, the situation changed dramatically. Sin and other Church officials reacted strongly and immediately to Aquino's death, sharply criticizing the regime both for its apparent culpability in the shooting and later for its clumsy efforts to stack the panel charged with investigating the assassination with Marcos loyalists. In coming out so forcefully against the regime in the wake of the slaying, Sin sent a critically important signal to the inert but politically alert Philippine middle and upper-middle classes. In his increasingly strident and frequent criticism of Marcos, Sin helped to articulate and shape public reaction to events, giving public voice to sentiments felt privately by many. He was offended and deeply embarrassed by the slaying and by what it said about the sorry state of Philippine democracy.

Sin's defection contributed greatly to the emerging sense of crisis and uncertainty that sustained the episode. This sense of generalized uncertainty was also linked to the emerging accounts of threat and opportunity

[1] Chapter 7 takes up the crucial issue of how revolutionary situations devolve into revolutionary outcomes, arguing that the key to this transformation is the process of elite defection and crossclass coalition formation. By this we mean the establishment of cooperative ties between political and/or economic elites formerly allied with the regime and traditional opposition groups. We use the case of the Sandinista revolution in Nicaragua to illustrate the process, but the Yellow revolution affords an eerie parallel to the former case. As in Nicaragua, the abandonment of Marcos by elites previously implicated in his rule – and the mass defection of the Philippine middle class – was key to the successful revolutionary outcome of the conflict.

that developed in the days immediately following the assassination. For the normally conservative middle class, the assassination came to be seen as a profound threat to the tattered remnants of Philippine stability. For the traditional leftist opposition – which had never doubted the threat posed by the Marcos regime – Aquino's death was seized on as a real "opportunity" to oust Marcos from power.

Despite various political maneuvers, Marcos was never able to reestablish the generalized sense of stability and political order that might have undermined the shared perceptions of threat and opportunity that fueled the unfolding conflict. Instead, as in the escalating phase of all episodes of contention, his actions only served to reinforce the growing sense of societal crisis and generalized uncertainty. Nor did Marcos' departure from the Philippines and Cory Aquino's ascension to the presidency immediately restore – in either a cognitive or structural sense – the political order and stability missing during the previous two-and-a-half years. On the contrary, lack of information about Cory Aquino's political leanings, combined with her call on April 23, 1986 for the drafting of a new Constitution, set in motion nearly a year of intense political mobilization and interaction by all parties interested in contesting the shape and substance of the new Philippine political order.

Vincent Boudreau (forthcoming: 10) captures the palpable sense of uncertainty and possibility that characterized the period immediately following Aquino's call for a formal restructuring of Philippine politics. "Into this vacuum rushed individuals and associations, avid to participate in the reconstitution of their government. It was a time of midnight phone calls, when political rumors chased one another around the capital, and activists marked time by the intervals between meetings and demonstrations." Only as the policies of the Aquino regime and the general shape of the emerging political status quo became clearer (with the approval of the new Constitution a key step in the process), did a generalized sense of uncertainty – and related perceptions of opportunity and threat – wane, and with it the high levels of mobilization and interaction characteristic of all contentious episodes.

Social Appropriation and Brokerage in the Yellow Revolution

In his rich study on popular mobilization in the Philippines during and immediately after the overthrow of the Marcos regime, Boudreau rightly takes scholars of social movements and revolutions to task for their failure to take seriously the dynamic processes by which ordinary citizens come to be mobilized in the service of broad national movements such as the Yellow revolution, and by which they are later demobilized as the struggle winds down. In short, Boudreau is concerned, in large part, with the dynamics of what we have termed *social appropriation* and *brokerage*. Born of this general theoretical interest, Boudreau has produced one of the richest accounts of mobilization and demobilization to be found in the literature.

Among the handful of other systematic investigations of social appropriation and brokerage is a second study that also takes the anti–Marcos movement as its focus of attention. However, this second study, by Eva-Lotta Hedman (1998), focuses on very different groups and social actors than Boudreau's study. Together, though, they encompass the two dominant patterns of oppositional mobilization and demobilization that characterized the episode. As such, they command our attention, both separately and in combination.

The general focus of Boudreau's research concerns the efforts of established left oppositional interests to recruit coalition partners from among grassroots organizations of the poor. Temporally, Boudreau is not strictly concerned with origins, but his account is so rich as to provide a general window into one important form of appropriation and brokerage, that both informed the struggle in the Philippines and is generally significant across many episodes of contention. Here, we see processes by which well-defined oppositional groups seek to appropriate the routine identities and everyday networks of shared fate and trust of previously inactive (or, at best, marginally active) social groupings.

Boudreau finds the complex blending of established and emergent actors that we have argued is the hallmark of many instances of transgressive contention. "The uprising," he writes (forthcoming: 8), "was a historical moment that depended both on two decades of opposition to government, and a period of more spontaneous turmoil and protest in the mid-1980s. The [final demonstrations in support of the military rebels] . . . as well as the rowdy electoral campaign that touched it off were notable in the degree to which they drew unorganized urban and middle class participants into collective demonstrations and protest. These protests, however, also depended on the organizational resources, and activist traditions, of several well-established, long-term political movements."

The ranks of various established oppositional organizations – students, farmers, labor, etc. – swelled during the episode. In addition, it created or revitalized several broad umbrella organizations representing the traditional Philippine left. These groups included: BAYAN (or New Nationalist Alliance), the chief Communist front organization active during the episode; KASAMA (The Federation of People's Organizations); and BISIG, which saw itself as a socialist alternative to the popular front activities of BAYAN. This rich mix of established sectoral associations (of students, farmers, labor, etc.) and broad umbrella organizations served as important agents of social appropriation and brokerage in the course of the anti–Marcos struggle.

Galvanized by the assassination, these small sectoral organizations engaged in targeted recruiting appeals designed to draw more of their immediate constituents into the fray. Moreover, this process was simultaneously going on at all levels of Philippine society. Local organizations of farmers and peasants used the assassination (and each succeeding "outrage" by Marcos) to recruit new members. Likewise, national farmer's associations, notably the Federation of Free Farmers, grew more aggressive in seeking to activate and expand the number of local affiliates nominally under their control.

But the simultaneous mobilization and aggregation of local, regional, and national sectoral interests during the unfolding conflict tells us only half – and the less interesting half – of the story. After all, these sectoral interests merely represented parts of the small leftwing opposition within Philippine society. The hallmark of the Yellow revolution was not so much stepped-up activity by traditional opposition groups as the active mobilization of the Philippine middle and upper-middle classes, worried about Communism but disgusted with Marcos. Hedman (1998) takes up this other half of the appropriation and brokerage story in her study.

As Hedman tells it, this latter segment of the movement was drawn into the struggle, not so much by the established sectoral associations, but by more moderate umbrella organizations that emerged during the struggle, and, to a lesser extent, as a result of direct appeals by institutions and figures central to the lives of the middle and upper-middle classes. Cardinal Sin's call for citizens to surround Camp Aguinaldo in the final days of Marcos' regime may have been the most dramatic instance of the latter dynamic, but conservative newspapers and national business associations played a role in this as well.

Among the more moderate – and typically ephemeral – umbrella organizations that drew the middle and upper-middle classes into the struggle, three in particular should be singled out for special mention. The first was

BANDILA, a social-democratic organization long allied with the Catholic Church. BANDILA's centrality in the episode again speaks to the important role that the Church played in legitimating movement participation on the part of the middle-class. The second group, JAJA (Justice for Aquino, Justice for All), emerged early in the struggle as little more than a vehicle for coordinating the street demonstrations that came to serve as the movement's hallmark.

Like JAJA, the third and final organization, The National Movement for Free Elections (NAMFREL), was also an ephemeral body designed less as an organized expression of sectoral interests than a temporary solution to a particular problem. The problem in question was how to insure that the "snap election" of February 1986 was conducted fairly and without the rampant voter fraud and intimidation that had long been a staple of the Marcos regime. NAMFREL was the response to this problem. But, though nominally nonpartisan, Hedman's research makes it clear that NAMFREL came to serve as a hotbed of anti–Marcos activism and a common pathway by which the middle class was drawn into the struggle.

The more general point that informs Hedman's study is that, unlike the patterns of recruitment and mobilization studied by Boudreau, the commercial and Catholic middle class eschewed the established sectoral organizations of the Philippine left in favor of moderate umbrella organizations of the type reviewed here, or recruitment via the established institutions (e.g., the Catholic Church, business associations) of Philippine society.

The Dog That Didn't Bark: The Absent Communists

Before we conclude our discussion of appropriation and brokerage, let us take up briefly what proved to be a highly consequential decision on the part of another key actor in Philippine politics *not* to play a significant role in the Yellow revolution. We refer to the decision by Communist insurgents to refrain from an active engagement in the events of 1983–1986 and beyond. We take up this issue not only in the interest of a complete accounting of the Philippine case, but to make the point that social appropriation and brokerage involves foregone framings and linkages as much as strategies and lines of action actually adopted. So it was with the Communists and the struggle to oust Marcos.

On the eve of that struggle the Communists were well established as a serious national threat both to the Marcos regime and to Philippine political stability more generally. "During the late 1970s and much of the 1980s," according to Benedict Kerkvliet:

> Political winds in the Philippines favored the acceleration of the New People's Army (NPA) and the Communist Party of the Philippines (CPP). Beginning in the late 1960s with a tiny number of members and even fewer rifles, the party and the guerrilla army had grown to become political and military forces in the nation then burdened by the Marcos regime and immense economic and political problems associated with that rule. By the mid 1980s the NPA had between twenty and twenty-four thousand members and controlled an estimated 20 percent of the country's villages and urban neighborhoods. . . . But by the early 1990s, the underground movement's fortunes had declined sharply. The NPA's "mass base" had diminished to 3 percent of the country's villages and neighborhoods . . . and the number of armed NPA had dropped to an estimated 10,600. [Kerkvliet 1996: 9]

The sharp decline in the fortunes of the Communist insurgents dates to the Yellow revolution and to the tactical choices made by movement leaders during the years of that struggle and the early days of the Aquino regime. Though these choices were vigorously contested, the decision to refrain from active engagement with the anti–Marcos movement and later with the Aquino regime was reaffirmed at every critical juncture. To this point, the impact of this arms-length posture has been disastrous:

> While the Communists could neither have instigated nor prevented the 1986 revolt even if they had wanted, internal and external critics of the CPP agree that the . . . movement would have suffered less from this change in political regime had they been participants in the process. If they had not opted for boycott, but instead joined with the broad opposition to defeat Marcos first at the ballot and then on the streets, then the revolutionary movement would have been in a better position to influence the course of events that followed. [Weekley 1996: 29]

What accounts for this serious failure on the part of the Communists? The rich body of ethnographic work produced by Roseanne Rutten (1991, 1996) on Communist organizing at the village level during the movement's heyday shows clearly that the failure cannot be attributed to any lack of skill at the related tasks of social appropriation and brokerage. On the contrary, the insurgents' efforts in this regard could well serve as a primer for peasant mobilization more generally. In the hacienda where she did her fieldwork, Rutten documents how organizers slowly and painstakingly succeeded in infiltrating and appropriating local Church and union structures and the collective identities on which they rested. The success of this effort turned, in part, on a classic example of what Snow and Benford (1988) have termed "frame bridging": the conscious effort to merge the ideology of the movement with an existing cultural framework. Rutten explains:

> The early activists, then, eventually reached hacienda workers by linking up with social networks of Church and unions that reached into many haciendas and villages in the province. Moreover, they connected to Liberation Theology, which matched to a large degree the ideological frame of the NPA. The CPP–NPA nationwide had developed an interest in Roman Catholic clergy opposed to the martial-law regime and committed to Vatican II's call for social justice. In Negros Occidental, progressive priests and nuns supported two militant unions, the Federation of Free Farmers . . . and the labor union National Federation of Sugar Workers. . . . NPA activists eventually began to recruit among local organizers of Basic Christian Communities and the labor union. [Rutten 1996: 120]

Having effectively appropriated these two key local institutions, NPA organizers had little difficulty in establishing strong bonds of trust and loyalty within hacienda society more generally and in translating these interpersonal resources into an effective village level structure of formal NPA positions. Then, by linking these village level positions into broader insurgent networks, local organizers brokered a strong (if regionally variable) national movement into existence.

With this structure in place, one could well have imagined the Communists actively embracing the crisis of 1983–1986 and attempting to build strong links – ideologically and structurally – to elements of the anti-Marcos coalition. Had they done so, the outcome of the episode and the structure of Philippine politics might look very different than it does today. Thus the decision of the Communists to boycott the Yellow revolution serves to underscore the contingent, interactive, context dependent nature of all episodes of contention. The assassination of Benigno Aquino fundamentally changed the context of Philippine politics. It was not the act that effected this transformation, but the interpretations and new lines of action fashioned, interactively, by various parties to the conflict that birthed the episode. Among the most consequential of these interpretations and, in this case, lines of *inaction*, were those that held sway within the NPA and CPP.

Finally, the case of the Philippine Communists allows us to note again the overweening importance of history and culture in shaping the actions of all parties to a contentious episode. Most of the time people experience culture as a set of binding cognitive, affective and behavioral constraints rather than as optional tools for action. So it would seem did the Communist braintrust during the Yellow revolution:

> The Party's history and its strategic situation prior to the surprise election announcement militated against a different decision. . . . Like any institution, the Party's own history and culture have always been strong determinants in its decision-making – they shape the way in which the Party sees the "objective, structural facts" of the world around it and in general, tend to slow down the process of adapting to exogenous change. At that particular moment in the political history of the Philippines and the revolutionary movement, key people in the CPP leadership could not read the changes outside the tried-and-true protracted people's war framework. [Weekley 1996: 29]

Their embedding in previous history misled Communist leaders as to what was possible in the volatile Philippine politics of their time.

Conclusion

The same basic mobilization mechanisms – *collective attribution*, *social appropriation*, and *brokerage* – appear in the two distinctly different episodes of contention we have compared. Considered separately and immediately, those mechanisms produce the same effects everywhere. Collective attribution, for example, always makes available new definitions of the possible and the probable, and thereby alters strategic choices. Yet overall trajectories and outcomes of mobilization by no means follow the same patterns everywhere. They differ because the sequence, combination, interaction, and context of these mechanisms' activation profoundly influence their joint consequences. To illustrate that variability, let us look at differences between the two episodes at hand.

Differences in Aggregate Effects of Brokerage

Consider the key agents of brokerage in Kenya and the Philippines. Despite the autocratic, corrupt, and violently repressive nature of Marcos' rule, the Philippines retained a rich array of local, regional, and national associations representing both the traditional left and the conservative business and Catholic communities. As Boudreau's (forthcoming) analysis makes clear, the former groups served as vehicles of social appropriation and brokerage in the wake of the Aquino assassination and, indeed, throughout the unfolding conflict; and as Hedman's work illustrates, the latter groups were mobilized against the Marcos regime as its death-knells began to toll. Not only were the central institutions of Church and business appropriated during the struggle; they helped to produce a host of newly created umbrella organizations – including NAMFREL – that would broker much of the popular mobilization.

The contrast with Mau Mau could not be clearer. In Kenya, few established political associations existed on the eve of the episode. The mass arrests accompanying the declared State of Emergency, furthermore, decimated those few (e.g., KAU and KCA) that were active. The absence of centralized mobilizing structures gave the movement its more reticulate, decentralized texture. It also confounded the colonial authorities. Steeped in a formal "chain of command" view of the world, they could not imagine any other form of social organization. Accordingly, against all available evidence, they kept insisting that the rebellion was a planned conspiracy. Kenyatta's trial was but the most visible manifestation of their search for the revolt's putative leaders.

This contrast in the locus and degree of centralized brokerage in the two cases (high in the Philippines; low in Kenya) may help to account for the much higher levels of violence in Mau Mau than the Yellow revolution. For example, formal organizations may be more inclined to avoid violence than insurgent groups that are organized less formally and in more decentralized fashion. The assumption here is that formal organization tends to imply some greater stake in the system and, thus, less willingness to deploy violence in the service of movement aims. This is, of course, conjecture on our part, but it is conjecture that is consistent both with certain strands of theory (Gerth and Mills 1946; Michels 1962; Piven and Cloward 1977) and the very different trajectories of the two cases under examination here.

Differences in Aggregate Effects of Certification and Decertification

The divergent outcomes in the two cases did not result entirely from initial differences in mobilization dynamics. Other mechanisms operating later in the episodes had profound effects on the very different trajectories and outcomes of contention in Kenya and the Philippines. Consider a pair of mechanisms – *certification* and *decertification* – that will receive much closer scrutiny in Chapters 5 and 7. Certification entails the validation of actors, their performances, and their claims by external authorities. Decertification is the withdrawal of such validation by certifying agents. The two episodes analyzed here present an interesting contrast in the dynamics and variable consequences of certification and decertification as a function of their intersection with other mechanisms.

Our discussion of Mau Mau touched on the trial and subsequent imprisonment of Jomo Kenyatta and other leading Kenyan nationalists. Rendered in terms of mechanisms, this trial effectively *decertified* Kenyatta, the moderate nationalist movement, and even the broader Mau Mau rebellion, which was depicted throughout the trial as a violent, atavistic cult. These successful decertifying efforts shaped the subsequent episode in highly consequential ways. Decertifying Kenyatta precluded his serving as an intermediary between colonial authorities and the insurgents. Had authorities worked with Kenyatta – in essence certifying him as a legitimate bargaining partner – we might have seen what social movement scholars have labeled a "radical flank effect," by which moderate actors take advantage of a polarized situation to gain leverage with authorities (see Chapter 6). The end result might well have been an acceleration of the independence process and Kenyatta's ascension to formal political authority. Instead, with all native actors decertified, colonial authorities were able to derail the independence movement temporarily, and isolate and repress the Mau Mau rebels with relative impunity.

Certification and decertification played an equally powerful, but generally facilitating role in the Yellow revolution. On the one hand, the burgeoning movement against Marcos benefited from certification at any number of critical junctures. Perhaps the most consequential was Cardinal Sin's early and unambiguous endorsement of the movement. If the critical hallmark of the movement was the mobilization of the moderate middle class, it was Sin more than anyone who signaled the legitimacy of participation in the struggle. But the episode was punctuated by other decisive instances of certification. For instance, findings of the Agrava Board, which implicated figures close to Marcos in the planning and execution of Benigno Aquino's assassination, simultaneously decertified the regime and certified the anti-Marcos forces.

Decertification also came powerfully from the former colonial power, one whose enduring political, economic, and cultural influence in the Philippines cannot be underestimated. The fact that Philippine householders could watch daily as their country was portrayed on American television as controlled by a corrupt, clientelistic, and criminal political class helped to powerfully decertify the regime. The official United States election watch team dispatched by President Reagan to ensure a fair and democratic election reinforced this decertification by the hegemonic ex-colonial power. As Carl Lande writes:

> Marcos has said that his greatest mistake was to call the February elections. Another mistake, surely, was to invite foreign observers, including several missions from the United States. The most prominent member of these missions was U.S. Senator Richard Lugar. Arriving with an open mind, Lugar by the end of election day was convinced that the election process was fatally flawed by massive government cheating. Hastening back to Washington, he played a crucial part in persuading President Reagan of that fact. [Lande 1987: 41]

In turn, President Reagan's decisive, if long overdue, withdrawal of support for Marcos in the final hours of the crisis, served as one final instance of decertification.

What can we conclude from these three sets of observations?

- First, that the same basic mobilization mechanisms – collective attribution of opportunity and threat, social appropriation, and brokerage – appeared in the two distinctly different episodes of contention suggests that they will turn out to be robust components of any process of mobilization and demobilization. That speculation needs to be refined, replicated, and tested, but it suggests attending less to differences in the forms and outcomes of contention than to the dynamic mechanisms and processes that they seem to share in common.
- Second, in calling attention to the significance of the three mechanisms across the two cases, we make no claim that these mechanisms produced identical joint effects in the two episodes or will do so anywhere else. On the contrary, the very different trajectories of the two episodes owed much to the different manifestations of the processes discussed here. Analysis begins with the identification of mechanisms on contention; it must extend to their sequences, concatenations, and contexts.
- Third, we do not maintain that our three mobilization mechanisms exhaust the dynamics of our two episodes or, for that matter, of any episode of contention. Certification, which played a key role in the Philippine case, will play an even greater one in the South Asian and South African cases we turn to in the next chapter. Still other mechanisms – identity shift and radicalization – will play key roles in Chapter 6's evocation of American antislavery and Spanish democratization.

Let us turn to those cases and to those mechanisms of contention.

5

Contentious Action

During the early 1960s, Amitav Ghosh lived in Dhaka, then capital of East Pakistan, where his father served in the Indian diplomatic mission. "There was," Ghosh remarks,

> an element of irony in our living in Dhaka as "foreigners," for Dhaka was in fact our ancestral city; both my parents were from families that belonged to the middle-class Hindu community that had once flourished there. But long before the Muslim-majority state of Pakistan was created my ancestors had moved westwards, and thanks to their wanderlust we were Indians now, and Dhaka was foreign territory to us although we still spoke its dialect and still had several relatives living in the old Hindu neighbourhoods in the heart of the city. [Ghosh 1992: 205]

For Hindus of India, Pakistan, and Bangladesh, the name Ghosh signals a family history of higher-caste standing. This Ghosh tells of a night in January 1964, when his father ordered their cook to sequester eight-year-old Amitav in their big house's master bedroom. As the fearful cook stole out to a nearby balcony for a look at what was happening below, young Amitav followed him, stared down, and witnessed a scene he recalled almost thirty years later in these terms:

> A large crowd is thronging around our house, a mob of hundreds of men, their faces shining red in the light of the burning torches in their hands, rags tied on sticks, whose flames seem to be swirling against our walls in waves of fire. As I watch, the flames begin to dance around the house, and while they circle the walls the people gathered inside mill around the garden, cower in huddles and cover their faces. [Ghosh 1992: 208]

In this half-remembered scene, people inside are Hindus, people outside Muslims, relations between them fear and hatred. That night the outsiders – who were insiders in Dhaka at large – finally did no more than toss rubble across the garden wall. By the following morning the assailants had departed, the refugees from their attack had settled down in the garden, and the cook had regained his composure:

> Later, we squatted in a corner and he whispered in my ear, pointing at the knots of people around us, and told me their stories. I was to recognize those stories years later, when reading through a collection of old newspapers, I discovered that on the very night when I'd seen those flames dancing around the walls of our house, there had been a riot in Calcutta too, similar in every respect except that there it was Muslims who had been attacked by Hindus. But equally, in both cities – and this must be said, it must always be said, for it is the incantation that redeems our sanity – in both Dhaka and Calcutta, there were exactly mirrored stories of Hindus and Muslims coming to each other's rescue, so that many more people were saved than killed. [Ghosh 1992: 209–210]

Since 1964, reports of contentious politics in this vein have arrived at a faster and faster pace from many parts of the world (Gurr and Harff 1994). Reporters commonly apply to events of this sort labels such as "communal conflict," "ethnic competition," "tribalism," "nationalism," "age-old hatred," and even "genocide." Such labels have become uncomfortably familiar in our time. Seen in the colder light cast by current analyses of contentious politics, nevertheless, three features of Ghosh's vivid account raise doubts: labeling of the outsiders (but not the insiders) as a "mob," description of the event and others like it as "riots," and taking of the terms "Hindu" and "Muslim" as unproblematic attributes of the individuals involved. Authorities, power-holders, and enemies typically use the word "mob" – from *mobile vulgus*, or fickle populace – to describe gatherings of which they disapprove. The word "riot" likewise conveys condemnation of collective action that direct participants almost invariably call something else: demonstration, march, gathering, retaliation, fight, and so on.

As for collective nouns such as Hindu and Muslim, people do in fact generally treat such words as if they designated essential, coherent attributes of other persons, and sometimes even of themselves. They adopt the implicit idea of a self-directed module bearing a single identifier. Although it has great attractions for would-be leaders of solidary communities, that idea carries little conviction as a basis for description or explanation of social behavior. It loses credibility when confronted with some contrary realities. Note the wide variety of identities an average person activates most days: spouse, parent, household member, traveler, consumer, worker, supervisor, member of this group or that. Witness how rarely anyone ever expresses all aspects of a complex self simultaneously – indeed how much people channel each other into expressing different identities selectively. Observe the exceptional socialization, discipline, and segregation that seem necessary conditions for making one identity predominate continuously over all others, as in military academy hazing, recruitment into a cult, or creation of a terrorist network. Even these extreme measures often fail to subordinate other identities of gender, kinship, or friendship. Recognize the ways that identities and their contents modify in the course of social interaction, with people adjusting their behavior as they acquire new identities, attempting to redefine the identities others attribute to them, and subtly negotiating who's who in such complex relations as worker-boss, courting couple, or in-laws. Consider finally the erratic, improvising, reflexive, negotiated, socially shaped character of individual action as it usually unfolds. Deliberate, effective, autonomous self-direction is rare. So are persons who live out their lives within just one identity.

The complexity of identities returns us to three fundamental questions about contentious politics we posed indirectly earlier:

Actors: Who makes claims, and why do they do so?

Identities: Who do they and others say they are, and why do they say so?

Actions: What forms do their claim making take and why?

This chapter pursues our three questions twice, first in a search for concepts to discipline any inquiry that asks them, then in identification of a handful of recurrent causal mechanisms that help answer the "why" questions across a wide variety of contention. In both pursuits, we are seeking not total explanations but useful, partial simplifications. Our simplifications, unsurprisingly, stress social interaction as the locus and basis of contention. They draw implicitly on parallels between political contention and argumentative conversation, which follows a dynamic that is irreducible to the initial intentions of the conversationalists. Above all, we break with the common assumption that intentions – or, worse yet, reasons given by participants – explain social processes. Yet, ironically, we end up observing that assertions of unitary actors and performances to validate those assertions play central parts in a great variety of contentious politics. The enactment of self-propelled unity turns out to be both a socially organized illusion and a profound truth of contention.

First, we explore these issues with respect to Hindu–Muslim conflict in South Asia since World War II, working our way gradually toward specification of mechanisms forming and transforming actors, identities, and actions. Then, much more briefly, we show that the same identity-related mechanisms appear in South African contention between 1985 and 1995. Finally, we make the case that the mechanisms in question – brokerage, category formation, object shift, and certification – operate in similar fashion across a wide range of contentious politics. They operate in similar fashion, that is, without in the least producing the same global trajectories or outcomes. Each mechanism involves the same immediate cause–effect connections wherever and whenever it occurs. But trajectories and outcomes of whole episodes differ because initial conditions, sequences, and combinations of mechanisms compound to produce variable global effects. Eventually, then, analysts of contentious politics will have to master the complexities of initial conditions, sequences, and combinations. For the moment, however, we can make a significant contribution simply by specifying crucial identity-connected mechanisms.

Hindus versus Muslims in Panipur

To see more clearly what is at issue, let us zigzag forward twenty-five years, then back ten years, from the 1964 conflict in Dhaka. During the years around 1990, American ethnographer Beth Roy spent repeated sojourns in the Bangladeshi village of Panipur. (Before successive partitions, of course, Panipur belonged to India, then to Pakistan.) In this village of absentee landlords, smallholders, and landless laborers, the Ganges basin's shifting waters exacerbated common peasant concerns about property rights and boundaries. The village included households labeled as Hindu or Muslim, but it lived from day to day with a much finer – and often cross-cutting – set of distinctions, notably of caste, class, property, and gender.

Although residents of Panipur that confided in Roy at first portrayed themselves as living in harmony with their multicultural neighbors, Roy eventually encountered evidence of deep conflicts in the village past. She met a local Mr. Ghosh, member of the high-ranking Kayastha caste. (Sudhir Kakar speaks cuttingly of "the Kayasthas, who are well known for their identification with the masters they have so ably served, whether the ruler be British or Muslim." [Kakar 1996: 10]) Mr. Ghosh first revealed to Roy that the village had experienced a whole series of violent conflicts (Roy 1994: 15–16). Like a robin that pulls at a loose thread for nesting material only to unravel a whole sweater, she kept asking questions about a 1954 incident until she had collected both a wide range of stories and a plausible reconstruction of the struggles that generated those stories. Once Mr. Ghosh had given her the opening, Roy pursued it relentlessly.

What happened in 1954? Golam Fakir's cow got loose, strayed across the limits of Golam's property, and ate lentils in Kumar Tarkhania's field. At that time, Panipur belonged to Pakistan, a predominantly Muslim state with a substantial Hindu minority; only later would its region, East Pakistan, acquire independence as overwhelmingly Muslim Bangladesh. In the village's broadest religious divisions, cow-owning Golam qualified as a Muslim, lentil-owning Kumar as a Hindu. Kumar's friends seized the cow, which Golam then forcibly freed over the protests of those who were guarding it. At that point the two men could have taken their dispute to a local court, which would no doubt have ordered Golam to compensate Kumar according to an established scale of damages.

Instead of settling their differences immediately, however, both farmers called in kinfolk, patrons, and allies. As a result, a minor dispute precipitated broader and broader alignments of bloc against bloc. The next day, for example, Golam provocatively tethered his cow in the same place before going off, but later returned to discover that someone had moved his cows (now multiple) into his own lentil patch. When Golam began to chase his cows out, Kumar's two brothers entered the field, attempted to take him off with the offending cow, heeded an elder Hindu's advice to release Golam, but grabbed him again when he threatened dire consequences:

> They again came rushing toward me. They caught me again. Again they tied me and started dragging me, and one of them hacked me with the sickle. He cut me on my right arm. I shouted. Some Muslims were standing a little distance away. Hearing me shout, they came running toward me. When they arrived, they freed me. [Roy 1994: 55]

Escalation continued. Partisans on one side and the other started seizing each other's cows. Supporters eventually took up knives, sickles, scythes, swords, sticks, shields, and spears, two groups lined up in parallel, hostile, facing rows, young people attacked each other, police intervened and eventually fired on the crowd. Their gunfire killed two or three people and dispersed the huge gathering. As each side demanded justice, as more previously peripheral outsiders joined the conflict, and as local authorities sought pacification, intervention moved up the Pakistani administrative hierarchy. With each step outward and upward, redefinition of the conflict proceeded; the farther and higher the incident went, the less it concerned complex, caste-and-class-mediated local relations among farmers and the more it became part of national level communal struggles between Hindus and Muslims (cf. Turner 1982: 69–70). As individual disputes escalate into inter-clan feuds in Corsica (Gould 1999), local arguments become intercommunal wars in South Asia.

Even local people redefined their conflict after the fact. Mr. Ghosh and his Muslim counterparts, for example, reported that initially they had nothing to do with the conflict except as distant observers, pacifiers, or mediators. For Mr. Ghosh, the Hindu side of the conflict began with Namasudras, members of a low-ranking caste of farmers and fisherfolk, not with respectable people like him; he himself stayed out of it. But people like him, both Hindu and Muslim, came to define the struggle not as a confrontation between Namasudras and their low-ranking Muslim equivalents but between Hindus and Muslims in general. The larger categories came to dominate collective memory.

As Paul Brass remarks of contemporary India:

> At the level of the village and its surroundings, *jati*, the local aspect of caste, may provide a basis for economic action, political organization, and social conflict. In a unit as large as a district, however, correspondingly larger units of political action or political coalitions across *jati* boundaries become necessary for effective political action. . . . At the national level, caste becomes virtually ineffective as a basis for sustained political mobilization for the available caste categories at this level lack appropriate social or economic content. Alternatives to caste as an organizing principle for political conflict also exist at every level in Indian politics, particularly from the district upwards. At those levels, categories such as Hindu and Muslim become more prominent, language loyalties become critical, one's status as a migrant or a "son of the soil" may be decisive, or factional, party, and ideological bases for political division may prevail. [Brass 1994: 155; for qualifications concerning language loyalties in India, see Laitin 2000]

Analyzing the Hindu-Sikh violence in Delhi that followed Indira Gandhi's assassination by two of her Sikh guards, Stanley Tambiah notes a remarkable parallel to Brass's observation:

> Who were the participants in the Delhi riots? It is tempting and comforting to say that the aggressors were strangers and enemies and not friends and neighbors. No such neat binary contrast quite fits the case in point. It can, however, be said that the more mob violence moved toward the active mobilization of people, equip-

ping them with the means of destruction and inciting them to violence, the greater was the likelihood of a guiding role by conspiring "outsiders," aided by informers and collaborators within. [Tambiah 1997: 1178–1179]

As she traced her elusive story, Beth Roy was uncovering South Asia's hierarchy of contentious politics.

Individualistic and Relational Views of Identities

In addition to its empathetic description and astute detective work, Roy's study fascinates by its patient unpacking of complexities in actors, actions, and identities. *Some Trouble with Cows* (the title echoes one of the first stories about the 1954 conflicts Roy collected) centers on questions of identity:

When I consider stories of village communalism, I want to know how people saw their world, how they placed their own desires within it, and how their sense of political possibility was influenced by distant winds of change. It has become common to assert that the most intimate domestic behaviors are in fact socially constructed. Collective experience is translated into psychological reality through a web of ideas internalized as invisible assumptions about the world. To unravel the psychological realities of collective behavior, I believe we must look to shared areas of understanding and social location. For instance, group actions are formulated from the experience of identity, that is, the complex construction of an individual's location in the community and her ties with others. Similarly, the will to action is born of detailed ideologies that often are experienced as common sense or unexamined assumptions about rights and powers. [Roy 1994: 3]

In this introductory passage and throughout her superb reconstruction of old conflicts Roy exhibits ambivalence between two points of view, sometimes treating identity and action as individual mental realities multiplied, sometimes locating identity and action in social relations: "an individual's location in the community and her ties with others." She thereby pinpoints a major difficulty in contemporary analyses of contentious politics (see Cerulo 1997: 393–394). The classic social movement paradigm that we are seeking to dismantle and improve suffers from the difficulty, as do the bulk of other schemes in rationalist, culturalist, phenomenological, and structuralist traditions.

Here is the difficulty: Humans live in flesh-and-blood bodies, accumulate traces of experiences in their nervous systems, organize current encounters with the world as cognitions, emotions, and intentional actions, tell stories about themselves in which they acted deliberately and efficaciously or were blocked from doing so by uncontrolled emotion, weakness, malevolent others, bad luck, or recalcitrant nature, and tell similar stories about other people. Humans come to believe in a world full of continuous, neatly bounded, self-propelling individuals whose intentions interact with accidents and natural limits to produce all of social life. In many versions, those "natural limits" feature norms, values, and scripts inculcated and enforced by powerful others – but then internalized by self-propelling individuals.

Closely observed, however, the same humans turn out to be interacting repeatedly with others, renegotiating who they are, adjusting the boundaries they occupy, modifying their actions in rapid response to other people's reactions, selecting among and altering available scripts, improvising new forms of joint action, speaking sentences no one has ever uttered before, yet responding predictably to their locations within webs of social relations they themselves cannot map in detail. They tell stories about themselves and others that facilitate their social interaction rather than laying out verifiable facts about individual lives. They actually live in deeply relational worlds. If social construction occurs, it happens socially, not in isolated recesses of individual minds.

The problem becomes acute in descriptions and explanations of contentious politics. Political actors typically give individualized accounts of participation in contention, although the "individuals" to which they attribute bounded, unified, continuous self-propulsion are often collective actors such as communities, classes, armies, firms, unions, interest groups, or social movement organizations. They attach moral evaluations and responsibilities to the individuals involved, praising or condemning them for their actions, grading their announced identities from unacceptable (e.g., mob) to laudable (e.g., martyrs). Accordingly, strenuous effort in contentious politics goes into contested representations of crucial actors as worthy or unworthy, unified or fragmented, large or small, committed or uncommitted, powerful or weak, well connected or isolated, durable or evanescent, reasonable or irrational, greedy or generous.

Meticulous observation of that same effort, however, eventually tells even a naïve observer what almost every combat officer, union leader, or political organizer acknowledges in private: that both public representations of political identities and other forms of participation in struggle proceed through intense coordination, contingent improvisation, tactical maneuvering, responses to signals from other participants, on-the-spot reinterpretations of what is possible, desirable, or efficacious, and strings of unexpected outcomes inciting new improvisations. Interactions among actors with shifting boundaries, internal structures, and identities turn out to permeate what in retrospect or in distant perspective analysts call actor-driven wars, strikes, rebellions, electoral campaigns, or social movements. Hence the difficulty of reconciling individualistic images with interactive realities.

Actors, Identities, and Actions

Who are the actors? What sorts of people are likely to engage in contentious politics? What sorts of people, that is, are likely to make concerted public claims that involve governments as objects or third parties and that, if realized, would visibly affect interests of persons outside their own number? In principle, any connected set of persons within a given polity to whom a definition of shared stakes in that polity's operation is available qualifies. In practice, beyond a very small scale, every actor that engages in claim making includes at least one cluster of previously connected persons among whom have circulated widely accepted stories concerning their strategic situation: opportunities, threats, available means of action, likely consequences of those actions, evaluations of those consequences, capacities to act, memories of previous contention, and inventories of other likely parties to any action.

In practice, furthermore, such actors have generally established previous relations – contentious or not – to other collective actors; those relations have shaped internal structures of the actors and helped generate their stories. In practice, finally, constituent units of claim making actors often consist not of living, breathing whole individuals but of groups, organizations, bundles of social relations, and social sites, such as occupations and neighborhoods. Actors consist of networks deploying partially shared histories, cultures, and collective connections with other actors. The "hundreds of men" who gathered outside Amitav Ghosh's family compound in January 1964, carrying torches and throwing bricks, formed just such a network.

Such actors, however, almost never describe themselves as composite networks. Instead, they offer collective nouns; they call themselves workers, women, residents of X, or United Front Against Y. Members of the crowd outside the Ghosh compound identified themselves as Muslims and those inside as Hindus. Other parties often contest those self-descriptions and substitute such collective nouns as rabble, misfits, or riffraff. In so doing they generally accept the implicit notion that actors have unitary identities. Census takers oblige by scooping whole people into religious categories. The Indian census of 1981, for example, enumerated 11 percent of the national population as Muslim, with the range running from 1 percent in Punjab to 64 percent in Jammu and Kashmir (Brass 1994: 231). Can we take those numbers as objective facts against which to assess Muslim–Hindu conflict? David Ludden states forcefully the problem in doing so:

> Like "Muslim," the term "Hindu" conjures an identity that is defined in many ways, and defined differently even by the same individual according to context. It is not known how many people in India would have identified themselves as Hindus, if asked, simply, "What is your religion?" in 1800, 1900, 1947, or 1993. But the vast religious tradition that we refer to as "Hinduism" has no single, unanimously agreed upon core set of institutions analogous to the Quran, *umma* (community of believers in Islam), the Bible, Catholic Church, or Talmud around which a Hindu religious identity could have been unified traditionally. Central philosophical tenets – *dharma* (religious duty), *karma* (fateful action), and *samsara* (the cycle of rebirth) – rationalize a divison of Hindu believers into four ranked ritual status categories (*varnas*) – Brahman, Kshatriya, Vaishya, and Shudra – and it is the distinctions, not the similarities, among countless caste groups (*jatis*) that form the primary basis of Hindu social identity. . . . Hindu identity is multiple, by definition, and India consists of many other religious identities as well, including those among Muslims, Zoroastrians, Sikhs, Christians, and Jews. [Ludden 1996: 6–7]

Those other ostensibly unitary groups, furthermore, also begin to look fragmented and various once we turn up the magnification for them as Ludden does for Hindus.

What's going on? Identities in general consist of social relations and their representations, as seen from the perspective of one actor or another. They are not durable or encompassing attributes of persons or collective actors as such. To bear an identity as mother is to maintain a certain relation to a child. The same person who bears the identity mother in one context easily adopts the identities manager, customer, alumna, and sister in others. A crucial subset of identities is categorical; they pivot on a line that separates Xs from Ys, establishing distinct relations of Xs to Xs, Xs to Ys, and Ys to Ys. Muslim/Hindu forms a widely influential categorical pair in Dhaka and Panipur. But so elsewhere in South Asia do Muslim/Christian, Hindu/Buddhist, and Buddhist/Christian, not to mention salient distinctions separating and binding pairs within the categories Muslim, Hindu, Buddhist, and Christian. Each pair defines not only a boundary but also a locally variable set of relations across that boundary.

Seen as social relations and their representations, all identities have a political side, actual or potential. Whether husband-wife or Muslim–Hindu, each categorical pair has its own historically accumulated forms of deliberation and struggle. Much identity-based deliberation and struggle raise questions that, when generalized, become problems of the common good: questions of inequality, of equity, of right, of obligation. Public debates and private identities often interact, as when men and women enact in their daily lives the issues and terms of great public struggles over gender inequality. Finally, all polities leave room for some claim-making on the basis of shared identity, and all polities build some identities explicitly into public political life; demands in the name of a religious minority illustrate the first phenomenon, installation of legal distinctions between citizens and aliens the second. Recognizing the ubiquity of identity politics in some senses of the term, we nevertheless call identities explicitly *political* when they qualify in both of these last two regards: when people make public claims on the basis of those identities, claims to which governments are either objects or third parties.

Identities are political, then, insofar as they involve relations to governments. Obvious examples are official, military veteran, citizen, imprisoned felon, and welfare recipient. Identities such as worker, resident, and woman likewise become political in some regimes, either where governments actually rule by means of such identities or where any set of people who subscribe to the same program have the right to voice collective demands. One of the most hotly debated questions in current Indian politics is whether, if it came to full power, the increasingly influential Bharatiya Janata Party (BJP), with its origins in Hindu nationalism, would inscribe religious categories into the previously secular Indian national governmental structure.

In the present Indian system, people who share routine religious identities already have the right to form parties of their own, so long as they represent themselves as embodying distinctive ways of life rather than creeds as such. Authorities currently contest any such right in Turkey, Algeria, Tanzania, Afghanistan, and parts of the former Soviet Union. To that extent many religious identities are already political identities in India. Indeed, as the observations of Amitav Ghosh and Beth Roy show, in some regards the Hindu/Muslim pair operates across South Asia chiefly in relation to government (see, e.g., Copland 1998). It designates a political distinction rather than separating two well-defined, unitary, transcendental world views from each other. To an unknown but probably large degree, shared orientations of category members result from, rather than causing, recurrent political relations between members of different categories.

Political identities vary, nevertheless, along a continuum from embedded to detached. *Embedded* identities inform a wide range of routine social relations, as in a village where membership in a given household strongly affects everyday relations with most other people. *Detached* identities inform only a narrow, specialized range of intermittent social relations, as when membership in a particular school graduating class (however powerful that identity was when its holders were young) dwindles in importance to an occasional reunion or chance encounter. Detached identities, however, sometimes matter greatly when activated, as in the cases of secret societies, military veterans, and illegitimate children. Embedded identities can detach, as when divisions by occupation or locality start superseding divisions by lineage, and lineage relations therefore shrink in scope and impact. Detached identities can also embed, as when residents of two adjacent neighborhoods begin to fight, draw sharp lines between themselves, and engage in harassment or vituperation at each encounter. The labels "embedded" and "detached," in short, do not describe the contents of identities, but their connections with routine social life.

Political identities figure in both routine social life and contentious politics; governmental officials, for example, typically hold jobs that engage them in a wide variety of noncontentious social relations as well as in contentious public politics. Yet some political identities originate or specialize in contention. Figure 5.1 schematizes the field of variation we have in mind. It points out that (despite some empirical correlation of routine with embedded identities and contentious with detached identities) the distinctions routine-contentious and embedded-detached are logically independent of each other. Households, it declares, usually provide the basis of embedded identities that operate chiefly in routine social life rather than in contentious politics. Household identities nevertheless take on political tones when government census-takers enumerate their members, militaries conscript or exempt young men on the basis of their relations to spouses and children, or someone organizes household-by-household responses to an urban renewal plan. All these relations to government easily become contentious. Membership in a jury likewise operates mainly in routine social life rather than in public contention, but bears a detached relation to most social interaction. Now and then jury membership provides the basis of participation in contentious politics, as when

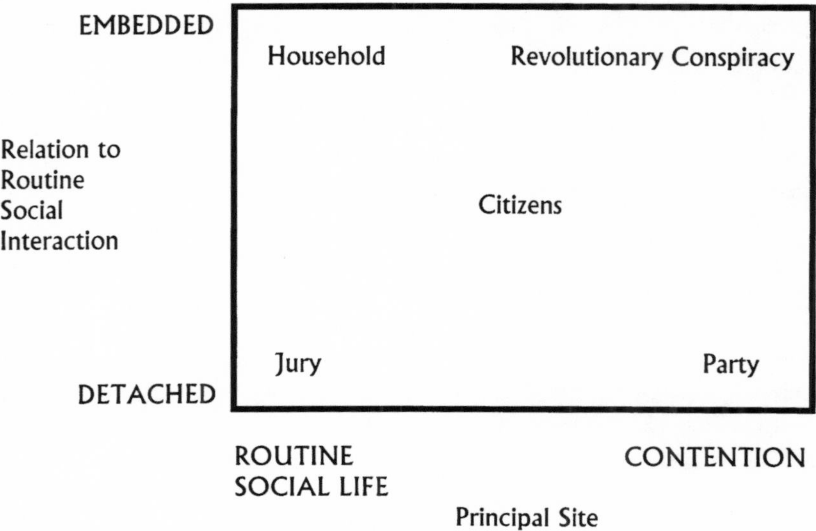

Figure 5.1. Loci of contentious Identities

disappointed parties to a verdict attack judge and jury. That is why we label it as a detached identity located chiefly in routine social life.

Why place revolutionary conspiracies in the upper-right-hand corner, combining embeddedness with siting in contentious politics? As a political identity, membership in a revolutionary conspiracy commonly embraces a wide range of social life – constitutes an embedded identity, that is – but takes much of its significance from contentious claims linking it to governments and other political actors. Although participation in some parties resembles membership in conspiracies, on the whole party membership activates intermittently, and chiefly in the heat of contentious politics. Hence its location in the detached/contentious corner. Citizenship appears in our diagram's very center to indicate that, even more than the other sorts of identities represented in the corners, citizenship ranges from mainly detached and routine (as in eligibility for state-administered welfare benefits) to largely embedded and contentious (as in recent struggles over who is a citizen of Yugoslavia, Serbia, Kosovo, Croatia, or Bosnia). Like other contentious identities, citizenship actually occupies an irregular space with respect to our two dimensions rather than the single point this simplified version assigns it.

Contentious Action

Over the course of contentious politics, actors take action in the names of identities. Identities define their relations to specific others. Their actions actually consist of *inter*actions with those others, interactions that center on claim making. They put on a performance of mutual, public claim making by paired identities. In the name of their asserted collective identity, interlocutors for actors demand, command, require, request, plead, petition, beseech, promise, propose, threaten, attack, destroy, seize, or otherwise make claims on assets that lie under someone else's control. When interlocutors for others reply in the name of their own political identities, an episode of contentious politics has begun. As the process continues, relevant identities often modify. The complex episode reconstructed by Beth Roy began as an altercation between two farmers identified as such but ended as a quasi-military engagement among Hindus, Muslims, and officials.

Repertoires and Political Interaction

Such a conversational, theatrical view of contentious interaction draws attention to the combination of scripting and improvisation in the actual making of claims. As compared with all the interactions of which actors are technically capable, in any particular setting and episode they employ a small set of routines repeatedly, innovating within limits set by the history of their previous interactions. India's Hindu-based BJP, for example, has jumped into national electoral contention with motorcades and chariot processions to publicize its cause:

> The chariots themselves are an amalgam of the old and new: temple chariot superstructures mounted on modern trucks and vans, equipped with loudspeakers, electrical generators, and so on. They are, in fact, composite modern elaborations that also include decorative elements borrowed from Peter Brook's film of the *Mahabharata*, as in the case of the chariot in which [BJP President Lal] Advani rode in 1990. The "religious" goals of "pilgrimage" and "holy war" were conflated with electoral calculations and pursuit of political power. Young recruits became voluntary "holy workers" (*karsevaks*); sadhus and *sants* mixed their ritual chantings with militant thuggery; and rituals of offerings called *pujas* and *yajnas* to deities were piously attended by politicians representing themselves as aspiring revivers of the Hindu nation and prospective ministers of state. [Tambiah 1996: 248; see also Davis 1996]

Thus not one routine, but a whole array of public performances, convey Hindu claims to BJP followers, rivals, the government, and indirectly to anxiously watching Muslims.

For this reason we can reasonably speak of contentious repertoires: limited ensembles of mutual claim-making routines available to particular pairs of identities. We borrow a theatrical metaphor – repertoire – to convey the idea that participants in public claim-making adopt scripts they have performed, or at least observed, before. They do not simply invent an efficient new action or express whatever impulses they feel, but rework known routines in response to current circumstances. Doing so, they acquire the collective ability to coordinate, anticipate, represent, and interpret each other's actions. Thus, people relating to each other as managers and workers in contemporary capitalist economies generally have available on-the-job production talks, grievance procedures, layoffs, job offers, demonstrations, strikes, appeals to governmental officials, and a few other routines for making contentious claims on each other. Outside their established repertoire lie routines that once occurred frequently in manager-worker relations of Western countries and remain technically possible, such as sacking the house of a reprobate boss or worker. Although strictly speaking repertoires belong to pairs of identities, for convenience we often generalize to a population, period, and/or place, referring for example to the prevailing contentious repertoire of Indian religious activists in the 1990s.

Performances within repertoires do not usually follow precise scripts to the letter; they resemble conversation in conforming to implicit interaction rules, but engaging incessant improvisation on the part of all participants. Thus today's demonstration unfolds differently from yesterday's as a function of who shows up, whether it rains, how the police manage today's crowd, what participants learned yesterday, and how authorities responded to yesterday's claims. Demonstrations that begin similarly end up as mass meetings, solemn marches, attacks on public buildings, or pitched battles between police and activists. Indeed, stereotyped performances ordinarily lose effectiveness in the same way that rote speech falls flat: They reduce the strategic advantage of their performers, undermine participants' claims of conviction, and diminish the event's newsworthiness. As a consequence, small-scale innovation modifies repertoires continuously, especially as one set of participants or another discovers that a new tactic, message, or self-presentation brings rewards its predecessors did not.

Consider the strategic circumstances of actors that already have well defined repertoires for the making of claims. Figure 5.2 simplifies the situation of a single participant in contention at the brink of action, for example an idealized summary of the refugees who huddled in Amitav Ghosh's family courtyard one night in January 1964. The previous history of interactions in the same category has laid down shared understandings represented by the interaction-outcome screen in Figure 5.2. Along the horizontal axis lie N possible interactions with assailants outside the courtyard walls, with Dhaka authorities, and with the Ghosh household. Available interactions probably included certain ways of fighting back, certain ways of fleeing, and certain ways of appealing to the authorities; only close historical study can tell us the actual forms of the then-available routines. Those possible interactions constitute the relevant repertoire for the current parlous situation, as seen from a single party's perspective. On the vertical axis appear likely outcomes of those possible interactions, similarly shaped by previous experience with such situations. Within each cell of this idealized matrix appear two linked items: (1) a probability that the initiation of interaction X will produce outcome Y, and (2) a causal theory connecting Y to X. Thus the actor reasons from outcomes to appropriate interactions, from interactions to likely outcomes, or more plausibly both at once. Even in this radical simplification we sense the great importance of previous experience in shaping highly selective repertoires of contention.

We could also complicate the scheme of Figure 5.2 and render it more dynamic. We might represent two claimants (say the refugees in the courtyard and the Ghosh household) and one object of claims (say the besiegers outside) and two sorts of interaction, cognitive and strategic. Two interaction-outcome screens would then figure in the diagram to register the fact that claimants and objects of claims read possibilities differently, because each has limited information concerning the other's resources, capabilities, and strategic plans and because each comes to the encounter from a somewhat different history of contention.

In this still-simplified sketch, claimants 1 and 2 already agree on the possibilities and likely outcomes of their joint action, although they may well disagree on the desirability of possible outcomes. Claimants 1 and 2 are engaging in cognitive interaction with their shared interaction-outcome screen, working out possible courses of action, while the object of claims is carrying on a similar cognitive process. Claimants 1 and 2 are interacting strategically – coercing or cajoling each other, creating a division of labor, and so on – as they contend with the object of their claims. Repeated many times as in frames of a movie, these interactions produce alterations in the proximity and contents of the two screens, which in turn

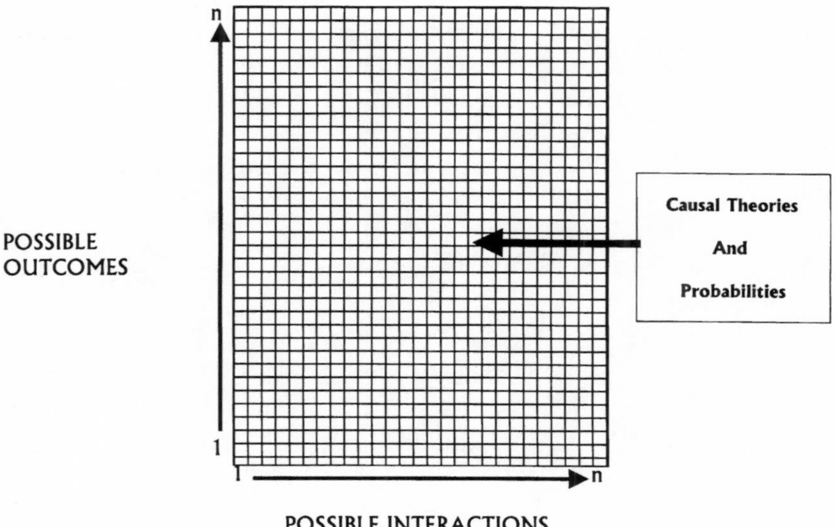

Figure 5.2. The Interaction–Outcome Screen

guide the next round of interactions. Small-scale innovation continues from beginning to end of the contentious episode. The model does not provide a realistic picture of contentious politics. It does show how we can incorporate history and culture into an account of contention without obliterating strategic interaction.

As we have seen in Panipur's struggles over cows and lentils, interactions that begin within the noncontentious repertoires of everyday life – routines for pasturing cows, marking field boundaries, and so on – sometimes move into the repertoires of contentious politics. They do not simply escalate, explode, or burst spontaneously into flames, but shift into a different interaction repertoire. Just as thoroughly bilingual friends often switch from one language to the other when signaling a shift of mood, subject, or context, they move into an alternative mode of communication (Gumperz 1982: Chapter 4). They do so because the social networks and shared understandings at hand channel participants into available definitions of what is happening, available means of communication and cooperation, available practices of conflict resolution, and available cultural idioms. When observers describe such events as "spontaneous," as they often do, they make an implicit distinction between episodes in which a systematic but subtle transition from non-contentious to contentious interaction occurs and those which result directly from prior deliberation and organization by at least one of the parties.

Contentious repertoires vary along three dimensions:

Particularism (as opposed to modularity): how specifically the forms of claim making in question attach to certain localities, groups, or issues

Scale: how many clusters of people who are readily distinguishable in routine social life participate in the making of claims

Mediation: the degree to which the communication of claims depends on privileged intermediaries, as opposed to direct confrontation with objects of claims

On the whole, contentious politics that builds on embedded identities features relatively particular and small-scale repertoires while bifurcating between direct confrontation (often violent) on a local scale and mediation by established authorities on the larger scale. Contentious politics building on detached identities more regularly involves modular, generalized forms of claim-making, large-scale coordination, and reliance on specialized representatives or political entrepreneurs. From a casual observer's point of view, contention based on embedded identities generally looks much more "spontaneous" than contention based on detached identities. From our analytic perspective, however, the difference concerns the sorts of switches that connect routine social life to contentious politics; where detached identities predominate in contention, political entrepreneurs, associations, extensive communication networks, and events of national scope play larger parts in the switch into contentious interaction.

Note the implications of this viewpoint, both negative and positive. Negatively, it denies that we can explain contentious politics by assuming the existence of unitary, self-conscious political actors who interact on the basis of game-like computations. Positively, however, it requires us to describe and explain the processes by which actors and their identities form – including, ironically, those special circumstances in which leaders of groups are indeed able to operate as if they were running or responding to unitary, self-conscious political actors who interact on the basis of game-like computations. It draws attention to the analysis of changing social relations as the basis of contentious politics.

Mechanisms

So far, we have emphasized conceptual problems: how to ask, not how to answer, questions about actors, identities, and actions. Our conceptual codification rests on rough parallels between contentious politics and conversation, especially argumentative conversation involving multiple interlocutors, auditors, and absent but relevant parties. Such parallels clarify recurrent causal mechanisms in contention. Let us illustrate our framework's utility by identifying four mechanisms, one each from the zones of actors, identities, and actions, plus one dealing with interplay among actors, identities, and actions. We can call those mechanisms brokerage, category formation, object shift, and certification.

Brokerage is the linking of two or more currently unconnected social sites by a unit that mediates their relations with each other and/or with yet another site. In the simplest version, sites and units are single persons, but brokerage also operates with cliques, organization, places and, at the limit, programs. In a simple version of brokerage, sites 1 and 2 (say Hindus in Panipur and in the neighboring village) have no current connection, but the broker (say Mr. Ghosh) not only connects the two of them but speaks on their behalf to the object of their claims (say the district police commissioner). In action, the model elaborates easily, for example, through the formation of direct connections between sites 1 and 2, the incorporation of additional sites, the introduction of bargaining between the broker and the initial object of claims, or movement of the two sites into overlapping positions with joint members and/or activities. Brokerage creates new collective actors. When newly connected sites harbor complementary resources, as Ronald Burt (1992) has pointed out, brokerage produces new advantages for the parties, especially for brokers. Similarly, the breaking of previously existing brokerage connections transforms politics and undermines the power of intermediaries (Gould 1998).

Brokers vary significantly in social location and modus operandi, with important consequences for the contention in which they participate. Names for different sorts of brokers include local elites, arbitrators, biculturals, interpreters, interlocutors, political entrepreneurs, nobles, priests, and chiefs. Some brokers deliberately keep their clients segregated from each other, while others actively merge them. Some decamp once they have made a crucial connection, while others build up their own positions through continued bargaining. Some undermine the capacity of certain sites for effective claim making by pairing them with ambitious rivals, by making unsavory deals with objects of claims, by diverting available resources to their own private ends, or by driving away supporters. Some don't know they are brokering, because they think of their activity as gossip, sociability, information-gathering, favor-giving, or mutual aid. In all cases, nevertheless, brokerage alters the connected sets of persons within a given polity to whom a definition of shared stakes in that polity's operation is available. Brokerage creates new boundaries and connections among political actors.

Category formation creates identities. A social category consists of a set of sites that share a boundary distinguishing all of them from and relating all of them to at least one set of sites visibly excluded by the boundary. Category formation occurs by means of three different submechanisms, through invention, borrowing, and encounter. Invention involves authoritative drawing of a boundary and prescription of relations across that boundary, as when Bosnian Serb leaders decree who in Bosnia is a Serb and who not, then regulate how Serbs interact with non-Serbs. Borrowing involves importation of a boundary-cum-relations package already existing elsewhere and its installation in the local setting, as when rural French revolutionaries divided along the lines patriot/aristocrat that had already split Paris and other major French cities. Encounter involves initial contact between previously separate (but internally well connected) networks in the course of which members of one network begin competing for resources with members of the other, interactively generating definitions of the boundary and relations across it. Norbert Elias and John Scotson (1994) describe the encounter of similar people in two nearly identical neighborhoods outside of Leicester who created a whole set of mutually hostile distinctions, labels, understandings, and practices separating the more recent arrivals from longer-term residents. They were creating new paired categories.

Or consider a Middle Eastern encounter. Amitav Ghosh, who spent years in Egypt as an ethnographer, retells a story his friend Isma'il had related in 1988 about Egyptian workers in Iraq:

> Earlier in the year Egypt had played a football match with Algeria, to decide which team would play in the World Cup. Egypt had won and Egyptians everywhere had gone wild with joy. In Iraq the two or three million Egyptians who lived packed together, all of them young, all of them male, with no families, children, wives, nothing to do but stare at their newly bought television sets – they had exploded out of their rooms and into the streets in a delirium of joy. Their football team had restored to them that self-respect that their cassette-recorders and television

sets had somehow failed to bring. To the Iraqis, who have never had anything like a normal political life, probably never seen crowds except at pilgrimages, the massed ranks of Egyptians must have seemed like the coming of Armageddon. They responded by attacking them on the streets, often with firearms – well trained in war, they fell upon the jubilant, unarmed crowds of Egyptian workers. [Ghosh 1992: 352–353]

At that point, Isma'il decided to leave oil-rich Iraq for his impoverished, labor-exporting Egyptian village. His experience with the process of category formation frightened him.

Neither invention, borrowing, encounter, nor their combination creates a complete perimeter or a homogeneous population on one side of the boundary or the other; mixed cases, further distinctions, and variable degrees of conformity always survive. Category formation takes time and occurs in discrete increments. But category formation powerfully affects the identities in the name of which participants in contention interact. Thus whether people in a given population make collective claims as women, citizens, Iraqis, or property owners depends in part on brokerage and in part on category formation.

Object shift significantly affects contentious repertoires. Object shift means alteration in relations between claimants and objects of claims, as when shifting parties and their brokers in Panipur moved up the Pakistani administrative hierarchy looking for allies and thus promoted militarization of their local conflict. Object shift often occurs in the short run, during the strategic interaction of contention; battling gangs unite against the police, the intervention of an official in a market conflict diverts customers' attacks to him, a besieged tax clerk calls in the mayor. Of course such shifts commonly alter the actors and the paired identities they deploy, but they likewise affect the forms of collective claim making that are available, appropriate, and likely to be effective. Object shift also occurs over the longer run and outside of contentious interaction.

When elected legislatures gain power vis-à-vis kings, warlords, and political patrons, for example, claim-making not only moves toward the legislature and its members, but shifts toward electoral campaigns, demonstrations of electoral power, and such devices as lobbying (Tilly 1997). This sort of parliamentarization generally promotes repertoire changes from particular to modular, from small-scale to large-scale, and from mediated by local notables to either direct or mediated by political entrepreneurs and legislators. The formation of the Indian National Congress in 1885 and its Gandhi-coordinated adoption of a hierarchical structure corresponding approximately to the British system of top-down administration both promoted and resulted from the increasing orientation of Indian leaders to the British Parliament; within their sphere of action, those moves generated modular, large-scale, relatively unmediated claims on British parties, administration, and Parliament (Johnson 1996: 156–162). During its early years, the Congress made its claims in the manner of an orderly British pressure group, by lobbying, petitioning, and drafting addresses (Bose and Jalal 1998: 116–117).

Object shift matters precisely because repertoires reside in social relations, not within individual actors or identities; a shift of objects selects or generates distinctive forms of mutual claim making. To be sure, long-run object shift intersects with a number of other formative processes. As relations between workers and managers change and as governments intervene more or less actively in management-worker disputes, all three parties undergo internal transformations, only some of which result directly from their interaction with each other; the government becomes a more prominent object of claims by workers and management, but that change occurs in interdependence with many others. Object shift also depends in part on brokerage and category formation, since brokers connect actors with distinctive objects of claims, and the formation of new categories produces new allies, enemies, and audiences for otherwise similar sets of claimants.

Certification refers to the validation of actors, their performances, and their claims by external authorities. It is the political version of a very general phenomenon. Pondering why weak, peripheral Sweden entered Europe's raging war in 1630, Erik Ringmar reflects on that general phenomenon:

> I will stress the social character of identities: people alone cannot decide who or what they are, but any such decision is always taken together with others. We need *recognition* for the persons we take ourselves to be, and only *as recognized* can we conclusively come to establish an identity. The quest for recognition will consequently come to occupy much of the time of people or groups who are uncertain regarding who they are. We all want to be taken seriously and be treated with respect; we all want to be recognised as the kinds of persons we claim to be. Yet recognition is rarely automatic and before we gain it we are often required to prove that our interpretations of ourselves indeed do fit us. In order to provide such proof we are often forced to *act* – we must *fight* in order to convince people regarding the applicability of our self-descriptions. [Ringmar 1996: 13–14]

Ringmar's language conveys the unfortunate implication that certification is chiefly a way of satisfying a psychological need. His analysis of

Sweden's intervention in the Thirty Years War, however, amply demonstrates that much more than national self-satisfaction was at stake: international recognition of Sweden as a Great Power because of its war-making prowess altered its relations to all other European powers, gave its diplomacy credibility it previously lacked, and affected the policies of its European neighbors. The treaties of Westphalia (1648) that ended the Thirty Years War, indeed, established a new set of powers, now identified as sovereign states, constituting both the certified major actors on the European scene and, collectively, the certifiers of arrivals and departures on the scene. For two centuries thereafter, successors of those powers continued the process of certification, and eventually extended it to all the world's states.

The process occurs in every polity, whether international, national, or local in scale. Every polity implicitly establishes a roster of those political actors that have rights to exist, to act, to make claims, and/or to draw routinely on government-controlled resources; it maps members and challengers. So doing, every polity also implicitly (and sometimes explicitly) broadcasts criteria for acceptable political organization, membership, identity, activity, and claim making. Some organizations specialize in surveillance and certification of acceptable or unacceptable versions of organization, membership, identity, activity, and claim making. To take an extreme but significant example, in 1945 the powers that settled World War II, redrawing the European map extensively as they did so, ceded their work of recognizing valid states to the United Nations. During the vast wave of decolonization that soon followed, United Nations officials spent much of their effort screening performances and claims in the form:

We are a distinct nation, and therefore we deserve a state of our own.
We are an unjustly oppressed people, and therefore we deserve a state of our own.
We were once an independent state and deserve to be independent again.
Our colonial masters are ready to concede independence to us.
Our claims to lead a new state are more valid than our rivals'.

Each claim entailed performances by aspiring national leaders – performances displaying evidence of legal rights, leadership, administrative capacity, popular support, internal military control, economic viability, and backing from at least some great powers. Those performances had to be polyvalent, establishing credibility with very different audiences, some of them at odds with each other. The minimum set included not only United Nations officials, but also leaders of former colonial powers, constituencies at home, rival claimants to represent the nation in question, and rulers of adjacent states, who were often making their own territorial claims at the same time. Coached by representatives of great powers, United Nations officials rejected far more claims in this vein than they accepted, but they still certified well over a hundred new states, with their proposed rulers and forms of government, between 1945 and 1990.

In this extreme case, the world's great powers created an international bureaucracy that radically standardized claim making in its arena. But similar processes operate less bureaucratically and at a smaller scale throughout the world of contentious politics. Every regime sorts forms of organization, publicly asserted identities, and forms of collective interaction along the continuum from prescribed to tolerated to forbidden. Indeed, a good deal of political struggle concerns which forms of organization, which identities, and which forms of collective interaction the regime in power should prescribe, tolerate, or forbid. What people loosely call Hindu nationalism in India centers on the demand for priority in these regards to Hinduism as defined by the Rashtriya Swayamsevak Sangh (RSS), a coordinating organization that originated in Nagpur in 1925. Since the RSS claims that Sikhs and Buddhists are actually Hindus, its program emphasizes state certification of the categorical pair Hindu/Muslim (Tambiah 1996: 244–245). It remains to be seen whether an RSS coalition in power would actually write its whole program into law.

Regimes, including South Asian regimes, differ momentously in which kinds of organization, identity, and collective interaction they prescribe, tolerate, and forbid. But all of them create procedures for public screening of acceptability in these regards; those procedures crystallize as laws, registers, surveillance, police practice, subsidies, organizations of public space, and repressive policies. As Isma'il's tale of 1988 implies, the repressive Iraqi regime of 1988 left no room for mass street demonstrations by Egyptian workers, which made those reveling workers fair game for attack by young Iraqis.

Because certification matters, important elements of contentious politics that a strict means–end calculus would render mysterious actually make sense. Why, for example, do participants in social movements spend so much of their energy in public affirmations of shared identities: marching together, displaying shared symbols, acting out solidarity? Many observers have thought that solidarity and shared identity bring intrinsic satisfaction, but that explanation ignores both the many occasions on which identity displays offer little but suffering to the participants and the effort that leaders invest in coordinating correct public performances in support of claimed identities. To make a successful claim of collective worthiness, unity, numbers, and commitment brings recognition as a credible political player with the capacity to make a difference in the next political struggle. In South Asia, group certification as a valid interlocutor for a major religious category gives serious weight to an organization or a network of leaders.

Intersecting Mechanisms in South Asia

All four of our mechanisms intersect in South Asia's Hindu–Muslim conflicts. Ayodhya, India, contained a sixteenth-century mosque, Babri Masjid, named for the first Mughal emperor, Babur. During the 1980s, militant Hindu groups began demanding destruction of the mosque and erection of a temple to Ram, the epic hero of the Ramayana. Just before the 1989 elections BJP activists transported what they called holy bricks to Ayodhya and ceremoniously laid a foundation for their temple. The following year, President Advani of the BJP took his chariot caravan on a pilgrimage (*rath yatra*) across northern India, threatening along the way to start building the Ram temple in Ayodhya. Advani started his pilgrimage in Somnath, fabled site of a great Hindu temple destroyed by Muslim marauders.

Advani's followers had fashioned his Toyota van into a simulacrum of legendary hero Arjuna's chariot, a familiar image that attracted flower petals, coconut, burning incense, sandalwood paste, and prayer from women as the caravan passed through towns and villages (Kakar 1996: 49). Authorities arrested Advani before he could begin the last lap of his journey to Ayodhya, but not before many of his followers had preceded him to the city. When some of them broke through police barricades near the offending mosque, police fired on them, killing "scores" of BJP activists (Kakar 1996: 51). As Sudhir Kakar tells it:

> Their bodies were cremated on the banks of the river Saryu and the ashes taken back by the BJP workers to the villages and towns in different parts of the country from which the dead men hailed. There they were eulogized as martyrs to the Hindu cause. Soon, Hindu-Muslim riots erupted in many parts of the country. [Kakar 1996: 51]

Those "riots," however, also centered on higher caste students' public resistance to the national government's revival of an affirmative action program on behalf of Other Backward Classes (Tambiah 1996: 249).

In the Hyderabad of 1990, reports Sudhir Kakar, violence continued:

> More than a thousand miles to the south of Ayodhya, the riots began with the killing of Sardar, a Muslim auto-rickshaw driver, by two Hindus. Although the murder was later linked to a land dispute between two rival gangs, at the time of the killing it was framed in the context of rising Hindu–Muslim tensions in the city. Muslims retaliated by stabbing four Hindus in different parts of the walled city. Then Majid Khan, an influential local leader of Subzimandi who lives and flourishes in the shaded space formed by the intersection of crime and politics, was attacked with a sword by some BJP workers and the rumor spread that he had died. Muslim mobs came out into the alleys and streets of the walled city, to be followed by Hindu mobs in their areas of strength, and the 1990 riot was on. It was to last for ten weeks, claim more than three hundred lives and thousands of wounded. [Kakar 1996: 51]

Although the Hyderabad incident's bloodshed far outstripped that of Panipur in 1954, the mechanism of escalation through object shift appears in both conflicts.

Nor did the conflict end there. On December 6, 1992, BJP militants actually destroyed Ayodhya's Muslim shrine and began construction of a Hindu temple on the same site. "Like all the previous movements and dates chosen," comment Chaturvedi and Chaturvedi,

> the choice of December 6 too had a covert Hindu connotation. It was the day on which the eighteen-day *Mahabharata* war had begun in which Lord Krishna had exhorted Arjun to do his duty and not count the cost. Once again, as on many previous occasions, the VHP [Vishwa Hindu Parishad] had used Hindu ritual symbolism to bring home a strong message of Hindu nationalism and Hindu identity to its great advantage. [Chaturvedi and Chaturvedi 1996: 182–183]

About the same time, BJP militants in Uttar Pradesh attacked and demolished a mosque in Faizabad, as well as recruiting followers for the Ayodhya campaign. In the Uttar Pradesh village of Baba ka Gaon, the very higher-caste exploiters of Scheduled Caste laborers sought (rather unsuccessfully, as it turned out) to recruit them to a pan–Hindu alliance for that purpose (Dube 1998: 212–214). The militants' work at Ayodhya issued from a combination of brokerage, category formation, and object shift. They then sought certification of the action from a hard-pressed central government. The incident set off Hindu–Muslim-police struggles through many parts of India, with deaths numbering perhaps 1,200 (Bose and Jalal 1998: 228; Brass 1997: 214–253; Chaturvedi and Chaturvedi 1996; Madan 1997: 56–58; Tambiah 1996: 251).

Brokerage, category formation, object shift, and certification all figured in these conflicts. Sandria Freitag points out strong parallels between the

Cow Protection movement of the 1880s–1890s and India's ostensibly communal struggles a century later. The "ability to link local identities and values to a broader ideology," Freitag remarks, "distinguished the Cow Protection movement from otherwise similar localized collective action of the period" (Freitag 1996: 216). In the movement:

> Itinerant preachers, under the patronage of local big men, called meetings at which printed posters told stories of the need to protect Mother Cow. Printed rules for new sabhas [cow protection associations] were held up as a model: as people in a locality established their own sabha, they would amend these rules to reflect local mores and the particular social frictions of the area. From the printed rules we discover that in some areas sabhas targeted Muslims, while in others they targeted low-caste, untouchable, or peripatetic groups. In the cities, the targets often became Christian converts. [Freitag 1996: 216–217]

Similarly, the Ayodhya agitation depended on brokerage from organizations and regional leaders, involved the accentuation and transformation of Hindu/Muslim categorical relations, entailed an object shift from local enemies to the national government, and – so far unsuccessfully – sought to establish certification for the stylized performance of recapturing presumably ancient Hindu religious sites from Muslim occupation. Although we need many more causal mechanisms to account for Hindu/Muslim conflict as a whole, our small battery of mechanisms helps explain significant features of the South Asian situation.

Brokerage, category formation, object shift, and certification need not occur together. Brokerage, for example, commonly plays a crucial part in strikes that bring several groups of aggrieved workers into coordinated action against the same set of employers. In such cases, categories often already exist, no shift in object takes place, and certification of the unions and workers involved as valid actors follows straightforward bureaucratic routines. Nor need the individual mechanisms produce the same general outcomes elsewhere. In South Asia's conflicts, object shift has repeatedly assimilated local conflicts that pitted gangs, speculators, or individual farmers against each other to the national repertoires, rhetorics, and categories of Hindu/Muslim conflict.

Object shift elsewhere, however, sometimes works laterally or downward – either transferring contentious interaction to another but parallel context or turning local enemies into victims of people who assembled on behalf of a national cause. In the first case, battling gangs sometimes unite to attack police sent to disperse them. In the second, looting that follows a concerted struggle between dissidents and authorities often has little to do with the original objects of the dissidents' claims or with demands dissidents were making. In either case, not only the interacting parties but also the repertoires, rhetorics, and categories shift significantly.

Identity Mechanisms in South Africa

South African experience between 1980 and 1995 provides many examples of brokerage, category formation, object shift, and certification as they operated in far different circumstances, in different combinations, and with different outcomes than in South Asia. Over the period as a whole, South Africa's elaborate system of apartheid collapsed as black Africans mobilized against exploitation, foreign governments and organizations organized more effective boycotts, demands for black labor increased and undermined existing systems of segregation, both domestic and overseas investment in the South African economy declined precipitously, prosperous whites fled the country, the ruling National Party itself split over competing programs of containment and accommodation, and some 30 percent of Afrikaner members left the party. During the 1980s, the government alternated between attempts to co-opt South Africans of mixed-race ("Coloured") and Asian background as well as compliant black leaders, on the one hand, and sustained repression, on the other. A complex series of strategic interactions connected competing black leaders, representatives of other constituted racial-ethnic categories such as Afrikaners or Coloureds, the regime's military forces, and members of the government itself.

Brokerage made a critical difference. Leaders of the militant Black Consciousness movement (BC, founded by Steve Biko in 1969 in deliberate contrast with the nonracial African National Congress, ANC), for example, started to form new coalitions during the 1980s. BC played a central part in organizing a resistance front called the National Forum. It also aligned itself closely with militant black-based unions. In competition and collaboration with the ANC, BC activists began organizing campaigns:

> Many BC activists, influenced by growing links with the ANC, concluded that a less ideological and more mass-based, locally organized resistance was now necessary. The state unintentionally encouraged this new strategy when in 1979, seeking to appease its opponents, it instituted reforms that provided breathing space for greater mass organization. Ironically, the emerging mass organizations benefited from reforms while publicly rejecting them to further bolster their popular appeal.

For example, when P.W. Botha later proposed a new tricameral parliament intended to attract back the loyalty of coloureds and Asians by giving them limited representation, activists used the proposal as the impetus for a national unification of localized resistance under the United Democratic Front (UDF), founded in 1983. [Marx 1998: 202–203]

This organizing effort occurred amid widespread formation of local civic associations and significant expansion of worker militancy in general (Price 1991: 162–182). The formation of a national United Democratic Front from 575 disparate organizations – itself a great feat of brokerage – drew on connections established by the now-illegal BC and ANC, but went well beyond them. In 1985 a similar (and, in fact, overlapping) coalition of trade unions formed COSATU, the Congress of South African Trade Unions. Those well-brokered organizations coordinated widespread resistance to the regime. Despite the government's declaring a state of emergency (July 1985) in most industrial centers, despite banning of many community organizations, and despite detention of thousands of activists without trial, black mobilization accelerated during the later 1980s. Resistance combined with international pressure to shake white control of public politics.

Under domestic and international pressure, even the Afrikaner bloc began to crack. In 1982, National Party MPs opposed to any compromise had already bolted the NP to form a smaller, determined Conservative Party. The NP's remainder made gingerly moves toward a settlement. In 1989, NP leader and premier F.W. de Klerk undertook negotiations with the previously banned ANC. By 1990, de Klerk was governing in close consultation with the ANC. Released from prison, ANC leader Nelson Mandela became a major participant in national politics. In 1991, COSATU activist Cyril Ramaphosa won election as the ANC's general secretary. Meanwhile, KwaZulu homeland chief Mangosuthu Buthelezi's Inkatha Freedom Party, which had previously received clandestine support from the government and the National Party, found itself increasingly isolated. Inkatha stepped up attacks on its ANC rivals, but by the 1994 elections was only receiving about 6 percent of the national black vote, as compared with the 75 percent that went to the ANC.

Nevertheless, the ANC had to negotiate between 1990 and its electoral triumph of 1994. The Soviet Union's partial disintegration in 1989 had reduced external diplomatic and financial support for the ANC, which had in turn encouraged the United States to press both sides for a compromise solution far short of revolution. As Joe Slovo, a major leader in the ANC and the South African Communist Party, reflected in 1992:

The *starting point* for developing a framework within which to approach some larger questions in the negotiating process is to answer the question: *why are we negotiating?* We are negotiating because toward the end of the 80s we concluded that, as a result of its escalating crisis, the apartheid power bloc was no longer able to continue ruling in the old way and was genuinely seeking some break with the past. At the same time, we were clearly *not dealing with a defeated enemy* and an early revolutionary seizure of power by the liberation movement could not be realistically posed. This conjuncture of the balance of forces (*which continues to reflect current reality*) provided a classic scenario which placed the possibility of negotiations on the agenda. And we correctly initiated the whole process in which the ANC was accepted as the major negotiating adversary. [Saul 1994: 178]

Thus a semi-revolutionary situation yielded to a remarkable negotiated compromise. We see Slovo analyzing a process combining (a) certification of the ANC by government authorities and by foreign powers with (b) brokerage inside the ANC as well as among the disparate forces of opposition that had mobilized during the 1980s.

Take the case of Inkatha mobilization in Natal. The KwaZulu homeland headed by chief Buthelezi consists of twenty-nine major and forty-one minor tracts of land scattered through the hinterland of Durban. KwaZulu exports labor to urban and industrial areas throughout Natal, the larger region pivoting on coastal Durban and enclosing all of KwaZulu. It also sends substantial numbers of migrant workers to the Rand, around Johannesburg. Many of its emigrants (especially in the Rand) live in hostels supplied by their employers, frequently within townships established for Africans under the system of apartheid. As all-male groups in segregated quarters, they have repeatedly clashed with township people, especially with young males.

Through much of KwaZulu and its areas of emigration, warlords who control their own enforcers play the classic games of indirect rule. Within their own territories, they recruit and discipline migrant workers, operate protection rackets, benefit from monopolies of such commodities as beer, and collect a variety of payments from local merchants. Chief Buthelezi's Inkatha Freedom Party had long enjoyed their financial, political, and (when needed) military support:

The various warlords tend to join Inkatha because in KwaZulu this relationship is based on a *quid pro quo* – as a reward for being left alone and allowed to follow

> their own devices they will undertake to deliver a certain number of men for Inkatha rallies and also provide "soldiers" for any fighting that needs to be done. Sometimes they bus vigilantes to other warlords who might need assistance or organise vigilante attacks on United Democratic Front/African National Congress . . . strongholds. [Minnaar 1992: 65]

Through the 1970s, an ANC/Inkatha alliance against apartheid seemed possible. By the early 1980s, however, Buthelezi and the ANC had become sworn enemies. The 1983 formation of the United Democratic Front, the 1985 establishment of COSATU, and their joint efforts to coordinate opposition to the regime in Natal threatened Inkatha hegemony over workers in and around KwaZulu. Inkatha struck back. When COSATU-affiliated unions began organizing workers in the Pietermaritzburg region of Natal, for example, Inkatha created and installed a rival union, engineered the firing of UDF-affiliated workers, and began an aggressive campaign of forced recruitment in nearby townships. UDF/Inkatha struggles accounted for some 691 deaths in the Pietermaritzburg region between 1985 and 1988 (Minnaar 1992: 7). Warlords and their followers figured importantly as Inkatha enforcers.

During the mobilization that followed the recognition of African-based political parties in 1990, however, many warlords became even more active agents for Inkatha, not only continuing their standard activities but increasing their payment of tribute to Buthelezi's party, supplying personnel for public displays of Inkatha support, and organizing attacks on ANC activists. (Nationwide, something over 5,500 people died in South Africa's political conflicts between 1984 and 1989, but that number swelled to 13,500 or more, mostly Africans killed by other Africans, between 1990 and 1993; Charney 1999: 184; see also Seidman 2000.) Meanwhile, Inkatha's opponents in the townships – especially students and unemployed ex-students – aligned themselves increasingly with the ANC. Civic associations formed widely to link young activists to older and more established members of their communities, as networks among civic associations formed connections from township to township. Thus webs of brokerage produced two formidable political forces in Natal.

As it does elsewhere, the mechanism of brokerage explains many alignments and realignments in South African politics between 1980 and 1995. Brokers connect previously unconnected sites, and thereby promote the creation of new collective actors and new relations with other actors, hence new identities. The enormous mobilization of Africans that surged immediately after the opening of 1990 relied less on the drawing of new people into contentious politics than on the integration of people who had been involved in struggle at a small scale into much larger political actors. Brokerage supplied the connections.

In the course of South Africa's turbulent history from 1980 to 1995:

- brokerage appeared repeatedly as political organizers drew disconnected factions and localities into common fronts
- object shift had political actors alternating their claim making among international actors, national authorities, and local targets, with corresponding shifts among repertoires, rhetorics, and categories
- certification figured centrally, both in the international response to successive national regimes, and in the recognition of previously banned political and economic organizations as valid actors within South African national politics
- category formation played a less salient part in South African public politics because most of the crucial categories had taken shape under apartheid or before

Perhaps the most important transformation of South African categories between 1980 and 1995 involved male-female relations within the African population. Massive entry of African women into paid labor coupled with declining male support for spouses and children to promote the emergence of women as a significant public category whose spokespersons declared them to have distinctive political situations, grievances, and interests from men. "As political organization spread and mobilization intensified," reports Gay Seidman,

> women began increasingly to organize their own groups. By 1986, separate women's organizations had been formed in most of South Africa. The United Women's Organization, for example, was formed in Cape Town in 1979, the Vaal Women's Organization was formed in 1983; and the Federation of South African Women, first founded in 1954, was revived in the early 1980s. By the late 1980s, many of these groups had begun to articulate a visible gendered perspective within the nationalist movement. [Seidman 1993: 306]

Even so, during the transition of 1989–1994, women did not obviously figure as a distinct political bloc or as a separate party to the new settlement. Feminist initiatives within the ANC generally failed when they came to votes within the Congress (Seidman 1993: 312–315). Up to that point, category formation proceeded slowly, and certification of women's representatives simply did not occur.

As the ANC came to power, however, the balance changed. Category formation and certification interacted. Parties to national negotiations over South Africa's future agreed in 1991 to creation of a Gender Advisory Board that would monitor the gender impact of proposals for political reorganization. Under Nelson Mandela's leadership, ANC national headquarters adopted a policy of including women in all significant committees as of 1992. During multiparty negotiations over the new constitution:

> In early 1993, ANC women activists decided that the gender advisory committee was inadequate and that more direct involvement of women was needed. Seeking to ensure that women's voices would be heard inside the negotiating chambers, in March 1993, in a little-publicized event, women ANC activists stormed the negotiation chambers, blocking talks until women were literally given places at the table. Amazingly, all 26 parties participating in the negotiation process accepted a gender quota – a decision that reflected the extent to which women on all sides had already raised issues of gendered representation in the construction of democracy. Fifty percent of each two-person team had to be female; thus, half of the negotiators who finally accepted a provisional constitution and set the elections in motion were women – a composition that had real implications for the kinds of institutions created under the new constitution. [Seidman 1999: 294]

The increasing salience of gender inequality, women's political voice, and public services for women resulted from the confluence of internal South African mobilization with connections to international feminist activism. In the 1990s, South African feminists could call on international allies and their own extensive international experience to insist that valid democratization required governmental support of women's rights. In 1995, the high level South African delegation to the United Nation's Beijing Conference on Women returned to South Africa publicizing the promotion of gender equality as an "internationally recognized obligation" (Seidman 1999: 297). In the background operated category formation, the creation of political identities as women amid the enormous ethnic, political, and economic fragmentation of South African life. Object shift occurred in the explicit targeting of the new government as the site of feminist demands. Certification figured remarkably, as South African leaders reshaped their gender politics to meet international standards. Brokerage by feminist leaders made it possible to frame programs in terms of gender at large despite enormous racial and ethnic disparities in the condition of women.

Close scrutiny of recent South Asian and South African experiences, then, shows us similar mechanisms altering actors, actions, and identities in both settings. Similarities end there, however. While in South Asia we witness an increasing tendency of nationally defined categorical divisions between Hindus and Muslims to preempt other bases of conflict and cooperation, in South Africa we see evidence of massive realignment in identities and their relations over a short period of time. More generally, both the environments in which they operate and their particular concatenation obviously make a large difference to the political outcomes of identity-affecting mechanisms. That similar causes and effects are working in disparate settings and forms of contentious politics by no means guarantees that they will produce similar structures and sequences on the large scale.

Brokerage, Category Formation, Object Shift, and Certification

Taken individually, our four identity-transforming mechanisms recur in essentially the same form across a vast range of contentious politics. Consider brokerage: linking of two or more currently unconnected social sites by a unit that mediates their relations with each other and/or with yet another site. Brokerage reduces transaction costs of communication and coordination among sites, facilitates the combined use of resources located at different sites, and creates new potential collective actors. Over time, brokerage establishes biases toward use of the same connections instead of other possible connections that would, in principle, produce different sorts of collective interaction. In the previous chapter, for example, we saw how itinerant traders connected Nairobi with highland centers of rebellion during Kenya's struggles of the 1950s. Those brokers helped produce a highly decentralized but quite effective communication structure that long baffled colonial authorities. Indeed, authorities kept searching for a nonexistent single, centralized, conspiratorial organization they thought to be led by Jomo Kenyatta.

We can think of *category formation* as a single mechanism or as a cluster of three closely related mechanisms. Category formation creates a set of sites that share a boundary distinguishing all of them from, and relating all of them to, at least one set of sites visibly excluded by the boundary. The variant of category formation we call *invention* entails authoritative drawing of a new boundary plus prescription of relations across that boundary. Category formation occurs through *borrowing* when people install locally a combination of boundary and cross-boundary relations that is already in operation elsewhere. *Encounter*, our third variant, forms categories when members of previously separate but internally connected networks come into contact with each other, begin competing for resources, and interactively negotiate definitions of a boundary and of relations across it. In its three variants, category formation figures in an enormous range of contentious politics, from nationalism to genocide to democratization. Chapter 6, for example, will show us category formation working in the early nineteenth century United States as pro- and anti-slavery forces created a fearsome boundary between themselves. At times, encounter, invention, and borrowing all contributed to that boundary's formation in different regions of the United States.

Object shift alters relations between claimants and objects of claims. Typical examples include generalization of an attack from local enemies to their presumed allies and appeals to third parties for intervention in a dispute. Object shift activates new or different social relations, thereby transforming available information, resources, and interaction scripts. It differs from its cousin brokerage because it centers on claim making, and therefore always alters previously activated answers to who's who questions. No claim occurs without at least implicit identification of claimant, object of claims, and relations between them. We have already seen object shift operating dramatically in the escalation of Panipur's conflict and in South African appeals for international sanctions against the apartheid regime. Chapter 6 will again show us object shift in operation as dissidents from Spain's Franco regime appealed to European allies for support.

As for *certification*, it refers to validation of actors, their performances, and their claims by external authorities. Remember that almost every person, social site, or constituted political actor maintains multiple relations with other persons, social sites, or constituted political actors, and therefore has multiple available identities, one per relation. Certification operates as a powerful selective mechanism in contentious politics, because a certifying site always recognizes a radically limited range of identities, performances, and claims. Thus, as we have seen, the United Nations evaluates performances on behalf of the claim "We Are A Nation," and rejects most such claims. Although thousands of actors have made claims in this vein since 1945, only a hundred-odd performances of this sort have brought their actors UN membership. The previous chapter showed us the United States acting as a certifying agent for the Philippine opposition to Ferdinand Marcos in 1986.

Our four mechanisms – brokerage, category formation, object shift, and certification – fall far short of providing a comprehensive model of contentious politics as a whole. We offer them as a sample of identity-shaping mechanisms that recur in a wide variety of settings, not as a neat interacting set that operates the same way regardless of setting. Having concentrated here on their place in transforming actors, actions, and identities, we have yet to explore their places in mobilization, demobilization, and trajectories of contention. The four mechanisms concatenate differently and produce contrasting results in different settings. Each one operates similarly, however, across a wide variety of eras, regions, social settings, and types of contention. We find them recurring in war, revolution, industrial conflicts, nationalism, social movements, and democratization.

That is the point: with respect to actors, identities, and actions, certain causal mechanisms operate across a broad range of contentious politics. They shed light on one of contentious politics' great paradoxes: how contingent assemblages of social networks manage to create the illusion of determined, unified, self-motivated political actors, then to act publicly as if they believed that illusion.

6

Transformations of Contention

In May 1856, Charles Sumner, a well-known Massachusetts abolitionist, was bludgeoned almost to death after delivering a speech in the United States Senate on "The Crime Against Kansas" (Sewell 1976: 279–280). Vituperative even for its day, Sumner's speech attacked a South Carolina Senator, Andrew Butler, for supporting the violent proslavery forces in Kansas. This so infuriated Butler's cousin, Representative Preston Brooks, that he came up to Sumner on the Senate floor, accused him of slandering both his relative and his state, and beat him senseless (Ransom 1989: 153). Sumner survived Brooks' assault. But coming as it did in the midst of attacks by pro-slavery forces on antislavery settlers in Kansas, "Bloody Sumner" joined "Bloody Kansas" as a symbol around which the coalition joining the issues of free soil, free land, and free people in the new Republican Party rallied. "Now is the beginning of the Second 'American Revolution,'" warned a correspondent of abolitionist Ben Wade (quoted in Sewell 1976: 280). He was right – but no one guessed the enormity of the bloody civil war that would follow.

On December 20, 1973, a greater act of violence exploded in Franco's Spain, where another civil war had ushered in a dictatorship three decades earlier. In a narrow street in Madrid, a bomb planted by the Basque terrorist group, ETA, killed the President of Franco's government, Luis Carrero Blanco (Payne 1987: 588–90; Reinares 1987: 123). With his close friendship to the dictator, and his determination that Spain stand as a bulwark against a Masonic-Communist conspiracy, Carrero Blanco was a buttress of the Franco regime's "bunker." His assassination seemed a grim portent of what might come when the aging dictator passed from the scene, a new civil war. That conflagration never came: What transpired instead was a peaceful transition to democracy. The resulting elite settlement spared stalwarts of the old regime, and indeed included many of them in the transitional government. It accepted the legitimacy of the Communist and Socialist oppositions, ushering in a process of depoliticization.

Elites, Institutions, and Contentious Politics

Not-quite-lethal violence in the U.S. Senate, and terrorist outrages in the streets of Spain. Why did the first contribute to a brutal civil war while the latter preceded a smooth transition to democracy? It is not enough to reply: "Spaniards had already *had* a civil war and would do anything to avoid another one." If hindsight were sufficient to prevent the repetition of disaster, this century would not have seen a second world war or the recurring sequences of strife in the Balkans. A better way of putting the question links it directly to the dynamics of contention. It runs as follows:

> Why did the trajectory of conflict in Spain, despite the fact that it transformed that country from dictatorship to democracy and involved enormous amounts of contention, resemble a peaceful protest cycle, while the conflict in America escalated to the logic of revolution?

Two approaches from opposite traditions in today's political science offer partial answers. Both turn on individual incentives and institutional compromises.

- Historical institutionalists such as Guillermo O'Donnell and Philippe Schmitter argue that Spain's transition should be seen as the result of successful bargaining of institutional compromises among political elites – of what came to be called a *reforma pactada* between government and opposition. [1986]
- Rational institutionalists such as Barry Weingast explain the collapse of the antebellum American polity as the result of a breakdown of an elite agreement that had produced an institutional compromise forty years earlier. [Weingast 1999; also see Riker 1982]

These analysts, to their credit, pay close attention to the interactions of individuals, groups, and parties. But in their emphasis on individual incentives and elite compromises, both accounts largely ignore the enormous amount of contentious politics that preceded and accompanied each episode, as well as the mechanisms of political change and conflict that created new actors and new identities, and transformed institutional politics. Despite a nod toward environmental mechanisms, the rationalist account adduces mainly *cognitive individual* mechanisms for the failure of the antebellum party system. Institutionalists who study the Spanish transition deal with one relational mechanism – brokerage – but limit it to elites and ignore the dynamics of contention (Pérez Díaz 1993: ch. 5).

Collapsing elite consensus was surely a critical variable in the breakdown of American unity, while the construction of a new elite consensus was critical to the Spanish transition to democracy. But we see broader mechanisms that engaged elites and non-elites in both countries during the crucial turning points of their respective conflicts:

brokerage, within and across the main cleavage lines that divided regime supporters and oppositions

identity shift (alteration in shared definitions of a boundary between two political actors and of relations across that boundary), as both countries approached the episodes we examine

radicalization, increasing contradiction between prevailing claims, programs, self-descriptions, and descriptions of others across such a boundary, and its opposite,

convergence, or what has sometimes been called "the radical flank effect," in which increasing contradictions at one or both extremes of a political continuum drive less extreme political actors into closer alliances

We do not argue that the two cases are similar. Indeed, we have chosen them precisely because they differ. Nor do we claim that these mechanisms, in combination, produced identical outcomes. On the contrary, they combined with very different environmental mechanisms to produce divergent outcomes. In America, the switch from the logic of a protest cycle to that of a revolutionary spiral can be traced through the formation of sectional mirror-image identities; through the growth of brokerage arrangements among antislavery activists, nativists, and western settlers; and through (a) radicalization of the views of North and South as the conflict approached and (b) convergence between moderate and radical forces on both sides. We then show that in Spain, driven by equally great identity shifts, new brokerage arrangements, and cleavages *within* the camps of regime and opposition, radicalization was balanced by convergence while contention was institutionally contained.

A Movement Cycle that Became a Revolution: Breakdown of the Antebellum Polity

To understand the dynamic of the antebellum American polity, we must look much further back in time than the Civil War (see Rustow 1970). In antebellum America, this takes us back to the 1820s, a period from which the abolitionist movement, as well as the dominant Jacksonian Democrats of the second party system emerged. So did the first major institutional conflict over slavery, triggered by the issue of whether the territory of Missouri should be admitted to the union as a slave or a free state. That issue was resolved by informal agreement to balance Missouri's admission as a slave state with Maine's admission as a free one (Poole and Rosenthal 1997: 94). This produced the "balance rule," which Weingast argues would curtail contention over the admission of new states to the Union for another forty years (Weingast 1999: 151). But that agreement was both imperfect and fragile, not only because it was frequently broken by defecting politicians, but also because issues other than slavery reinforced the cleavage between North and South and an assertive new actor – the West – shifted the balance toward the North.

To understand both the containment of contention and its eventual transgression, it is necessary to remember that, except for the infamous three-fifths rule, the founders of the Federal Constitution tiptoed around the issue of slavery, leaving its regulation in the hands of the states.[1] Northerners, it is true, held a preponderance of seats in the popularly elected House of Representatives. But to entice the (generally less populous) slave states into the Union, the founders created a Senate that allocated two seats to each state, large or small. While antislavery activists in the House periodically offered antislavery resolutions, equal representation in the Senate allowed the South just as regularly to block them. Only if the number of free states came to seriously outweigh the slave states in the Senate or if other issues combined with antislavery to bring North and West together would the balance shift. This provided an incentive for stability-seeking politicians from North and South to balance the entry

[1] The three-fifths rule held that for purposes of electoral apportionment of congressional seats, unfree individuals would be counted as 3/5 the weight of free individuals. Other key decisions were Article I, section 20, which placed the control of labor contracts in the hands of the states, and Article 4, section 2, which prevented slaves from gaining their freedom by escaping to the North.

of new free states with simultaneous or near-simultaneous admission of slave states.

Why would they want to do so? For most of the period after 1828, the Democrats, solidly based in the South, controlled Congress and the Presidency. They used their position to defend slavery. The Whig party divided: With substantial support from northern commercial interests who made money financing and shipping southern cotton to England, they were reluctant to oppose the institution. Moreover, both Democrats and Whigs had substantial electoral representation even in regions in which they were in the minority; allowing slavery to polarize political debate would risk the loss of the enclaves of Whigs in the South and of Democrats in the North and West. Each party also required a majority of national electoral college votes to elect a presidential candidate. For those reasons, leaders of both parties had incentives to keep the sectionally divisive issue of slavery off the political agenda (Ransom 1989: 29–32; Silbey 1985). There was a "partisan imperative" to leave slavery in the hands of the states, one that underlay the informal balance rule and reinforced the institutional rules laid down by the Constitution.

There were exceptions to the regulation of slavery by the states: the slave trade, slavery in the District of Columbia, and the transportation of slaves between states. These issues roiled the Union throughout the antebellum period, but none had the capacity to break it apart. The slave trade became illegal in 1808; slavery in the District of Columbia was a relatively minor issue, though it held symbolic value; while the transportation of slaves was largely in the hands of the courts. This did not make it a non-issue, but returning escaped slaves to their owners could safely be left to the Supreme Court, which was largely sympathetic to the slaveholding interest.

Westward expansion held the greatest potential for conflict, and everybody knew it. As immigration swelled the population of the North, the balance of population and economic dynamism between North and South began to shift (Ransom 1989: 131). Conversely, as fear spread among southerners that their region was losing parity, they looked to the creation of new slave states to keep up with the North's expansion. As long as the balance of slave and free states remained stable, political conflict would be contained. Until the mid-1850s, only the disputes over Texas' entry into the union and the Mexican war seriously threatened this equilibrium.

But if that was all that the antebellum party system was about, why did it collapse when it did? The North's more dynamic and expanding economy is one traditional explanation. But on its own, economic expansion is no explanation for political change. Think of how the South African economy flourished during decades of apartheid. Weingast's argument that politicians had incentives to defect from the intersectional balance rule provides another reason. But why would elites defect if their voters were indifferent to slavery? Our argument is fourfold:

- First, northern and western voters were increasingly *not* indifferent to slavery, though that does not mean they were friendly to slaves.
- Second, opposition to the institution encapsulated other issues in an emerging political identity that stimulated a mirror-image identity shift in the South.
- Third, these identities combined with nativism and expansion of the free-labor western economy in a series of new political formations and culminated in the brokerage of the interests of North and West in the new Republican party.
- Though Republicans were by no means all antislavery advocates, their electoral presence in the North and West gave them incentives to unify around economic interests shared by the two regions, while their ability to craft an electoral majority in the two regions gave them no further incentive to compromise with the South.

These four claims depend upon our reading of changes in contentious politics outside the political elite. Let us turn to these now.

From Moral Abolition to Political Antislavery

While Congress was avoiding the slavery issue through institutional compromise, it was growing increasingly intense outside of Washington. It gravitated around a number of issues: slavery in the District of Columbia, the guerrilla war waged between proslavery and antislavery factions on the frontier, the illegal movement of slaves across state boundaries and the fugitive slave act that was passed to stop it. As in many such cases, an unpopular issue was insistently forwarded by a small and active minority: the abolitionist movement.

Abolitionism as a social movement was never more than a tiny minority, derided for its utopianism and regarded as an irritant even in the North. It arose out of the same 1820s "second great awakening" as enthusiastic religion, temperance, Sabbatarianism, women's rights, and antimasonry. It retained a family resemblance to these movements. The "new"

American historians of the period have taught us not to romanticize abolition or exaggerate its importance (Silbey 1985: 88–91). It is true that the abolitionists were numerically weak and ideologically divided from the beginning (Sewell 1976: 40). But they nevertheless had an effect on politics in two indirect ways. First, abolitionism offered a language of sin and damnation to characterize an institution that most Americans regarded as a form of property (Davis 1969; Foner 1995: ch. 3). Second, it helped to produce a generation of antislavery politicians, who gravitated in large numbers into the surge parties of the 1840s and 1850s and then into the Republican party (Barnes 1957; Sewell 1976). Although the most famous moral abolitionist, William Lloyd Garrison, rejected politics for most of his career, antislavery became a political persuasion with the electoral potential to cut across the cozy lines of Whig and Democratic partisanship. To return to our typology in Chapter 1, it produced transgressive politics within institutions.

The evolution of antislavery from a movement of moral outrage into a form of political activism occurred gradually and unevenly. First came the lobbying and petition campaigns of the 1830s (Barnes 1957), then the formation of the Liberty and Free Soil parties in the 1840s and 1850s (Sewell 1976: chs. 1 and 3), finally emergence in 1856 of a majority faction of the Republican party that rose to national power with Lincoln's election in 1860. While moral abolitionists isolated themselves in splendid uprightness, political antislavery activists worked within politics, forging coalitions with moderate opponents of slavery and others whose interest in slavery was minimal. Their political acumen was revealed when Democrat Stephen A. Douglas attempted to build a national constituency for his presidential ambitions in 1856 by admitting slavery north of the Missouri compromise line of 1820. "Nearly all [the antislavery forces] were quick to perceive the political opportunities it afforded and hastened to capitalize upon them" (Sewell 1976: 260).

But political antislavery would have remained impotent had it not been for a set of broader changes in American society: first, a set of structural changes that bound North and West closer together and set them increasingly apart from the South; second, an identity shift in both regions that contributed to the radicalization of the conflict; and third, the brokering of a coalition among antislavery, nativism, and western settlement that destroyed the arrangements of the antebellum party system and produced the new Republican party and the Civil War.

Structural Change

Between 1845 and 1854, just under three million people entered the United States – most of them coming from Ireland and Germany, many of them hard-drinking and urban (Ransom 1989: 131). The majority settled in the North, driving down wages and inducing many northerners to move west, in a powerful economic/demographic vacancy chain of migration and replacement. That expansion left the South, with its more static rural society, far behind.

Not only did the population of North and West increase much faster than that of the South. Most westerners came from the nonslave states of the northeast, sharing their Protestant background and their spirit of enterprise. Though earlier periods of economic growth had linked North and South, as the North expanded, "the Northern economy increasingly became integrated as more trade traveled along an east-west axis than along a north-south axis" (Weingast 1999: 184).

Tensions proceeded alongside integration. New Americans of foreign stock were widely blamed for an increase in social disorder and drink (Ransom 1989: 133; Silbey 1967: 47–63) and temperance was an important cognate product of the Second Great Awakening. The fact that many (especially the Irish) were electorally mobilized by the Democratic machines of the eastern cities identified the Democrats with the foreigners by northern and western Protestant voters. In the new, enterprising, mainly Protestant western states, a population base was becoming available for nativism as well as for opposition to southern slaveholders competing for land with northern farmers.

Identity Shift, North and South

If demographic and economic change provided a structural foundation for political change, it promoted collective action through the formation of new identities. Antislavery activists came together with nonabolitionist northerners around a program of settling the West by free men on free soil. The political party that did the lion's share of the work in preparing the country for division tellingly called itself the Free Soil party (Sewell 1976: ch. 8). Free Soil represented a generation of farmers and would-be farmers who looked with apprehension upon the competitive westward drive of slaveholding farmers from the South. Whatever they thought of slaves – and many westerners despised them – admitting slavery into the new states of the West would give southerners economic advantages that the northerners lacked. The Free Soil party was the direct result.

But "free soil" was more than a party ideology: It became the master frame of western politics, connecting those who had entered politics as moral abolitionists with those whose major concern was with the settlement of the West and the creation of a non-slave-owning society. From the former came the moral fervor that gave mid-century politics its apocalyptic air; from the latter the pragmatic desire to keep the competition of slave agriculture out of the West. As ties formed among political abolitionists, western farmers, and eastern merchants and Protestants, their societal vision and political identity broadened to that of free men employing free labor on free soil, opposing "slavery's illegitimate coercions and the condition of labor in the North" (Foner 1995: xxiii). As Foner writes:

> Political anti-slavery was not merely a negative doctrine, an attack on southern slavery and the society built upon it; it was an affirmation of the superiority of the social system of the North – a dynamic, expanding capitalist society, whose achievements and destiny were almost wholly the result of the dignity and opportunities which it offered the average laboring man. [Foner 1995: 11]

Antislavery gave a moral gloss to this new identity. Like abortion in the 1980s, it was a symbolic issue that encapsulated positions on a number of dimensions. "We are opposed to the extension of slavery," wrote the *New York Post* in 1857,

> because it degrades labor; it demoralizes the character; it corrupts the young . . . it is an obstacle to compact settlements, and, as a consequence, to every general system of public instruction, literary or religious; it develops bad passions without providing any means of disciplining or controlling them, and generates a lawless state of society. [Quoted in Sewell 1976: 293]

The conflicts of the 1850s produced a mirror-image process of identity shift in the South. Before 1830, according to Fredrickson, "Open assertions of permanent inferiority [of blacks] were exceedingly rare" (Fredrickson 1971: 321). But as antislavery advocates trumpeted the virtues of free labor against the "Slave Power" of the South, southerners shaped an image of northerners as soulless, money-grubbing, and self-righteous, and of their own civilization built around the symbols of family, religion, and respect for tradition (Genovese 1969: Part 2 and 1992; Wyatt-Brown 1979). As Fredrickson ironically observes: "It took the assault of the abolitionists . . .

to force the practitioners of racial oppression to develop a theory that accorded with their behavior" (Fredrickson 1971: 321).

Southerners were outraged at being fed moral sermons inviting them to relinquish their property without compensation. Novels such as *Uncle Tom's Cabin* provoked an even angrier response and rebuttals from the North that "kept slavery before the reading public for years to come" (Sewell 1976: 235). After journalistic ties between the regions were shut down, North and South depended on one-sided reports of Congressional debates, grim testimony from families forced to flee hostile environments, and tales of the increasingly violent encounters between proslavery and antislavery settlers on the frontier, especially in "bloody Kansas."

The Kansas dispute between slave and free, abolitionists and proslavery vigilantes encapsulated the growing polarization of northern and southern identities. As Michael Fellman writes:

> Most of the settlers who came to Kansas were westerners who may not have had strongly developed proslavery or antislavery sentiments. . . . But general preconceptions, day-to-day friction, and battle turned vague feelings into strident sectional identities. [Fellman 1979: 289]

Brokerage and Radicalization

The "new" political historians of the 1960s saw slavery issues such as "bloody Kansas" as an exception to the largely local focus of national politics until the eve of the Civil War. But "local issues" reflected crucial regional economic interests that were not so much opposed to antislavery as orthogonal to it – making possible alliances across regions (Weingast 1999). It was not the moral attack on slavery that brought about the collapse of national unity; it was the convergence of political antislavery with Free Soil and their brokering by a new generation of political entrepreneurs. Added to this was the nativist reaction to the migration of European working-class Catholics that produced the so-called Know-Nothing movement and laid the foundations for the formation of a crossregional, transissue political coalition (Ransom 1989: 135).

The disruptive effects of nativism and westward expansion on the party system became evident in the 1854 congressional election, when both the Know-Nothings and Free Soilers burst on the political scene. Though neither party won a single Senate seat, between them they gained forty-three seats in the House, threatening the electoral balance between Whigs and Democrats and triggering a cycle of radicalization. The Democrats regained their losses in the presidential election of 1856 (Ransom 1989: 137), but nativism, Free Soil, and antislavery combined to begin the collapse of the second American party system.

This was no mere partisan realignment: the 1856 election came amid a classical cycle of protest, one in which previously different axes of conflict fused. As Stephen Douglas (who bore a share of responsibility for it) wrote at the time, the Democratic defeat came from

> a crucible into which was poured Abolitionism, Maine Liquor lawism, and what there was left of Northern Whiggism, and then the Protestant feeling against the Catholic and the native feeling against the foreigner. [Quoted in Ransom 1989: 135]

The result was sectional, ideological, and partisan polarization of the American polity, breakdown of the balance rule, and polarization into rival sovereignties.

Lincoln embodied this new coalition and its crystallization in the election of 1860. A westerner, at best a tepid antislavery advocate, and at worst a negrophobe, his campaign in the 1860 election nevertheless brought together a coalition of North and West, nativists, free soilers, Whigs, and northern Democrats. Southerners read his election as the conquest of the party system by the slavery cleavage. It was never so simple, but with their chance of expanding slavery into the West blocked and a sectional coalition party in control of the Presidency and Congress, which no longer needed southern votes, the states of the lower South either had to bow to Republican hegemony or secede. Rather than a cycle of protest ending in renovation of the existing policy, what had been a political conflict contained within institutional routines produced a revolution.

Convergences Against Compromise

Neither South nor North were unified, but the distance between the regions widened through radicalization within each political camp. In the South, as secession approached, and the big slave owning states of the Deep South lined up their forces, they understood the need for regional unity and leveraged the hesitant Border States into joining the secession (Crofts 1989). In the North and West, radical antislavery advocates in the Republican party pushed their more moderate colleagues toward confrontation, with speeches like the one that led to Sumner's caning. Foner sums up:

> As conservative tendencies appeared in the Republican party, radical leaders intentionally made inflammatory speeches in Congress, bringing out more forcefully than ever the religious and moral issues in the anti-slavery movement. [Foner 1995: 111]

By 1858, the realignment of American politics along sectional lines was complete, as North and West formed a solid majority and the Democrats emerged more and more as a regional party (Poole and Rosenthal 1997: 99).

Brokerage, identity shift, radicalization, and convergence: no short list of causal mechanisms explains all episodes of contention, nor do particular sets of mechanisms concatenate in the same way in every context. Brokerage and identity shift may combine with totally different overall outcomes under different conditions, for example when some groups radicalize while others converge around the center. This we can illustrate by turning to our second episode – the Spanish transition to democracy – which shows how these mechanisms combined in a peaceful, incremental, and remarkably civil replacement of one sociopolitical system by another.

A Civil War that Never Happened: The Spanish Transition to Democracy

If ever a polity seemed in danger of exploding into civil war, it was Spain in the last years of the Franco dictatorship. Carrero Blanco's assassination in 1973 not only attacked a buttress of the old regime; it initiated a steady increase in polarization that triggered memories of the devastating civil conflict of the 1930s many feared would explode again (Aguilar Fernández 1995). Stanley Payne estimates that over 100,000 executions and murders from both sides had taken place during that war (1987: 219). Pérez Díaz reminds us that in the Republican zone almost 7,000 priests were murdered during its first months (Pérez Díaz 1993: 129). This was a cataclysm every bit as searing in Spanish political memory as the war between the states in the United States.

The Franco regime that emerged from that war ruthlessly repressed supporters of the Republic. The postwar prison population swelled to 270,000 in 1939 (Pérez Díaz 1993: 223). Though mass Nazi-style executions were rare, nationalist authorities went methodically from town to town, arresting republican sympathizers, trade unionists, and those guilty of "grave passivity" (Maravall 1979: 67). The state church engaged in a policy of moral cleansing, mounting "parades, processions, panoplied entrances, dedications to the Sacred Heart and to the Virgin, protestations of Catholic faith and obedience to the Pope" (Pérez Díaz 1993: 131). Regional autonomists retreated into internal exile, the use of their languages officially discouraged and their cultural expressions reduced to folklore, popular songs, and dances (Buxo i Rey 1995: 126; Johnston 1991: ch. 4; Pérez-Agote 1987: 3–10).

Nor did repression end with normalization (Linz 1973: 181). As late as 1958–1961, a period when opposition was at its nadir, the European Committee for Amnesty reported some 600 political prison sentences (Maravall 1979: 90). The industrial strife of the late 1960s and early 1970s unleashed a new wave of arrests of both unionists and ordinary workers (Maravall 1979: 73). Well into the 1970s, police and civil guards responded to workers' protests with arrests and beatings.

Yet Spain moved from an authoritarian regime to a democratic monarchy through a largely peaceful process of liberalization that some have called "a pacted break" (*ruptura pactada*). By the accounts of most experts, by the early 1980s, the country had largely consolidated its democratic system (Linz and Montero 1999; Linz and Stepan 1996: 108; Morlino 1998: 19). These authors see a transition largely effected by elites associated with the old regime, largely ignoring the process of polarization marked by extremist violence and increasing labor militancy (but see Maravall 1979; Reinares 1987: 127).

Of elite convergence there was plenty. After the failure of a repressive strategy following Carrero Blanco's murder, the most central figure in the transition was the first post–Franco Prime Minister, Adolfo Suárez, who built a democracy "with the bricks of the authoritarian system" (Linz and Stepan 1996: 93–96; Preston 1986: ch. 5). It was Suárez who fashioned the pacts between moderate elements of the Franco regime and the opposition parties and unions, making of Spain "the very model of the modern elite settlement" (Gunther 1992), and launching the process of autonomization of the regions in the constitution (Pérez Díaz 1990: 198–201).

Among students of democratization, the Spanish experience fed a healthy reaction against the structural models that had animated earlier debates. Those who feared a recurrence of the interwar conflicts found welcome relief in its peaceful transition and drew from it the lesson that "pacted," elite-led transition could constitute a model for successful transitions to democracy elsewhere (di Palma 1990; Gunther 1992; Karl 1990; but see Linz and Stepan 1996: 56). But (like new institutionalist accounts of the American Civil War and in the face of the violent insurgency in the Basque country) these accounts had surprisingly little to say about contentious politics or about the mechanisms of transition other than elite negotiation.

Institutional Containment of Contention

The story of Spain's transition has the following major components: small groups of "seceding" authoritarian elites taking advantage of a liberalizing process within an eroding dictatorship that was unable to stop the logic of liberalization once it had began. By involving moderate elements progressively in pacts and agreements, these groups built bridges to the opposition, convincing them that they could well afford the risk of playing the democratic game. Their participation in the process, and the concessions they were willing to make, in turn convinced reactionary elites – the well-known "bunker" – that they had nothing to fear by going along with liberalizing of the old regime.[2]

Once begun, so the argument continues, the process of liberalization snowballed as various groups from both inside and outside the regime saw their interests served by participation in the constitutional negotiations, and convinced their followers to go along, in order to limit their losses in the outcome. The period from the pre-constitutional negotiations of July 1976 (when the Suárez government was installed) to June 1977 (when the first general elections were held) was the most critical phase of the process, serving to build confidence and reduce uncertainty among formerly divided elites (Linz and Stepan 1996: 91–98; Pérez Díaz 1993: 218–225).

Pact making went beyond political reform; the keystone Moncloa pact pledged the government to a continuing program of reform both of institutions and of economic life. The participation of the Communists and Socialists in the process assured management that the workers over whom they had influence would refrain from excessive strike activity and from extreme demands. At least so the story goes. Military intervention was sidestepped by careful preemption of key issues by Suárez and by the fact

[2] Of course, there are variations and permutations in the story as it is told by various authors. While Giuseppe di Palma and Donald Share emphasize elite transactions and O'Donnell and Schmitter emphasize the liberalization of the Francoist system from within, Maravall and Preston emphasize the struggle both in Spanish society and within the Francoist elite, which made possible the democratic pacts of 1976–1979.

that no significant political faction came forward to urge the military to intervene (Gunther 1992: 66). The process built up the authority of organized business (the CEOE), and strengthened the two major union confederations (the Communist-led CC.OO and the Socialist-led UGT), at the cost of more radical smaller unions (Pérez Díaz 1990: 225). It culminated in the disappearance of the politician who had begun it – Adolfo Suárez – and of his party, the UCD, after its term of office and its replacement by the now moderate PSOE. That turnover led to an early and peaceful alternation between government and opposition and thus to democratic consolidation (Linz and Montero 1999: 21–31).

Like the balance rule in the United States Senate, the pacts and institutional compromises made by the outgoing Spanish elite and their competitors in the opposition exchanged compromising each actor's optimal policy outcomes for a set of institutional arrangements through which each could pursue its goals (Przeworski 1986). But just as the balance rule depended on the alignment of the party system and contained contention within American society, the pacts that underlay the Spanish transition are difficult to understand in isolation from the nature of the old regime and from the contentious politics within Spanish society.

An Authoritarian Regime

What kind of a regime was this? With the defeat of the Republic and the triumph of reaction in Europe, Spain's new rulers at first adopted many of the trappings of fascist totalitarianism: blue-shirted militants marching in serried ranks in support of the dictator; a corporatist syndical organization designed to transmit state priorities to hand-picked representatives of capital and labor; a National Movement designed to represent "sound" opinion; a rubber-stamp *Cortes* with no right to initiate legislation and hardly any power to influence it; repression of the regional autonomies that the Republic had promised the restive Basque and Catalan regions; governing bodies filled with military men and a higher civil service drawn predominantly from the upper class; a state church that not only enforced moral order but served as a bulwark of the regime (Maravall 1979: 4–6; Payne 1987: 517: ch. 12; Pérez Díaz 1990: ch. 3).

But Franco was too shrewd and too prudent a leader to embrace fully the single-party model urged on him by his European fascist allies. As the tide of war turned against the Axis powers, he held the firebrands of the

Falange at arm's distance, forming cabinets through a judicious juggling of factions, and ruling through a set of weak institutions led by men whose loyalty was predominantly personal. The regime could best be characterized as "authoritarian," with limited pluralism, a conservative mentality rather than a rigid ideology, the cultivation of apathy rather than mobilization, and a mass party with little real power (Linz 1970, 1973; Linz and Stepan 1996: ch. 3).

Isolation from western cultural and political trends was an important weapon in maintaining state control. Convinced that Spain stood almost alone against a worldwide Masonic-Communist conspiracy, the Francoists strove to keep out dissenting or modernizing currents. Their success can be measured by the low level of ordinary criminality up until the years of transition and by the high degree of religiosity registered by surveys. The proportion of Spaniards declaring themselves to be "fervent" or "practicing" Catholics was 77 percent as recently as the late 1960s (Fundación FOESSA 1970: 448; Montero 1997).

Economic autarchy was the second mechanism through which Spain was cordoned off from the corrupting currents of the West (Maravall 1979: 66–69). As in Fascist Italy, however, it had perverse effects: encouraging an uncompetitive private sector and a clientelistic and crony-ridden financial system, and creating a large and protected public sector in a regime hostile to collectivism. Wages were low and the vertical syndicates left workers little autonomy, but they could be fired only with difficulty. A sort of unofficial collective bargaining was allowed to grow up during the 1960s to take the steam out of industrial conflict.

A third resource was Spain's capacity to hold itself aloof from the conflicts and alignments of international politics. We remember the horrors of Guérnica and the intrusion of foreign Communists and fascists in Spain's civil war but easily forget that Franco, unlike Mussolini in Italy, kept Spain from sharing the costs of Hitler's war. As the Cold War emerged, the United States became Spain's major international sponsor, providing a crucial legitimation for the regime and, allowing the dictatorship a longer lease on life than it might otherwise have enjoyed.[3]

[3] In a personal communication, Davydd Greenwood points out that "from what we know, in 1949, Franco was ready to fall, when Truman's ambassador told Truman that Spain could be had for a song. Hence the pseudo–Marshall Plan after 1949 and the U.S. bases on Spanish soil. From that moment on, the U.S. became one of Franco's greatest patrons."

Structural Change

With the launching of the European economic miracle, the Spanish economy began to profit from the expansion of its neighbors – among other things, from tourism. But it became increasingly clear that the economy would suffocate if it remained in sacred isolation. Industry and tourism were favored with lavish subsidies; workers were encouraged to emigrate to other countries, where they became a source of foreign exchange, and were also exposed to subversive ideas (Malefakis 1982: 219). Between 1964 and 1973, the economy grew at an enormous rate – in real terms at a rate of 7.3 percent a year – while GNP per capita rose from less than $300 in 1960 to $3,260 in 1970 (Gunther, Sani and Shabad 1986: 24). By the 1960s, from the "dictatorship of the victory," Spain had become "a dictatorship of development" (Carr 1980: 165). The boom did not subside until the two post-oil-shock years of 1974 and 1975.

Population movement was the most dramatic marker of structural change (Maravall 1979: 25). Between 1961 and 1968, over 2.9 million people changed residence, and from 1950 to 1970 the farm population fell from 42 to 25 percent (Maravall 1995: 71). This shift from the countryside to the cities was accompanied by a decline in traditional forms of large landholding as well as by a disappearance of Spain's once-radical agricultural proletariat (Linz and Montero 1999: 82; Malefakis 1970). As a result, there was both an increase in the size of the industrial work force and a sharp growth in the service sector and a rise in real incomes. In real terms, income per capita tripled between 1960 and 1975.

But between the country's stubborn corporatist institutions and this new spurt of growth a number of contradictions arose. The lack of a modern fiscal system, the precariousness of social policy, dependence on the prosperity of its neighbors and on a reservoir of low-wage workers combined with the regime's fear of destabilization to obstruct its adaptation to its new economic status. One indicator among many was severe income inequality. By 1970, a group of American political scientists wrote that

> the top 1.23 percent of the Spanish population in terms of income possessed a larger portion of the total national income (22.39 percent) than did the bottom 52.2 percent of the population (who possessed only 21.62 percent of the national income). [Gunther, Sani and Shabad 1986: 26]

The economic crisis that swept over the West in 1973 would hit Spain particularly hard, just as Franco's grip was slipping and a new wave of contentious politics was gathering steam.

Contentious Politics in an Authoritarian Regime

Did the thirty-odd years of Franco's rule and the economic growth of the postwar years erase the heritage of conflict of the Civil War? What would happen to Spain's traditional political cleavages after Franco left the scene? Juan Linz, Spain's most authoritative interpreter, projected in 1967 that the Communists and left–Socialists might gain 41 percent of the vote in a post–Francoist election, while the right would gain 14 percent. Linz hoped a strong Christian Democratic party along Italian lines would fill the void (1967: 267).

As the 1960s ended, the resurgence of industrial conflict in Western Europe provided models for collective action in Spain too (Crouch and Pizzorno 1978), with the difference that here clandestine Communist-led workers' commissions (CC.OO) were the major organized force in the factories. From the mid-1960s on, the Spanish working class sustained a level of strikes "that fell well within the broad Western European pattern even though such industrial conflict [in Spain] was illegal." The number of working hours lost through strikes rose from 1.5 million in 1966 to 8.7 million in 1970 (Fishman 1990: 88). These were not just economic protests. By 1965, a new form of collective action, the *huelga general local*, developed, combining economic and political demands and demonstrating that the workers had a high capacity for political – and not just occupational – mobilization (Maravall 1979: ch. 2).

Though the workers' tactics were moderate (Durán Muñoz 1997), and their tactics self-restrained (Pérez Díaz 1993: ch. 5), this vast wave of industrial conflict signaled to the political opposition the existence of a mass base for democratization. Contention diffused across industrial areas and demonstrated the unity of the working class through an increasing number of solidarity strikes, which rose from 4 percent of all strikes in the mid-1960s to over 45 percent after 1967. Particularly in old industrial regions (mining in Asturias, metal working in the Basque country, in Catalonia and in Madrid), but even in new industrial areas, solidarity strikes became more and more common during the early 1970s. They were particularly effective in the Basque country, where, during one 1974 conflict, 80 percent of the active population went out in a regional general strike (Maravall 1979: 37).

In that region, but also in Catalonia, the regime faced resistance of a much fiercer kind. These were, after all, highly developed industrial regions in which Francoist cultural policy had repressed regionalist aspirations. Separatist movements grew up in both regions that combined economic claims with resentment at Madrid's centralizing policies. It was from these two regions that both violent and symbolically important resistance developed. Between 1960 and the year of Franco's death, ETA (the clandestine Basque terrorist movement) caused forty-three deaths (Linz and Stepan 1996: 99) and crystallized a culture of violence (Pérez-Agote 1987: ch. 1). After Franco's death the violence intensified, rising to sixty-seven deaths in 1978, the year in which the new constitution was passed, and seventy-six in 1979, the year of the second general election and the passage of the Basque autonomy statute (Reinares 1987: 127). Catalan nationalism was more pacific, but it produced a subtle and symbolically important resistance in this most "European" of Spain's regions (Buxo i Rey 1995: 95; Johnston 1991; Pérez Agote 1990: 194–7).

Opposition formed far outside the factories and the two large minority regions. After Vatican II, Catholic churchmen, and especially the lower clergy, involved themselves increasingly in the democratic movement. Clerical opposition (and its convergence with other sectors of opposition) first became visible with the condemnation of the official workers' syndicates by the Spanish Bishop's Conference and its call for the legalization of trade unions (Preston 1986: 16). This new attitude of the hierarchy encouraged the radicalization of young priests associated with the JOC (*Juventudes Obreras Católicas*) and of worker priests, many of whom shared the lives of migrant workers in the peripheries of the large cities (Preston 1986: 18–19). A new religious activism, disdainful of the Church's "national Catholicism" and anxious for a "morality of authenticity" developed in the shadow of the regime (Pérez Díaz 1990: 157–61).

At the same time, in the universities, a new generation of students, fed by economic development, challenged by foreign study, and stimulated by the loosening of press controls, was producing illegal left-wing groups, permanent assemblies, and mass demonstrations. By the late 1960s, it was as easy to find Marxist tracts in the universities of Madrid or Barcelona as it was in Rome or Paris (Payne 1987: 519). "The universities gradually became a subcultural ghetto within Spanish society," writes Maravall, "and, in these enclaves, the dominant ideas were the ideas of the student movement" (1979: 117).

The neighborhoods of an expanding urban society were another source of growing mobilization. In 1964, the regime had introduced the *Ley de Asociaciones*, legalizing associations of parents, neighbors, consumers, and other groups (Bier 1980: 27–32). Popular organizations grew up outside this semiofficial framework, giving rise to competitive, often semiofficial ones promoted by municipal authorities (Blyth 1999: 9). By the early 1970s, neighborhood groups were organizing all over Spain, around issues ranging from police brutality and high property prices all the way to poor Christmas lighting and the lack of green spaces (Blyth 1999: 10). By 1974, official and unofficial groups were beginning to coordinate their efforts on a citywide basis, broadening their claims from strictly neighborhood problems to "corrupt and undemocratic local officials, lack of investment" and even demanding changes in the local political class (Bier 1980: 40–44; Blyth 1999: 10–11).

How could an authoritarian regime hold the lid on a society that was mobilizing economically, ethnically, and intellectually and organizing from the factories to the minority regions to urban neighborhoods? In the mid-1960s, the answer was seen in economic development and in the absorption of so-called "technocratic" elements into the ruling circles, to the detriment of traditional stalwarts of the regime such as the Falange. The shadowy secular Catholic group, Opus Dei, owed its ascent within Spanish politics to this *apertura*. So did the loosening of press censorship and the launching of a number of refreshing new journals (Maxwell 1983). But as strikes proliferated and ETA violence intensified, increased repression was the chosen course.

Advocates of the "elite transition school" sometimes forget the savagely repressive atmosphere that preceded the transition. By 1973, convictions by the Tribunal of Public Order had grown 250 percent over the early 1960s (Maravall 1979: 41; Payne 1987: 502). Fed by fear of rising terrorism in the Basque region, the regime struck back with suspensions, dismissals, and arrests (Maravall 1979: 41). The low point came with a wave of arrests following the assassination of Carrero Blanco. Rather than broaden his government to rally the various sectors of the regime, Carrero's successor Carlos Arias Navarro appointed a cabinet "largely composed of remnants of the bureaucratic inner core of the regime." Excluded were both the military and the Opus Dei technocrats who had entered the government during the reform period (Payne 1987: 592–3). From 1973 to the end of 1975, over 6,300 Basques were arrested (Payne 1987: 601).

Repression and the Diffusion of Contention

Though repression was triggered by Basque terrorism, it had the effect of isolating the regime not only from that region but from labor, the Church, political opponents, other regional minorities, and from key industrialists, who would have preferred to settle their industrial disputes on economic terms. It also isolated Spain from Europe, and from the emerging European Economic Community, which Spanish business elites hoped to enter (Marks 1993). The Burgos trial against Basque nationalists in 1970 caught the attention of sympathizers all over Europe (Reinares 1987: 123).

Repression failed to contain contention. Not only did ETA terrorism continue through 1974 and 1975 (Pérez Díaz 1990: 200), by 1975, the working days lost to strikes had risen to 14.5 million. In 1976 (year of the most critical political negotiations), strike days rose to 150 million. And while economic demands made up the bulk of the strikes in the 1960s, an escalating proportion were now political (Maravall 1979: 33–37). Contention also moved outside the factories; almost 800 collective actions were reported in *El País* between May 4, 1976, and the end of 1978. Precisely as the transitional pacts were being negotiated, Spaniards were exploding into the streets. In 1974, a scattering of leftwing groups, such as the FRAP and the short-lived MIL, came to light. ETA, once divided between a military and a political-military wing, split and came under the control of its armed militants (Reinares 1987: 124–5). Right-wing groups, trade unions, neighborhood associations, students and "alternative" groups all joined the fray.[4]

Repression also gave rise to its own wave of contention. Even before Franco's death, thousands of Spaniards demonstrated for "a full amnesty for political prisoners of the Francoist dictatorship, a demand that in many cases was accompanied by one for a labor amnesty (Aguilar Fernández 1997: 89). Collective action in favor of an amnesty was closely linked to the collective memory of the civil war, and largely accounts for "the obsession of collective actors . . . with convincing authorities that these actions would be *peaceful*" (Aguilar Fernández 1997: 89). This wave of demonstrations shows the intricate ways in which mass protest and elite politics intersected. As Nancy Bermeo concludes:

> Elite pacts were certainly key to the democratization of Spain, but these pacts were forged in a situation in which extremism and moderation existed simultaneously. [Bermeo 1997: 309]

[4] The more complex Basque nationalist movement – so often reduced to the armed attacks of ETA – also drew on working-class and Catholic dissent. Three important treatments are Azurmendi 1998, Garmendia, Parraluna and Pérez-Agote 1982, and Pérez- Agote 1987.

Not only did extremism and moderation co-occur: Elite and nonelite contention were reciprocally related to each other – "interstitial choices," in Pérez Díaz's lexicon (Pérez Díaz 1990: 6). If Spain's elites and counterelites managed the transition through a measured process of negotiation in conference rooms, it was due in part to the pressure of transgressive politics in the streets, in the factories, and in the minority regions.

Identity Shift

Then why was the politics of transition so contained? Part of the reason was the continued coercive capacity of the Spanish state, made plain by its continued repression of dissent, right up to and during the transition (Durán Muñoz 1997: chs. 5–6). Part was due to the determination of the opposition to keep a lid on mobilization so as to deny the military a pretext for a preemptive coup (Aguilar Fernández 1997). A third element involved the moderate goals of the demonstrators themselves, and their genuine support for democracy (Fishman 1990; Pérez Díaz 1990: ch. 5). But there is a deeper answer that we can only grasp by understanding something of the profound changes occurring within Spanish society before the regime neared its end. From a country that stood on the periphery of Europe and saw Europe as "abroad," Spain had undergone a paradigm shift in the mentality and behavior of both its elites and the country at large. This "European reference, and the construction of a European identity for Spain, has been one of the most crucial mechanisms at work throughout the entire process" (Pérez Díaz 1990: 5).

Consider religion: Encouraged by the changes in the Vatican in the 1960s, the leaders of the Catholic Church went through a process of reform from within. But reform was led by a younger generation of priests and devout laymen responding to a society that was beginning to evolve in a secular direction. By the end of the 1960s, the priesthood had become less popular as a career and the presence of the church in society had declined (Fund. FOESSA 1970: 470; Pérez Díaz 1990: 165). Although a majority of the population still claimed to be practicing Catholics, church attendance was in sharp decline in the cities, as well as among younger age cohorts (Fund. FOESSA 1970: 442–444; Linz and Montero 1999: 88–90).

As religiosity declined, both secular education and cultural exposure to Europe expanded. The number of university students rose from 76,000 in 1961 to 229,000 ten years later (Maravall 1995: 71) and many went to study abroad. By Franco's death the university had developed a culture of political dissent and been in a state of continuous unrest for most of the preceding fifteen to twenty years. Moreover, with an easing of censorship in a press law passed in 1966 (Payne 1987: 511), Spaniards could learn more about what was happening in the world and in their own country. This was symbolized by the newly emerging media, most strikingly by the appearance of *El País*, which emulated *Le Monde* and symbolized Spain's Europeanization (Edles 1998: 46; also see Maxwell 1983).

Spain was not only becoming more like Europe; Spaniards were increasingly identifying *with* Europe. This was first obvious in the opposition to Franco. Throughout its history of exile, the PSOE argued forcefully in favor of joining Europe (Marks 1993: 3–4). But it was also the case for business, which saw itself falling rapidly behind its competitors without access to European markets and technology. This was already clear in the 1960s, when the research of de Miguel and Linz showed Spanish managers rejecting paternalism and accepting modern models of industrial relations (reported in de Miguel 1976).

In contrast to the sharply diverging left–right identities of the Republican period, middle-class Spaniards experienced the transition to democracy having constructed a new political identity. This could be seen in the victory of Gonźales's moderate faction of the PSOE over its competitors; in the surprising victory of Suárez' virtually unknown party in the first post–Franco elections; in the weakness of Communism in the first post–Franco elections; and in the failure of the Christian Democratic parties. These had long histories in Spain, but their vestiges of integralism turned off secular Spaniards while the Church hierarchy refused them its support (Edles 1998: 68–69).

Not only identities oriented toward Europe emerged in the transition period. There also was a crystallization and broadening of autonomist identities. The inclusion of regional autonomy in the new constitution was no elite concession from on high. In fact, in Catalonia, Suárez "*avoided* making pacts with the political parties, and reached an agreement with Josep Tarradellas [a historic Catalan leader] on the restoration of the Generalitat [or government] of Catalonia" (Pérez Díaz 1993: 199). By including autonomism prominently in the constitution, Suárez was reacting to regional movements in which "the democratic evolution of the institutions was slowly permitting the emergence of an earlier discourse of autonomism" (Buxo i Rey 1995: 127).

Catalonia and the Basque country were also major regions of working-class and Catholic opposition to Francoism. In Catalonia, for example, the nationalist movement was transformed in the 1970s into "a legitimate anti–Francoist opposition" by its contact with "the many Catalan workers who were active in the working-class movement" and through its relationship to progressive Catholicism, which made it more acceptable to the middle class" (Johnston 1991: 123–124). The movement for the Autonomies was part of a more general identity shift in Spanish society that was constructed through the processes of contentious politics. Even regions such as Andalusia, which knew little regional nationalism in the past, began to stir as the result of the government's strategy of regionalization (Pérez Díaz 1990: 200–202).

Brokerage

Like population movement in the antebellum United States, secularization and economic modernization are no more than structural processes producing the boundaries for potential change. Identity shift does no more than signal the frames within which moves can be made. As in the formation of an antislavery coalition in antebellum America, these parameters had to be turned into working agreements to permit Spain to transcend a regime that had governed the country for forty years.

The elite negotiation model of the Spanish transition captures an important part of that process, the portion that could be observed at the moment of transition. Brokerage occurred both within the opposition, as its leaders negotiated first the Plataforma de Convergencia Democratica and then the Coordinación Democratica. It occurred later between the opposition and moderate regime forces. But elites were not merely *choosing* formulas for constitutional revision from above; they were brokering agreements *on behalf of* the groups they represented, or claimed to represent.

It is true that the leaders of the opposition made compromises with representatives of the old regime in order to restrain "excessive strike activity" in return for commitments for political reform (Gunther 1992: 55). Yet these arrangements would have foundered had it not been for the support of a highly mobilized working-class base whose shop-floor militants were "self-constrained" because they largely accepted the goal of democratization (Pérez Díaz 1990: 222). Gunther rightly observes that the major gain from the Moncloa Pact was increased integration of the elite and the legitimation of the Communist party. But the parties of the left were able to broker such a deal precisely because they had the threat of their working-class base behind them.

Brokerage also operated among organized Catholics. After Vatican II and the development of a generation of Catholic activists who rejected the role of state church, a new generation of leaders moved into positions of power in the Spanish hierarchy. Among them was the so-called Tácito group, "a group of Catholic civil servants and professionals . . . finally becoming a source of leaders and a laboratory for political formulas for the democratic transition" (Pérez Díaz 1993: 169). Between 1975 and 1978, the church "made a decisive contribution toward easing the hostility of the conservative right to the new democratic regime" (Pérez Díaz 1990: 171).

Brokerage also worked its way below the summit. Spain in the 1960s possessed a number of sites that linked opposition groups to one another. The CC.OO took advantages of changes in industrial relations practices to bring workers from different factories and sectors into contact with one another. Younger clerics provided sanctuaries for antiregime activists to meet and organize. By the early 1970s, clerics were even offering sanctuary to priests, students, and workers demonstrating for Basque nationalism (Payne 1987: 499, 562–563).

The most important site of brokerage was one that the elite negotiation model largely ignores: between the two main opposition parties. Historical enemies with memories of vicious infighting and betrayal in the civil war, the PCE and the Socialist party signed a series of pacts in the early 1970s that permitted them to present a united front when negotiations opened with the regime. This would of course have been impossible if not for moderate views of their bases; but this simply tells us that the mechanisms of identity shift and brokerage worked hand-in-glove to produce a relatively united opposition faced by a regime coalition riven with cleavages between a hardline "bunker" and the proponents of liberalization.

Convergence and Radicalization

In antebellum America, as North and South moved further apart, a polarization occurred within each region. In Spain radicalization on the extremes brought moderate regime and opposition groups together. There were strategic reasons for convergence: Opposition leaders remembered well the ravages of the civil war – and which side had won it. Fearing a preemptive strike from the bunker, they worked hard to find sources of agreement with moderate sectors of the regime.

But convergence was also a result of deep-seated and long-standing changes in Spanish society. Consider as one example the changed relationship between clericalism and right-wing voting, on the one hand, and anticlericalism and support for the left. In Spanish history, the clerical issue had envenomed relations between left and right (Cruz 1997). To be on the left virtually meant being anticlerical, while support for the secular dominion of Catholic values was a sine qua non of conservatism. The degree of religiosity still varies between left and right in Spain, as it does in all Catholic countries (Linz and Montero 1999: 88). But by the early 1990s, José Ramón Montero shows, the co-occurrence of right–left ideology and the level of religiosity had narrowed sharply (1997: Table 6).

But convergence had a counterpart in the radicalization of both extreme right and left. On the one hand, as the transition evolved, right-wing groups on the margins of the regime opposed the "permissive" policies that allowed contention to emerge. Adell Argilés' data shows that 10 percent of the demonstrations and 24 percent of the participants in Madrid protests that he studied in 1976 involved extreme right-wing groups.[5] Groups with names such as Fuerza Nueva and Guerrilleros de Cristo Re began to appear to the right of the regime.

On the other hand, right-wing mobilization was triggered by and coincided with an increase in Basque violence. In April 1975, a state of emergency was declared in the Basque country and, in August, a new antiterrorist law was passed. In September of that year, five ETA and FRAP militants were executed. In January 1977, ten people died in Madrid's black week, and in May, six more were killed in a new wave of violence in the Basque country. In 1978 (the year the constitution was approved), deaths by extremist violence escalated to sixty-five (Linz and Stepan 1996: 99). In 1981 a right-wing coup by parts of the military – triggered by ETA outrages and the government's inability to contain them – threatened the survival of democracy itself.

But in Spain radicalization had the opposite effect to its effects in antebellum America – it produced a "radical flank effect" that isolated the extremes, forced the unions and the parties of the left to define their projects as peaceful, and reinforced collaboration between the opposition parties and the regime. Although support for the independence of Catalonia and the Basque country rose at the beginning of the transition, it

[5] Ramon Adell Argilés kindly provided these figures on Madrid's extreme right-wing protests from his original research.

fell sharply as ETA terrorism mounted and a referendum created the popular basis for the passage of Spain's autonomy statute (Linz and Stepan 1996: 103–5; Pérez Díaz 1990: 198–204). Each turn in the armed struggle between ETA terrorists and the police brought greater revulsion among the mass public and helped to bring about a convergence around the center of the political spectrum.

To summarize: structural change created the bases for a society that was capitalist, secular, and pragmatic; identity shift oriented Spaniards to Europe and away from the past; brokerage created links within the oppositions and between them and moderate sectors of regime supporters; and radicalization isolated the extremes instead of dividing the society. What might have been a revolutionary convulsion resembled a cycle of protest intertwined with elite transaction.

Nineteenth Century America and Twentieth Century Spain

There are ironies in the outcomes of these two episodes. Though launched in the context of a formally democratic system and mainly visible through institutional politics, America's political conflicts of the 1850s over free soil and slavery linked up with identity-transforming and cleavage-widening processes at the base of American society to produce truly transgressive politics and a national conflagration. Although it involved simultaneous waves of labor, ethnic, religious, and civic contention, the Spanish transition produced its outcome through negotiated pacts with a minimum of institutional disruption. Violent American tragedy, peaceable Spanish transition: two very different – and in traditional terms, incomparable – situations. But concerted, comparative attention to the mechanisms of contention within them have helped to comprehend their outcomes as well as to lower the walls that normally separate the analysis of nominally different forms of contention.

This comparison between two very different episodes has shown how placing similar mechanisms (in this case, identity shift, brokerage, radicalization, and convergence) within their historical contexts can help explain why some episodes end in civil war or revolution while others take a more circumspect route resembling a protest cycle. But we aim at more than contextualization. Though some have seen the collapse of the antebellum polity in America as primarily a partisan realignment (Gienapp 1987) with antislavery little more than a sideshow, and others have seen the transition in Spain as little more than a "transition by transaction"

(Share 1986), both processes were part of broader episodes of contention linking elites with key sectors of an actively mobilized public.

In both cases, institutional and elite politics were the visible evidence of sea changes beneath the surface. Those changes can only be understood by looking as well at the actions of social movements and social actors. In both cases, what began as weak and inchoate movements of minorities converged with changes in elite and institutional politics to produce major episodes of contention and essentially new polities – inclusive but decentralized in Spain, and in the United States a strong federal system rather than one dominated by the states.

The short-term results varied from their long-term outcomes. In Spain, the first stage after Franco's death was a pacted liberalization under the leadership of elements associated with the more pragmatic sector of the old regime. In the United States, the first outcome of the Civil War was ascendancy of the radical Republicans and a reconstruction of the South that promised equal rights for former slaves. But the long-term results were rather different: the disappearance of the centrist UCD and consolidation of democracy in Spain under leadership of the anti–Francoist PSOE; a consolidation of the stronger federal state after Reconstruction by a regime that returned the South to white hegemony, though without slavery.

If the Spanish transition was effected by elites through largely peaceful means, it was made possible by a shift of identities, brokerage between segments of the society, and a combination of radicalization at the extremes and convergence at the center. If the United States left African Americans unrepresented in the South, it was largely due to the concentration of the new majority in the North and West around a dynamic project of capitalist expansion (Bensel 1990). In both cases, contention transgressed the borders of conventional politics and, in both, the transformation of contention brought about the transformation of their polities.

What's Going on Here?

Notice what is happening in this outlandish comparison of nineteenth century United States struggles and twentieth century Spanish political transformations:

First, similar causal mechanisms – identity shifts, brokerage, radicalization, and convergence – played significant parts in producing very different episodes of contention.

Second, the larger scale effects of those mechanisms depended heavily on the settings in which they operated, the sequence in which they activated, and the combinations in which they occurred.

Third, their analysis forced us to break down the provisional barriers we initially erected among actors, mobilization, and trajectories. Identity shift, for example, seems at first glance to concern actors alone, but soon turns out to be a spur to mobilization and a shaper of trajectories.

In Part II of this study, we have come a great distance from where we began in Chapter 2: asking mobilization questions about the American civil rights movement, identity questions about the Parisian revolution of 1789, and trajectory questions about Italian conflict in the late 1960s. By identifying partial parallels between mobilization or demobilization in Kenya's Mau Mau and the Philippines' Yellow revolution in Chapter 4, between actor–action–identity features of Hindu–Muslim conflict and the end of apartheid in South Africa in Chapter 5, and between trajectories of American antislavery and Spanish exit from the Franco regime in this chapter, we have followed the trail of identical causal mechanisms across two different kinds of boundaries: among ostensibly unlike episodes, settings, and types of contention; and among actors, mobilization, and trajectories.

Consider the mechanisms and processes we have emphasized in these three chapters:

- attribution of threat or opportunity, social appropriation, brokerage, and certification in the Kenya/Philippines comparison
- brokerage, category formation, object shift, certification in the South Asia/South Africa comparison
- identity shift, brokerage, radicalization, and convergence in the U.S./Spain comparison

The overlap is significant; brokerage explains significant features of all six episodes, while identity shift, object shift, certification, and social appropriation form an interacting bundle of mechanisms. Most of the mechanisms connect with radicalization and convergence. Despite their labels, none of them belongs exclusively to any of the separate domains – mobilization, identities, or trajectories – with which Part I began.

The three new mechanisms introduced in this chapter (identity shift, radicalization, and convergence) clearly work in a much wider range of contentious politics than democratic transitions and regressions. Conceived of as alteration in shared definitions of a boundary between two political actors and of relations across that boundary, identity shift makes a difference in war, nationalist mobilization, revolutions, and many other forms of political struggle. Recall how rapidly and decisively identity shift occurred in Paris during July 1789, as the French regime and its subjects negotiated new definitions of their relations to each other. Reflect on how new subjects, collectively defining themselves as the nation and individually belonging to the category of citizens, altered French politics. Identity shift matters.

So, obviously, does radicalization – increasing contradiction between prevailing claims, programs, self-descriptions, and descriptions of others across a boundary between political actors. During the early phases of the Italian postwar protest cycle that we examined in Chapter 2, the increasing contradiction separated mobilizing students and workers from the regime's stalwarts. We also witnessed radicalization in South Africa, Mau Mau, the Philippines' Yellow revolution, and elsewhere. Radicalization, like identity shift, is a robust, wide-ranging mechanism.

Finally, convergence, where increasing contradictions at one or both extremes of a political continuum drive political actors between the extremes into closer alliances. For students of social movements, a classic case is one we examined in Chapter 2 as well: the civil rights movement in the United States. There the emergence of black nationalists on one side and diehard segregationists on the other promoted coalitions among newly self-styled moderates who opposed each other vigorously before the 1960s. Later phases of postwar Italy's protest cycle brought just such radical flanking into play as the opposition Communists joined the governmental majority. But such effects occur far outside the range of social movements. In nationalist mobilizations, for example, convergence commonly brings together former rivals who fear destructive action, and discredit to their cause, from others they label as extremists. Once again, a mechanism we have discerned in a particular pair of episodes turns out to work across a wide range of contentious politics.

Compared to this book's starting point, we count that recognition in advance. The classic political process agenda for explanation of social movements featured boxes labeled social change, mobilizing structures, framing processes, political opportunities, repertoires, and movement emergence. Unlabeled arrows connected the boxes. We have, in effect, been placing those arrows under microscopes to observe what goes on inside them. We find mechanisms and processes – cognitive, relational, and environmental – within them.

The examination of mechanisms and processes in Part II of this study helped us overcome three frequently criticized drawbacks of the standard agenda identified in Part I: its static character, its poor representation of interplay among actors, and its reduction of complex experience to framing and strategic calculation. It has offered the additional advantage of escape from the compartmentalization of social movements, revolutions, democratization, and other forms of contention as *sui generis* phenomena with separate literatures and different ground rules. By doing so, it fortifies resistance to the seductions of general laws and general models: how the ideal social movement works, how the ideal revolution works, and so on. Whatever its own weaknesses, this approach to mechanisms, processes, and episodes drives us inexorably to observation of dynamic, contingent interaction among actors that are themselves undergoing continuous creation and transformation. That is the task of Part III.

PART THREE

Applications and Conclusions

7

Revolutionary Trajectories

Let us begin to put the approach developed in Part II to a greater test. There we settled for showing that similar mechanisms can be identified in dissimilar episodes and used to clarify causal connections within those episodes. Now we ask if the sorts of mechanisms we uncovered within those episodes can illuminate the complex processes that others have lumped together as "revolutions," "nationalism," and "democratization." We will see that they do. To make our case, we extend the comparison of episodes to very large transformations that are usually compared only to each other. Chapter 7 compares revolutionary processes and their successes and failures in late twentieth century Nicaragua and China. Chapter 8 compares state integration and disintegration in nineteenth century Italy with their counterparts in the twentieth century Soviet Union. Chapter 9 closes the trilogy by comparing processes of democratization (and sometimes of de-democratization) in nineteenth century Switzerland and twentieth century Mexico. In Chapter 10 we turn to some unanswered questions and further test the robustness of our approach by applying some combinations of mechanisms that we identified from one set of cases to others in our repertoire as well as to three entirely new episodes.

Between Origins and Outcomes in the Comparative Study of Revolution

In an influential review essay, Jack Goldstone described two early generations in studies of revolution, the first focussing on "natural histories" of revolution and the second on "structural strain" (Goldstone 1980). In the first, scholars pictured trajectories of revolution in rigid stages; while in the second, no attention was paid to process at all, with the origins of revolutions deduced directly from underlying social strains. Goldstone went on to describe what he called a "third generation" of theory in the study of revolution – a comparative approach emphasizing the role of structural factors in the origins of revolution. Among the most important factors in that tradition were broad political, economic, and demographic changes that undermine the stability of established regimes (Goldstone 1991; Skocpol 1979).

Whether recent theoretical schools are best described as "generations" is an open question (after all, the "structural approach" to revolution goes back many generations to the work of Marx and Engels). But Goldstone's essay captured, even as it contributed to, a clear shift in orientation among scholars of revolution. It was explicitly comparative; it looked beneath the surface of events for underlying causes of revolution; it was internationally rooted; and it went beyond the question of origins to examine revolutionary outcomes. Indeed, it was one particular kind of outcome that interested both Goldstone and Skocpol – the social revolution.

This third generation of revolutionary studies accomplished much, but also left much to accomplish. For a start, its structuralist cast left little room for actors to seek to fulfill their dreams, make alliances, learn from one another, and make mistakes. Reflecting the cultural turn of the past two decades, a "fourth generation" of scholarship grants more attention to the role of human agency and cultural construction in the emergence of revolution.[1]

The attention we have given to such factors as the attribution of threat and opportunity, social appropriation, and identity shift in earlier chapters should make our sympathy to that turn obvious. But this fourth generation shared some of the same problems as the third. By narrowing attention to great social revolutions, both of them elided the factors that distinguish social revolutions from other successful revolutions, and failed to examine the transformative mechanisms that produce revolutionary outcomes out of revolutionary situations. As Goldstone points out in a more recent article, successful revolutions are not a genre apart, but share characteristics with social movements, rebellions, failed revolutions, and cycles of protest (1998).

[1] Among those stressing the need for such attention are Foran (1993), Goodwin (1994), Keddie (1995), Selbin (1993), Sewell (1985) and Wasserstrom (1995).

This truncated conception of the central subject matter in revolutionary studies had two negative effects. First, it limited the number of systematic investigations of how revolutionary situations turn into revolutionary outcomes. Second, it conflated revolutionary origins with trajectories. A full theoretical accounting of revolutions requires answers to three progressive questions:

1. under what conditions and through what processes do viable contenders to state power emerge?
2. under what conditions and through what processes do those contenders succeed in displacing the incumbent regime?
3. under what conditions and through what processes does the ongoing struggle for control of a new state result in a social revolution?

Only the first of these questions can be examined through an analysis of revolutionary origins. To answer it, furthermore, would require a representative sample of revolutionary situations – not merely those that resulted in success. Questions 2 and 3 can only be examined by systematic attention to trajectories – that is, to what happens *after* a revolutionary situation has appeared. Moreover, they require very different samples of episodes: the first a sample of revolutionary situations (only some of which succeed) and the third by a sample of revolutionary outcomes (only some of which result in social revolutions). This chapter ignores the first question to focus on the trajectories of a successful and a failed revolution and turns its attention centrally to the processes that shape the fate of revolutionary contenders.

In pursuing this agenda, we are not without help. The few systematic comparative studies that address the question of revolutionary outcomes within a population of revolutionary situations tell a similar story: Timothy Wickham-Crowley's *Guerillas and Revolution in Latin America* (1992) and Charles Tilly's *European Revolutions, 1492–1992* (1993) both show that few successful cases result from a large sample of revolutionary situations. Wickham-Crowley's eleven revolutionary Latin American cases yielded only two revolutionary outcomes; Tilly's 709 revolutionary outcomes in European history produced no more than a score of successful ones. (Were we to turn to Question 3, we would find an even tinier proportion of transforming social revolutions.) Something must be happening – not in the origins or structural conditions but in the trajectories of contention – to produce so few successes out of so many revolutionary situations.

When we turn to these trajectories, neither the structuralists' emphasis on origins nor the culturalists' focus on agency take us very far, for neither deals with the crucial interactions within contentious politics that result in new alignments, new identities, and the collapse of oppressive regimes. By now it will cause no surprise that we think what happens within a revolutionary trajectory can better be understood as the result of the intersection of a number of causal mechanisms. We do not offer a systematic account of all such mechanisms and their interaction in a sample of revolutionary situations. Instead, we use a paired comparison of the Nicaraguan revolution of 1979 and the Chinese student rebellion of 1989 to zero in on one process in particular: the defection of significant elements from a dominant ruling coalition. We define this process of regime defection as "a sustained process by which significant elements of a previously stable ruling coalition align with the action programs of revolutionary or other opposition groups."

We are particularly interested in regime defections that link regime allies with broadly based opposition groups. These groups, though not these alone, seem to be most involved in successful revolutions. As we will see, such a coalition emerged in Nicaragua over a decade of revolutionary politics, but was absent in China, despite a tradition in the Chinese party state of regularly using popular contention to achieve its policy goals. We will not trace every element in the protracted struggle between the regime of Anastasio Somoza Debayle and the Sandinista National Liberation Front (from here on, FSNL) or in the defeat of the Chinese student insurgency of 1989. Instead, we limit ourselves to underscoring how some key mechanisms of regime defection worked, or failed to work, emphasizing the role of contingent events within each episode and describing the revolutionary turn of the one and the revolutionary reversal of the other. Our aim is to highlight the process that produced such contrasting outcomes.

The Trajectory of Revolution in Nicaragua

The 1979 overthrow of the Somoza regime brought to an end nearly five decades of brutal, corrupt rule by the Somoza family. It also ushered in a period of significant democratization, as the Sandinistas sought – ultimately unsuccessfully – to share power with elements of the moderate anti–Somoza opposition with whom they had forged a fragile revolutionary coalition. But if the Sandinistas' hold on power was short-lived, the democratic reforms they instituted were not. For all its various woes (including the devastation of Hurricane Mitch) Nicaragua has become a very different and far more democratic society today than it was under the Somozas. If the 1979 regime transfer does not qualify as a true Social or Great Revolution, it nonetheless must be counted as a significant revolutionary outcome. Our task in this section is to search the history of the revolution for the dynamic processes and mechanisms that help account for how a fairly typical revolutionary situation in the context of late twentieth century Latin America developed into a successful and significant transfer of state power.

First we must establish when Nicaragua entered a revolutionary situation. We define a revolutionary situation as one involving three elements (Tilly 1993: 10):

- appearance of contenders, or coalitions of contenders, advancing exclusive competing claims to control of the state, or some segment of it
- commitment to those claims by a significant segment of the citizenry
- incapacity or unwillingness of rulers to suppress the alternative coalition and/or commitment to its claims

Though the application of this definition obviously requires further specifications (e.g., what constitutes a "significant segment of the citizenry"?), it seems clear that by 1970 the FSLN had mobilized enough popular support and shown itself to be sufficiently resilient to repressive campaigns by the National Guard to satisfy all three criteria (Black 1981; Booth 1982; Christian 1986; Farhi 1990; Parsa 1999; Vilas 1986; Wickham-Crowley 1992). Thus Nicaragua can be characterized as having lived through a revolutionary situation for the entire decade of the 1970s. But as Wickham-Crowley's comparative work makes clear, Nicaragua was hardly alone among countries in Latin America in this regard. By his accounting, Latin America produced ten other revolutionary situations in the post World War II era alone. But in only one other of these ten cases – Cuba – did the process of revolutionary contention yield a successful transfer of state power. Like Cuba, Nicaragua is the exception rather than the rule.

How do we account for this exception? The process of regime defection figures prominently, not only in most of the empirical accounts of that revolution (see Black 1981; Booth 1982; Christian 1986; Foran 1990; Parsa 1995; Selbin 1993), but in more general comparative analyses differentiating trajectories of successful from those of unsuccessful revolutions (Dix 1984; Midlarsky and Roberts 1985; Russell 1974; Wickham-Crowley 1989, 1992). As a result, by 1979 Somoza found himself confronting a broad opposition movement composed not only of elements of the traditional left – students, labor unions, peasants, and the vanguard FSLN – but also of the country's Catholic hierarchy, the mainstream press, and much of the business elite. Among the key institutional actors who typically figure in revolutionary dramas, only the military remained substantially loyal to *somocismo*.

We want to identify the key mechanisms implicated in that process. Three mechanisms seem especially significant. They are *infringement of elite interests*, *suddenly imposed grievances*, and *decertification*. We regard these mechanisms as neither the single key to events in Nicaragua nor, more boldly, as a Rosetta Stone for decoding all revolutionary outcomes. We claim only that they played an important role in encouraging the critical process of regime defection. Other consequential mechanisms were operating as well, some of which we will mention in passing. We see our task as pushing the explanatory agenda back a step from "regime defection" to ask: "What different mixes of mechanisms shape it and with what subsequent effects?"

Mechanisms in Revolutionary Contention

If the FSLN established a viable revolutionary presence in Nicaragua in 1970, it did so without benefit of significant elite allies. Though they had expanded far beyond their humble beginnings in the early 1960s, the Sandinistas were still little more than the vanguard of a small collection of Nicaragua's most disadvantaged social groups. Moreover, as the 1970s dawned, the remote north central region of the country remained the movement's only real stronghold. More important, the FSLN attracted only a limited following among students, radical labor, and the urban poor. But by 1977 the Sandinistas would be the undisputed revolutionary wedge of a broad opposition coalition that included representatives of most of the country's elite institutions. How had this happened in a scant five to six years, when the bulk of Latin American guerilla movements failed?

Existing literature on Nicaragua suggests that the lion's share of responsibility for the wholesale defection of elite elements to the cause of the revolution resulted from the routine practices and actions of Somoza and his agents. Thus, our interpretation of the unfolding of the episode over the crucial decade of the 1970s resonates with the two generalizations offered by Jeff Goodwin in his stock-taking article on studies of revolutions. Writes Goodwin:

> First, most of these studies demonstrate how repressive or disruptive state practices, including putatively well-intentioned ones, may have the unintended consequence of both concentrating or fusing disparate popular grievances and focusing these on the state itself . . . Second, all of the studies examined above suggest that one type of authoritarian regime is especially vulnerable not only to the formation of strong revolutionary movements, but also to actual overthrow by such movements, namely, autonomous, corrupt, and repressive personalist dictatorships. . . . By alienating elites and middle strata as well as popular classes [he concludes] these dictatorships have become the target of broad, multiclass protest movements. [1994: 757–58]

And so it was in Nicaragua. Two of the three mechanisms described below center on the effects of Somoza's actions in driving Nicaragua's elite and middle strata into an uneasy revolutionary partnership with the Sandinistas.

Infringement of Elite Interests

Virtually all enduring regimes are rooted in relatively broad coalitions of elite actors, the alliance sustained by mutual recognition and support for each other's interests. This appears to have been true even of the Somoza regime, at least up to a certain point. Writes Black:

> From its earliest days, Somoza power had rested on the family's ability to achieve dominance within the ruling class and then reach mutually beneficial agreements – political pacts on one hand, commercial alliances on the other – with the remaining bourgeois sectors. Accepting these rules, the bourgeoisie grouped itself into BANIC and BANAMERICA [two broad commercial networks], and flourished. With their consolidation, their need for Somoza grew. Agribusiness, commerce and industry were allotted, with each group enjoying certain preserves, and the crude monopolistic control they exercised over the mass of the Nicaraguan people produced an increasingly violent class conflict which a unified bourgeoisie relied upon Somoza to suppress. [1981: 62–63]

Save for Costa Rica, in its basic contours the Nicaraguan political economy differed little from those of the other Central American countries, most of which experienced but survived revolutionary movements akin to Nicaragua's (Paige 1997, Yashar 1997). The clear implication: Gross class disparities and economic exploitation may help to trigger revolutionary situations but are clearly not sufficient in themselves to produce revolutionary outcomes. For that to happen, the material/political interests of segments of the dominant regime coalition must be seriously compromised.

By all accounts, the decisive break came in the aftermath of the massive earthquake that leveled the capital city, Managua, on December 23, 1972 (Black 1981; Booth 1982; Christian 1986). Somoza himself described the earthquake as a "revolution of possibilities." He certainly knew what he was talking about. He exploited these possibilities with naked greed, cornering the various markets created by the rebuilding of Managua and aggressively denying to all but a few trusted cronies any share of the action. In the end, the Somoza clan exercised monopolistic control over demolition, real estate speculation, road work, and the construction of new homes and commercial buildings, the latter selling at four or five times their original value. Somoza's personal avarice and unwillingness to share the windfall created by the crisis precipitated another of even greater consequence. Black writes:

> Overnight, patterns of economic control and Somoza's relationship with the bourgeoisie were transformed. . . . The aftermath of the earthquake also introduced a new phrase into the vocabulary of the bourgeois opposition: *competencia desleal*, unfair or disloyal competition. The rules of the game, and with it the fragile consensus which held the dictatorial state together, had been broken. [1981: 59–61]

The first serious cracks in the ruling alliance appeared almost immediately following the quake, but were clearly visible by early 1973. By then the two main organizations representing elite business interests had assumed strong policy positions in opposition to the Somoza regime. The two organizations, the Superior Council of Private Initiative (Consejo Superior de la Iniciative Privada, or COSIP, later COSEP) and the Nicaraguan Development Institute (Instituto Nicaraguense de Desarrollo, or INDE), further distanced themselves from Somoza in 1974 through their cosponsorship of a convention of Nicaragua's economic elite that demanded an end to government corruption and issued a call for reforms to aid the "great dispossessed majorities." In the same year, a third major organization, UDEL, appeared and soon established itself as an even stronger opposition force than either COSIP or INDE. Cobbled together from various political and trade union groups, UDEL's stridency was attributable both to its independence from elite economic interests and the visibility and charisma of its founder and nominal leader, Pedro Joaquín Chamorro, the editor of *La Prensa* and one of the very few public figures who commanded a degree of national visibility and respect.

But despite the clear rift that had developed between the regime and key elements of the traditional ruling class, none of these organizations were prepared to call for revolution. Certainly none of them viewed the FSLN as an ally. But three more years of notorious outrages at the hands of the regime, including Somoza's imposition of a uniquely savage brand of martial law in December 1974, pushed the regime's elite opponents ever leftward. By 1977, the third year of Somoza's "state of siege," the rift between the regime and its former elite allies had become a chasm. With the imposition of new business taxes and the removal of a host of tax exemptions in the same year, the chasm grew wider still. As Booth writes,

> Most major business interests still preferred a "national unity" reform that would get rid of the Somozas but keep the basic political structure intact – including the National Guard and the PLN. . . . One key group of Nicaraguan capitalists . . . helped to broaden the revolutionary coalition and established business . . . links with the FSLN. Among them were industrialist Emilio Baltodano Pallais, lawyer businessman Dr. Joaquín Chamorro, supermarket magnate Felipe Mántica, and international banker Arturo Cruz Porras. Their contacts with and mid-1977 endorsement of the FSLN allegedly led the guerrillas' leadership to propose them along with eight others for cabinet posts in a revolutionary government. This "Group of Twelve," exposed in 1977, fled Nicaragua for safety. From exile, they began to lobby against international aid for Somoza and to organize the anti-–Somoza coalition within Nicaragua. [1982: 102]

The defection of The Twelve escalated the polarization of Nicaragua's traditional ruling class. The murder of Pedro Joaquín Chamorro on January 10, 1978, marked the point of no return for many in the bourgeoisie. Having eschewed direct action to this point, COSIP, INDE, and a host of other private sector organizations took an active role in a succession of nationwide strikes and business shutdowns designed both to protest Chamorra's assassination and to force Somoza from office. Over the final sixteen months of his regime the full weight and diversity of Nicaragua's elite defections was felt by Somoza. Indeed, with most of his former elite allies arrayed against him, it was only through repression that he survived in office as long as he did.

Suddenly Imposed Grievances

In an influential 1983 article, Edward Walsh and Rex Warland introduced to social movement research the concept of "suddenly imposed grievances." The specific event to which they applied the concept was the accident at the Three Mile Island nuclear power plant. But they felt that the accident was but a single instance of something more general: singular events that dramatize and heighten the political salience of particular issues (in their case the perils of nuclear energy). Other examples mentioned by the authors shared the "act of God" quality of the Three Mile Island accident. The events did *not* result from purposive human activity. But it seems reasonable to broaden the concept to include purposive actions that mobilize opposition through the same mix of alarm and outrage noted by Walsh and Warland in connection with Three Mile Island.

Such actions figured prominently in Nicaragua. They must be counted as another important mechanism facilitating the regime defections so crucial to the revolutionary outcome there. As was true with the infringement of elite interests, it was Somoza and his agents who were responsible (or were believed to be responsible) for the series of "celebrated" atrocities that served to dramatize and render more salient the oppressiveness and arbitrary nature of his rule.

None of these suddenly imposed grievances was more consequential than assassination of *La Prensa* editor, Pedro Joaquín Chamorro, which galvanized elite and popular opposition to the regime. The popular response to the slaying was immediate. Within hours of the murder, some 50,000 mourners/demonstrators appeared outside Chamorro's home. Two days later, during the funeral procession, angry mobs totaling 30,000 burned Plasmafersis and other Somoza-owned businesses. More important, as Paige writes,

> Chamorro's assassination was a critical turning point for the Nicaraguan bourgeoisie. He had been at the center of a dense network of Conservative Granada families and was a national symbol of opposition to Somoza. His death indicated to many members of the bourgeoisie that no one was safe. [1997: 38]

The organized expression of this broader, more militant elite opposition was the general business strike launched on January 24, 1978. Even the Conservative party, an official partner in the Somoza-led government, signaled its opposition to the regime of which it was a part by urging its members to boycott the regular municipal elections held in February of the same year.

The context, circumstances, and eventual impact of this event are similar to those that characterized the assassination discussed in Chapter 4 – the 1983 murder of Benigno Aquino in the Philippines. In the Nicaraguan case, the evidence suggests that the assassination was ordered by the owners of the firm, Plasmafersis, in retaliation for a *La Prensa* exposé concerning the company's export of scarce blood plasma. One of the firm's owners, Anastasio Somoza Portocarrero, was Somoza's son and likely heir to the family political dynasty. The immediate effect of the two slayings on the mobilization of popular and elite opposition to the respective regimes suggests a relatively robust causal link between a form of suddenly imposed grievance and the process of regime defection.

But for all the climactic significance of the Chamorro slaying and its aftermath, the event was not the only instance of suddenly imposed grievances during the unfolding revolutionary process. Here we note another similarity and a difference between events in the Philippines and Nicaragua. The similarity was that in both cases, the process of crossclass coalition formation was punctuated and, in large part, fueled by a succession of ill-conceived regime actions. The difference was that in the Philippines, the series of outrages began with the assassination, whereas in Nicaragua the slaying came near the end of this punctuated process. In particular, several earlier catalyzing actions were significant reference points in the rising revolutionary tide among Nicaragua's traditional elites.

The most important of these actions was Somoza's suppression of political and press freedoms during the thirty-three-month State of Siege waged by the regime. To understand the importance of Somoza's actions, it is worth remembering that a majority of the Nicaraguan bourgeoisie had probably supported martial law when it was first declared in late December of 1974. For that declaration was issued in the midst of an event that shook the Nicaraguan elite to its core, even as it galvanized popular support for the FSLN. The event was the successful Sandinista raid on December 27, 1974, on a holiday party thrown by Somoza's Minister of Agriculture, José María Castillo.

That raid netted the Sandinista commandos an impressive collection of hostages drawn from the upper reaches of the regime, foreign diplomatic circles, the Somoza family, and Nicaraguan society in general. It also afforded them a national and international forum for their views, and in the end, a stunning revolutionary triumph when Somoza acceded to all of their demands, including wage increases for a broad array of workers (including his own National Guard), the release of several key political prisoners, a ransom of $2 million dollars, and safe passage to Cuba. The cheering crowds that greeted the FSLN commandos as they were transported to the airport underscored the depths of the humiliation visited upon Somoza by the raid.

For many in the Nicaraguan bourgeoisie, the raid did not so much humiliate as frighten them. Until then the insurgency in the North had been a distant concern. While opposition to Somoza's excesses had grown within their ranks, the elite still backed the regime in its war against the Sandinistas. But if fear of the FSLN prompted many affluent Nicaraguans initially to support the declaration of martial law, Somoza's blatant use of the siege to wage war – not only against peasant rebels in the North, but against moderate opposition leaders as well – quickly radicalized a good many of their followers. The dictator's intentions became clear with his arbitrary jailing of several UDEL leaders, punitive restrictions on national labor unions, and imposition of complete press censorship. In the end, the raid and resultant martial law declaration "aggravated the political crisis of the Nicaraguan bourgeoisie. It delineated more clearly than ever before those sectors . . . who would ultimately stick by the dictatorship and those other bourgeois groups whose opposition would grow more outspoken" (Black 1981: 88). Instead of using the fears generated by the raid to stem the tide of elite defections, Somoza's undifferentiated reaction to it pushed elite opponents into an ever stronger, if wary, embrace of the FSLN.

Decertification

To this point we have stressed the role of Somoza and his agents in unwittingly encouraging the elite defections we think were key to the revolutionary outcome in Nicaragua. But lest we seem to argue that state actions alone shape revolutionary trajectories, let us examine a mechanism placing a very different group of actors – what we will call certifying agents – at the center of action. *Certification* we defined in Chapter 5 as validation of actors, their performances, and their claims by external authorities. By *decertification*, we mean the withdrawal of such validation by key certifying agents. Without the support of prominent elite groups, not even the most ruthless dictatorship will long survive.

Regimes are embedded in a secondary structure of validation as well; one that links them to the international system of nation states via their relations with other regimes and transnational bodies. As we saw in Chapter 4's Yellow Revolution, withdrawal of support by significant other states commonly exerts both direct and indirect effects on the regime's stability. Direct effects range from withdrawal of vital financial or military support to imposition of severe economic sanctions to granting of aid to insurgents to direct military intervention by foreign states. Indirect effects center on the impact that withdrawal of foreign support has on key domestic actors. Decertification often emboldens insurgents to escalate their operations against the regime, or prompts once-supportive elite groups to abandon a regime they now view as irreparably damaged. Both kinds of effects were clearly visible in the Nicaraguan case.

Five countries' actions, over time, destabilized and effectively decertified the Somoza regime. The five are: Costa Rica, Venezuela, Panama, Mexico, and especially the United States. For its part, the United States was an unwilling ally of the Sandinistas. That is, while consistently opposed to the FSLN, the United States, under President Carter, did take several actions that clearly abetted the revolutionary process. Among these actions, the one that drew the most attention was the sharp reduction in U.S. aid to Somoza following Carter's accession to office in 1977. Reflecting the President's efforts to link foreign aid to human rights practices, U.S. economic assistance to Nicaragua was cut by 75 percent between 1974–1976 and 1977–1978 (Atkins 1977; Congressional Research Service 1979). Military aid fell by 43 percent over the same period.

These cuts had both direct and indirect effects on the stability of the regime. The direct effect of the U.S. human rights policy "was to reduce National Guard resources and to diminish the regime's military capability" (Booth 1982: 129). The indirect effects were perhaps even more important. The sharp cut in economic aid simultaneously reduced state subsidies to various key sectors while triggering a significant exodus of foreign investors from the Nicaraguan economy. The net effect of these developments was to exacerbate a mechanism – the infringement of elite interests – discussed earlier.

The growing rift between the United States and Somoza emboldened the Sandinistas. To quote Booth (1982: 129): "The rebels, meanwhile, feared less that they might have to confront the United States in combat, and became bolder as the dictatorship's political edifice crumbled." But just as the insurgents were growing more active, a second U.S. action further weakened the regime's hand in dealing with them. Under pressure from Carter, Somoza agreed, in September of 1977, to lift the thirty-three-month State of Siege he had implemented during the raid on the Castillo house. From a strictly strategic point of view, the move was clearly a mistake. While corrosive of domestic political support, the Siege had, in fact, effectively limited rebel activity. With the repressive lid off, the Sandinistas were freer to mobilize at precisely the moment the U.S./Somoza rift encouraged them to do so. In October and November of 1977 the insurgents launched their largest and most sustained actions to date. Much the same scenario was repeated nine months later when, in June of 1978, Somoza acceded to U.S. pressure and invited the leaders of the moderate opposition – the Twelve – who had fled the country the previous year to return to the country. Again hoping to curry favor with the Carter administration, Somoza's action only backfired. No increase in U.S. aid was forthcoming and the return of los Doce touched off a tumultuous airport rally and wave of generalized unrest.

The Marcos regime depended mainly upon American support, but Nicaragua was embedded in a more complex regional structure, albeit one dominated by the United States. Among the other countries facilitating the revolutionary process, perhaps none contributed more to the decertification of the regime than Costa Rica. Motivated by a long and acrimonious history of conflict with its neighbor to the North, Costa Rica aided the revolution in a number of ways. No contribution was more important than the freedom given to the FSLN by three successive presidents to operate freely in the country's remote northern region bordering Nicaragua. There the rebels were free to operate training bases and launch strikes into Nicaragua.

Costa Rica also allowed arms shipments bound for the Sandinistas into the country from Panama, even discreetly allowing Ministry of Public Security personnel to transport the shipments directly to the rebels (Booth 1982: 131). Besides harboring FSLN guerrillas, Costa Rica also served as the home in exile for los Doce, where the group engaged freely in anti–Somoza propaganda and international fund-raising efforts. These tacit decertification efforts became official on October 23, 1978, when Costa Rica became the first country to sever diplomatic ties with the Somoza regime.

Less important, though still significant roles were played by several other countries in the effective decertification of the Somoza government. As noted above, Panama – perhaps the strangest of Sandinista bedfellows – directly assisted the insurgents by serving as the entry point and main transportation artery for arms purchased by the FSLN from Cuba and elsewhere. Under Omar Torrijos, the Panamanian government also granted asylum to the Sandinista commando team that, in an embarrassing setback for Somoza, captured the Nicaraguan National Palace in August of 1978. Torrijos also lent weapons and the promise of military assistance to Costa Rica in an effort to dissuade Nicaragua from taking military action against that country in retaliation for sheltering the FSLN.

Venezuela and Mexico were among the region's most active and vocal opponents of the Somoza regime. For its part, Venezuela acted even earlier than Mexico, issuing its first public call for OAS (Organization of American States) sanctions against Somoza in February of 1978. Eventually, in May of 1979, Venezuela persuaded all its Andean Pact neighbors to follow its lead and sever diplomatic ties with the Somoza regime. Late in 1978, Mexico joined Venezuela in using the OAS as a forum for denouncing Somoza and calling for investigations into alleged human rights abuses. Mexico also pressed the International Monetary Fund (IMF) and other financial institutions to suspend credit to Nicaragua. This range of actions by its neighbors left the Somoza regime increasingly cut off from the international sources of political, financial, and military aid so crucial to the long-term viability of small and dependent states. Just as important, the erosion of external support encouraged all of the internal dynamics our analytic narrative has highlighted.

The trajectory of the Nicaraguan revolution was exhausted neither by the general process of regime defection nor by the three mechanisms whose role in that process we have highlighted. Although we regard the occurrence of significant ruling elite defections as a powerful predictor of regime collapse, the mechanisms we have identified are neither the only ones relevant to the case nor necessarily present in all successful revolutionary outcomes. But it is difficult to imagine such outcomes in the absence of significant regime defections of the sort we have found in Nicaragua. We illustrate this claim by reference to a dramatic case of failed revolution.

Contentious Politics in China 1973–1989

It would be hard to imagine a revolutionary situation coming to any more abrupt or public a failure than the 1989 Chinese student movement. In the full glare of international media attention, the climactic crackdown of June 3–4 effectively resolved any questions concerning the capacity of the Communist hardliners to govern – even as it provoked worldwide condemnation of their behavior. For all the publicity attendant upon the events of 1989, however, surprisingly little in the way of systematic scholarly analysis of the origins and dynamics of the movement has been produced to date (but see, Black and Munro 1993; Calhoun 1994; Wasserstrom 1991; Zhao 1997, 1998, 2000). Moreover, most academic work on this episode has focused exclusively on the events of spring 1989 and ultimately the decision of Chinese leaders to repress the demonstrators. Our approach differs in two main ways:

- we begin by examining the links between elite factional conflict and mass mobilization – to allow us to investigate the role played by coalitional politics between these levels
- we place the 1989 events in the context of the broader history of factional conflict that followed the "restoration" of Deng Xiaoping in 1973 and the series of popular movements that preceded the 1989 student movement; this ongoing conflict gave the movements life

Let us begin with a brief historical account of this broader period and then turn our attention to the events of 1989 proper. We focus on the interaction of elite and mass contention.

Elite and Popular Contention in China

Throughout this volume we have stressed the inextricable link between elite and popular contention. This relationship is reciprocal in nature. Not only do most instances of popular contention grow out of temporally prior episodes of elite conflict; the latter have the capacity to influence these episodes and significantly reshape the broader systems of institutionalized power in which they occur.

While the linkage between elite and popular contention is a ubiquitous feature of social life, its strength varies from polity to polity. Earlier we sought to differentiate regimes along two dimensions: state capacity and protected consultation. All things equal, we expect the relationship between elite and popular contention to be stronger in high-capacity than in low-capacity states, and greater in less than in more democratic states. Combining these dimensions yields an especially stark prediction: *Elite and popular contention will couple most tightly in high-capacity, nondemocratic regimes.* The history of "mass struggle" and factional conflict within party-state circles in China since 1949 would certainly seem to support this prediction. Indeed, within the category of high capacity, nondemocratic states, it is hard to identify a state that exemplifies the principle better than the People's Republic of China (PRC).

The link between elite and popular contention in the PRC is reinforced by two particular features of Chinese political and social life. The first concerns the interdependence of party-state relations. Even forty years after the Communist ascension to power, there was no Chinese state apart from the Chinese Communist Party (CCP). Whoever controlled the Party effectively controlled the state. The second feature is the extraordinary degree of penetration of the party-state apparatus into most realms of Chinese society. To implement and insure conformity with their vision of a true revolutionary society, Mao and other Communist Party elites set about building a highly elaborated system of party-state control, organized hierarchically within all major segments of Chinese society (Oi 1991; Walder 1986; Walder, Li, and Treiman forthcoming). Historically, this system has served to constrain autonomous grassroots political activity, while affording Party elites at all levels an extraordinary vehicle for mobilizing popular support for all manner of state initiatives.

These two features of Chinese politics have, in turn, shaped the character of popular contention in the PRC. Quite simply, for Chinese leaders popular contention – or "mass struggle" in the Chinese lexicon – has long served as a conventional means of waging factional war against their enemies within the Party. The reasons for this are twofold. First, the extent of Party penetration into the everyday lives of ordinary citizens grants elite factions the control necessary to mobilize mass action. This accounts for the "how" of popular contention, but not the "why." *Why* would Party elites risk mobilizing the masses in the first place? Ironically, how the CCP exercises its monopoly on power constrains strategic action by Party elite. Lacking any independent political institutions (e.g., free elections, an autonomous judiciary, or independent trade unions), the Party actually has few vehicles available for resolving internal factional conflicts. The extraordinary control that Party elites enjoy over most sectors of Chinese society makes orchestrated mass struggle a logical response to the problem.

Does this mean that every instance of popular mobilization is orchestrated purposively from above? Reading the work of many Sinologists, one could be forgiven for coming to this conclusion. But in fact, the answer has to be negative. The strength and efficiency of the party-state system is variable by region, thus allowing more grassroots autonomy and greater potential for popular unrest in some areas (e.g., rural more so than urban) than in others. But even where the system is strongest and most elaborated, there is a potential for spontaneous popular mobilization. If there were not, we would be hard pressed to explain the lengths to which the party-state had to go in 1989 to restore order. Nevertheless, a baseline model of popular contention in the PRC should probably proceed on the assumption that most instances of mass action begin life as orchestrated extensions of factional struggles among party-state elites. Certainly the major instances of popular contention one sees in the years following Deng Xiaoping's remarkable resurrection at the CCP's Tenth Congress in September 1973 would seem to conform to this model.

The April 5th Movement

Though remarkable in itself, Deng's return to prominence in 1973 hardly signaled an end to factional conflict within the Party. Instead the period 1973–1977 was marked by a tense war of nerves as Deng, Premier Zhou Enlai, and other Party pragmatists struggled at all levels to regain control of the party-state from the Maoist zealots – especially the so-called Gang of Four – who had gained ascendance during the Cultural Revolution. Until Mao's death in September 1976 the outcome of this intense factional struggle was very much in doubt. In fact, on the eve of Mao's death, it appeared as if the Gang of Four was perhaps more firmly in control than it had been earlier in the period. The control of the Gang of Four appeared to have been solidified in the internecine warfare set in motion by Zhou Enlai's death in January 1976. Though second only to Mao in the Party's pantheon of revolutionary heroes, Zhou's death occasioned none of the solemn mourning and funeral services normally reserved for high-ranking Party officials. The reason: As the very embodiment of pragmatic party politics, Zhou had long been anathema to the Gang of Four.

Elite and popular discontent with the shabby treatment accorded Zhou's death was crystallized on March 25, 1976, when the official Shanghai daily, *Wenhui Bao*, attacked Zhou as a "capitalist roader".[2] Aided by students, workers, and others angered by this attack, Deng's faction struck back. Students and workers in Nanjing took to the streets the day after the attack and sustained protest for nearly a week. Events unfolded a bit later in Beijing, facilitated by the portentous approach of Qing Ming, China's traditional festival honoring the dead. Though official pronouncements railed against the "superstitious affair" and barred workers from taking part in unauthorized mourning ceremonies, the first day of the festival, April 4, saw hundreds of thousands of demonstrators take to

[2] A rhetorical staple of antirightist campaigns, the term "capitalist roader," is used to impugn those who have strayed from the revolutionary path and are suspected of harboring bourgeois or capitalist tendencies.

Tiananmen Square in an outpouring of grief and affection for Zhou and, as the day wore on, increasingly open opposition to the Gang of Four.

The episode escalated dramatically on April 5, 1976, following overnight removal by security forces of the wreaths and tributes the demonstrators had laid at the foot of the Monument to the People's Heroes the previous day. Angered by the action, a crowd of perhaps 10,000 to 15,000 people demanded the return of the wreaths and tributes, and then defied repeated orders to disperse, forcing the Public Security Bureau to clear the square through a series of pitched battles that stretched well into the evening. Official reaction to this first Tiananmen Incident was quick, reflecting in unmistakable terms the close connection between popular contention and the struggle for control of the Party and Chinese state. In a carefully worded statement issued on the night of April 5, Beijing's hardline mayor identified Deng Xiaoping as the "black hand" behind the protest.

Within days of the incident, Deng was once again stripped of all his official posts. However, this second banishment was to prove much shorter than the first. Mao himself died in September 1976 and Deng's pragmatic faction regained the upper hand. Barely a month after Mao's death, the Gang of Four was arrested and subsequently tried in connection with their actions during the Cultural Revolution. Still, reflecting the hierarchical nature of party-state control, Maoist hardliners remained in positions of power throughout the country. What followed in 1977–1978 was a concerted campaign by Deng's faction to root out the Maoists and to reassert broad ideological control over Chinese society. This latter aspect of the campaign involved a dramatic rewriting of recent political history in China.

In the summer of 1978, scores of political prisoners jailed by the Gang of Four were released. Some 200,000 people persecuted during the Anti-Rightist Campaign of 1957 were officially rehabilitated. Next the Party turned to rectifying the position of the protesters in the wake of Zhou Enlai's death. First the Nanjing protests received official praise. Then came the stunning climax of the campaign. On November 15, 1978, the Party resolved that the Tiananmen protests had been

> "a wholly revolutionary action of the masses" against the Gang of Four. For the first time since 1949 the Party had given its blessing to a spontaneous popular action free of official control. "Long live the people!" was the headline of the *People's Daily* editorial. . . . The April Fifth . . . [protesters], wrote the editors, had prevented China from "being turned into a fascist state manipulated by a handful of ambitious leaders." Yesterday's bad elements became today's heroes. [Black and Munro 1993: 40–41]

The authors' claim that the April 5th Movement was "a spontaneous popular action free of official control" may well understate the involvement of Deng's faction in the 1976 demonstrations. Still, the reality of those protests was less significant to democratic elements in Chinese society than the state's reversal of official opinion. In seeming to embrace popular democratic action, Party pragmatists not only delivered a stinging rebuke to their Maoist enemies within the Party, but gave aid and comfort to those who hoped to see Deng's fiscal measures matched by limited political reforms. Ironically, the symbolic end of one conflict marked the beginning of another, this one pitting Party pragmatists against an embryonic democratic movement set in motion by Deng's reforms and his opportunistic embrace of popular protest.

In this struggle, Deng must be credited with a role similar to the one played by Mao in the Cultural Revolution. Deng facilitated the rise of the democratic movement, using it as a weapon in his struggle with hardline Maoist elements within the Party. But wary of real political reform, Deng was at best opportunistic in his response to the movement, encouraging it when it seemed useful to his broader modernizing agenda, but countenancing repression when the movement appeared to threaten the stability of Party rule in China.

The Democracy Wall Movement

This oscillating pattern of elite facilitation and repression is evident in regard to the major democratic moments preceding the 1989 events. The first of these was clearly set in motion by – if it was not an intentional extension of – the climactic anti–Maoist campaign of 1978. Quickly dubbed the Democracy Wall movement, the episode began in earnest just four days after the November 15 *People's Daily* editorial, when a wall poster appeared in the Xidan area of Beijing daring to criticize Mao himself for errors committed in his later years. The brazenness of the poster and the unusual restraint shown by the authorities in dealing with the criticism ushered in a extended period of public debate and dissent. Posters proliferated at Xidan. On November 27, 1978, demonstrators occupied Tiananmen Square for two days of wide-ranging debate and public speech making.

In early December, independent publications began to be offered for sale at Xidan. Though tame by western standards, the magazines and other publications were unprecedented in the People's Republic, creating new avenues for public expression and criticism of established policies. So why were the magazines allowed to survive? The apparent answer again highlights the close connection between elite and popular contention. If the ongoing struggle between Deng's reform faction and Maoist hardliners within the Party encouraged the movement in the first place, the movement in turn appears to have been used, at least initially, by Deng to aid and abet his reform agenda.

More specifically, the protests of late 1978 and early 1979 occurred in the context of two events key to Deng's program and long-term political survival. The first was the Party's Third Plenum in mid–December, 1978, at which Deng was able to solidify his hold on power, in part by drawing on the demonstration of popular support afforded him by the movement. Even more momentous was Deng's historic visit to the United States in January to February 1979, a visit taken to demonstrate his country's pragmatic opening to the West. The visit proved a triumph for Deng, in part because the restraint shown the Democracy Wall movement by the Party helped reassure a skeptical Congress and foreign policy establishment of China's willingness to grant limited political reforms.

With these two events behind him, Deng tacked leftward, both to rein in the movement and to undercut the criticism of Party hardliners. On March 16, 1979, he delivered a speech that reiterated the Party's commitment to Four Cardinal Principles – the socialist road, the people's democratic dictatorship, the leadership of the Communist Party, and Marxism–Leninism–Mao Zedong Thought – and effectively set limits on the kinds of discourse and criticism the Party was prepared to tolerate. Within a matter of days, authorities arrested two of the Movement's most radical leaders (Wei Jingsheng and Ren Wanding) for failing to heed the warnings implicit in Deng's speech. Over the spring, authorities kept a tight reign on the movement; by summer, "the Wall itself was closed down and an alternative venue provided in a park far from the city center where all posters had to be registered with the authorities and their contents approved in advance" (Black and Munro 1993: 52). The movement soldiered on into the fall but, saddled with these new constraints, it was never again a force of any significance.

The Gengshen Reform Period

Popular mobilization developed for a second time in late 1980 following Deng's announcement of his Gengshen reforms.

The centerpiece of the Gengshen program [write Black and Munro] was the 1980 election campaign. Deng explained that the newly elected Congresses were part of "a system of mass supervision so that the masses and ordinary Party members can supervise cadres, especially the leading cadres." Like Mao, Deng saw "democracy" as a useful tool for mobilizing people in support of Party policies. [Black and Munro 1993: 58]

Once again, Beijing's fragile coalition of democratic forces responded to Deng's reform initiative. In its form, no less than its timing, this latest democratic "moment" revealed the by-now familiar stimulus/response relationship between Party and popular politics. Whereas the earlier two episodes had involved little more than public expressions of protest, the 1980 movement took the form of a popular electoral campaign. Veterans of the April 5th and Democracy Wall movements, as well as other prominent reform figures, participated enthusiastically in the one month campaign season that lasted from November 3 until early December. Although few of the progressive candidates were elected, there were many in the broader democratic movement who saw the elections as a watershed for Chinese politics.

This third thaw was to prove short-lived. Within a week of the election, the Party's Central Committee went behind closed doors and hammered out an official directive (with the innocuous title of Document No. 9) outlawing all illegal organizations and publications. Concerned that the election had once again loosed worrisome democratic elements (and mindful of the Solidarity crisis then gripping Party officials in Poland) Party hardliners pushed for and got Deng's backing for the measure. Deng then used the measure to orchestrate a severe crackdown against the tattered remnants of the Democracy Wall movement and progressive election campaigns.

Beijing, December 1986

The third and final democratic episode preceding Tiananmen took the form of a brief, but intense, flurry of protest activity in December of 1986. Though the immediate precipitant to the protest was a speech on December 4th to the students of Hefei by noted astrophysicist (and Party gadfly) Fang Lizhi, the episode coincided with another high-water mark in reform influence within the Party. Earlier that year, in anticipation of the Sixth Plenum, Party officials announced a New Hundred Flowers movement to open up China's scholarly establishment to all manner of outside influences. At the Plenum:

> Deng himself gave the keynote speeches, resuscitating the failed "Gengshen spirit" of 1980, and Hu Yaobang [Deng's longtime protégé and designated successor] orchestrated the attack [on the hardliners]. . . . But perhaps the most outspoken of Hu Yaobang's associates was the Party's new propaganda chief, Zhu Houze. . . . Zhu was the only senior cadre who dared to tackle the thorny issue of the degree to which China should risk what the leftists called "wholesale Westernization." He told his colleagues, "No one single country or people can monopolize all the best fruits of thought, culture, and technology." Thinly coded, this meant borrowing not only the money and scientific know-how of the West, but elements of its political system too. [Black and Munro 1993: 91]

It was in this context that the student protests of December 1986 were launched. If Fang's speech provided the spark, it certainly was not one he had intended. But the students seized on one line from his speech in which he had rhetorically reminded the students that: "Democracy is not a favor bestowed from above . . . [but] won through people's own efforts."

Once under way the protests spread rapidly. By mid–December twelve cities were affected, including the key industrial city of Shanghai. With workers in that city threatening to join in, Deng again took decisive action. Ever mindful of the delicate factional balance needed to sustain his economic reforms, Deng acted to preempt the spread of what had come, in Party circles, to be known as the Polish disease. Democratic movements rooted in serious linkages between workers and students (or other elements of bourgeois reform) were to be repressed at all costs. The costs in this case included the expulsion of Fang Lizhi from the Party, the selective prosecution of activist workers, and most dramatically, the forced retirements of the Party's two most prominent reformers, Hu Yaobang and Zho Houze.

Beijing, Spring 1989

We have accorded the events of 1976–1988 as much space as we have because the 1989 movement is only comprehensible when viewed in the light of both Deng's sporadic (if opportunistic) embrace of political reform over the previous twelve years, and of the democratic episodes that greeted Deng's moves. Indeed, in most respects, the 1989 movement is very much a piece with the four previous episodes. Recall that, in its origins, that movement resembled nothing so much as the April 5th movement. The earlier movement was set in motion by the popular expression of grief and anger that accompanied the death of Zhou Enlai and the disrespect accorded his passing by the Gang of Four and their allies. It was the death of the discredited reformer, Hu Yaobang, on April 15, 1989, that set events in motion this time. Then, as before, the movement began with thousands of ordinary Beijing citizens entering Tiananmen Square on April 16 and 17 to lay wreaths and tributes to Hu Yaobang at the foot of the Monument to the People's Heroes.

But if the origins of Beijing Spring recall the April 5th movement, there were important differences. Most significantly, the earlier movement occurred in the context of a clear factional struggle between Maoist hardliners and Deng's more pragmatic faction. Despite efforts to read a similar factional struggle into the events of 1989, the evidence for such a conflict is weak at best. We will review this evidence below. For now, the important point is that whereas the events of March to April 1976 were almost certainly encouraged – if not orchestrated – by Deng and his allies, the available evidence does not support a similar role for Zhao Ziyang, the Party's most visible reformer, in 1989.

An important logistical difference was also evident in 1989. Those who had demonstrated in 1976 never occupied the Square. But this time, fearing that security forces would once again try to remove the tributes overnight, thousands of the mourners/protesters occupied the Square on the night of the 17th to prevent the reoccurrence. The battle for Tiananmen Square and, by extension, for the Party and Chinese state had been joined.

This chapter's analytical purpose precludes a detailed accounting of the events that took place over the next seven weeks. The broad outlines of the episode are reasonably well known and available elsewhere (Black and Munro 1993; Brook 1998; Calhoun 1994; Zhao 1997, 2000). In quick summary, the students occupied the Square more or less continuously from April 17 until the climactic events of June 3–4. This seven-week period was marked by a seemingly mixed set of signals from Party officials, leading to the widespread belief among observers and demonstrators alike that a major struggle for control of the party-state was in progress. Party officials acted with uncharacteristic restraint in the days leading up to, then during the official state funeral for Hu Yaobang. Not only were the students allowed to occupy the Square throughout this period, but were permitted to cross police lines on the day of the funeral to present a petition intended for Premier Li Peng.

Three days later, however, all restraint vanished when official Chinese television (CCTV) broadcast a strongly worded editorial (intended for publication in the April 26 *People's Daily*) from Beijing's hardline Mayor, Chen Xitong. The editorial described the movement as a planned antigovernment, antisocialist conspiracy, threatening grave consequences to all those who continued to support the protests. The editorial only angered students all the more and helped to revive the flagging movement. April 27 saw the largest demonstration to date, as an estimated 150,000 students defied the government directive and marched past the Square (Brook 1998: 31).

Having failed to short circuit the movement through intimidation, Party officials moderated their tone over the next few weeks. Drawing the most attention during this period were the two conciliatory speeches delivered by Zhao Ziyang on May 3 and 4. The second of these, to an important meeting of the Asian Development Bank, praised the students for their basic loyalty and support of the system and simultaneously urged more openness in the official Chinese media. Building on the goodwill engendered by Zhao's speeches, it looked as if the movement was winding down, with most student participants satisfied to quit the Square and accept the government's offer to engage in an official "dialogue" scheduled for May 14. With Soviet President Mikhail Gorbachev scheduled to arrive the very next day for the first Sino–Soviet summit in thirty years, the apparent agreement with the students would have been welcome news to party-state officials.

Those officials – and most movement adherents – had not counted on radicalization, the resolve of a relatively small number of student activists to sustain the occupation of the Square. They did so by launching a hunger strike two days before Gorbachev's scheduled arrival. Mindful of the embarrassment and disruption that such a campaign would occasion during Gorbachev's visit, Party officials tried through intermediaries to persuade the strikers to abandon their plan and quit the Square. But the restraint shown during these negotiations further reinforced the radicals' belief that reformers were exercising considerable influence within party-state circles.

Official restraint continued throughout Gorbachev's visit. But far from confirming a major factional split within the Party, the restraint seems to have been the result of a desire on the part of state officials to see the summit come off without incident. This interpretation accords well with the government's actions on the night of May 19–20. Just a day after

Gorbachev's departure from Beijing, a Chinese military force of at least 100,000 attempted to retake the Square by force, only to be rebuffed by citizens acting spontaneously to protect the students (Brook 1998: 70). After a tense forty-five hours of military–citizen standoffs throughout Beijing, the troops were ordered back to base. When coupled with the surreal stalemate of the next two weeks, this action lent further credence to the factional struggle interpretation. Then came the climactic events of June 3–4. On that night, troops broke through the makeshift barricades and desperate legions of Beijing citizens, who for two weeks had blocked the major roads leading to Tiananmen, and retook the Square amidst much chaos and violence (see Brook 1998: ch. 5–6 for a detailed account of the events of fateful night). The quasi-revolutionary situation ended rapidly.

The 1989 Chinese student movement displays significant linkage between elite and popular contention. Like the episodes summarized earlier, the mass mobilization that occurred during the spring of 1989 appears at first glance to have issued from elite contention. But it involves far more autonomy of the grassroots struggle than characterized earlier episodes. The movement did not stem from deep factional divisions within the Party. On the contrary, few signs of factional division emerged during the struggle. That fact helps account not only for the tragic resolution of the episode, but also for the relative political stability seen since 1989. Let us explore further the apparent contradiction between 1989's events and general characteristics of Chinese contention. We take up the connection between elite and mass action first.

Party Struggle and Mass Action

There are a number of important ways in which the 1989 movement might be seen as the product of prior elite contention. First and foremost, it developed within the broad "democratic community" nurtured by Deng's reform program and the series of popular mobilizations reviewed above. Though opposed to explicitly political reforms, Deng's modernizing vision required an expansion and liberalization of certain institutional spheres (e.g., education, state-sponsored research, and publishing). In turn, the loose networks that developed within and between these spheres facilitated the rise of an amorphous democratic community united by a desire to see China's economic reforms matched by a comparable expansion in political freedoms. Besides its functional origins in China's modernizing economy, the community's contentious capacity also owed much to Deng's opportunistic facilitation of the earlier democratic episodes. That is, by encouraging these prior democratic moments, Deng and his allies had fostered hope among the democrats as well as invaluable experience in the art of mass politics.

The immediate precipitant of the 1989 movement also reflects the close connection between mass and elite politics in the PRC. It was, after all, the death of the reputed reformer, Hu Yaobang, that first set the students in motion. By taking to the streets to honor Hu, the students were signaling their support for the kinds of political reforms he was thought to have favored. More important, they were also aligning themselves with Hu's presumptive political heirs, most notably Zhao Ziyang, and his principal aide Bao Tong.

In the time-honored tradition of Chinese Communist politics, for their part, Zhao, Bao and other reform minded Party officials probably did try to use the movement both to press for limited political reforms and to advance their standing within Party circles. Toward these ends, Zhao Ziyang seized the occasion of the high profile meeting of the Asian Development Bank in Beijing to deliver a keynote address in which he legitimized many of the student's concerns (e.g., official corruption), while pledging to "use democratic and legal avenues to resolve [the conflict]" (Black and Munro 1993: 167). The fact that the speech was delivered on the highly charged seventieth anniversary of the May 4 student movement only added drama and significance to Zhao's remarks.[3] In a related action several days earlier, Zhao had reversed an earlier Party directive, and authorized the editors of nine major newspapers to provide full and objective coverage of the student demonstrations, adding that the Party was sympathetic to many of the student aims. It is hard to read these actions as anything other than a set of strategic moves designed to embolden the students, galvanize broad public support for the movement, and make it more difficult for the hardliners to repress the demonstrations.

But why would Zhao play with fire in this way? Black and Munro (1993: 164) offer an explanation:

[3] On May 4, 1919, thousands of students gathered in Beijing to protest the terms of the Versailles Peace Conference and, more significantly, to call for a general societal embrace of the Western ideals of democracy and science. This unprecedented mobilization of Chinese students was subsequently appropriated by the Communists and, later, by "democratic forces," as a key event in the heritage of each.

> When Zhao looked out at the crowds in the street, he saw a source of political leverage . . . a little, perhaps, as Deng Xiaoping had seen the crowds at the Democracy Wall in 1978. Zhao felt that his hand was strengthened by the coming anniversary of the May Fourth movement, which was certain to mark a new climax for the student movement. This year the date was important for another reason, too: Hundreds of international bankers would flock to the Great Hall of the People on that day to hear Zhao's keynote speech to the Asian Development Bank. He felt confident that the hard-liners would not risk a crackdown at such a time.

There is even suggestive evidence that Zhao's aide, Bao Tong, leaked word of the Party's plan to impose martial law and forcibly clear the square on May 20, thereby allowing ordinary Beijing residents time to erect barricades leading to Tiananmen Square. This advance word thwarted the Party's plan and prolonged the crisis for another two weeks. Whatever the truth of this incident, Party hard-liners certainly believed the charge and used it to imprison Bao Tong for three years for "leaking state secrets" to movement forces.

Finally, whatever the reality of the situation, in the course of the movement, observers and activists alike came to *believe* that a climactic battle was underway for control of the Party. The battle, it was believed, was being waged by reformers such as Zhao, against both Deng's pragmatists, and Maoist hard-liners still opposed to Deng's modernizing (read: capitalistic) reforms. It was in this shared and highly charged context that the movement unfolded. It was this popular view that shaped the interpretation of the mixed messages coming from the Party during the struggle, messages that in their inconsistency only reinforced the popular attribution of political opportunity to the episode.

In contrast to that view, we see little evidence of titanic factional struggle in the events of April to June. In his book, Dingxin Zhao (2000) makes a persuasive case against Party factionalism as the key to the movement. The centerpiece of Zhao's argument is a careful analysis of the backgrounds and actions of thirty-one key Party figures during the Tiananmen struggle. The thirty-one include all seventeen Politburo members at the time as well as fourteen "veterans" known in 1989 to still be highly influential in party-state circles. Zhao concludes from the data that there is little hard evidence to attribute strong reform views to anyone on the list other than Zhao Ziyang. But if not factional struggle, then how do we explain the fits and starts and mixed signals conveyed by the regime during the seven-week episode? Our answer is straightforward: Contingent events and the mechanisms they activated, not factional struggle, conspired to constrain party-state response to the movement at three critical points in the unfolding episode.

The first "fit" in the government's response to the crisis came between April 17 and 22 when funeral preparations and the actual ceremony prevented officials from aggressively repressing the movement. The first "start" in party-state response came in the immediate aftermath of the funeral with the April 25 broadcast of the aggressive *People's Daily* editorial. A return to a more accommodating line came during the two-week period defined by the meetings of the Asian Development Bank (May 4) and the Sino–Soviet summit (May 15–18). But the planning for the initial May 19 military crackdown was clearly already going on during Gorbachev's visit. The same applies to the climactic "invasion" of Beijing on June 3–4. As Brook (1998) argues in his authoritative book on the assault, the final lull in official response to the crisis was probably owed to nothing so much as the logistical requirements of the campaign.

Regime Defection in the Chinese Student Movement

To apply the concept of "regime defection" to China requires that we understand the distinctive way in which power is structured in the PRC. Here the contrast between China and Nicaragua is instructive. Nicaragua's ruling class had long been comprised of a fairly broad coalition of the nation's economic elite (Booth 1982; Paige 1997). Overlaid on this economic foundation were a set of nominal opposing political factions, embodied most notably in the Conservative and Liberal Nationalist (PLN) Parties. Within these overlapping spheres there had always been rivalries, tensions, and coherent divisions. Prior to the 1970s, however, these cleavages had never been so strong as to threaten the stability of the Somoza regime. But by the end of the earthquake episode and the murder of Chamorro, however, signs of elite defection were clear. By then, the regime had become more a liability than an asset to most of the ruling class. The result was the gradual defection of more and more elements of the regime's traditional ruling coalition, reluctant alignment with the Sandinistas and other opposition forces, and the eventual overthrow of Somoza.

As our analysis of factional strife in 1989 Beijing suggests, nothing resembling this pattern of defection from the regime was present there. This is not to say that the students were alone; broad segments of the Chinese population showed sympathy for the demonstrators. Among them were small but significant groups of independent workers, a healthy representation of academics and affiliated professions, a significant, if unknown, proportion of Beijing's ordinary citizens, and, for a time, even representatives of the official Chinese media. What was crucially missing was any significant representation by the one segment of Chinese society that has, since 1949, controlled the state and, indeed, all aspects of Chinese life – the Chinese Communist Party. Though Zhao Ziyang, Bao Tong, and others within the Party clearly had sympathies with the students and tried, in various ways, to use the movement to advance their own agendas, none of the reformers can be said to have defected to the ranks of the insurgents.

Significant defections from one other segment of Chinese society might well have altered the course of the episode. We refer to the Chinese military, which remained overwhelmingly loyal to the regime during the crisis, thereby short-circuiting one of the key mechanisms evident in revolutionary outcomes. Brook explains that

> Many Democracy Movement activists in May assumed that the professionalization of the PLA officer corps, combined with appeals to noble traditions of serving the people, would inhibit the Army from coming to Li Peng's defense. . . . The error in the Chinese assumption was to neglect the decisive power of the senior officer corps. The PLA is still run by men who owe their power and allegiance to Deng Xiaoping's faction within the Communist Party. Their allegiance is not abstract; most of them personally served in Deng's Second Field Army during the 1940s. [1998: 206]

Why elite-mass solidarity failed to emerge in China is a question that is beyond the scope of this chapter. What we can say is that none of the three mechanisms invoked in accounting for the success of the Nicaraguan revolution were triggered in the events of 1989, nor indeed, over the course of the thirteen-year series of democratic moments reviewed here. If we view the Party as affording the regime its crucial social-structural foundation, the relevant question with respect to the infringement of elite interests is whether Deng's economic (or other reform) policies in any discernible way undermined the power and privilege traditionally enjoyed by Party members. The clear answer is "no."

Similarly, in stark contrast to Somoza's capacity for suddenly imposing grievances on a broad and undifferentiated range of targets, Party authorities generally avoided the kind of arbitrary and crude forms of repression and self-aggrandizing policies that were Somoza's hallmark. The Tiananmen massacre could arguably be thought of as the one exception to this pattern. But even here, the regime clearly tried over a period of weeks to defuse the situation without recourse to force. When it finally did make use of force, the actual loss of life was relatively small, so far as we can tell (see Black and Munro 1993: ch. 15; Brook 1998: ch. 6) suggesting a degree of restraint consistently absent in Nicaragua. Finally, despite diffuse international support for the Chinese students and scathing condemnation of the June 3–4 government crackdown, no foreign government or major international body ever decertified the regime in any significant way.

Conclusions

What else can we learn from comparing these two cases of a successful and a failed revolution? No doubt plenty. But in closing we emphasize two main factors: the first relating to the role of contingency in the dynamics of contention; and the second to the analogies between revolutionary and other contentious processes.

Contingency and Context

Against the long-standing structural bias in the field of comparative revolutions, William Sewell (1985, 1996) has called for more attention to liminal events, citing the assault on the Bastille (and the subsequent battle over the meaning of the event) as exhibit A in his case for a more "eventful" analysis of political contention. In both Nicaragua and Beijing, as we have seen repeatedly, there were, first, contingent events, second, strategic leadership decisions that sometimes had unexpected effects, and third, an intersection of causal mechanisms that led to outcomes that could not have been predicted with either structural or cultural determinism.

With respect to contingent events, two in particular constituted crucial switch points that foreclosed some paths and opened others:

- the Managua earthquake and Somoza's kleptomaniacal response to it
- the death of Hu Yaobang and the near-simultaneity to it of Gorbachev's visit

Both of these events produced sudden and unpredictable decisions, high levels of uncertainty, and new combinations of threat and opportunity. In Nicaragua the earthquake produced unprecedented opportunities for corruption and the exercise of monopoly power. In China, Hu Yaobang's death placed severe constraints on the regime's social control options. Both responses triggered mobilization – the first through threat and the second through opportunity. The quiet mobilization of the portion of the Nicaraguan business elite that was shut out from profiting from reconstruction contracts brought many into opposition to a regime that had succored their interests in the past, while the opportunity of Hu's funeral gave the Beijing students the chance to take advantage of the state's restraint.[4]

But contingent events are not only happenstance; they trigger mechanisms that shape the subsequent dynamics of contention. Somoza's crackdown aggrieved a portion of the populace that had provided important support for his regime, thus encouraging defection by growing numbers of the Nicaraguan bourgeoisie; the Chinese Party elite's hesitation to use repression for many weeks was attributed as an opportunity by the students. Both developments triggered other mechanisms: The state of seige in Nicaragua hastened the Carter administration's decertification of Somoza; while by allowing the Tiananmen conflict to stretch out for five long weeks through the Sino–Soviet summit, the Chinese leaders created an appearance of divided sovereignty, encouraging ever widening circles of popular support, but also providing time for conflicts to develop among the students.

Finally, much of the contingency unfolding in our narratives results from the concatenation of different mechanisms. In the interest in demonstrating our mechanism-and-process-based approach, we have generally left the issue of mechanism-interaction to one side. (We return to it in Chapter 10.) But even brief reflection on our two cases shows how similar mechanisms can yield very different outcomes when they combine with other mechanisms. Consider radicalization, a mechanism that we have seen in many of our episodes. The exasperation of the Nicaraguan bourgeoisie combined with regime decertification by Washington that allowed a powerful crossclass coalition to develop with the lower-class-based Sandinistas. But in China, in the absence of decertification, the radicalization of a portion of the Tiananmen demonstrators weakened the coalition and helped turn a revolutionary situation into a revolutionary failure. Like

[4] As Fang Lizhi pointedly noted:

> Hu Yaobang himself wasn't that important, and the regard heaped on him was excessive. But in China, leader's death serves as an excuse for people to assemble. The Party can't very well tell the people not to mourn a Party leader! Since a funeral is the only [culturally legitimate] situation when people can assemble, you take advantage of the opportunity. [quoted in Brook 1998: 21]

American antislavery and Spanish democratization, both episodes contained strong mechanisms of radicalization; but in the presence of other mechanisms the one led to revolutionary success and the other to revolutionary disaster.

Culture and the Comparative Study of Revolutions

This takes us to the lessons of these two stories for the comparative study of revolution. Returning to the generations of revolutionary research we sketched at the outset, we see nothing resembling the rigid stage theory of the first generation of scholars in either episode. Nor is there much trace of the structural strain identified by the second generation. Neither does the structural determinism of the third school explain in any probabilistic sense the events we have studied. Our response to the fourth generation of culturally sensitive scholarship is more nuanced. On the one hand, our brief summary of key events in both cases underscored the central importance of cultural processes and human agency in the episodes we have studied. Where we part company with our more resolutely culturalist colleagues is in asserting that history, culture, and interpretive processes operate not like external shrouds but through the interactions of the major players in each drama.

Consider the case of Tiananmen. History, culture, and international political and economic factors combined to shape the strategic interpretations and actions available to Chinese authorities. Historically, the parallels between the April 5th movement and the events following Hu Yaobang's death could not have been lost on Deng, Li Peng, and his allies. The rituals and normative conventions governing the deaths of high Party officials acted as a second set of strategic constraints on the regime. But to these historical and cultural constraints must be added the strategic aims of those in power. These interests and the political and economic relationships implicated in their realization acted as a final influence on the interpretations and actions of movement adherents and opponents alike. It was not "Chinese culture" acting as a deus ex machina, but the impact of history, culture, and strategy on the interactions of the combatants that produced the outcomes we have studied.

History, culture, and strategic calculations came together in the substantive and symbolic stakes surrounding the Sino–Soviet summit. Substantively, China hoped to put the long period of conflict with the Soviets behind it and perhaps even to take advantage of the economic opportunities and markets expected to open up in a liberalizing USSR. But the very process of liberalization, which promised these new markets and made the summit possible, posed dangers to the regime. Much as they disparaged the Soviets for going soft on dissidence, Party officials could ill afford to appear out of step with their long-time rival. Symbolically, the stakes were high as well. Having long criticized the Soviet Union for deviating from the "true socialist path," Party officials were loath to initiate a bloody crackdown in the full media glare assured by the summit. Nothing would call into question the regime's claim to be a "true" People's state more than a massive campaign of repression directed against the people.

Revolutions are not A Single Thing. A rounded account of contentious dynamics in the Beijing episode requires us to pay simultaneous attention to long-term structural shifts (e.g., economic liberalization, regime realignment), to the cultural framing of each player's interpretations of opportunity and risk, and to the short-term strategic interaction around contingent events. But structure, culture, and strategic calculation are not outside of the mechanisms of contention but the raw material for their action and interaction. In the next two chapters, we apply this perspective to two other broad historic processes – nationalism and democratization.

8

Nationalism, National Disintegration, and Contention

"Nationalism," writes Arthur N. Waldron, "in general is a powerful and comprehensible idea. Yet while it defines general situations, it is not very useful in explicating specific events" (1985: 427). The "adjective 'nationalist' has been attached to people, movements, and sentiments in a way that is usually taken (without explanation) as distinguishing each of them meaningfully from some other variety." Waldron's analytical stance suffices so long as we take no interest in the dynamics of nationalism or in its interaction with other forms of public politics. Nationalism is part of struggle – contentious politics, in our lexicon. As we have argued repeatedly, we cannot understand any episode of contentious politics as the expression of any single discourse, ideology, or nominally distinct form of contention.

To understand why nationalism arises, we must understand its varied political sources. We need to know when and why they sometimes converge in nationalist outcomes. We must also ask to what extent nationalist episodes are the result of structural factors, institutional constraints, and cultural constants, and to what extent they emerge from cascades of contention. When we do so, we are likely to find that nationalist outcomes intersect with motives, movements, and state policies having little to do with nationalism. We are thus likely to find similar mechanisms to those that drive other forms of contention. As a corollary, we should discover that similar mechanisms underlie what history has coded as contrary nationalist processes – such as national disintegration and nation-state building.

This chapter focuses on the apparently contrary processes of national unification and national disintegration, using two large, portentous, dissimilar episodes – nineteenth-century Italian unification and twentieth-century Soviet disintegration – to identify mechanisms and processes of contention that recur in a wide variety of national and ethnic settings. When Italy unified in the 1860s, it occurred through an apparently lightning-fast process of annexation of a plethora of petty states to Piedmont–Sardinia, producing a weak, if centralized state and an imperfectly integrated elite. Yet the next 140 years would see little separatist nationalism – either on the peninsula or on the two big islands, Sicily and Sardinia, with their distinct languages and cultures.

In contrast, when Russian tsarism fell, the Soviet Union under Lenin and Stalin built a monolithic state welded together by a single party, in which regional languages acquired official standing and regional political elites trained in Moscow and returned to their regions as Moscow's agents. These same elites formed the basis of state disintegration that occurred every bit as rapidly as the Italian state came into being, causing even more astonishment. How the once titanic Soviet monolith disintegrated along the lines of once weak national boundaries in many ways forms the converse of how the weak and dispersed Italian state took shape.

We will find similar mechanisms at work on these two ostensibly contradictory political processes. Within each, we will see combinations of opportunity spirals, identity shift, competition, and brokerage. That similar mechanisms combine differently in different contexts will not surprise readers of our book; that they are found in such patently contrasting political processes as nation-state building and national disintegration renders the comparison more interesting and more provocative. It is more provocative because it suggests that standard ways of coding major historical episodes depend more on political outcomes than on the processes involved. It is more interesting because it shows that we gain more explanatory leverage by examining the mechanisms that drive a wide range of contentious episodes than by classifying them as if they operated according to their own distinct laws.

Nationalism in Discourse, Nationalism in Practice

Nationalism is most often analyzed as a sentiment or a belief, but less often as a species of contentious politics. Even Miroslov Hroch, who identifies a Phase C of nationalism – the phase of mass national movements – sees such mass based action "merely as an externalization of nationalist ways of thinking brought into being well before the onset of nationalist action" (Hroch 1985: 22–4). Like Mark Beissinger (forthcoming: 9), we argue against such cognitive determinism, claiming not only that the passage from Phase B to Phase C is problematic and interesting, but that even the nationalist identities and predispositions Hroch finds only in Phase B form interactively in the contentious politics of nationalist episodes.

But we go further. Even when it is described as a "movement," little attention is given in the literature on nationalism to its resemblance to and interaction with other forms of contention. Definitions frequently turn on the subjective/objective dichotomy of national feeling, on the imagination of nations, and on good versus bad nationalism – all discursive, rather than interactive properties. A large number of scholars have been agitated over the question of whether the nation is essential or invented (Eley and Suny 1996) and whether it corresponds to language, ethnicity, or communal groups. We sidestep the subjective/objective debate, agree that nations are imagined, but think that this is a less interesting question than nationalism's interaction with other conflicts and other forms of politics – both prescribed and contentious – as it takes root in different political contexts.

In its most general terms, nationalism involves the twin claims that distinct nations have the right to possess distinct states, and that rulers of distinct states have the right to impose national cultural definitions on inhabitants of those states. Nationalist politics therefore divides into two interdependent forms: attempts of self-identified members of nations that do not currently control their own states to acquire independent states, and efforts of rulers to make their definitions of national interest and culture prevail within their own territories. In either case, obviously, political disputes concern both who has rights to control what territories, and who has rights to speak for what nations. Following Haas (1986) in large part, we proceed from the following definitions:

A nation is a body of individuals who claim to be united by some set of characteristics that differentiate them from outsiders, who either strive to create or to maintain their own state.[1]

A nation-state is a political entity whose inhabitants claim to be a single nation and wish to remain one.

[1] Haas uses the modifier "socially-mobilized," a term we prefer to avoid because of its overlap with our term "mobilization." The modifier is crucial to Haas' theory because of his embrace of the idea that nationalism relates to modernity and leads to rationalization.

Nationalism is a claim by a group of people that they ought to constitute a nation or that they already are one; but this generic category divides into:

a. National sentiment, a claim that people on one side of a categorical boundary ought to exercise self-determination at some point in the future;

b. Nationalist ideology, a body of arguments and ideas about a nation advocated by a group of writers and activists embodying a political program for the achievement of a nation-state; and,

c. A national myth, the core of ideas and claims that most citizens accept about a nation-state beyond their political divisions when a nation-state is successfully created.

A nationalist movement (and here we add to Haas' definitions) is a struggle between (a) activists that embrace a nationalist ideology and (b) states and/or other groups which either oppose or are indifferent towards their claims.

Language, Ethnicity and Nationalism

Haas gets us this far without tying nationalism irrevocably to either language or ethnicity – although these are frequently the content of national sentiments, ideologies, myths, and movements. But like nationalism itself, their centrality is contingent and linked to the process of nation-state building. Through contentious politics language, ethnicity, or other symbols of categorical distinctiveness become mobilized forms of political identity.

Take language. According to an old jibe, a language is a dialect that has acquired its own army. At least for European experience over the last few centuries, the correlation is clear but the lines of causation are not. While some linguistic groups created states and endowed them with armies, others shaped and consolidated the national languages and cultures that were then claimed to be the origin and justification for those borders and those armies. In states such as France, England, and Italy, languages that were regarded as standard and were learned in school were made into favored means of communication, while poor linguistic cousins, such as Breton and Auvergnat, Welsh and Cornish, Sicilian and Ladino, lost ground. In the eastern part of the continent, small groups of intellectuals shaped "national" languages out of old dialects and imagined them to have been eternal.

However important a common language is to nation and state building, the idea of a single linguistic group for every state is peculiarly recent. Though the preference for monolingualism had emerged in Europe by 1800, most governments did nothing dramatic about it for the next fifty years, and early nineteenth-century national movements worried less about linguistic conformity than about national viability (Hobsbawm 1990: ch. 1). If there were agreed-upon criteria allowing a people to be classified as a nation, they were three: historic association with an existing state or with one with a fairly lengthy past; the existence of a long-established cultural elite; or "a proven capacity for conquest" (Hobsbawm 1990: 37–38). The principle that states be defined by distinct languages is inscribed neither in history nor in nature.

Nor has the mapping of language into state power always prevailed. The Great Frederick of Prussia and Catherine of Russia spoke French to their peers, while Manchu long remained the confidential language of China's Qing rulers. Cavour spoke French more comfortably than Italian, while the ruler of the Kingdom of the Two Sicilies was most comfortable speaking the local Neapolitan vernacular. Even today, French, Italian and, to a lesser extent, Romansch flourish alongside German (itself coupled with numerous local variants of Schwyzerdütsch) as full-fledged languages of Switzerland. Swiss practices reveal the contingent nature of language as a criterion of nationality.

Nor have minority languages disappeared at an equal rate for all purposes in all fully established nation states. Sicilian and Venetian survived in united Italy for generations as household languages. In many recently independent countries, a formula of "two +/– one" languages seems to be emerging, rather than the linguistic homogenization that was expected to prevail there (Laitin 1992, 2000). Of the major European and European-derived nation-states only France and Israel have made a fetish of linguistic purity (Hobsbawm 1990: 21).

A similar ambiguity relates nationality to ethnicities. Ethnicity is a constructed claim to common origin, shared culture, and linked fate but, unlike nationality, it affords adherents no necessary political standing and has a shifting and nonessential relation to nationality. "Nationalism and ethnicity are related," write Stephen Cornell and Douglas Hartmann, "but they are not the same. What most clearly distinguishes nationalism from ethnicity is its political agenda" (Cornell and Hartman 1998: 37). Like other identities, nationality and ethnicity refer to social relations rather than individual attributes, rest on socially organized categories, and involve claims to collective rights-cum-obligations.

In the case of ethnicity, claims to rights and obligations vary in degree and type, from passing recognition of kinship all the way to legal singling out for special treatment, negative or positive. Nationalist intellectuals, clerics, language teachers, bureaucrats, soldiers, and rent-seekers have at one time or another hitched their wagon to an ethnic star, seeking to elevate it into a nationality by distinguishing it from others. Others have constructed ethnicity as the foundation for an existing state they hoped to erect in their own images. Still others have cordially ignored it, building national identity on criteria that emerge from common life together, on common suspicion of neighbors, or on state-made boundaries.

Statebuilding and Nationality

But in the case of nationality, rights and obligations connect people to each other on one side of a categorical boundary – a state boundary – and to agents of the state that defends the boundary. Not all processes of nationality construction are purposive; many are the unintended products of states' institutional development or of national expansion. Long before invention of the term "nationalism," the rise of high-capacity states and high-intensity economies remade the world's cartography. Those twin processes standardized national languages, imposed a few of those languages as tools of commerce and empire, swept many widely spoken idioms to the peripheries of public life, and produced substantial territories in which most people only spoke a single recognized language. As they created uniform and standardized categories of citizens and their duties, states created national languages. As they created national languages, nationally certified cultural forms were evolved. As these forms were created, others were relegated to the categories of ethnicity, dialect, and folklore (Duara 1996).

Nineteenth-century Europeans followed a model set earlier by the conquering French, who under expansionist revolutionary and Napoleonic regimes encouraged local groups of patriots to rebel in emulation of the French nation. When these succeeded, they established French-style governments on conquered territory, no more wishing to stimulate nationalism in these areas than to accord them real autonomy. But nation building was infectious. After the French retreat and the restoration of the old regimes, small groups of conspirators – many of them former administrators for the French – developed ideologies of republicanism and democracy. In a classical example of opportunity spirals and modeling, state-*led* French nationalism gave rise to state-*seeking* national movements on the territories that the French defined and led to state disingegration through the same processes that produced new states.

State-led nationalism incited state-seeking nationalism in three ways:

First, by generating resistance and demands for political autonomy on the part of culturally distinctive populations living within the perimeters of a nationalizing state.

Second, by proselytizing among culturally related citizens of neighboring states – or at least providing support for their aspirations.

Third, by providing clear, advantageous models of statehood for the envious gaze of would-be leaders of stateless would-be nations.

Newer forms of state-led nationalism followed, competing with state-seeking nationalists by combining versions of their own discourses with the legitimacy and the military and administrative resources of existing states – such as the Savoy-ruled Kingdom of Piedmont–Sardinia and the old Tsarist Empire.

Within Europe, picking apart of the Austro–Hungarian and Ottoman empires produced multiple opportunities for both kinds of nationalism. The former threatened the hegemony of traditional states and empires, leading in part to their breakup and in part – as in the Turkish empire – to redefinition as national states. Outside of Europe the same models of state formation increasingly held sway in the Americas and East Asia. State-seeking nationalism led to state disintegration and to the redefinition of dynastic states and empires as nation-states. We see their interaction in the two cases chosen for analysis in this chapter.

Nationalism and Contention

What has all this to do with contentious politics? Plenty, though you wouldn't know it by reading much of the work on nationalism.

For reasons that have more to do with intellectual fashion than with history or politics, both traditional students of nationalism such as Hayes (1966) and Kohn (1955) and their modern successors such as Anderson (1991) and Balibar (1991) have focused on nationalism as a form of discourse. They have seldom troubled to discriminate among Haas' national sentiments, ideologies, and myths and have cordially ignored the politics of nationalist contention as well as its intersection with other forms of politics. In the case of the traditionalists, this took the form of studying the explicit ideologies of nationalist theorists, though national sentiments were frequently canvassed too.

In the case of modernists, nationalism as discourse indifferently conflated sentiments, ideologies and myths under a social constructionist umbrella. Unlike the case of traditionalists – who invariably focused on nationalist ideologues – it was often difficult to tell *who* was doing the construction – ideologues, movements, or the analysts themselves! In both cases, it was not always clear whether the construction was occurring in people's heads, in their classrooms, or in interaction with significant others. Where contention does figure, "culture wars" take the place of political struggle (Smith 1996: 123), removing nationalism from politics. "Constructivism," observes Mark Beissinger, "has generally not interrogated the ways in which collective action itself may be constitutive of nationhood" (Beissinger forthcoming: 10).

The nationalism literature has also engaged in the kind of sectoral partitioning of the world of contentious politics that we reject. Consider our second case – the disintegration of the Soviet Union. "*Glasnost'*," writes Mark Beissinger, "did not begin as a nationalist explosion. It became one. . . . The first major eruption of nationalism to occur in the *glasnost'* period did not take place until almost a year-and-a-half after *glasnost'* had begun . . . and had nothing to do with the secessionist issues that ultimately came to dominate the agendas of nationalist movements" (Beissinger forthcoming: 47). As Beissinger's work shows, we will learn more about nationalism by connecting it to other forms of contention than by segregating it for specialized treatment.

Our object here is not to survey the world's nationalisms, but to connect nationalism more securely to contentious politics in general. To do so, we begin with the contexts of nationalist movements in each of our widely diverse cases: Italy on the eve of national unification and the Soviet Union as it tottered on the edge of disintegration.

When Italy unified in the 1860s the question of languages other than Italian was never considered and the administrative model chosen was designed to annex a dispersed and disconnected plethora of petty states to Piedmont. The national state that emerged was centralized but weak – precisely what might have been expected, other things being equal – to give rise to waves of peripheral resentments and mobilizations. But though revolution was an Italian household word in 1860 (Grew 1996), movements of regional nationalism have been both weak and sporadic, and not even the 1960s cycle of protest produced a serious regional revolt. How did Italy keep an imperfectly integrated peninsula and two distinct island cultures together in the absence of a strong state? This puzzle can only be solved by examining the political interactions surrounding the process of state making and the mechanisms through which the new state was constructed and national unity maintained.

In contrast, for over seventy years the Soviet Union organized much of its regional government around principles of nationality. Regions such as Tajikistan and Uzbekistan were named for one of their major populations, and languages of those nominal nationalities given formally equal standing with Russian. Moscow-trained party and administrative leaders were recruited from each region's putative nationality, and systems of regional patronage were built up within ethnic lines. Organization of regional politics around nationality lined up claimants for leadership of successor states as the Soviet Union disintegrated. It also made the role of the great connector language, Russian, politically controversial in every post–Soviet territory except Russia itself.

Did a national myth ever develop across the sprawling Soviet empire? Were national sentiments – both inherited and constructed by Soviet nationalities policy – so robust that they bubbled to the surface when the Soviet state weakened? Or did the Communist apparatchiks, who were formed by Moscow to rule their regions, transform into nationalists in the process of contention? How the once-titanic Soviet monolith became vulnerable to minority language groups is in many ways the converse of how the weak and dispersed Italian state formed. Let us begin with the earlier episode.

Italy: State-Building without Hegemony

When Italy unified in the 1860s, rather than accommodate to the peninsula's and the two islands' heterogeneity, Piedmont's King Victor

Emmanuel and his Prime Minister, Cavour chose, French-style, to annex the rest of the country. They brooked no compromise with the varied administrative and cultural traditions of the annexed regions. The results were predictably stormy: In Rome, still under papal domination, plots were hatched to bring back the Bourbons to Naples and to subsidize organized banditry in the continental South. In Sicily, a virtual state of siege was the only way the new rulers could keep peasant violence, republicanism, and banditry in check (Riall 1998). Still the map of Italy today looks much as it did in 1861, except for the accretion of the Veneto, the Papal domains, and the acquisitions of World War I.

Most discussions of Italian national unity begin predictably by rehearsing Massimo d'Azeglio's famously reductive aphorism: "We have made Italy; now we have to make Italians." But this deceives as much as it enlightens. It enlightens because it was indeed true that the bulk of the population on the Italian peninsula and the two major islands had little knowledge of Italy and few spoke Italian before 1860, but it deceives because of its unstated assumption that this state of affairs was unusual. When we consider that popular nationalism would have been difficult to find among the masses of most future nation-states, Italy's uniqueness becomes quite relative. National unity formed through the resources, opportunities, and mechanisms that have given the Italian state both its durability and its weakness ever since.

The classical social movement paradigm helps us to see the resources and opportunities that brought Italy to unify when it did. Four main ones were:

1. Italian unification combined state-led with state-seeking nationalism: Cavour and Victor Emmanuel already *had* a state that they wanted to extend; the Mazzinians wanted to create one *ex nihilo*; and anti–Bourbon southerners – especially in Sicily – had one that they wanted to be rid of (Riall 1998; Romeo 1963). In Sicily especially, the movement toward acceptance of one set of foreign rulers (Victor Emmanuel's Kingdom of Piedmont-Sardinia) was advanced by the collapse of another (the Neapolitan Bourbons).
2. Piedmont-Sardinia had European approval for its designs. (Lyttleton 1991: 232; Mack Smith 1985: chs. 2–3). Cavour was able to manipulate the rivalries of Piedmont–Sardinia's neighbors – France, Prussia and Austria – and take advantage of Britain's interest in having a strong counterweight in the Mediterranean to its rival France.

3. Italy's intellectual and professional elite had a literary and administrative language. Italian – like many of the languages of nationalism – "created unified fields of exchange and communication below Latin and above the spoken vernaculars" (Anderson 1991: 44).
4. Nationalism came to be supported by many people whose interest in national unity prior to 1860 was questionable or nonexistent, and was the product of, and not the precondition for, the contentious episode we examine below.

Revolution in the South

From the familiar story of Italy's unification, the South largely has been excluded as a primary actor. While the northern elite disparaged the South as a paradise inhabited by devils, its conquest by Garibaldi was preceded by a vigorous indigenous revolt, and it played a crucial role in the decertification of the Bourbon state in Naples and in the making of the new state. The outcome of its revolution against the Bourbons embodied in particularly acute form the mechanisms that constructed the new polity.

Throughout the South, aristocratic decline, the formal end of feudalism in 1812, and Bourbon land reform policies had created a new provincial middle class. Everywhere in the region, peasants profited little from the Bourbon reforms, and in fact suffered from the hated *macinato* tax that they imposed. From 1820 on, waves of violent but largely ineffective insurrections broke out – most dramatically in 1847–1948. But the Kingdom of the Two Sicilies was, as one English wag put it, "protected by salt water on three sides and by holy water on the fourth." It survived due to sufferance of the Habsburgs, after 1815 the dominant power on the peninsula, and to divisions among possessing classes in Sicily and on the continent.

In Sicily, alongside a proud and insular nobility that had long hated the domination of Naples, the Bourbon reforms created a new middle class of landowners, who both resented control for Naples but took advantage of it to gain control of the land and monopolize local administration (Riall 1998: ch. 1). Autonomist and separatist sentiment was encouraged by the distance of the capital, by the sheer incapacity of the Bourbons to rule the island effectively, and by small groups of democrats on the eastern side of the island. But the same land reform that enriched the middle class denuded the peasantry of the common-use rights on which they had depended under the old regime. "By the mid-nineteenth century," writes

Lucy Riall, "the peasants in Sicily had become a revolutionary force" (Riall 1998: 57).

All of this made for an unstable and explosive mixture. As Riall writes,

> It involved a multi-cornered and overlapping struggle among traditional and not-so-traditional elites, liberals, democats, autonomists, Bourbons, clerics, and the urban and rural poor. . . . It was in Sicily that the revolution against the Bourbons started, and it was here that the collapse of political and administrative authority in 1860 was most dramatic. [Riall 1998: 27]

Riall's specification supports our view that nationalism must be seen in relation to politics – contentious and otherwise; that its most interesting episodes go well beyond the imaginings of nationalist intellectuals; and that contention over nation building is far more palpable than a "culture war." Indeed, much of it results from the interaction of claims and conflicts that are not self-consciously nationalist.

We cannot rehearse all of this long and tangled history here. Let us focus on the brief cycle of 1859–1961 in Sicily. During that period, Cavour's policy of piecemeal annexation went from halting success to success. Garibaldi and his *mille* stunned the world with their invasion of Sicily; and Cavour – in a brilliant but cynical preemptive strike – marched south, ostensibly to prevent the red-shirted Garibaldi from entering the Papal States, but actually to seize control of the revolution Garibaldi had made. We focus on the episode that erupted at its core: Garibaldi's conquest of Sicily, the social and political conflicts that it triggered, and the cooptation of his victory by Cavour. The major groups were the democrats supporting Garibaldi, the moderate liberals behind Cavour, the Sicilian poor who seized the opportunity of his coming to attack their landlords, and middle- and upper-class Sicilians whose original instinct was for autonomy but ended with support for annexation. The interaction of these actors reveals the mechanisms that led to the success of unification and to many peculiarities of the Italian national state that emerged.

Sicily in 1860: A Contentious Episode

At the dawn of 1859, it would have been difficult to see Cavour and Victor Emmanuel emerging as rulers of the entire peninsula and especially of this distinct island culture. With the Austrians ensconced in Milan and the Po Valley fortresses and a French garrison protecting the papal domains,

Cavour's aim went no further than the exclusion of Austria from the Po Valley and gaining Piedmontese control over Lombardo–Veneto. He did so in 1859 by provoking a war with Austria when that country was weakest, and by outflanking the Milanese radicals who dreamed of a Republic. Support was gained in France by ceding Nice to Louis Napoleon, in Prussia by the blow dealt its rival, Austria, and in England by the prospect that an independent Italy would balance French power (Mack Smith 1954: 1).

So far, it was nothing more than a small state trying to become a middle-sized one with the sufferance of its betters – no contentious politics here; little sign of nationalism. But ever the opportunist, Cavour annexed the central Italian duchies by encouraging local democrats to stage plebiscites in the name of Italian nationalism. Each of these acquisitions was added piecemeal to the existing state by what one wag called Cavour's "artichoke" strategy (Mack Smith 1954: 50). Mazzini's dream of creating an Italian identity by a cathartic national uprising seemed to be dissolving by a gradual process of tidying up the border. Cautious Cavour still thought national unity to be a chimera, but that was before Garibaldi's expedition and the conflicts and claims that it triggered.

Sicily was the great exception to the "royal conquest" model of Italian unification. Ruled from Naples for most of the past 300 years, it had enjoyed a brief moment of constitutional freedom between Napoleon's defeat and the return of the Bourbons, and another in 1847–1848, when its bourgeoisie took a leading role in sparking the European revolutions of those years (Romeo 1950: 306). But since Sicily was, or saw itself as, a colony of Naples, that revolution had strong separatist overtones and left behind a tradition of autonomism among the island's upper classes (Riall 1998: ch. 1; Romeo 1963). This was an era in which Sicilian intellectuals began retelling the island's glorious, if tragic, history of repeated invasions and publishing dictionaries in the Sicilian vernacular. Few Sicilians thought seriously of carrying the flag of Italian nationalism for the Piedmontese Victor Emmanuel.

But while the municipal insurrections and rigged plebiscites that accompanied Cavour's conquest of central Italy were little more than adjuncts of royal policy, Garibaldi's invasion of Sicily, his swift march across the island, and the political struggles that accompanied his arrival in Palermo constituted a dramatic contentious cycle creating new identities and forging new alliances. Triggered by both an autonomous revolt of middle-class democrats in the cities and by uprisings of embittered peasants against landholders and Bourbons (Riall 1998: ch. 2), it brought 1848 exiles back to the island as missionaries to make contact with bands in the hills and organize revolutionary activities in the cities. As the revolt spread from Palermo to the other major centers and into the countryside, these emissaries urged Garibaldi to launch his expedition.

With no support from Cavour – who actually ordered the Piedmontese navy to stop it at one point – and with a rag-tag army of Mazzinians, republicans, democrats, unemployed intellectuals, and adventurers, Garibaldi's landing at Marsala actually came as the earlier revolts were losing their momentum. News of the landing triggered an even broader wave of peasant uprisings, incited municipal revolts in the major cities, fomented breakdown of local government and communication, and thus brought withdrawal of the Bourbons to the continent.

Like many nationalist episodes all over the world, the Sicilian revolution was no homogeneous imagining of a national revolution. It was a wave of contentious politics that included many actors whose goals were far from nationalist and others who became nationalist in the course of contention. Sicilians rallied to Garibaldi and his *mille* from a variety of standpoints and with a variety of motives: nobles opposing Bourbon land reforms, taxes and usurpation of the island's autonomy; urban middle-class democrats seeking a representative system of government; impoverished peasants hoping to find in the red-shirted Garibaldi a liberator from landowner pressures; and numerous local landholding and officeholding opportunists who defected from the collapsing Bourbon regime as soon as it seemed Garibaldi would win. Liberal nationalists who saw in Piedmont the best hope for a regime of progress and freedom were barely a presence as the cycle of contention began.

These different standpoints led to inevitable conflicts both under Garibaldi's "dictatorship" and afterward, when the Piedmontese set up a provisional *Luogotenenza*. While the peasants sought ownership of the land and the democrats hoped for a constituent assembly that might win Sicily better terms from Cavour, autonomists sought a Sicilian state and landholders wanted to hold on to – and possibly increase – their local power. Autonomists, democrats, and peasants all lost out. With respect to the first, Cavour hinted (falsely, as it turned out) that he would look kindly at local autonomy if the electorate would agree to annexation. The democrats were likewise defeated by annexation, which attached the South and Sicily to the centralized administrative structures of Piedmont and by the moderates' political success in splitting them (Riall 1998: 127–8).

With regard to the peasantry, Garibaldi's government – still engaged in winning control of the continental South – turned back on his initial promises to distribute the land as he allied with the local landowning class to stamp out anarchy (Riall 1998: 89–90). As for the latter, they took advantage of easily rigged auctions of Church and Bourbon lands to aggrandize themselves and supported annexation to prevent rural anarchy. Though few had had any notion of Italian nationalism when Garibaldi landed, fear of disorder rallied them to the Piedmontese cause. As Lampedusa's young hero, Tancredi, tells his aristocratic uncle: "If people like us don't get involved, others [that is, mafiosi and mischief-makers] will give you a republic" (Tomasi di Lampedusa 1960: 42). When a plebiscite took place in October, annexation won by an overwhelming margin. A barely imagined Italy became a reality as the outcome of a complex game of class confict, fear, ambition, uncertainty, and military force.

Why did Sicilians accept annexation so quickly? Were they swept up by Cavour's blandishments? Discouraged by Garibaldi's alternating grand flourishes and hesitations? They were surely not revealing a deep love of Italy! As social disintegration seemed to threaten property, Cavour's agents (not above stimulating demonstrations against Garibaldi's government) gained support for annexation from middle- and upper-class groups petrified at the danger of rural and urban insurrection. What had begun as a homegrown popular insurrection and democrat-led guerrilla warfare ended, via an episode of contention, as a royal conquest supported by the island's social elite under the guise of a well-managed plebiscite. As Lampedusa's young hero also tells his uncle: "If we want everything to remain as it is, it is necessary that everything change" (Tomasi di Lampedusa 1960: 42).

As it took power in Sicily and the continental South, the new regime rigidly applied Piedmont's market economy, legal system, and centralized administration to the conquered regions. To this was added a series of ruthless military incursions into the countryside to stamp out banditism and Bourbonism. In the continental South, whole villages that supported insurgent brigands were destroyed (Mack Smith 1969: 55–59); in Sicily, a series of military operations were mounted to destroy resistance to unification (Riall 1998: chs. 5–7). In 1866 a full-scale urban and rural insurrection broke out, supported by Bourbonists, democrats, the urban poor and rural bandits (Riall 1998: ch. 8).

Integration was more than military: The crushing weight of a modern fiscal system and Piedmont's debts from the Austrian war were applied without relief to a region that lacked modern economic resources (Romeo 1950). A liberal customs union opened the South to northern commercial penetration, snuffing out the few infant industries that the Bourbons sponsored and destroying much of the livelihood of Palermo's merchants and artisans, as that capital city was reduced to the status of a provincial town. The fact that the Sicilian insurrection of 1866 was mounted with the slogans "Long Live the Republic!" and "Long Live Religion" indicate how narrow the government's base was in the island (Riall 1998: 207).

But integration of a peculiar kind resulted, with profound results for Sicily's and the South's place in the unified state. From the appointment of Garibaldi's government on, the need for local interlocutors to establish the new government, collect taxes, and control rural disorder brought local elites who had no prior adhesion to either the democrats or the moderate liberals to the national cause. In addition to gaining protection for a brutal system of landholding, these elites benefited from the payoffs that would accrue from the control of local and regional government. In some towns, the local governing elite consisted essentially of members of the same family, colluding for their mutual enrichment and to keep their enemies out (Riall 1998: 95–100). The new regional governors appointed by Garibaldi and his successors, as Riall points out,

> used their powers to pursue independent policies of their own rather than obeying instructions from Palermo. . . . Some governors used their considerable powers to pursue personal goals. . . . Those who had been mayors, electors, decurions, *capi-urbani*, *sotto-capi*, and even known spies under the Bourbons were now presidents or members of local councils and commanders of National Guards under the democrats [Riall 1998: 95, 96, 99].

As insurgent challenges continued well into the 1860s, while police and carabinieri seemed incapable of dealing with them, the government saw no alternative to coopting local elites of all ideological stripes. The culmination came after the revolt of 1866, when the police chief of Palermo "resumed the Bourbon practice of colluding with criminals as a means of maintaining public order." For Sicily's rural elites, "control and manipulation of local government became central to their power within the community as a whole" (Riall 1998: 227). This situation undermined the national state's strength and legitimacy even as it increased local elites' dependence on central government.

It was not until 1876 that the parliamentary Left came to power under Depretis, but by that time it was unified by little else than its opposition to the Right, its hunger for place and power (Lyttleton 1991: 223), and its resentment of Piedmont's hegemony. Depretis' chief strength lay in the South, where prefectoral interference in elections, the "transformation" of deputies from the Right into supporters of the Left in return for favors, and a series of deals with local elites turned the tactics that the Right had used to restore order into a mechanism of consensus. Not only the democrats and Mazzinians on the Left, Catholics of all stripes, but also conservatives on the Right – and of course, those who had sought regional autonomy – felt betrayed by a regime that realized few of the hopes of those who had fought to make it. By the 1870s, we witness no more publication of Sicilian dictionaries. A proto-nation without a state had produced a state with little authority and linked the Sicilian elites who might have led a revolt of the periphery to it through clientelism, payoffs, and protection.

Mechanisms of Unification

It would be easy to end our story here, having shown that Italy was made, not through a "culture war" and not through a distinctly nationalist movement, but through a combination of political and military maneuvering, class conflict, and a variety of forms of contentious politics. The episode sped toward its climax by mechanisms that are familiar from nonnationalist episodes. We focus on four that will reappear in our case of national disintegration in the second part of this chapter: opportunity spirals, identity shift, competition, and brokerage.

Opportunity Spirals

At different phases of the story, Garibaldi's electrifying invasion, the changes in Cavour's policy, the land occupations of the Sicilian peasants, the rallying of the autonomists to annexation, all demonstrated the mechanism of shifting and expanding opportunity – a mechanism familiar to many scholars of contentious politics. Opportunity spirals operate through sequences of environmental change, interpretation of that change, action, and counteraction, repeated as one action alters another actor's environment.

The opportunity offered by the uprising in Sicily in April 1860 convinced Garibaldi to lead his rag-tag army on what seemed to Cavour a hopeless and dangerous mission. In turn, Garibaldi's initial successes triggered land occupations by the peasants, sending police and local officials fleeing to the cities and weakening the Bourbon resolve. These successes convinced Cavour to take advantage of both. Mack Smith deftly summarizes this catalytic moment:

> The national movement was not strong, but for a brief while it coincided with a social movement of great strength. As the [Bourbon] government was paralyzed by the noncooperation of the leading families in each village, political rebellion joined hands with social revolution and spread from Palermo into the countryside. This in turn brought about the collapse of local authorities all through the island; the police fled for their lives; family feuds and social grievances came out into the open, and society was soon in a state of more or less complete dissolution. [Mack Smith 1954: 9]

Identity Shift

But revolutions are not made of opportunities alone: A process of transformation of identities and affiliations was triggered by the dramatic events of April and May 1860. While before Garibaldi's expedition, few believed that Italy could be made, by the end of April the British minister in Naples remarked on the "amazing development which the notion of annexation and a single Italian kingdom has acquired within the last six months" (quoted in Mack Smith 1954: 8). Little of this must have affected Sicily's numerous landless poor, whose concerns were more social than political, but their uprising helped drive a large number of propertyholding Sicilians from autonomism into the royalist camp.

Garibaldi had at first played for peasant support, "but he soon found that his sole chance of permanent political victory lay in the support of the landlords" (Mack Smith 1969: 42), who flocked to the annexationist party for protection against their own peasants. "By its own logic, therefore, a movement which had grown out of peasants rebelling against landowners ended upon the side of the landowners against their peasants" (Mack Smith 1969: 42), and thence on the side of annexation against autonomy. Their enthusiasm for Italy would rapidly cool under the broken promises of decentralization, but in 1860 the autonomist upper classes became enthusiastic annexationists (Romeo 1950: 339).

Not only the Sicilian elite, but Cavour himself demonstrates the power of contentious politics to transform identity. An advocate of no more than a confederation of Italian states until 1860, he had seen outright unification as a Mazzinian illusion fraught with dangers of foreign intervention and republican revolution (Mack Smith 1954: 23). But as news of Garibaldi's successes filtered north and word arrived from France assuring him of noninterference, Cavour's attitude turned around 180 degrees, as he called the exploit "the most poetic fact of the century" and sent reinforcements and arms to support the campaign (Mack Smith 1954: 29–30). From then on, Cavour was an outright advocate of annexation, turning his back on the Bourbons and planning for the construction of a unified Italian state.

Competition

Cavour was driven by more than enthusiasm for Garibaldi's exploits and territorial ambitions. Political competition between the moderates and the democrats was a mechanism that shot through the entire episode and helped to push the cautious Cavour and Victor Emmanuel toward a more aggressive policy. As soon as word arrived in England that the *mille* had landed, Mazzini slipped away from his police watchers and arrived in Italy, to pepper Garibaldi's lieutenants with militant advice and attempts to give the entire enterprise a republican allure.

Cavour's advisers responded by urging him to outdo Mazzini in his support for the expedition or risk allowing "the reds" to have an open field for their schemes. In Sicily, his agent La Farina worked to undercut the radical position by stimulating fear of social revolution. The moderates' fear of radical success also drove them to immoderate actions, ultimately leading Cavour to take the bold step of entering the Papal States, risking French displeasure, and alienating Catholics from the new state for decades.

Brokerage

From the Garibaldian dictatorship on, "the relationship between central government and local elites tended to be based more on short-term, private gain than on any principle of public service or bureaucratic rationality" (Riall 1998: 227). This, plus the criminalization of opposition, deprived the national state of any legitimacy it might have had in Sicily; but it increased the dependence of local elites on central government. That situation was renewed and perfected after World War II, in the system of power constructed by Christian Democracy (Chubb 1982; Schneider and Schneider forthcoming). The implicit deal that the Piedmontese moderates made with Sicilian elites in exchange for their support for annexation set a pattern of clientelistic brokerage that would govern North–South relations for decades.

We asked rhetorically at the beginning of this chapter "how a weak and inefficient polity built from a dispersed and disconnected set of petty states avoided violent outbreaks of regional separatism." We can now hazard a hypothesis based on the conception of brokerage developed in earlier chapters. As Lyttleton writes of the southern political class in the unified state, "They formed the mercenary army of local politics . . . following whoever could promise them a job as municipal clerk or tax inspector. The skills they cultivated were particularly those of the mediator" (Lyttleton 1991: 234). Those who rose into national politics became the political brokers between North and South, using their control of local clienteles as their political stock-in-trade (Lyttleton 1991: 246; Salvemini 1955: 383–404).

Elites who could achieve their personal and political goals through brokerage with northern political party leaders might make poor patriots, but would have little incentive to pursue autonomist or regionalist programs that might once again trigger rural revolution. "Deprived of a true mass base and wedded to old local and clientelistic forms of representation," concludes Lyttleton, "the liberal strategy became essentially one of mediation" (Lyttleton 1991: 250).

Opportunity spirals, identity shift, competition, and brokerage were some of the mechanisms at work in the creation of a unified state that superimposed a highly centralized administration upon a society rife with regional differences. If life were simple, these differences would have produced recurring movements of peripheral nationalism.

Instead, they produced a nation-state without hegemony. Critics like Gramsci and Salvemini criticized the obvious costs and dysfunctions of this weak pattern of integration – and particularly the fact that integration took place through elites, encouraged corruption, and at the margins blended with criminality (Schneider and Schneider forthcoming). It left many ordinary southerners the prey of landowners, mafiosi, and corrupt politicians.

Looking at the big picture, and leaving moral considerations aside, the Italian pattern of unification shows a tradeoff between legitimation and state strength, on the one hand, and between durability and state weakness, on the other. We now turn to a case in which state strength was high but ultimately contributed to state disintegration.

The Soviet Union and its Successors

Similar mechanisms operated with entirely different general outcomes in the Soviet Union. In this once-monolithic party-state, an opportunity spiral raced from top-down liberalization to democratic movements to nationalist stirrings to separatism and disintegration. Identities that were partly created by Soviet nationalities policy and a Republic structure organized to implement that policy mutated into nationalist ideologies. Competition between Republic and less-than–Republic nationalities and among state and economic elites for a share of the spoils eroded the Center's capacity to respond to the crisis. Here, too, forms of brokerage – some inherited from the old regime, some forming anew – filled the vacuum of the collapsing Center. Here, too, what seemed impossible a few short years earlier came to be seen as inevitable with the virtues of hindsight.

But Soviet experience poses a rather different set of empirical problems from its Italian counterpart, notably:

1. How did a political economy that seemed so solid, centralized, authoritarian, and resourceful disintegrate visibly in five or six years?
2. Why did so much of the contentious claim making funnel into ethnic and national self-assertion?
3. How then did so many old regime power holders reappear in positions of power after the great transformation?

Coherent explanation of the critical moment of transition requires knowledge of what went before (Bunce 1999). Our account of the Soviet past exaggerates the centrality of nationalities policies as compared with control of enterprises and party structure. Without claiming for a moment that nationalism alone destroyed the Union, we focus on the mechanisms that gave nationalism its significant place in Soviet collapse.

The Soviet Union formed in the ruins of war and revolution. Its imperial predecessor took heavy losses from its battering by Germany and Austria in World War I, losing control of Russian Poland and the Baltic provinces in the process. Workers' strikes and soldiers' mutinies in 1917 coupled with resistance of the Duma (national assembly) in driving the Tsar to abdicate and a conservative–liberal provisional government to take power. Soon insurrectionary counter-governments of workers and soldiers were forming at the local and regional level, as Bolshevik leaders such as Lenin and Trotsky returned from exile. Struggle swirled around multiple factions and issues, but by November 1917 the Bolsheviks had gained enough ground to seize power from the provisional government.

Between 1917 and 1921, the Bolsheviks had their hands full simply keeping what remained of the Russian empire together. In a great effort, Lenin, Trotsky, and their collaborators returned the country to civilian control by locating a tightly disciplined Communist party (itself recruited in part from former or present military men) within a large centralized bureaucracy. With Stalin's takeover (and expulsion of Trotsky) in 1927, the Soviet Union moved into a phase of forced-draft industrialization, agricultural collectivization, bureaucratic expansion, and increasingly authoritarian deployment of the Communist party as an instrument of central power.

World War II produced an enormous demographic shock, extensive nationalist bids for autonomy, and a major centralization of political power. Even more so than before World War II, the postwar Soviet economy and polity depended on the combination of three elements: (1) maintenance of formidable military might, (2) large-scale coordination and division of labor in the production and distribution of subsistence goods, and (3) close surveillance and control of all political expression. Yet that imposing system collapsed during the 1980s.

How did it happen? At the time, Soviet assistance in Afghanistan's left-leaning military coup of 1979 seemed like just one more Cold War contretemps, but it proved crucial. As the United States poured in support for a variety of Afghan rebels, the Soviet military suffered a frustrating and humiliating stalemate. Under Leonid Brezhnev, the Soviet Union began efforts to stimulate the economy through various forms of decentralization and devolution of power. In 1985, liberalizer Mikhail Gorbachev arrived at the party's head. He soon began promoting *perestroika*, a shift of the economy from military to civilian production, toward better and more abundant consumer goods, and in the direction of higher productivity. Gorbachev also moved hesitantly into a program of opening up public life – releasing political prisoners, accelerating exit visas for Jews, shrinking the military, reducing external military involvement, and ending violent repression of demands for political, ethnic, and religious autonomy.

Reduction of central controls over production and distribution eventually began to promote:

- proliferation of small enterprises
- attempts to set up collaborative enterprises with foreign capitalists

- more open operation of the black markets, gray markets, and mutual aid networks that had long linked individuals, households, and firms
- massive slowdowns of payments and goods deliveries to central organizations
- diversion of government-owned stocks and facilities into profit-making or monopoly-maintaining private distribution networks to the benefit of existing managers, quick-thinking entrepreneurs, and members of organizations already enjoying preferential access to desirable goods, facilities, or foreign currencies
- substitution of private media and systems of exchange for public means

All this happened as the government was attempting to generalize and liberate national markets. As a consequence, the capacity of the central state to deliver rewards to its followers declined visibly from one month to the next. In response, officials and managers engaged in what Steven Solnick calls a run on the bank. Wherever they could divert fungible assets to their own advantage, they increasingly did so; they set about "stealing the state" (Solnick 1998). The process was well advanced by the time overt nationalist movements became visible.

On the political front, a parallel and interdependent collapse of central authority occurred. The results of Gorbachev's economic program alienated not only producers who had benefited from emphasis on military enterprise, but also consumers who did not have ready access to one of the new distribution networks and officials whose previous powers were now under attack. In a classical process of polarization, his political program opened up space for critics and rivals such as Boris Yeltsin, who, from a Moscow base, rose to control the Russian federation. Gorbachev's own effort to check the threatened but still intact military and intelligence establishments through conciliation, caution, and equivocation alienated reformers without gaining him solid conservative support. Simultaneously, he sought to acquire emergency powers that would free him to forward economic transformation. That brought him into conflict with rival reformers, political libertarians, and defenders of the old regime alike.

Although demands for guarantees of religious and political liberties arose in 1987, nevertheless, it was the rush of nationalist and nationalizing leaders to gain assets and autonomy to assure their position in the new regime that overwhelmed the old one. Russia's Communists had dealt with non–Russian regions by coopting regional leaders who were loyal to their cause. They integrated them into the Communist party, recruited their successors among the most promising members of designated nationalities but trained them in Russia, and dispatched many Russians to staff new industries, professions, and administrations. Russian language and culture were promoted as media of administration and interregional communication, while regional power holders were granted substantial autonomy and military support within their own territories just so long as they assured supplies of state revenue, goods, and conscripts. Any individual or group that called for liberties outside of this system was quickly suppressed. Such a system could operate effectively so long as regional leaders received powerful support from the center and their local rivals had no means or hope of appealing for popular backing.

The system's strength also proved to be its downfall. Gorbachev and collaborators simultaneously promoted opening of political discussion, reduced military involvement in political control, tolerated alternatives to the Communist connecting structure, made gestures toward truly contested elections, and acknowledged diminished capacity to reward faithful followers. As that happened, both regional power holders and their rivals suddenly acquired strong incentives to distance themselves from the center, to recruit popular support, to establish their credentials as authentic representatives of the local people, to urge priority of their own nationalities within territorial subdivisions of the USSR they happened to occupy, and to press for new forms of autonomy. In the Baltic republics and those along the USSR's western or southern tiers, the possibility of special relations with kindred states and authorities outside the Soviet Union – Sweden, Finland, Turkey, Iran, the European Community, and NATO – offered political leverage and economic opportunity the Soviet Union itself was decreasingly capable of providing.

Time horizons contracted rapidly. On the large scale and the small, people could no longer count on payoffs from long-term investment in the existing system; they reoriented to short-term gains and exit strategies. When Gorbachev sought a new union treaty, with greater scope for the fifteen republics but preservation of a federal government's military, diplomatic, and economic priority in a referendum of March 1991, leaders of six republics (Latvia, Lithuania, Estonia, Moldavia, Armenia, and Georgia, all of which had started the process of declaring themselves independent) boycotted the proceedings. Results for the other republics confirmed the division between Russia and non–Russian portions of the tottering federation. From outside, venture capitalists, development economists, world financial institutions, and powers such as the United States, Turkey, Iran, and the European Union all strove for their pieces of the action and/or for containment of ugly spillover from Soviet turmoil.

In the face of ethnic disaggregation, economic collapse, undermining of the old regime's powers, and Gorbachev's refusal to engage in vigorous repression, many observers and participants on the Soviet scene feared a bid of the military, intelligence, and Party establishment to reverse the flow of events. History realized their fears. In August 1991, a shadowy Emergency Committee sequestered Gorbachev, but failed in a coup as Yeltsin led resistance to them in Moscow. Over the next four months Yeltsin sought to succeed Gorbachev, not as Party secretary but as chief of a confederation maintaining a measure of economic, military, and diplomatic authority. Even that effort ended with dissolution of the Soviet Union into an ill-defined and disputatious Commonwealth from which the Baltic states absented themselves entirely, while others began rushing toward exits.

Once the Soviet regime collapsed, Russian nationalists (including the opportunistic nationalist Yeltsin) faced a fierce dilemma. On the one hand, they claimed the right of Russians to rule the Russian federation, which actually included millions of people from non–Russian minorities. Such a claim supported the principle that titular nationalities should prevail. On the other hand, they vigorously criticized the treatment of Russians outside the Russian federation – for example, the large numbers of self-identified Russians in Estonia, Lithuania, Ukraine, and Kazakhstan – as second-class minorities facing a choice among assimilation to the titular nationality, lesser forms of citizenship, and emigration (Barrington 1995). Unsurprisingly, newly independent neighbors often accused the Russian federation's authorities of imperialism.

Mark Beissinger's catalog of protest events from 1987 through 1992 throughout the Soviet Union's space identifies a crucial shift in popular mobilization. Protest demonstrations increased rapidly in numbers from 1987 to 1989, then reached their peak in 1990, only to swing wildly but in a generally downward direction thereafter. Mass violent events, in contrast, reached a minor peak in mid-1989, but began a powerful upward surge in 1991, remaining frequent through 1992. By 1992, the dominant issue of protest events had become the drawing of borders among republics (Beissinger 1998: 294–305). The shift corresponded to a switch from relatively peaceful, if massive, demands for reform and national representation to bitterly fought struggles over national rights. As in Italian unification, state-seeking nationalism (on the part of republics seeking exit from the Union) and state-led nationalism (on the part of republic leaders seeking to establish hegemony within their own territories) interacted powerfully, but with opposite results.

Mechanisms of Contention

No single episode of contention contains exactly the same mechanisms as any other – even in the case of episodes that are more similar than our two. In the Soviet case, internal threats and external opportunities figured much more prominently than they had in Italian unification. But all four of our mechanisms – opportunity spirals, identity shift, competition, and brokerage – operated with a vengeance in Soviet disintegration.

Opportunity Spirals

In the Soviet case, several spirals succeeded each other. Looking closely at nationalist contention, Beissinger identifies four phases in the development of secessionist mobilization within the USSR (Beissinger forthcoming: 141–144). As early as 1986, demands for autonomy and protection arose not only from Estonians, Latvians, Lithuanians, and Ukrainians, but also from Kazakhstan. Diffusion resulted in part from deliberate proselytizing by the Balts, but it was also transmitted by media reports and by elites who were beginning to look over their shoulders and look for state resources to buttress their positions (Beissinger forthcoming: 139).

Emulation at first followed the pattern of a chain reaction:

> Unrepressed mobilization by Jewish refuseniks and Russian nationalists influenced the decision by Crimean Tatar dissidents to conduct a protest campaign, which in turn influenced attempts by Baltic dissidents to organize demonstrations, which in turn influenced the behavior of Armenian activists, and so on down the line. [Beissinger forthcoming: 48]

The earliest outbreaks of nationalist contention depended heavily on prior group resources (e.g., population size, urbanization) and on institutional constraints (e.g., ethnic groups with Republic status were more likely to participate than those with less-than–Republic status). But as the contention spread, these structural and institutional factors faded in importance, as smaller, less urbanized and non–Republic ethnic groups took advantage of the weakening Center to emulate the actions of the early risers. So rapidly did nationalist contention diffuse that it soon came to resemble a single "tide," in Beissinger's language. As a Soviet journalist wrote in 1990, "Sometimes it seems as if the whole country has gone to one rally, one demonstration." Beissinger concludes: "Eventually, acts of nationalist contention grew normalized and constituted a vast tide of nationalist disruption that moved in significant ways according to its own logic" (Beissinger forthcoming: 47–48).

Opportunity spirals extended beyond outright contentious politics to the behavior of elites and managers: first through bids for external support of profit-making and rent-seeking enterprises under declining central controls, then outright assertions of rights to national autonomy on the parts of existing regional leaders and their local rivals, finally seizure of fungible state resources by whoever could make off with them.

Identity Shift

Considering previous images of the Communist system as an unshakable block, identity shift occurred with startling rapidity, with longtime beneficiaries of Communist control backing off from identification with the Party and its legacy in favor of a series of improvised alternatives among which ethnic labels (including Russian) assumed ever-increasing scope. Beissinger describes a visit to Soviet Moldova in 1987, in which he and his wife were assigned three guides: a Moldovan who sang the praises of the Soviet system, a Jew who was suspicious of Beissinger's own Jewish identity, and a Ukrainian "whose main purpose seems to have been to watch over the Moldovan and the Jew." Returning in 1990 after two years of upheaval, Beissinger found the Moldovan had become a rabble-rousing Moldovan nationalist, the Jew had emigrated to Israel, and the Ukrainian had moved back to the (nearly independent) Ukraine. "These Moldovan encounters," he concludes, "are a metaphor for the massive reimaginings of self that characterized the Soviet Union in its final years" (Beissinger forthcoming: ch. 4).

Competition

Competition operated on two fronts: in attempts to gain external economic and political support; in related attempts to seize organizations and assets previously firmly under state control. In political subdivisions containing more than one well organized national population, threats mounted rapidly to those who lost the competition for certification as authentic regional citizens. Those who moved first could gain more. Escalation began, with each concession by the central government to some nationalities giving new incentives and precedents for further demands by other nationalities, increasingly threatening any connected population that shared a distinct identity but failed to mobilize effectively. Within such heterogeneous regions as Nagorno–Karabakh, a primarily Armenian enclave within Azerbaijan, militants of neighboring ethnicities battled for priority, and did not scruple to kill. In addition to Azerbaijan, Moldavia, Georgia, and Tadjikistan grew mean with intergroup conflict. Between January 1988 and August 1989, ethnic clashes claimed 292 lives, leaving 5,520 people injured and 360,000 homeless (Nahaylo and Swoboda 1990: 336). Even in republics with little claim to a distinct national tradition, such as Byelorussia, a competitive bandwagon effect produced an imagined national history, a currency that soon ran out of national heroes to portray and turned to local animal life instead, and what eventually turned into a quasi-state utterly dependent on its Russian neighbor.

Brokerage

Brokerage may be less obvious, but it made a big difference in three regards. First, Republican governments like the Ukrainian one took on the brokerage role in reforming the Soviet state into a confederation that political parties might have occupied in less authoritative states (Beissinger forthcoming: 36). Second, brokerage helps account for the remarkable continuity of rulers through apparently revolutionary turmoil. Although gangsters and tycoons have appeared from the shadows of Soviet society, for the most part the people who run things in the former Soviet Union are the same sorts of people – and in many cases the very same people – who ran things during the 1980s. That is because as connectors in a vast centralized system they had privileged access to information, resources, and other centers of power; it was extremely difficult for anyone to match the advantages afforded them by their institutional positions (see Willerton 1992). The third regard is the converse of the first: once regional leaders, entrepreneurs, work groups, and ordinary citizens started to resist yielding goods and services to central authorities, those authorities lost power as brokers; they could no longer redistribute resources to sustain their own positions, their allies, and the activities to which they were most committed.

Thus opportunity spirals, identity shifts, competition, and brokerage interacted powerfully, but with dramatically different outcomes than in the creation of an Italian state where so many political fragments had lived before.

Kazakh Contention

Consider Kazakhstan as a vantage point for closer viewing of both national disintegration and national identity formation. Although apparently unpromising ground for either state-led or state-seeking nationalism, late– and post–Soviet Kazakhstan underwent internal struggles and major transformations in the name of nationalist claims. In Kazakhstan, dizzying opportunity spirals shifted the relations of regional leaders to local and international actors simultaneously, identity shift occurred as those same regional leaders came to claim a distinctive national heritage, competition for control of the territory and its national heritage grew intense, and brokerage by former Soviet functionaries built connections around which a new country organized. Kazakhstan offers an exemplary case of opportunistic yet effective top-down nationalism – the same sort of nationalism that arose widely in the Soviet Union after 1985, not to mention the Italian peninsula after 1859.

What sort of place is Kazakhstan? As Martha Brill Olcott sums up the background:

> Kazakhstan is an accidental country, a nation that was carved out of a Soviet republic whose boundaries were never intended to be those of an independent state. Independence has shaped the nature of Kazakhstan's politics, and not always in ways that are supportive of democratic principles. Although the home of one of the first glasnost-era popular protests, the Almaty riots of 1986, prior to independence Kazakhstan did not make the same strides toward democratization that neighboring Kyrgyzstan did. While independent political groups were organized, they lacked real influence on the political process. [Olcott 1997: 201]

Olcott's accurate summary calls for background and explanation.

The territory people now call Kazakhstan centers on the steppe crisscrossed for centuries by caravans between China and Europe. Today's Kazakhstan touches the Caspian Sea, Turkmenistan, Uzbekistan, Kyrgyzstan, and China. Across a vast border with the Russian federation it also abuts Siberia, the Urals, and the Volga region. At 2.7 million square kilometers, Kazakhstan covers about the same amount of territory as Argentina. Over most of the last millennium, nomadic Turkic pastoralists have predominated within its territory. (The Kazakh language includes a number of terms, mostly derogatory, for settled peoples, but none for nomads.) Kazakhstan's pastoralists have endured conquest after conquest.

Conquered by expanding Mongols in the thirteenth century, the region sustained its own khan from the later fifteenth century. Forcible integration of the region into the Russian empire during the eighteenth and nineteenth centuries, followed by extensive immigration of Russian-speaking farmers from the north, greatly increased Russian cultural and political presence in Kazakhstan: "About 1.5 million new colonists from European Russia came to Kazakhstan at the end of the 19th century and in the beginning of the twentieth century" (Khazanov 1995: 157). Those changes marginalized the region's nomadic herders and drove many of them into settled agriculture. Self-identified Kazakhs took advantage of the Bolshevik Revolution to create an autonomous republic that lasted from 1918 to 1920. Those Kazakh nationalists, however, soon succumbed to Soviet military might.

Come to power, Stalin eventually established his characteristic pattern of governing the region through Moscow-oriented Kazakhs; between 1924 and 1933, Kazakhs grew from 8 to 53 percent of the region's Communist party (Suny 1993: 103). Stalin's regime created a full Soviet republic of Kazakhstan in 1936. In that republic, well situated titular nationals – certified Kazakhs – gained preferential access to jobs, higher education, and party membership. But Stalin and his successors also built an economic system that made Kazakhstan's major industrial and commercial nodes tributaries of centers in Russia and Uzbekistan rather than connecting them with each other. The early 1930s brought forced collectivization of agriculture and fixed settlement of the remaining Kazakh nomads; in response to pressure, Kazakhs destroyed 80 percent of their herds (Suny 1993: 107; see also Viola 1996). During resistance to collectivization, perhaps a quarter of the Kazakh population, some twenty million people, died of violence or famine.

Successive Soviet regimes shipped in technicians, peasants, and political prisoners from Russia, Byelorussia, Poland, Ukraine, and the Caucasus as displaced Turkic nomads died out or fled to China. Unsurprisingly, Russian-speakers concentrated in and around the Russian-oriented nodes, which meant that ethnic balances varied enormously by region within Kazakhstan. In 1989, only 0.9 percent of all ethnic Russians in Kazakhstan claimed knowledge of Kazakh (Smith, et al. 1998: 150).

To be sure, the system looked very different from the bottom up than from the top down. "Among the Kazakhs," remarks Ronald Suny, "Soviet power was a façade that disguised the real structure of local power underneath" (Suny 1993: 114). In rural areas at the local level traditional leaders adapted to the Soviet presence, fashioning their own accommodations with regional and national power. But that changed relation to regional and national power constituted a deep alteration of existence. In cities and in Russian-dominated regions, furthermore, the whole way of life altered, obliterating the structures left by centuries of nomadic existence.

Kazakhs themselves divided into three large and sometimes competing clans, or *zhus*: a Great Horde concentrated chiefly in southern Kazakhstan, a Middle Horde in the north-central region, and a Lesser Horde, in the west. Ethnic Kazakh Dinmukhamed Kunaev became regional party boss in 1964, allied himself closely with Leonid Brezhnev, and eventually acquired full membership in Soviet Union's Politburo. Kunaev brought a number of Kazakhs (especially from his own Great Horde) into his administration. On the whole, Central Asian national leaders, Kunaev among them, opposed Gorbachev's liberalization, which threatened their systems of patronage and control.

In 1986 Gorbachev replaced Kunaev with Gennadi Kolbin, an ethnic Russian unconnected to Kazakhstan. Students and others thereupon demonstrated against the regime in the capital, Almaty (Olcott 1997: 205–206). "Kolbin's inability to master either Kazakhstan's economy, which continued to decline, or Kazakhstan's complex social and demographic make-up," reports Olcott, "led within three years to Kolbin's being replaced by Nursultan Nazarbaev, an ethnic Kazakh who since 1984 had been chairman of the republic's Council of Ministers" (Olcott 1997: 206).

Nazarbaev worked with Soviet authorities to initiate economic reorganization, but within Kazakhstan he consolidated power by stressing Kazakh nationalism. A Nazarbaev-sponsored bill of August 1989, for example, made Kazakh the state language, stepped up Kazakh language instruction, and shifted public business into Kazakh. He then had to hold off Russian resistance organizations, on one side, and more radically Kazakh nationalist organizations, on the other. At the same time, he made a series of attempts to organize parties that could serve as successors to the Communists while providing him with support; those efforts failed, especially because they became vehicles for rivals to challenge Nazarbaev's dominant position. Nevertheless the 1989–1990 elections generally brought Communist incumbents back to power from local to national levels.

Nazarbaev's commitment to what remained of the Soviet Union did not prevent him from shifting sides adroitly during the uncertainty following the failed coup of August 1991. As Francis Clines reported from Moscow on August 26 of that year:

> Signaling the republic's refusal to be under Russian influence now that the central Government was collapsing, Mr. Nazarbayev told the nation, "Kazakhstan will never be anyone's younger brother." The shocking reversal of fervor for retailoring the union could be seen in the fact that, little more than a week ago, Mr. Yeltsin and Mr. Nazarbayev were close colleagues pushing the union treaty. They were preparing to sign the compromise pact in which Mr. Gorbachev vowed to begin a new era of power for the republics last Tuesday, two days after the coup was launched. [In Gwertzman and Kaufman 1991: 556–557].

That was not Nazarbaev's last switch. By November 1991, Nazarbaev was collaborating with Gorbachev in a failed last-ditch effort to create a Union of Sovereign States including Russia, Belorussia, Kyrgyzstan, Tajikistan, Turkmenistan, Azerbaijan, and Kazakhstan. Many observers thought, in fact, that Gorbachev planned to make Nazarbaev his deputy as well as Union president.

During the Soviet Union's last moments, in December 1991, Nazarbaev gained election as Kazakh president. In 1992, after the Soviet Union's collapse, Nazarbaev finally succeeded in creating a party, the People's Unity Party, that harnessed popular support (at least among self-identified Kazakhs) to his personal interest. That party continues the dangerous struggle to hold central power in the face of Russian resistance on one side and Kazakh nationalist mobilization on the other. It has the help of a predominantly Kazakh government that closely manages candidates, elections, and parliaments (CSCE 1998). In March 1995, indeed, Nazarbaev had the election of the incumbent parliament annulled and assumed emergency powers until he held new elections late in the year. By 2000, he had consolidated power sufficiently to grant himself a life term as president.

In the splintering Soviet Union, regional politics took on ethnic nationalism in a form strongly influenced by the Soviet regime's definitions of titular nationality – even where, as in Kazakhstan, regional leaders sought to maintain their membership in the Soviet Union or its successor. For the most part, Central Asian nationalism depended much less on bottom-up mobilization of shared national sentiment than on top-down creation of national institutions and identities. Speaking of Central Asian states Kazakhstan, Kyrgyzstan, Uzbekistan, and Turkmenistan together, Graham Smith and collaborators remark that:

> In addition to drawing on Soviet bureaucratic structures and institutions, the Central Asian states have underpinned their independence by elaborating nationalising policies and practices that seek to assert the hegemony of their respective titular nations. Despite formulations in the constitutions and other legislative acts guaranteeing the equality of all citizens, nationalising policies and practices are manifest in, *inter alia*, the iconography of the new regimes, the privileged status accorded to the local languages, newly revised histories and the exclusion of members of non-eponymous groups from the echelons of power. [Smith et al. 1998: 139]

Struggle, then, centers on neither the form nor the cultural frames of the regime, but on who has the right to speak for the titular nationality assigned to the region by Soviet authorities. That struggle, however, leads to resistance – a form of state-seeking nationalism – on the part of ethnic Russians and Russified elites. On behalf of both groups, Russia continues to press Kazakhstan for dual citizenship and for protection of the Russian language. Russian nationalist figures such as Alexander Solzhenitsyn step up the pressure by advocating formation of a Greater Russia including not only Ukraine and Belarus, but also northern Kazakhstan. Meanwhile, leaders of other self-identified nationalities make parallel demands for autonomy or even secession. Cossacks, for example, have entered politics contentiously and energetically in Kazakhstan's Northwest.

Having ridden the rapids of the Soviet Union's downstream rush and deploying resources originally afforded him by Soviet federalism, Gorbachev-appointed Nazarbaev still rules Kazakhstan with a heavy hand. His strategy of rule combines ruthless patrimonialism in the domestic arena with pragmatic nationalism in the international arena. His powerful daughter married the son of Askar Akaev, Kyrgyzstan's president. While tolerating (and possibly benefiting from) a great deal of rent seeking by former and present state officials, Nazarbaev has sought to advance a definition of Kazakh national identity without alienating either a large domestic Russian minority or the great Russian power to his north.

No doubt with an eye to intermittent civil war in nearby Tajikistan and the volatility of ethnic, linguistic, regional, and religious factions in neighboring Uzbekistan and Kyrgyzstan (Atkin 1997; Fane 1996; Fierman 1997;

Huskey 1997; Juraeva and Lubin 1996), Nazarbaev has handled ethnic-linguistic divisions with kid gloves. He expresses uncertainty about language as a basis for political identity:

> I do not accept the concept of "Russian-speaking population." Which of us is not a Russian speaker? After all, the whole of Kazakhstan speaks Russian, including 99 percent of Kazakhs. [Beissinger 1995: 170]

The only nationalist groups Nazarbaev's regime has actively suppressed are some Russian activists and the militant Alash party, which advocates a great state uniting all the Turkic peoples. Meanwhile, the regime resists pressure from outside (especially Russia) for recognition of dual citizenship, recruits ethnic Kazakh immigrants from China, Mongolia, Iran, Turkey, Uzbekistan, and Russia, as it presses its self-identified Russians to declare themselves either foreigners or dedicated citizens of a Kazakh state.

Without actively suppressing or expelling members of other categories, titular Kazakh authorities have treated Kazakh nationality as a patronage system that should advantage those who are willing to live within its limits. For whoever can claim to control the country, the stakes are high. Including its share of the Caspian, Kazakhstan contains enormous potential wealth in minerals, including estimated oil reserves of 40 to 178 billion barrels, equivalent to a quarter century of total U.S. oil consumption (Ingwerson 1997: 1). While not quite rivaling Afghanistan in drug production, rural Kazakhstan grows substantial amounts of cannabis and opium. Cocaine, other drugs, and a wide range of valuable contraband flow across the country, with mobsters and officials dividing large profits. Before the economic crises of the 1990s, furthermore, Kazakhstan supplied a substantial portion of the Soviet Union's commercial grains. If the state ever establishes an effective system of taxation and investment, it will have abundant revenues to spend, not to mention fortunes to be made in capitalist enterprises (see Feige 1998).

Claimants to that state actually divide sharply by ethnic category. As of the early 1990s, demographers enumerated 44 percent of the republic's population as Kazakh, 36 percent as Russian, and about 10 percent as "Europeans" of other varieties. The remaining tenth fell into a hundred other nationalities, chiefly Asian in origin (United Nations 1995: I, 6). By 1997, Kazakh officials were claiming 50.6 percent of the population as Kazakh and only 32.2 percent as Russian (Smith, et al. 1998: 153). The proportion identified as Kazakh was rising through a combination of differential fertility, exits of Russians, in-migration from other parts of Central Asia, and (most likely) shifts of declared identity on the parts of people with mixed ancestry. Nevertheless, the 1995 constitution's drafters had to contend with the fact that the country's ostensible nationality still accounted for no more than half of its population, and that the country's lingua franca was not Kazakh, but Russian.

In fact, many officially designated Kazakhs have grown up as Russian monolinguals, and are only learning their smattering of Kazakh under pressure. The most Kazakh authorities can hope for is that a new generation will grow up bilingual in Russian and Kazakh; even there, the prospect seems dim without a much larger effort at cultural transformation and a great diminution of ties to Russia. Kazakh nationalism does not reside in the population's widely shared identification with a unitary culture. It pivots on claims of national leaders to represent that population on the international stage.

In Kazakhstan, we again see the mechanisms of opportunity spirals, identity shift, competition, and brokerage, but from a very different angle. Kazakh leaders' claims to be Communist, Kazakh, and/or rightful rulers of a sovereign entity shifted with dizzying speed in response to changes in the external environment, notably relations to Russia and to other Soviet republics. Identity shift occurred multiple times in the same process, as the capacity and propensity of Soviet central authorities to certify and support the identity of loyal Union members shifted and waned. Competition entered the scene twice, both in struggles to seize resources within Kazakhstan and in shifting coalitions among the forces of Nazarbaev, Gorbachev, Yeltsin, and other republic leaders. Brokerage remained crucial on the same two fronts: both as the connection between Kazakh identity and state power within Kazakhstan, on one side, and as Nazarbaev's generally successful monopolization of relations between Kazakhstan and the rest of the world, on the other. Nazarbaev's agile alternation among Russian patrons and no patron at all itself constituted a tour de force of brokerage.

Italian Integration versus Soviet Disintegration

Considered as a whole and certainly in its outcome, the contentious unification of Italy between 1859 and 1870 seems quite a different phenomenon from the disintegration of Soviet unity between 1985 and 1995. It was. In the first case a regional power with poor legitimation integrated a diverse set of regions into a weak but centralized state through conquest, contention and brokerage, and avoided separatist nationalism for most of its unified history; in the other a strong state that had exercised apparently strong hegemony over a far-flung empire for seventy-four years disintegrated rapidly.

Yet both momentous episodes involved the interplay of state-led and state-seeking nationalism and national integration and disintegration. In both, claims and conflicts that it would be strained to define as essentially nationalist converged in episodes that history has labeled "nationalism." More important for our purposes, though they moved in opposite directions, the two episodes involved some of the same causal mechanisms. Operating in different contexts in different sequences and combinations, they produced massively different outcomes: a new and durable, if weakly integrated, state glued together by brokerage, on one side; a score of more or less independent states on the other.

We could obviously point to other mechanisms the two episodes had in common, for example the commitment, identity threat, repression, tactical innovation, and radicalization we have stressed in other contexts. We single out opportunity spirals, identity shift, competition, and brokerage for two reasons: first because they played such salient parts in these episodes; second because they help explain puzzling features of the same episodes.

In the case of Italy, it should no longer be puzzling that such a scattered, heterogeneous set of polities coalesced around a nationalist program and a constitutional monarchy – especially over the opposition of a powerful church. Mobilization and countermobilization of competitors for the national mantle (e.g., Cavour, Garibaldi, Mazzini, and their respective followers) followed the logic of an opportunity spiral, produced rapid identity shifts for political activists who had initially mobilized against local or regional enemies, involved direct competition for internationally recognized national power, and depended heavily on brokerage supplied both by veteran revolutionaries and by regional power holders. Long-standing regimes like the Bourbons' in southern Italy were decertified by a combination of internal revolt and international de-certification. Temporary alliances crystallized into durable arrangements of government. A ramshackle but durable state with grudging but effective acceptance of its priority over other authorities emerged from struggles that could easily have ended in losses of territory to adjacent states, creation of several rival states committed to antithetical programs, or return to the previous status quo.

In the Soviet Union's debacle, the puzzles we identified earlier were

1. How did a political economy that seemed so solid, centralized, authoritarian, and resourceful disintegrate visibly in five or six years?
2. Why did so much of the contentious claim making take the form of ethnic and national self- assertion?
3. How then did so many old regime power holders reappear in positions of power after the great transformation?

Opportunity spirals, identity shift, competition, and brokerage do not by themselves provide full answers to these questions. Yet a clear understanding of how brokerage worked during the Soviet Union's later years helps explain how regional leaders whose power depended on negotiation between Moscow and their favored regional constituencies shifted so rapidly from apparently dogged commitment to outright resistance. The rapid rise of ethnic and national assertion and their almost equally rapid turn to violent confrontation depended on all four mechanisms in concatenation – as, for example, the threat of one republic to exit from the Union increased the effectiveness of another republic's threat to exit. Old regime power holders reappeared in part because they appropriated pieces of the old state, which is not one of the mechanisms we have discussed at length in this chapter. But they also responded to and helped create identity shifts from Communist and Soviet to national, not in terms of age-old identities, but in terms already made available by the broker-mediated government of the disintegrating Soviet Union.

Although we might try to assimilate Italian unification to existing models of democratization or state formation and Soviet disintegration to existing models of revolution or imperial decline, the teaching of our analysis runs in precisely the opposite direction. Instead of considering these whole episodes as instances of distinct large-scale processes that operate according to their own laws, we gain much more explanatory leverage by examining them closely for political mechanisms that operate in a wide range of contention. The same lesson emerges from analysis of our third large-scale process, democratization.

9

Contentious Democratization

Decorous Switzerland and tumultuous Mexico make an odd couple. Yet comparison of their contentious, erratic paths toward democracy contributes to linking democratization with contentious politics. It establishes that for all their difference, both Switzerland and Mexico came to the unequal degrees of democracy they now experience through intense popular contention. It shows that initial paths in one direction or another – through French-led centralization in Switzerland and popular revolution in Mexico – need not determine future directions. It underscores the fact that strikingly different itineraries toward democracy exist, with each trajectory leaving significant marks on prevailing forms of public politics. It finally identifies recurrent mechanisms that figure importantly in democratization as they do in other contentious political processes.

In Switzerland, Mexico, or anywhere else, explaining democracy requires identification of recurrent causal mechanisms that democratize a polity, plus specification of conditions that affect emergence and concatenation of those mechanisms (Tilly 2000). Most theories of democratization either stop at the specification of conditions (e.g., socioeconomic modernization) or leap to the description of how it is effected (i.e., through successful transactions among elites). This chapter identifies some broad processes (combinations and sequences of mechanisms) in the analytical space between conditions and descriptions. In particular, it identifies processes that (a) insulate public politics from prevailing categorical inequalities and/or (b) integrate trust networks into public politics. Following the precedent of previous chapters, it singles out a few mechanisms for particular attention: coalition formation across classes, central cooptation of intermediaries, dissolution of patron-client networks, and the by now familiar mechanism of brokerage.

A comparison of Switzerland and Mexico also reveals the severe limits faced by all singular explanations of democracy:

- as a standard sequence of tests passed or failed
- as an expression of prevailing public attitudes or political culture
- as craft work by skilled leaders
- as a more or less likely outcome of economic growth
- as some combination of those elements

We emphasize the role of contentious politics in democratization, pointing to some paradoxes and tipping points that help to explain democracy's detours. We follow by specifying two broad paths of democratization – a weak state path and a strong state one, illustrating the two in the cases of Switzerland and Mexico. We finally focus on two processes that help explain the dynamics of the two paths and compare their contrasting outcomes in our two uncommon cases.

Definitions and Pathways

How will we know democratization when we see it? Working definitions of democracy divide into three overlapping categories: *substantive* criteria emphasizing qualities of human experience and social ties; *constitutional* criteria emphasizing legal procedures such as elections and referenda; *political-process* criteria emphasizing interactions among politically constituted actors (for reviews and critiques, see Bratton and van de Walle 1997; Collier and Levitsky 1997; Dawisha 1997). Our preferred definition falls squarely within the political-process category. For present purposes:

> A regime is democratic insofar as it maintains broad citizenship, equal and autonomous citizenship, binding consultation of citizens at large with respect to governmental activities and personnel, as well as protection of citizens from arbitrary action by governmental agents.

We prefer such a political-process definition on the grounds that (a) it captures much of what theorists of democracy from Aristotle onward have been trying to describe without the usual inconveniences of substantive and constitutional definitions, (b) it locates democracy within a causally coherent and more general field of variation in characteristics and practices of regimes, (c) it clarifies causal connections between popular contention and democratization, a much misunderstood but crucial relationship.

Regimes vary, among other ways, in *breadth* (the proportion of all persons under the government's jurisdiction that belong to polity members), *equality* (the extent to which persons who do belong to polity members have similar autonomy and access to governmental agents and resources), *consultation* (the degree to which polity members exercise binding collective control over governmental agents, resources, and activities), and finally *protection* (shielding of polity members and their constituencies from arbitrary action by governmental agents). Breadth, equality, consultation, and protection change in partial independence of each other; authoritarian populist regimes, for example, have commonly created relatively broad and equal polity membership in combination with limited consultation and little protection. To simplify matters, nevertheless, we can combine breadth, equality, consultation, and protection into a bundle of variables we call *protected consultation*. When protected consultation reaches high levels, we begin to speak of democracy. Strictly speaking, then, democratization is not a consequence of changes in public politics but a special kind of alteration in public politics.

If democracy entails high levels of protected consultation by definition, as a practical matter it also requires the institution of citizenship. Citizenship consists, in this context, of mutual rights and obligations binding governmental agents to whole categories of people who are subject to the government's authority, those categories being defined chiefly or exclusively by general relations to a specific government rather than by reference to particular connections with rulers or to membership in categories based on imputed durable traits such as race, ethnicity, gender, or religion. Citizenship fortifies breadth and equality of political participation as it defines boundaries between segments of the population that are and are not eligible for different degrees of binding consultation and protection. Democratization means any net shift toward citizenship, breadth of citizenship, equality of citizenship, binding consultation, and protection.

Figure 9.1 schematizes the line of reasoning that follows. Where low governmental capacity and little protected consultation prevail, political life goes on in fragmented tyranny: with multiple coercive forces, small-scale despots, and competitors for larger-scale power, but no effective central government.

The diagram's opposite corner contains the zone of citizenship: mutual rights and obligations binding governmental agents to whole categories of people who are subject to the government's authority, those categories being defined chiefly or exclusively by relations to the government rather

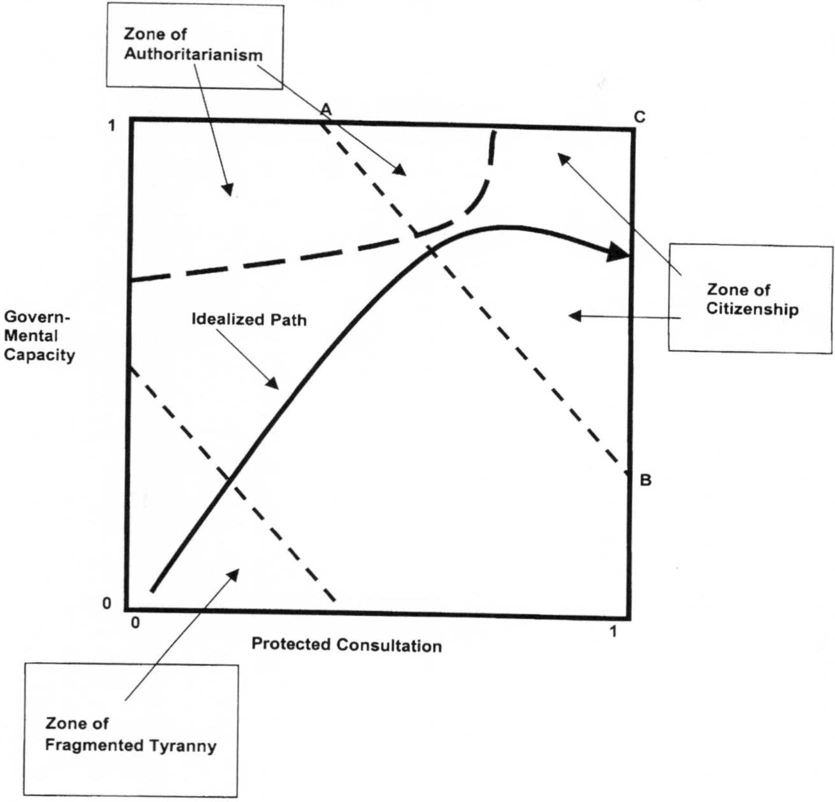

Figure 9.1. Effective Democratization

than by reference to particular ties with rulers or membership in categories based on imputed durable traits such as race, ethnicity, gender, or religion.

At point A of the diagram's triangular citizenship zone, a combination of little protected consultation and extremely high governmental capacity describes a regimented state, one we might call totalitarian. Nazi Germany illustrates political processes at the apex – or the nadir – of that point. At point B, protected consultation has reached its maximum, but governmental capacity is so low the regime runs the risk of internal and external attack. Nineteenth century Belgium never reached that point, but veered repeatedly toward it (Deneckere 1997). Point C – maximum governmental capacity plus maximum protected consultation – is probably empty because of incompatibilities between extremely high capacity and protected consultation. This line of reasoning leads to our sketching a zone of authoritarianism in the diagram's upper left, overlapping the zone of citizenship but by no means exhausting it. It also suggests an idealized path for effective democratization giving roughly equal weight to increases in governmental capacity and protected consultation up to the point of entry into citizenship, but then turning to deceleration, and ultimately mild reduction, of capacity where protected consultation has settled in.

Contention and Democratization

This takes us to contentious politics. To say that democratization means any net shift toward protected consultation signifies at a minimum, that (a) some groups want such a shift to take place and are willing to make vigorous efforts to effectuate it; (b) those groups may consist of governmental elites, counterelites, people demanding it for themselves, or some combination of these; (c) others who see their vested rights and privileges threatened are likely to oppose it; but that (d) except in retrospect, many of those efforts may not be thought of either by claim makers or by those who receive them as demands for democracy. Democratization, in other words, is not A Single Thing, but the contingent outcome of interactions among a number of claims and counterclaims. Contending claims produce new grids of relationships that work through protected consultation among claimants and counterclaimants for public goods. All of this means that (e) like our trajectories of contention, democratization is not a finite and linear process and that (f) various forms and processes of contention familiar from earlier chapters – social movements, revolutions, war, nationalism, labor conflict – can combine to produce protected consultation.

Contentious processes can also combine to detour polities from democratization, not only because some people oppose democracy itself, but also – and probably primarily – because claims made in the name of democracy threaten their vested interests. Such counterclaims have so frequently detoured countries away from democracy that some well-meaning observers interpret contention itself as a threat to democracy. They have plenty of cases to support them: struggles of the Spanish Republic leading to civil war and Francoism; collapse of the Weimar Republic and the opening it gave to German National Socialism; the combination of rural revolt and urban militancy that allowed Mussolini to take power in Italy (Linz and Stepan 1979).

But those are cases of democratic detours. Democracy results from, mobilizes, and reshapes popular contention. Two features of that interdependence help account for the mistaken impression that the two are incompatible. First, on the whole, democratization greatly limits life- and property-threatening forms of public, collective claim making, substituting for them highly visible but less directly destructive varieties of interaction. Second, in democratic regimes, on the average, threats and declared intentions to act in a certain way (instead of nonnegotiable direct actions) occupy much more central positions in popular politics than they do in nondemocratic regimes. Yet in fact such threats lead to open conflict from time to time, and would lack credibility if they did not.

Our analytic problem, then, is to discover how and why regimes make net moves toward protected consultation, especially those net moves that bring them into the narrow zone of citizenship and democracy. Our empirical problem is to understand how and when contentious politics leads polities toward this zone. Since many regimes that edge toward democracy later veer away, we can hope that solution of our primary analytic problem will also help explain why de-democratization occurs. Since some spectacularly contentious processes produce democracy while others do not, and still others do so with fragility, tracing processes of contention comparatively will address our analytical problem as well.

Strong and Weak Paths to Democracy

Movement toward protected consultation intersects with another important dimension: *governmental capacity.* Capacity is the extent of the control governmental agents have over changes in the condition of persons, activities, and resources within the territory over which the government exercises jurisdiction. Beyond a very small scale, no democracy survives in the absence of substantial governmental capacity. That is true for both internal and external reasons. Internally, maintenance of protection, consultation, equality, and breadth against the maneuvers of powerful domestic actors who have incentives to subvert them rests on substantial governmental capacity. Externally, governments lacking substantial capacity remain vulnerable to subversion, attack, or even conquest by bandits, rebels, guerrilla forces, and outside governments.

Within the space of Figure 9.2, we can imagine two extreme trajectories from petty tyranny to some sort of democracy:

A weak-state path featuring early expansion of protected consultation followed only much later by increase in governmental capacity at the large scale, hence entry into the zone of effective citizenship from below; only a few modern states followed this trajectory completely because most of them that started succumbed to conquest or disintegration.

A strong-state path featuring early expansion of governmental capacity, entry into the zone of authoritarianism, expansion of protected

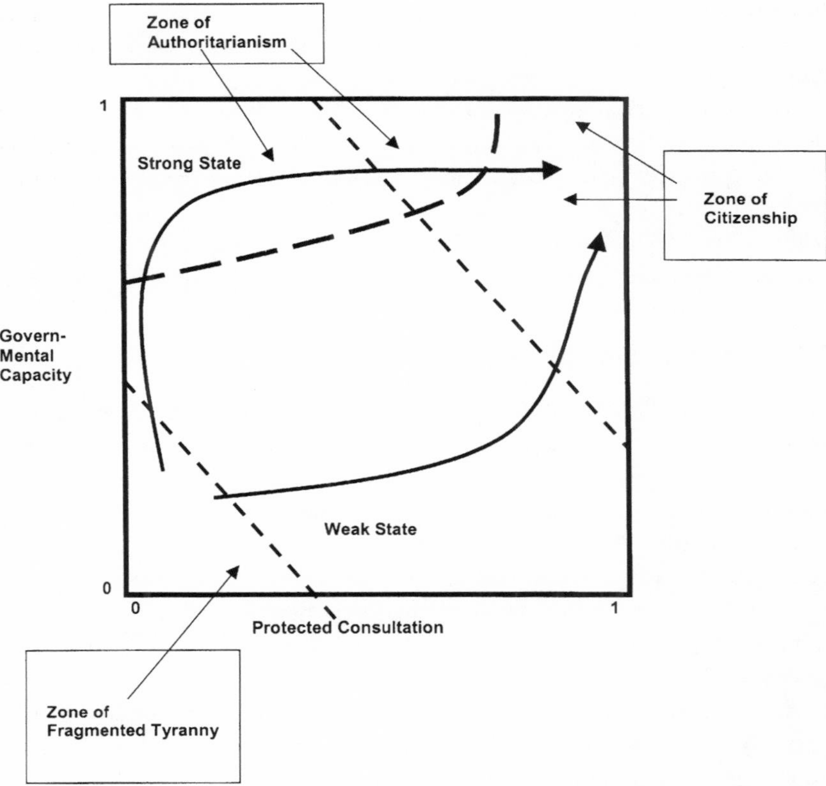

Figure 9.2. Strong-State versus Weak-State Paths to Democracy

consultation through a phase of authoritarian citizenship, finally the emergence of a less authoritarian, more democratic, but still high-capacity regime.

Two brief examples of democratic detours along weak and strong state paths suffice to illustrate how many ways there are to leave the road between tyranny and protected consultation. From the perspective of its large noble class (although certainly not from the perspectives of its merchants and peasants), eighteenth century Poland's government bristled with protected consultation. With heavy-handed intervention from neighboring powers, after all, Polish nobles elected their king, sometimes deposed him, and usually maintained armed forces of their own far surpassing the royal army. As a composite state, Poland notoriously lacked capacity, so much so that rebellions of Cossacks and others almost destroyed the state in the mid-eighteenth century. Conquest by Russia, Prussia, and Austria from without choked off Poland's existence as an autonomous state from 1795 to World War I.

Venice followed a startling version of the strong state trajectory, but came nowhere near democracy until the later nineteenth century. Venetian merchants, pirates, and warlords built up one of Europe's most predatory and effective states between the tenth and fifteenth centuries, creating a fragmented empire extending around much of the Adriatic and Eastern Mediterranean. A tight, stratified oligarchy grew wealthy from trade and predation, but allowed the bulk of the Venetian population – at home and abroad – no say whatsoever in public affairs. Elected doges came only from the highest levels of the Venetian patriciate. Even during the relative decline of Venetian commercial power after 1600, Venice's republic remained the instrument of a small ruling class. With Napoleon's invasion of 1797, to be sure, Venice participated temporarily in the new Italian regime of representative institutions. The restored republic fought beside Europe's democrats, and lost, in 1848, before falling into Austrian hands until 1866. Only after joining the newly forming Italian kingdom did Venice move into a limited but relatively durable regime of protected consultation.

Over the past few centuries, few real histories have demonstrated such dramatic extremes as old regime Poland and fourteenth- to nineteenth-century Venice. Most described more erratic courses with reversals and sudden shifts in both dimensions. The vast majority entered or approached the zone of authoritarianism at one time or another. In all cases of democratization, however, some versions of three critical processes took place: partial insulation of public politics from material inequalities, partial integration of private trust networks into public politics, and installation of protected consultation into the routines of public politics. For regimes following the strong-state trajectory, these processes entailed dismantling the apparatus of authoritarianism. For regimes following the weak-state trajectory, sheer creation of state capacity and its commitment to protected consultation played central parts. In between, conversion of expanding state capacity to democratic politics generated struggle after struggle.

Democratization, then, never happened without intense contention. But only under special conditions did contention yield net movements toward democracy. In all three idealized trajectories toward protected consultation – strong-state, weak-state, and intermediate – insulation of public politics from material inequality, integration of trust networks into public politics, and alterations of public politics occurred. Within each of these processes, characteristic mechanisms such as crossclass coalition formation appeared repeatedly.

We use two uncommon cases – one of them establishing rudiments of democracy over a century ago, and the other nibbling at its edge today – to examine some of the processes and mechanisms typical of strong-state and weak-state routes toward protected consultation. To further our analytical goals, we skim lightly over the early histories of the two countries, ignore most of the change mechanisms that contribute to democratization, and zero in on two processes that constructively contrast them: insulation of public politics from material inequality and integration of trust networks into public politics. Within those two processes, we single out just four important causal mechanisms: crossclass coalition formation, central cooptation of intermediaries, dissolution of patron-client networks, and brokerage.

At the threshold of the twenty-first century, Switzerland stands as one of the world's older democracies. It has retained from the nineteenth century an oligarchic air and a mosaic structure, but it carries on public business through consultation of the citizenry, provides substantial protections to people who qualify as its citizens, and generally contains contention within the prescribed and tolerated forms of expression 150 years of democratic experience have laid down as the norm. For most of its postrevolutionary history, in contrast, Mexico filled its quasidemocratic institutions with authoritarian content. Although elections produced regular turnover in presidents and other public officials, losing parties frequently challenged the honesty of those elections, opposition parties until recently could not shake national dominance by the governing coalition, *guerrilla* sputtered and occasionally exploded in several regions, and citizens still suffer dramatically unequal treatment by government officials from police to presidents. Only in the year 2000 did a peaceful alternation in presidential power take place. Yet by comparison with its autocratic nineteenth century history, Mexico has moved toward democracy.

Our comparison of Switzerland and Mexico raises questions about the various paths that lead away from tyranny or oligarchy toward democracy. Figure 9.3 locates idealized Mexican and Swiss trajectories from 1750 to 1990 within the space. It shows Mexico more closely approximating the strong-state path, Switzerland the weak-state path, with neither one

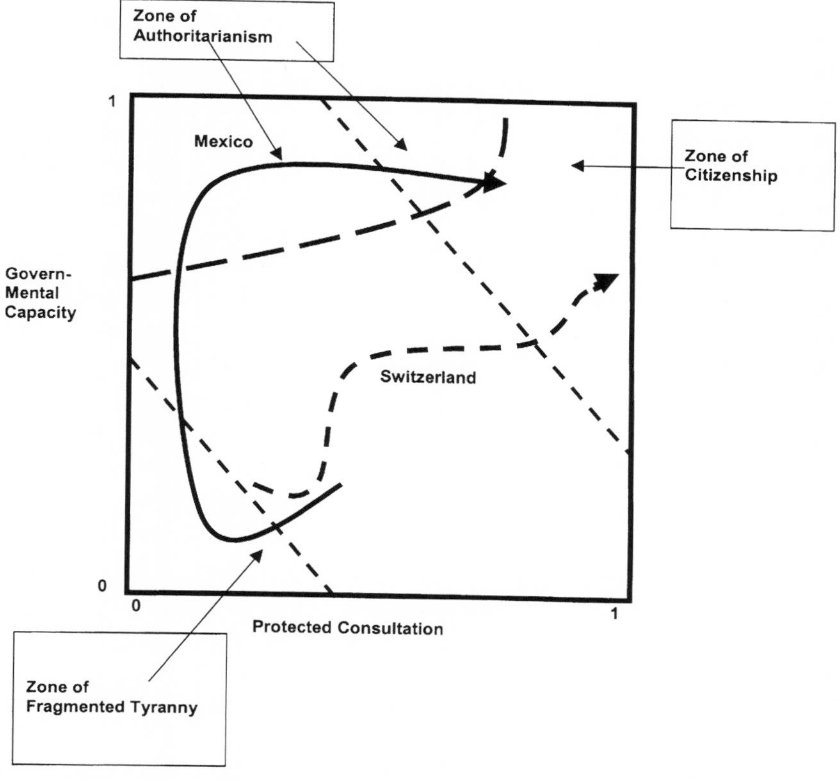

Figure 9.3. Mexican and Swiss Paths Toward Democracy, 1750–1990

cleaving tightly to the extreme version of the paths that we sketched in the cases of Poland and Venice. But that is all that it shows; it leaves vacant the processes that produced Switzerland's precocious semidemocracy in 1848 and Mexico's semiauthoritarianism after 1928.

Processes and Mechanisms of Change

Where should we look for explanations? Democratization emerges from interacting changes in three analytically separable but causally interdependent sets of social relations – public politics, inequality, and networks of trust – all connected to changes in the regime environment. In the course of democratization, the bulk of a government's subject population acquires binding, protected, relatively equal claims on a government's agents, activities, and resources. In a related process, categorical inequality declines in those areas of social life that either constitute or immediately support participation in public politics. Finally, a significant shift occurs in the locus of interpersonal networks on which people rely when undertaking risky long-term enterprises such as marriage, long-distance trade, membership in crafts, and investment of savings. Such networks move from evasion of governmental detection and control to involvement in the polity and the presumption that government agents will meet their long-term commitments. Where the three sets of changes intersect, effective and durable democracy emerges. Conquest, confrontation, revolution, and colonization sometimes accelerate democratization not because of their *sui generis* properties but because they intensify and accelerate the same mechanisms that promote democratizing alterations of trust networks, categorical inequality, and public politics in the course of incremental change.

Table 9.1 lists combinations and sequences of mechanisms and processes that in principle, according to this argument, are likely to play a part in democratization. In this first encounter of our analytical scheme with complex historical episodes, we will not demand evidence for the operation of each hypothetical mechanism. We will count results as encouraging if most of the following apply:

- changes in trust networks and categorical inequality affect the extent and character of protected consultation
- shifts within public politics likewise affect the extent and character of protected consultation

Table 9.1. *Sample Mechanisms and Processes Promoting Democratization*

1. Inequality
• dissolution of coercive controls supporting current relations of exploitation and opportunity hoarding
• education and communication that alter adaptations supporting current relations of exploitation and opportunity hoarding
• education and communication that supplant existing models of organization, hence alter emulation of inequality in formation of new organizations
• equalization of assets and/or well-being across categories within the population at large
• insulation of existing categorical inequalities from public politics
2. Networks of Trust
• creation of external guarantees for government commitments
• incorporation and expansion of existing trust networks into the polity
• governmental absorption or destruction of previously autonomous patronclient networks
• disintegration of existing trust networks
• expansion of the population lacking access to effective trust networks for their major long term risky enterprises
• appearance of new long term risky opportunities that existing trust networks can not handle
• substantial increase of government's resources for risk reduction and/or compensation of loss
• visible governmental meeting of commitments to the advantage of substantial new segments of the population
3. Public Politics
• coalition formation between segments of ruling classes and constituted political actors that are currently excluded from power
• brokerage of coalitions across unequal categories and/or distinct trust networks
• central co-optation or elimination of previously autonomous political intermediaries
• bureaucratic containment of previously autonomous military forces
• dissolution or segregation from government of nongovernmental patronclient networks
• imposition of uniform governmental structures and practices through the government's jurisdiction
• mobilization-repression-bargaining cycles during which currently excluded actors act collectively in ways that threaten survival of the government and/or its ruling classes, governmental repression fails, struggle ensues, and settlements concede political standing and/or rights to mobilized actors
• extraction-resistance-bargaining cycles during which governmental agents demand resources under control of nongovernmental networks and committed to nongovernmental ends, holders of those resources resist, struggle ensues, and settlements emerge in which people yield resources but receive credible guarantees with respect to constraints on future extraction

- mechanisms and processes in those changes generally alter involvement of governmental agents with trust networks
- mechanisms and processes in those changes generally alter insulation between categorical inequality and public politics
- mechanisms and processes in those changes generally affect the breadth, equality, binding influence, and protection of political participation
- confrontation, colonization, conquest, and revolution produce their effects on protected consultation by accelerating some of the same mechanisms and processes
- similar mechanisms and processes affect paths of democratization and dedemocratization in both Switzerland and Mexico
- no obviously simpler, more powerful, or better known scheme clearly accounts for both episodes

It would complicate our analysis excessively to elaborate each of these claims. Let us examine two of them in Switzerland's and Mexico's very different paths toward democratization – the effects of changes in trust networks and categorical inequality on the extent and character of protected consultation. We argue that the combination of (a) trust networks becoming involved in the polity and (b) insulation of categorical inequalities from the state – but not necessarily their reduction – help to produce democratization. More narrowly, we claim that:

- crossclass coalition formation (creation of coordinated action across a major class boundary) promotes insulation of categorical inequality from public politics.
- central cooptation of intermediaries (integration of previously autonomous brokers and leaders of subordinate categories into governing coalitions) promotes integration of trust networks into public politics.
- dissolution of patron-client networks (breaking of asymmetrical and personalistic chains of relationship connecting power holders with subordinates) likewise promotes integration of trust networks into public politics.
- brokerage (linking of two or more currently unconnected social sites by a unit that mediates their relations with each other and/or with yet another site) facilitates the first two mechanisms – crossclass coalition formation and central cooptation of intermediaries.

Yet these mechanisms and processes combined very differently in Switzerland and Mexico. They contributed to long-limited but relatively stable democratization in Switzerland, but have not yet produced stable democracy in Mexico. We see an earlier, weak-state route in this direction in Switzerland; we see a later, and still deeply contested, strong-state route in Mexico.

Switzerland

The Swiss experience stands out for yet another "dog that didn't bark": its transition to representative government in the presence of consistent linguistic and religious differences. Important distinctions have long existed between Switzerland's Germanic-speaking northern and eastern cantons, its French-speaking western border cantons, its Italian-speaking southern rim, and its Romansch-speaking enclaves in the southeast. Within nominally German-speaking regions prevail sharp town to town differences in the Alemannic dialects known generically as Schwyzerdütsch, which actually serve as languages of choice for spoken communication. With a dominant cleavage based on religion and inherited from the Reformation, nevertheless, the Swiss have rarely fought over linguistic distinctions.

Switzerland is even more remarkable for the vitality of representative institutions in company with fairly weak state structures. Similar regimes elsewhere in Europe generally succumbed, like Poland, to conquest by higher-capacity (and less democratic) neighbors. Switzerland's topography, its ability to summon up military defense when pressed, and rivalries among its powerful neighbors gave it breathing room similar to that enjoyed by Liechtenstein and Andorra. Whatever else we say about the Swiss itinerary toward democracy, it certainly passed through intense popular struggle, including extensive military action. The same process that produced a higher-capacity central government, furthermore, also created Switzerland's restricted but genuine democracy: as compared with what came before, relatively broad – if unequal – citizenship, binding consultation of citizens, and substantial protection of citizens from arbitrary action by governmental agents. But it veered away early from the strong-state path to democracy favored by the French occupiers, and made the transition to democracy by encapsulating enclaves of local oligarchy and inequality in its federal system.

Long a scattering of belligerent fiefs within successive German empires, most Swiss areas acquired de facto independence at the Peace of Basel

(1499) and de jure recognition as a federation at the Peace of Westphalia (1648). Their control of major transalpine routes for trade, travel, and troop movements gave Switzerland's segments the means of political and commercial survival, but also made them objects of incessant intervention by neighboring powers. "The peculiarity of Switzerland's former social order," observed Karl Deutsch,

> expressed itself in the singularity of its mountain cantons. A mountain canton such as Uri is a peasant canton with moneyed, armed, superbly informed peasants; it is a natural city with mountains instead of city walls and mountain passes instead of city gates. It is also an agricultural region that hosts an urban style of government that conceives of itself as a self-governing city. Below, in the Midlands exists the league of burghers of city-states such as Bern and Zurich with the peasants of their own canton, hence another relation between urban citizens and rural residents. Thus the rights of small towns were well established and the self-government of those towns all the more respected. [Deutsch 1976: 34–35]

Until the eighteenth century's end, the federation remained no more than a loose alliance of thirteen cantons with strong ties to allied territories of Geneva, Grisons (Graubünden), and Valais, plus subject territories (e.g., Vaud, Lugano, Bellinzona, and Valtellina) of their component units. From the sixteenth to eighteenth centuries, Switzerland withdrew almost entirely from international war on its own account, but supplied crack mercenary troops to much of Europe. During that period, Switzerland's politics operated chiefly at the local and cantonal levels: outward-looking efforts to hold off other powers, inward-looking efforts to deal with enormous disparities and particularities of privilege.

Over this entire era, individual cantons featured a degree of democratic deliberation that stood out from almost all of Europe, but only limited state capacity. "The old Confederation in its last decades," remarks Jonathan Steinberg,

> was a marvellous thing, a patchwork of overlapping jurisdictions, ancient customs, worm-eaten privileges and ceremonies, irregularities of custom, law, weights and measures. On the shores of Lake Luzern, the independent republic of Gersau flourished with all of 2,000 inhabitants and enjoyed much prestige among political theorists of the time as the smallest free state in Europe. The famous Göttingen Professor Friedrich Christoph Schlosser seriously toyed with the idea of writing a multi-volume history of the republic under "a universal-historical" aspect as a microcosm of all of European history. [Steinberg 1996: 39–40]

Conquered by Napoleon (with assistance from Swiss revolutionaries) in 1798, then receiving a new constitution that year, the Swiss briefly adopted a more centralized form of government. The national government remained fragile, however; four coups occurred between 1800 and 1802 alone. At the withdrawal of French troops in 1802, multiple rebellions broke out. Switzerland then rushed to the brink of civil war; only Napoleon's intervention and imposition of a new constitution in 1803 kept the country together. The regime of 1803, known interestingly as "the Mediation," restored considerable powers to cantons, but by no means reestablished the Old Regime. Switzerland's recast federation operated with a national assembly, official multilingualism, relative equality among cantons, and freedom for citizens to move from canton to canton.

Despite some territorial adjustments, a weak central legislature, judiciary, and executive survived Napoleon's defeat after another close brush with civil war (this time averted by Great Power intervention) from 1813 to 1815. By the war settlement of 1815, Austria, France, Great Britain, Portugal, Prussia, Russia, Spain, and Sweden accepted a treaty among twenty-two cantons called the Federal Pact as they guaranteed Switzerland's perpetual neutrality and the inviolability of its frontiers.

Switzerland of the Federal Pact operated without a permanent bureaucracy, a standing army, common coinage, standard measures, or a national flag, but with multiple internal customs barriers, a rotating capital, and incessant bickering among cantonal representatives who had no right to deviate from their home constituents' instructions. Let us stress that weakness of state capacity in the 1830s. Writing from Bern to Claude-François de Corcelle on July 27, 1836, Alexis de Tocqueville declared that:

> In my quality as an *American* I have already developed proud disdain for the Swiss federal constitution, which I frankly call a league and not a federation; a government of this sort is the softest, most powerless, most awkward, and the least capable of leading people anywhere but to anarchy that one can imagine. The kingdom of England is a hundred times more republican than this so-called Republic. [de Tocqueville 1983: 70]

At the national scale, the Swiss lived within a system better disposed to vetoes than to concerted change. With a Protestant majority concentrated in the richer, more industrial and urban cantons, an approximate political split Protestant-liberal-radical versus Catholic-conservative became salient in Swiss politics by the 1830s, with pockets of anticlericalism in the cities. In regions dominated by conservative cities such as Basel, the countryside often supported liberal or radical programs. In centers of growing capital-intensive production such as Zurich, conflict pitted a bourgeoisie much attached to oligarchic political privilege against an expanding working class that bid increasingly for voice in public politics and allied increasingly with dissident radicals among the bourgeoisie.

The political problem became acute because national alignments of the mid-1840s pitted twelve richer and predominantly liberal–Protestant cantons against ten poorer, predominantly conservative–Catholic cantons in a diet where each canton had a single vote. (Strictly speaking, some units on each side, products themselves of earlier splits, qualified as half-cantons casting half a vote each, but the 12 to 10 balance of votes held.) Thus liberals deployed the rhetoric of national patriotism and majority rule while conservatives countered with cantonal rights and defense of religious traditions. Three levels of citizenship – municipal, cantonal, and national – competed with each other (see Prak 1998).

Contention occurred incessantly, and often with vitriolic violence, from 1830 to 1848. As the Belgian and French revolutions of 1830 rolled on, smaller scale revolutions took place in the Swiss towns and cantons of Aargau, Lucerne, St. Gallen, Schaffhausen, Solothurn, Thurgau, Vaud, and Zurich. Thereafter, republicans and radicals repeatedly formed military bands (often called free corps, or *Freischärler*) and attempted to take over particular cantonal capitals by force of arms. Such bands failed in Lucerne (1841), but succeeded in bringing new administrations to power in Lausanne (1847), Geneva (1847), and Neuchâtel (1848).

Given Switzerland's later staid reputation, the chronology makes startling reading. During 1831, 1832, 1833, 1834, 1839, 1841, 1847, and 1848, armed struggles over forms and prerogatives of government shook one part of Switzerland or another. The largest military engagement took place in 1847, when Switzerland's federal Diet ordered dissolution of the mutual defense league (Sonderbund) formed by Catholic cantons two years earlier. When the Catholic cantons refused, the Diet sent an army to Fribourg and Zug (whose forces capitulated without serious fighting), then Lucerne (where a short battle occurred). The Sonderbund had about 79,000 men under arms, the federation some 99,000. The Sonderbund War ended with thirty-three dead among Catholic forces and sixty dead among the attackers. Its defeat consolidated the dominance of liberals in Switzerland as a whole, and led to the adoption of a cautiously liberal constitution, on something like an American model, in 1848.

The settlement of 1848 only occurred as the result of outright civil war. Yet that peace settlement laid the foundations for a long period of limited but stable democracy at the national level. It resulted from a compromise between the cantons of relatively direct democracy at the local and cantonal scale – Lucerne, Uri, Schwyz, Unterwald and Zug – and those that had set up representative systems – Geneva, Fribourg, Vaud, Bern, Solothurn, Aargau, Zurich, Schaffhausen, and Ticino.

Two paradoxes, then: popular armed struggle that issued in democracy, and the fiercest opposition to national democracy from those who had practiced direct democracy at home. Resolution of the second paradox helps resolve the first. The "direct democracy" of regions that opposed federal reform really consisted of government by assembly based on jealously guarded equality within a restricted class of qualifying citizens. In direct parallels to those parts of urban Europe where cities enjoyed considerable political autonomy, male citizens of Swiss communes and cantons had rights and obligations to bear arms in civic militias – so much so that well into the nineteenth century eligible voters commonly carried a sword, dagger, or bayonet as signs of their distinction. For centuries before the 1840s, armed assemblies frequently formed on their own initiative to protest actions by one authority or another. Sometimes they overturned regimes by force, created temporary assemblies to judge or debate authorities' actions, or coerced authorities themselves to call assemblies of citizenry (Head 1995).

Behind public equality stood oligarchy, chauvinism, and coercion. Although an assembly's majority could and sometimes did reject proposals by a commune's or canton's officers, in practice wealthy men generally dominated high public office and rarely let serious opposition to their role reach public expression. Where the sheer scale of local polities inhibited routine government by direct assembly, cantons commonly adopted the veto (in which only a majority of qualified voters could overturn a formal proposal, regardless of how many actually voted) or the referendum (in which a majority of those voting on a proposal carried the day, regardless of how many actually voted) as a substitute for face to face, *viva voce* deliberation. No matter what the procedures, Swiss versions of direct democracy typically involved narrow participation, relatively equal rights within the charmed circle of participants, binding consultation of those participants, and limited protections for anyone outside their number. Swiss direct democracy also coupled with fierce protection of local and cantonal politics from outside interference. The system protected not individual liberty so much as collective autonomy.

The Protestant, liberal, commercial, and industrializing cantons that adopted representative democracy, in contrast, generally expanded popular participation in cantonal politics and sought a stronger national union to protect and promote trade and hold off Switzerland's aggressive neighbors. Switzerland's armed struggle between 1830 and 1848 resulted largely from efforts of urban activists for representative democracy to beat down the oligarchic politics of direct democracy. In so doing, they willy-nilly became advocates of a stronger central state as well. But their need to forge some kind of national unity and the stubborn resistance of the mountain cantons led the burghers of Zurich and Bern to integrate cantonal autonomy permanently within the new federal settlement.

The hard-won Swiss constitution of 1848 thus established a federal system, not a unitary state on the French model. It split sovereignty between the federal government and the cantons. It created a bicameral representative system in the American style, with equal representation of cantons in the upper house, roughly equal representation of voters in the lower house and protection of local language rights. Despite the victory of 1848, Swiss constitution makers still had to get their proposals past a majority of cantons, then past a majority of voters in a national referendum. In the process, they lost proposals for a strongly centralized army, a national public school system, a national road system, and a single national language (Ruffieux 1983: 9).

As compared with late nineteenth-century French or British models of democracy, the Swiss federal system looks extraordinarily decentralized and heterogeneous: a distinctive constitution, dominant language and citizenship for each canton; multiple authorities and compacts; a remarkable combination of exclusiveness with the capacity to create particular niches for newly accepted political actors. "Not so long ago," remarked Lionel Gossman in 1999, "old Baselers still spoke of 'going to Switzerland' just as they might speak of going to France or Germany" [Gossman 2000: 6]. Swiss cantons perform many activities that more centralized systems assign unambiguously to direct agents of a national state structure. For example, even the Swiss national army lies partly under cantonal control: Cantonal authorities can promote officers up to the rank of captain. Civil servants and university professors must live and pay taxes within the canton where they work. When we speak of the national scale or the federal state, then, we are using a shorthand for political activity involving either the federal Diet, its direct agents, or coordinated action among cantons. Through all subsequent constitutional changes, those residues of Swiss political history have persisted. They continue to exercise profound effects on contentious politics within

Switzerland (Giugni and Passy 1997; Kriesi, et al. 1981; Kriesi, et al. 1995, Trechsel 2000).

In terms of the federal government's trajectory within our capacity-protection space, by the end of 1848 Switzerland at the national scale had moved significantly toward broadened political participation, arguably extended political equality among groups and individuals, maintaining binding consultation and protections while considerably augmenting the central state's capacity. At that point, we can reasonably speak of nonauthoritarian Swiss federal citizenship. In between, the Swiss federal state had suffered grievous attacks on its capacity, protections had declined, and civil war had torn the country apart. But in the course and aftermath of that civil war, the federal state built its capacity to a level unprecedented except perhaps under French hegemony between 1798 and 1803. Swiss political history from 1830 to 1850 followed a struggle-filled version of the weak state trajectory toward democracy.

Let us concentrate, then, on the critical period from 1830 to 1848. During those nineteen years, Switzerland (considered as a whole) went from an uneasy federation among cantankerous, unequal, internally oligarchic cantons connected politically by no more than exiguous central institutions to a relatively solid semidemocratic federation. On the way, it passed through repeated armed conflicts, multiple small-scale revolutions, and a civil war that could have split the country permanently.

For centuries before the 1840s, local oligarchies insulated themselves from what passed for a Swiss national state through limited local direct democracy (Head 1995). Switzerland's armed struggle between 1830 and 1848 resulted largely from efforts of activists for representative democracy to beat down the oligarchic politics of direct democracy. In so doing, they not only created a stronger central state but brought these oligarchies into the broader Swiss polity that they were creating. They did not, in doing so, increase equality; but they did insulate the new national state from the deep inequalities that marked Swiss society and geography and begin to weave trust networks across a segmented polity.

Swiss Inequality

Categorical inequalities translate easily into differences in political rights and obligations as well as providing bases for collective contention. But the inscription of prevailing categorical inequality by gender, religion, race, class, or other dividing principles inhibits democratization. It fosters inequality in political participation, promotes inequality in rights and obligations of citizenship, compromises binding consultation, and enfeebles protection from arbitrary action by state agents. Although democratization does not depend on elimination of material inequality in the population as a whole, it does depend on the formation of buffers between major day-to-day inequalities and public politics. In very unequal early nineteenth century Switzerland, then, the question was what might create buffers between public politics and deep divisions by language, religion, class, and locality. In the account that follows, we pay particular attention to the mechanism of crossclass coalition formation. That coalition formation originally occurred within religious divisions, but eventually breached even those divisions. It only happened because of powerful brokerage by Swiss cantonal leaders.

Let us focus fixedly on the national scale. Switzerland's relative democratization of national politics after 1830 resulted in part from local and regional seizures of power by democrats of various stripes, but it did not always entail democratization of local and regional politics. In the highly industrial half-canton of Appenzell Ausserrhoden, for example, a semiannual outdoor general assembly (*Landsgemeinde*) of male citizens long held ultimate political authority. But as typical ages of school attendance and work shifted, the canton actually raised its minimum age for participation from sixteen to eighteen in 1834, and again from eighteen to twenty in 1876 (Tanner 1982: 396); with respect to age, the canton dedemocratized.

What is more, Appenzell's major cantonal officers, who actually set the agenda for general assemblies, came overwhelmingly from leading mercantile and industrial families. When it came to officeholding in parish government, the town of Bühler actually included more poor men in 1810–1820 (after French hegemony had extended political participation) than toward 1840 (Tanner 1982: 382–383). Increasing material and political inequality in villages, towns, and cantons could cohabit with increasing political equality in national politics so long as the spheres remained partially insulated from each other.

On the small scale, indeed, Switzerland featured startling combinations of equality and inequality. Fellow citizens of cities or of villages, speakers of the same dialects, comembers of religious congregations insisted on equal public standing. So long as Switzerland relied on agriculture, small crafts, transalpine shipping, and the export of troops for its livelihood, its localized governments fitted forms of rule to patterns of material inequality like glove to hand. During the eighteenth century, however, the expansion of cottage textile production created new classes of workers and entrepreneurs who escaped the usual relations of urban masters, merchants, and landlords, on one side, with artisans and peasants, on the other. By 1774, for example, in the hinterland of Basel only 17.6 percent of all household heads were farmers, 27.3 percent were day laborers, and the remaining 55.1 percent industrial producers in homes and shops (Gschwind 1977: 369; cf., Braun 1960).

Conquering French forces and their Swiss revolutionary allies abolished urban guilds, those mainstays of material inequality. After 1800, machine-based urbanization of cotton textile spinning left an increasingly dissident body of hand-loom weavers in the countryside; mechanization of weaving after 1840 then began to wipe out those weavers in turn. Urban concentration of textile production also shaped a classic if small-scale conjunction of industrial bourgeoisie and proletariat in Switzerland's major centers of cloth production (Braun 1965, Gruner 1968). Organized crafts and their masters lost much of their predominance in the politics of those centers. Correspondences among wealth, landowning, and political power declined.

Not that Swiss industrialization reduced material inequality. On the contrary; in the short run extremes of poverty and wealth increased. But by maintaining landed oligarchies in political power, as industrialization caused a shift in population from farm to urban centers, the Swiss system of segmented, privileged public politics grew increasingly insulated from prevailing material inequalities. It was precisely against partial exclusion from public politics and against the domination of landed elites that merchants, professionals, and industrial bourgeoisie banded together in favor of political reform and sometimes even dared to ally themselves with industrial workers in radical politics. Expansion and nationalization of citizenship promised to increase their power vis-à-vis old landed elites, but only at the expense of giving poorer workers direct access to government. In this way, transformations of inequality – and especially its relation to public politics – gave a small boost to Swiss democratization during the 1830s and 1840s.

Here we focus not on the waxing, waning, and alteration of categorical inequality in general, but on its intersection with public politics. Of the checklist in Table 9.1, Switzerland's changing inequality promoted democratization chiefly through three mechanisms: (1) dissolution of coercive controls supporting current relations of exploitation and opportunity hoarding, (2) insulation of existing categorical inequalities from public politics, (3) crossclass coalition formation. We will say little about the first case, but it is clear that the abolition of guilds and expansion of factory production dissolved the previously close connection between Swiss governmental institutions and craft organization. In this sense, Switzerland's political transformation did not differ much from any of the democratic-capitalist revolutions of Western Europe.

In the second case – insulation of existing categorical inequalities from public politics – Swiss retention of political institutions based on the implicit assumption of fixed local populations organized around relations to landed property blocked immediate translations between economic and political power and thus acquired and preserved the consent of the rural oligarchies to a stronger national unity. From this descend many of the peculiar characteristics of Swiss politics until well into the twentieth century: the installation of the old institution of the referendum alongside more indirect forms of representation, the exclusion of women from the franchise until quite recently, a set of policies designed to defend the survival of rural ways of life. These compensated for the growing domination of national politics by the bourgeoisie of the victorious Protestant cantons. They did not, nor were they meant to, inhibit large increases in material inequality generated by Switzerland's industrialization. But they did erect buffers between class, gender, linguistic, and religious divisions, on one side, and public politics, on the other.

Our third mechanism, crossclass coalition formation, figured repeatedly in the nineteenth-century foundation of Swiss democracy. The liberal (and predominantly Protestant) elite that most actively promoted democratic constitutions between 1830 and 1848 could not act alone. They had little choice but to seek support against their Catholic conservative rivals among the workers and peasants who formed the majorities of all cantons, but who had hitherto usually accepted the guidance of their local priests, landlords, and merchants. Thus in cantons Basel and Schwyz coalition-based popular rebellions against urban oligarchs produced small-scale civil wars well before the general war of 1847, and resulted in formal secessions of the more liberal half-cantons from their previous dependency. Those coalitions in turn promoted two democracy friendly outcomes: empowerment of workers and peasants in national politics and strengthening of the central state's capacity.

Swiss Trust Networks

Alterations of trust networks played a large part in promoting Swiss democracy. Here we concentrate on effects on democratization produced by central cooptation of intermediaries, dissolution of patron-client networks, and brokerage. But we also encounter a number of the other mechanisms listed in Table 9.1 – for example, creation of external guarantees for governmental commitments and expansion of the population lacking access to effective trust networks.

From the late sixteenth century onward, the Swiss had organized much of their lives within segments defined by trade, language, dialect, and religion. Patron–client ties linked richer and poorer members of those segments. Religion in particular etched sharp boundaries within Swiss social life. Communal and cantonal citizenship often depended on religious affiliation. Up to the French conquest of 1798, for example, "with the exception of most Calvinist refugees, no Catholic or non–Zwinglian Protestant could become a citizen of Basel, whether the city or the countryside" (Gschwind 1977: 423). Although minorities, including Jews, lived in the interstices, religious affiliation mattered enormously to public standing.

Over the long run of 1750 to 1840, however, Switzerland's two-stage industrialization undermined trust networks built on religion, language, craft, and perhaps those built on older forms of transalpine trade as well. First, the dynamic expansion of cottage industry drove a large increase in rural landless populations. Then, after 1820 or so, concentration of textile production in factories – first for spinning, then for weaving as well – generated a movement of workers to industrial towns as well as a shorter term rise and fall of hand-loom weaving in the countryside. Both French abolition of guilds and competition from manufacturers operating outside of established crafts undermined the networks of journeymen that had previously organized small-scale production (cf. Rosenband 1999: 457).

Although new workers generally came from old rural families, their altered social situations detached them from established rural networks of reciprocity and patronage. In Zurich's hinterland, for example, incremental effects of industrialization combined with the struggle of liberal bourgeois to reduce the control of Protestant ministers over family law, charity, schools, Sunday entertainment, and local finances (Joris and Witzig 1992: 26; see also Joris 1994). It is most likely that similar processes eroded networks of credit and mutual aid among village women.

Before 1848, these processes proceeded earlier and farther in Switzerland's predominantly Protestant regions than in its regions of Catholic hegemony. Switzerland's early industrialization concentrated in Protestant-dominated cantons such as Bern and Zurich rather than in Catholic cantons such as Lucerne and in high mountain areas. Historians have not so far examined the effect of this difference on trust networks. In addition to the usual difficulties of reconstructing interpersonal networks from historical sources (see, e.g., Bearman 1991, 1993; Gould 1995; Kalb 1997), historians of Switzerland must cut through powerful myths of social disintegration that saturate commentaries of the time (Braun 1965: 41–43). Still, we can plausibly infer that Catholic networks of kinship, parish membership, friendship, mutual aid, and godparenthood retained greater salience and greater insulation from public political life at the large scale than did their Protestant counterparts. Similar differences seem to have separated liberal Protestants and secularists of industrial cities, such as Zurich, from conservative Calvinists in their agricultural hinterlands.

Our analysis therefore runs as follows: In large portions of Switzerland, rural industrialization, proletarianization of rural populations, then urban implosion undermined the operation of trust networks that had connected local groups in marriage, credit, mutual aid, gossip, and trade as well as sustaining patron–client ties between richer and poorer households. Those processes activated most of the destructive mechanisms enumerated under the heading of trust networks in Table 9.1: disintegration of existing trust networks, expansion of the population lacking access to effective trust networks for their major long-term risky enterprises, and appearance of new long-term risky opportunities that existing trust networks could not handle.

At the same time, continues our account, a prospering bourgeoisie invested itself in higher capacity governments that could abolish internal customs barriers, create protections against external competition, establish standard measures, build commercial infrastructure, and expand public education. State-building activities then activated mechanisms attaching trust networks to public politics, even to government itself. Bourgeois leadership interacted with expanding state capacity in (1) creation of external guarantees for governmental commitments, (2) incorporation of existing trust networks into the polity and their expansion, (3) governmental absorption or destruction of previously autonomous patron–client networks, (4) substantial increase of government's resources for risk reduction and/or compensation of loss, and (5) visible governmental meeting of commitments to the advantage of substantial new segments of the population.

These mechanisms extend from government to institutions of public politics that depend on government – political parties, elections, special interest associations, labor unions, and so on. Incorporation of such institutions into people's trust networks enables and commits the same people to monitor governmental activity and press for collective voice. The shift from government as a shield for existing local privileges and hierarchies to government as a fulcrum of mediation – a shift that, to be sure, went much further in France and Prussia than in Switzerland – served as a solvent and transformer of trust networks.

We witness, then, a general process of integration between trust networks and public politics. Within that process, central cooptation of intermediaries played a crucial part, especially as the Sonderbund War's settlement integrated Catholic and conservative leaders, with their cantons, far more firmly into Swiss national politics at the price of a federal system and extensive concessions to cantonal autonomy. Dissolution of patron–client networks occurred on both sides of the Sonderbund line, with industrialization, commercialization, and the very creation of central political institutions all working against the old landlord-and-priest-dominated systems of patronage. Brokerage facilitated both mechanisms, crucially connecting parties during the peace settlement of 1848 and providing new connections of ordinary Swiss citizens with national political institutions.

Before 1848 among Catholic Swiss no such incorporation seems to have occurred, but among Protestants more readily and others some movement in that direction had already begun with the Helvetian Republic of 1798, and continued thereafter. Between 1798 and the 1840s, the federal state became especially the state of Protestants; the more Catholics in general resisted federal power, the more Protestants clung to it. Detailed evidence of such a tendency would in principle show Protestants more readily investing in federally backed securities, paying federal taxes, reporting for military service, placing children in careers depending on federal support, and demanding federal mediation of disputes more energetically than Catholics.

No one, so far as we know, has yet assembled the crucial evidence. In a country where so many public powers remained in the cantons, furthermore, nineteenth century Swiss had relatively few opportunities to commit themselves in these regards. Nevertheless, it is at least suggestive that during the Mediation government of 1803–1813, the mainly Protestant cantons of Zurich, Bern, Basel, Solothurn, Schaffhausen, Aargau, and Vaud paid higher per capita taxes than their Catholic neighbors (de Capitani 1983: 166). Those cantons were also, to be sure, generally more industrial and commercial than their neighbors. On the whole, capitalism and Protestantism coincided in nineteenth century Switzerland. The advance of capitalism fragmented older trust networks and made the state more central to the enterprises of entrepreneurs and workers alike.

One could also tell a tale of Swiss democratization as reflexes of rational action, cultural determination, or structural change: as the outcome of canny negotiation among representatives of the civil war's victorious and defeated elites during winter-spring 1848, as an inevitable longterm expression of Swiss civic culture, with only the precise path of institution building open to contingency, or as a characteristic by-product of advancing capitalism. The troubled history we have reviewed, however, makes clear that the formation of 1848's limited democracy resulted from widespread popular contention. Military, diplomatic, and popular confrontations from 1830 through 1847 came close to shattering the Swiss federation forever. The creation of democratic institutions at a national scale, far from simply adapting smaller scale democratic practices, occurred through partial curtailment of the consultative forms that had governed public life in most cantons. The shock of civil war accelerated transformations of inequality, trust networks, and public politics that had been occurring sporadically for half a century. Swiss citizenship and democracy, with all their limitations, emerged as contingent products of popular struggle.

Mexico

While Mexico does not form a mirror image of Switzerland, it comes pretty close. Through the centuries when the Swiss were successfully defending their mountain cantons from external invasions, Mexico suffered conquest, settlement from Spain, and decimation of its native peoples. The *conquista* lasted three centuries, went through many stages, and was never homogeneous. For example, while Cortez destroyed the Aztecs, he allied himself with their indigenous enemies; while the Church was the handmaiden of domination, its missionaries were more likely to defend their Indian charges than the *crioles* who exploited their labor; and while the Habsburgs followed their homegrown instinct to rule at the center and leave much autonomy to regional officials, the Bourbons followed a more centralizing policy and left a patchwork of corporate privileges behind them. That combination of central rule, provincial autonomy, and corporate privilege laid shaky foundations for the long history of revolts, rebellions, revolutions, coups, and foreign occupations that have marked Mexico's modern history.

First came:

- independence, won in 1821 after eleven bloody years of conflict that began with the revolt of a Creole–Indian majority against a peninsular elite and continued with the construction of a professional army of independence, leading to the first "constitutional assembly" in Michoacán in 1814. Both movements failed and Mexican independence was actually established by the conservative Agustin de Iturbide.
- decades of struggle between liberal and conservative elites punctuated by waves of foreign intervention and occupation and the loss of the country's richest territories to its northern neighbor.
- a period of solidly entrenched authoritarianism (the *Porfiriato)* when formal constitutional guarantees and putative federalism were undercut by administrative centralization and personal rule.
- a revolutionary decade beginning in 1910 dominated by struggles among a succession of military/revolutionary *caudillos* that saw the tumultuous eruption of the rural poor into regional and national struggles.
- a regime crisis in 1928–1929 when assassination of President-elect Alvaro Obregón led to a pacted solution in the mid-1930s centering around the formation of a what became a one-party-dominant state.

All this produced a more or less steady state elective authoritarianism through five decades of economic growth, internal peace, and increasing centralization from the 1930s until the 1970s.

Then exposure to the international economy, massive urbanization, and a series of regime crises increased inequalities, eroded networks of trust around the ruling party, opening the way to the mobilization of independent peasant, worker, urban, and teachers' movements, producing the period of democratizing contention we examine below.

From Mexico's long, tortured post-conquest history, let us extract three observations. First, even under the height of Bourbon power and certainly thereafter, Mexico never operated as a unified society (Rubin 1997). Second, locally born Creoles – not the indigenous population – led the drive to independence, and dominated Mexican politics for the next half-century. Except for brief and usually futile intrusions into military conflicts, Mexico's Indians remained subjects of Mexican politics and not challengers. Third, like Switzerland's eventual weak-state path to democracy, Mexico's strong-state one was not written in the stars.

Its first attempts at democracy were made by liberal and conservative elites who produced exquisitely democratic constitutions.

These constitutions usually remained dead letters or were easily manipulated by centralizing leaders. In the fifty-odd years between independence and its first authoritarian experience, Mexico lurched from one destructive internal war to another, from liberal to conservative rule, and from shaky independence to successive interventions – by the Americans in 1847 and the French between 1862 and 1867. There followed a brief protodemocratic period under the indigenous Benito Juarez – the so-called *Republica restaurada* – in which there were reasonably free and fair elections, and a division of power between the executive and the legislature (Cosio Villegas 1973). But under Porfirio Diaz, who gained power in 1876, the liberal constitution passed in 1857 was used to establish a political order that was technically representative, liberal, and federal, but centralized power and filled both legislature and judiciary with presidential cronies. Formal federalism, which recognized Mexico's large size and vast regional differences, was undercut by a centralized administrative system, and the president served virtually at his pleasure. Diaz, as sociologist Andrés Molina Enríques put it, ran an "integral" government, by "integrating into the person of the President the real powers . . . as well as the formal powers . . . and by neutralizing dissident voices" (quoted in Krauze 1997: 10).

With the outbreak of the Revolution in 1910, however, mass conflict made a sudden and spectacular intrusion into Mexican politics. That revolution combined a liberal desire for true representative government and free and fair elections leading to alternation in office, nationalists' interest in independence from economic domination from the North, workers' demands for union recognition and decent salaries and working conditions, and peasant demands for land rights, overlaid with regionally based conflicts among military/political *caudillos*. Through movement and countermovement, coup and countercoup, and personal conflict among the generals of the "revolutionary family," the conflict dragged on for nearly a decade. It was followed by succession of military presidents from northern Mexico – the so-called "Sonoran dynasty" – who centralized power through the construction of a central bank, the expansion of public education, and the professionalization of the army. They held power uneasily until 1928, when the assassination of Alvaro Obregón led to fear of a coup. This was resolved by a coalition among literally hundreds of small parties within the Revolutionary Family (Knight 1992: 131ff). The eventual outcome was the formation of a corporatist-personalist party under a strong president, the forerunner of the long-ruling Partido Revolucionario Institucional, which aggregated major elite groups (excluding the church) through a centralized and highly politicized use of state machinery. A more informal pact with business exchanged certain property and policy concessions for a free hand in running the government for the ruling party.

This sequence of events gave rise to a fairly stable system of elective civilian rule without effective opposition, low autonomy of organized groups, and a lack of civil liberties that lasted well into the postwar period (Whitehead 1995). To solve the problem of recurring military coups, dampen labor and peasant demands, and unite the groups that had emerged from the revolution and create a common front against their enemies, Mexico's political elite put together a system of power based on the following elements:

- an all powerful president elected every six years without possibility of reelection but with the right to name his successor from within the Revolutionary Family and with strong control over both the legislature and the judiciary
- a single (or almost single) party that served the monarch-president in multiple controlling functions: social, electoral, and political (Krauze 1997: 243)
- a weak federal system that served as a transmission belt for central governmental policies, the allocation of patronage, and control of the ruling party's electorate, and gave some scope for local power structures to develop autonomously
- a coalitional/corporatist structure that claimed virtual representation of all the major social groups in whose name the revolution had been fought – workers, peasants, the middle sectors, and the military

- use of mass mobilization as a tool of the regime, both to signify its popular roots and as leverage for conflictual policies, and tolerance for limited autonomous dissent that frequently led to reformist efforts if not outright cooptation

At the heart of this structure was a set of center-periphery linkages that delivered state services to, and mobilized the vote of citizens through networks of bureaucratic and political officials and local bosses (vaguely known as *caciques*). The latter were chosen and controlled from the center, could call in the repressive forces of the state when necessary, but were most useful in distributing state resources in return for providing solid electoral results and maintaining social peace. (In these regards they resembled the Soviet Union's leaders of ethnic republics, which we saw in Chapter 8). To this vertical clientelist pyramid was joined a horizontal corporatist pact among party, interest group, and bureaucratic leaders, held together by the desire to preserve the fragile stability achieved in 1928–1929 and share the spoils of office. The ruling party assured its continuity by judicious bargains among elite groups, electoral legislation designed to prevent new parties from competing nationally,[1] and a mixture of repression with toleration of contention.

The 1928–1929 pact had brought together potential contenders around the center and began the practice of excluding opposition leaders politically rather than physically (Knight 1992). The strategic decision to avoid conflict by incorporating important elite groups in a single party crystallized into a permanent *camarilla* around the center, not unlike the recurring pattern of *trasformismo* that we saw in Southern Italy in the last chapter. This opened space on left and right for opponents to organize – but not sufficient political space or access to resources to seriously challenge the ruling party until the 1980s and 1990s.

Relative toleration of contention set the Mexican regime off from most other authoritarian regimes in Latin America. Through the first twenty years after the revolution broke out, contention was both violent and incessant, ranging from military coups led by victorious revolutionary generals to attacks on the secular state by the integralist *cristeros*, to sometimes

[1] The key electoral provision seems to have been aimed at preventing parties from mounting even local slates unless they could demonstrate a minimum degree of national presence. The revision of this electoral provision facilitated both the PRD's and the PAN's local and regional electoral successes and thence the latter's presidential victory in 2000. See Cadena–Roa 1999 for a summary.

violent labor struggles, to presidentially approved peasant mobilization in the name of land reform under Cárdenas in the 1930s. The 1940s and 1950s, in contrast, were periods of relatively peaceful coexistence, but the 1960s and 1970s saw an increase in labor and peasant organizing and the appearance of an organized student movement that, in 1968, triggered the savage repression of Tlatelalco Plaza.

By the 1980s, contention had become a more or less steady accompaniment of routine politics. This was heightened by the crushing tragedy of the Mexico City earthquake, which gave rise to a wave of autonomous community organizing, and by a split in the ruling party and the formation of the progressive Partido Revolucionario Democratico (PRD) under Cuauhtémoc Cárdenas, son of Mexico's reforming 1930s president. Though most attention has focused on opposition in the popular sectors, a key group that began to move away from the regime in these years were international sectors of the business community, outraged by the nationalization of the banks in 1982.

As long as it did not threaten the PRI's hegemony, a high degree of social contestation was permitted and even useful. Even when protest went too far, repression was swift but reform was its frequent concomitant; PRI elites preferred to suborn the subjects of protest campaigns rather than leave them open to the political opposition. "The leadership of the PRI," wrote Anderson and Cockroft in 1972, "rather systematically attempts to make dissidents give at least qualified and partial support to the party, and . . . is willing to give dissidents a hearing and certain concessions in return for such limited support" (Anderson and Cockroft 1972: 232). Contentious politics of a limited kind became one of the mechanisms of Mexico's incomplete democratization, providing occasions for the ruling party to use the state to extend its reach and avoid the formation of a concentrated opposition.

Since the 1960s, the democratic forms established in modern Mexico's founding pact have begun to break out of their authoritarian carapace. From peasants and indigenous groups to workers to urban middle-class movements to independent business groups and opposition parties, Mexicans began to expand the limits of democratic participation. Voting and civil rights expanded as groups outside of the government's corporatist family produced a vital and remarkably contentious civil society – symbolized on the one hand by the Assambleas de barrio formed after the Mexico City earthquake and, on the other by protracted semi-insurgency in Chiapas in the 1990s. From a centrist coalition that occupied political space on right and left, state elites grudgingly ceded political ground on both sides while shifting economically away from their populist roots and dealing reluctantly with autonomous groups in the periphery (Cornelius, Eisenstadt and Hindley 1999; Rubin 1997).

The period from 1988 to the present has seen the convergence of opposition groups into two strong, nationally based parties – the center left PRD and the center-right Partido de Acción Nacional (PAN). The first gained a majority in the legislature in the 1990s while the second gained the presidency in the three-way race of 2000. Each party has strong regional redoubts, but they both draw from a variety of constituencies and practice internal coalition politics. The pair has come to resemble a typical democratic-capitalist pattern of left versus right, in opposition to the centrist monopoly established by the PRI during the 1930s.

Mechanisms of Change in Mexico

Switzerland's partial but definitive democratization occurred over two decades despite exclusion of half its adult population from the vote. Why has that of Mexico taken since 1910 to do so despite inclusion in the electorate of both halves of its adult population, a now-competitive party system, and a robust fabric of contentious politics? An inadequate answer is that authoritarianism is sticky – even the electoral kind installed in Mexico. But the fact that phenomena have origins does not explain their persistence or even the changes within them. A more historicized answer is that the initial solution to Mexico's problems gouged out troughs through which later developments automatically flowed. But if path dependency was sufficient, why did Mexico not follow the original liberal instincts of its Creole liberators or follow the paths of its French or American occupiers? Mexico's trajectory can better be seen in terms of the interaction of shifts in inequality, trust mechanisms, and the uses made of public politics by new social actors.

Again, we emphasize four relevant mechanisms: crossclass coalition formation, central co-optation of intermediaries, dissolution of patron-client networks, and brokerage. In the case of Mexico, crossclass coalition formation occurred, it did foster insulation between deep categorical inequalities and public politics. Both central cooptation of intermediaries and dissolution of patron-client networks did, when they happened, favor integration of trust networks into public politics. Brokerage, however, produced antidemocratic alliances in Mexico at least as often as it nudged the regime toward democracy. Unlike Switzerland's settlement of the Sonderbund War, Mexico's exit from its revolution installed an oligarchy in power on the basis of a giant patronage system and extensive use of the state for rent seeking. It also excluded most of the huge Indian population and Indian-based trust networks from public politics. That settlement set serious obstacles to further democratization.

We look for the start of the modern Mexican system of governance not in 1910, as most observers do. Instead, we date it from Obregón's assassination in 1928 when – to protect the conquests of the revolution from its enemies – a pact establishing social peace was made including virtually every major elite group in the Revolutionary Family, with the Church on the sidelines. It also established a system of state-led corporatist organizations to solder these actors together at the national level; and it extended a vertical hierarchy of clientelist dependencies to integrate a wide-ranging and widely disparate periphery to the center through expanded state capacity.

This was no thin statist cover-up for a right-wing conspiracy. Not long after its establishment President Lazaro Cárdenas brought the impoverished peasantry into the PRI's coalition (albeit at a subaltern level) with a sweeping land reform and system of state-financed cooperatives (*ejidos*) that effectively tied peasants to the regime and forestalled their autonomous organization (Sanderson 1984). This incorporation of peasants held off rural insurgencies for generations to come and created a state-impregnated agricultural sector. At the same time, the regime held labor in a captive embrace through its corporatist union confederation, moved closer to business, and even made its peace with the Catholic Church. In a delicate balancing act that depended much more on the distribution of benefits than it did on repression, the party-state developed an elaborate territorial-clientelist network. The network became crucial "in directly processing vast portions of the relations between rulers and ruled, as well as in structuring the internal operation of corporatist institutions themselves" (Heredia Rubio 1997:10). It also deflected Mexican political development from democratization for over five decades.

In terms of our first key process – insulation of public politics from categorical inequality – what happened with the creation of the PRI's system was:

- direct involvement of the state to temper Mexico's highly unequal territorial and social system through systematic transfers from wealthy

to poorer regions and from independent landowners and industrial sectors to dependent peasants and workers
- equally great use of the state to exclude from effective participation those sectors of the population that fell outside of its broad coalition and those political groups that contested its hegemony

In terms of our second key process (integration of trust networks into public politics), there was:

- connection of the state with private trust networks via powerful brokers through vertical clientelism and horizontal corporatism, which paradoxically undermined public politics except as engineered by the state
- exclusion of large segments of the population – labeled paternalistically as Indian – and their trust networks from public politics
- creation of enclaves of autonomy from political interference in the banking, academic, and business sectors [Heredia Rubio 1997]

Ironically, the partial integration of trust networks into day to day state operation blocked those trust networks (and those of excluded categories) from integration into public politics outside the state. This combination of state-influenced social equalization, state-created political inequality, and broker-mediated trust networks kept the PRI elite in power uninterruptedly for seven decades.

But although no shocks as great as conquest, colonization, or revolution shook Mexican society during this period, the system began to break down in the 1960s. Four kinds of changes deeply affected inequality, networks of trust, and public politics, thus democratization:

First, fed by the oil boom and reflected prosperity from Mexico's neighbor to the north, postwar economic change produced a vast wave of immigration from the countryside to the cities. There former peasants, freed from obligation to local *caciques*, and a new middle class – technically trained and more oriented to the market than to the state – thinned their dependency on the PRI system. Especially in northern Mexico, where independent economic growth was strongest, this new middle class produced a vigorous conservative party, the PAN, that gained solid buttresses of power both from practicing Catholics and from organized business in that region. But even within the ruling party, it produced an elite anxious for technocratic solutions to the nation's problems and impatient with the rent-seeking institutions of PRI power.

Second, greater involvement in the international economy accompanied economic growth and technocratic management. International capital and finance – largely held at bay under previous administrations – stimulated Mexico's growth during the 1960s. When damaging financial crises hit in 1982 and 1995, the government was forced to cut deeply into public spending. The cuts had devastating effects on personal income and on the capacity of PRI's corporate structures to deliver the patronage on which the party's power depended (Cook, Middlebrook and Molinar Horcesitas 1994; Hellman 1994a). Signature of the North American Free Trade Agreement on January 1, 1994, capped this process of economic liberalization. These changes undermined the efficacy of the PRI's corporatist/clientele structures, replacing them with a more unmediated relationship between the market and the citizen (Fox 1994).

Third, both economic development and internationalization opened Mexican society to transnational cultural and political exchange. This was not a simple reflex of economic liberalization. The student movement that erupted in 1968 and the wave of citizens' movements that gathered force in the 1970s both preceded liberalization. But internationalization exposed state-aided Mexican firms to competition. International exchange exposed Mexican politics and criminality to international press coverage, but it also pumped cultural and political resources into the country. For example, in Oaxaca, a region of great poverty but high political tension, migration to the United States underlay the development of one of the most innovative social movements, the California/Oaxaca based Frente Indigena Oaxaqueno Binacional.

Fourth, and as a result, the regime itself became increasingly susceptible to international pressures. An example: While the police had been so indifferent to the gaze of an international press corps assembled for the 1968 Olympics that they openly massacred hundreds of students in Tlatelolco Plaza, by 1994 the government refrained from repressing the rebellion in Chiapas, partly through fear of an international backlash (Hellman 1999). Less dramatically, the same opening to international gaze nudged the government to accept a series of electoral reforms and foreign poll watching that made it possible for opposition parties to contest effectively, and eventually win, in national elections (Cadena-Roa 1999).

Mexican Inequalities

The literature on neo-liberalism in Mexico has emphasized its devastating effects on broad sectors of the Mexican population. World Bank-induced reductions in public spending were heavily skewed toward reducing transfer payments to poor peasant producers and reducing real wages for workers in unorganized sectors. But what made these sudden wage shocks so politically explosive was that they attacked at their heart the state policies that had maintained consent among lower-class urban and rural sectors for many decades. With liberalization, real salaries plummeted even in heavily unionized state sectors like petroleum production and refining; even civil servants and university professors saw real declines in their incomes.

Small farmers were particularly hard hit by these policies. In the export sector of coffee production, the state withdrew its marketing agency, INMECAFÉ, from the market, leaving thousands of small producers without protection from middlemen and from the late 1980s collapse of world coffee prices (Snyder 1999). The advent of NAFTA in 1994 then left small producers of maize and beans open to competition from cheaper North American imports. While large producers of irrigated tree fruit, melons, and tomatoes gained from freed access to American markets, the withdrawal of the state from protecting farm prices was especially devastating to small producers who had been part of the PRI's peasant confederation and opened it up to competition from autonomous groups.

The decline of the PRI's corporatist/clientele network reduced the power of the brokers who had previously mediated the distribution of state goods and services. It opened new possibilities for mobilizing around categories of identity that previously had not been recognized in relations between center and periphery of the Mexican state. Mexico's indigenous population divides into hundreds of ethnic groups, each in their own locality, with their own languages and traditions. This fragmentation dovetailed well with the PRI's vertical system of power, in which many local *caciques* had indigenous roots, or at least used their positions in the PRI national machine to protect and advance the interests of local supporters (Rubin 1997: ch. 3). These relationships were vertical and implicitly competitive; there were few incentives for translocal indigenous alliances or identification of common interests. With the decline of the PRI's corporate/clientele system, more opportunities opened for integration of local groups, and greater openings for translocal alliances appeared. This takes us to networks of trust.

Mexican Trust Networks

Mexico before its Revolution was marked by strongly local and corporatist trust networks laid down by the segmented pattern of Spanish colonization, reinforced by the hacienda system, and exacerbated by the long period of disorder following the revolution of 1910. The major significance of the installation of the PRI system in the 1930s was to connect local and regional networks with a national corporatist/clientele system through brokers who enjoyed exceptional power as a consequence. Mexico's networks of trust bifurcated: Indian networks remained out of the system almost entirely, while those that connected with the state built around the ruling party's corporatist and clientele structures. Brokers gained power by mediating between state agents and local clienteles. By organizing networks of trust through and within the state, Mexico's politicians created barriers to the development of alternative autonomous ones (Fox 1994). The Mexican process inhibited connections between trust networks and public politics except as manipulated by the state itself.

The new technocratic elite that inherited the highest levels of PRI and state power in the 1970s and their neoliberal response to the financial crises of the 1980s began to unravel these state-impregnated trust networks. As the state increasingly withdrew from key sectors of economic activity while opening up electoral competition and grudgingly allowing non–PRI governors and mayors to take office, leaders of PRI-linked organizations lost the certainty that their party ties could assure their futures, their clients lost the confidence that their votes could produce economic security, and new, independent networks began to develop. Established patron-client ties began to dissolve.

In the labor, peasant, and neighborhood sectors, autonomous popular organizations began to challenge the official corporatist arms of the ruling party, using their power of mobilization to bargain for benefits for their adherents (Hellman 1994b). Organized business emerged as an autonomous player in the political game, offering its financial support to the PRI nationally, but supporting PAN candidates in local and gubernatorial elections. In the labor sector, new groups like the FAT (Federación autonoma de trabajo) emerged to challenge the official (Confederación mexicana de trabajo). Even within the latter, an old guard that still thought of itself as part of the revolutionary family began to be replaced by more militant and more professional labor organizers.

A powerful irony has therefore appeared in Mexican public politics. Many of Mexico's new opposition leaders learned their trade in PRI's patron-client politics. As they have created opposition parties and independent organizations, they have commonly built, or even transferred, their own patron-client networks. They have also sought clients among previously excluded segments of the population. But their very action begins a process of substituting autonomous trust networks for government-dominated patron-client chains. To the extent that it creates connections between widespread trust networks and public politics, it has contributed to democratization.

Once the linchpin of state control over trust networks began to falter, not only neoliberal policies but selective social policies designed to sop up dissent became opportunities for autonomous organizations to gain access to state resources. The PRONASOL solidarity program, put in place by the Salinas government to provide infrastructure and social services, targeted regions of the country with ties to the opposition. Where possible, local political elites were given control over PRONASOL spending in their areas, but elsewhere independent groups gained access to the program too (Fox and Aranda 1996). In Oaxaca widespread indigenous forms of self-governance were given authority by a state-level constitutional reform that resulted in part from the challenge of the Zapatista rebellion in Chiapas.

Clientelism has not disappeared from Mexican politics as it has become more competitive. In parts of the South, for example, even in the face of the Zapatista insurgency, governors are still able to manipulate public resources for political gain (Heredia Rubio 1997). Whether Mexico emerges as a democratic, high-capacity regime – the final stage in our "strong-state path" – is still an open question. But its public politics are coming to represent something like the combinations of different forms of prescribed, tolerated, and forbidden contention that we see in democratizing systems, as some challengers begin to use successfully inherited forms as they find them, others extend them to new uses, while still others attempt to constitute a new polity.

Comparisons and Conclusions

As promised, the macrohistories of democratization in Switzerland and Mexico follow fundamentally different trajectories to significantly different destinations. Switzerland comes about as close to our idealized weak-state trajectory as any viable existing state, and Mexico offers a fairly good approximation of our idealized strong-state trajectory. For all its oligarchy and particularism, Switzerland now lives with a relatively stable democratic regime. Mexico, meanwhile, in moving into the zone of citizenship and democracy experienced a decline in state capacity, and suffered serious problems of criminality, corruption, and rightwing backlash in response.

Switzerland and Mexico have arrived at their current political situations through very different relations to the international system – Switzerland long hemmed in yet preserved by the cross pressures of multiple great powers, Mexico, long living in the shadow of the capitalist giant to its north, now wedded to it economically through the North American Free Trade Agreement. After centuries of exporting war and settling local issues through armed force, nineteenth century Switzerland accomplished the historically rare feat of firmly subjecting its military forces to civilian control. Even today, it is not certain that Mexico's rulers have effectively subordinated their military and police forces to civilian control. Yet with respect to the relative timing and extent of changes in state capacity and protected consultation, Mexico's overall history since 1800 more greatly resembles the early paths of those states that now qualify as democratic than does Switzerland's unusual itinerary.

At two levels, nevertheless, our comparison of Switzerland with Mexico contributes to an explanation of democratization in general. At one level, we find that alterations of inequality, trust networks, and public politics interacted, as expected, in those changes that moved Switzerland and Mexico closer to citizenship and democracy. More precisely, our reviews identify three sites of change as crucial: (1) at the interface of inequality and public politics, (2) at the interface of trust networks and public politics, (3) within public politics itself. To say so is not to declare that economic transformation and shifts of public opinion were irrelevant to democratization, but to argue that insofar as they promoted democratization, they operated largely or exclusively through alterations of inequality, trust networks, public politics, and their interplay.

At a second level, we find a number of the same mechanisms recurring in Swiss and Mexican democratization. Table 9.1 listed a large number of mechanisms that seem likely to figure in democratization, divided by their relative impact on inequality, networks of trust, and public politics. Our analysis has singled out just four of those mechanisms: crossclass coalition formation, central cooptation of intermediaries, dissolution of patron–client networks, and the old familiar brokerage. Few political analysts will be stunned to learn that brokerage makes a difference. Still, it clarifies both democratization in general and differences between Switzerland and Mexico in particular to recognize how crucial to democratization are brokerage activities that reduce the relative prominence of particular ties between subjects and rulers while connecting whole categories of the state's subject population to agents of the state.

Two strong conclusions emerge from this analysis of contention and democratization in Switzerland and Mexico:

1. the two interact incessantly: democratic polities form through contentious politics and reshape contentious politics as they form
2. the same sets of mechanisms that explain action, mobilization, and trajectories in contentious politics also explain those rare sets of political changes that produce democracy

Democratization is not a *sui generis* phenomenon – to be analyzed alongside contentious forms of politics and only touching base with them at rare and dangerous moments of transition. Nor is democratization a simple matter of elites deciding for a society when and how it should be more democratic, as some scholars of democratization seem to believe. That was what happened in Mexico in the 1930s, with the democratic detour we have seen resulting. Democratization occurs through the same kinds of mechanisms we found in social movements, cycles of contention, revolutions, and nationalism.

Similar mechanisms – but in different combinations – appear in other forms of contention that are usually singled out for separate treatment. These may concatenate in similar patterns across nominally different forms of contention. In Chapter 10 we apply some of these combinations that have emerged from one or another of the forms of contention we examined to others of nominally distinct character.

10

Conclusions

We have kept our promises – at least some of them. We have moved from the static standard agenda for the study of social movements, with its bias toward treating one actor at a time, mainly from the West, to a more dynamic and relational account of contentious politics within and across world regions. While drawing our main illustrations from episodes of transgression, we have highlighted the incessant interplay between contained and transgressive modes of contention. We have insisted on the uselessness of choosing among culturalist, rationalist, and structuralist approaches to contentious politics but adopted insights from all three where we found them helpful. We have presented a program of inquiry centered on detection of robust mechanisms and processes in contentious episodes.

We have also blurred established boundaries among actors, mobilization, and trajectories, finding that similar mechanisms and processes appear in all three. We have developed and illustrated our arguments by means of fifteen wildly divergent episodes, working hard to cross boundaries among ostensibly different types of contention – democratization, nationalism, social movements, revolutions, and so on – by identifying similar mechanisms and processes within them. We have, finally, avoided any claims to create a new general model for all contentious episodes or for particular families of contentious episodes.

Recall how the book has unfolded. Part I (Chapters 1–3) reviewed existing analyses of contentious actors/action, mobilization/demobilization, and trajectories, assessing strengths and weaknesses of prevailing approaches to various forms of contention. It pointed to the need for more dynamics, more relational analyses, and more causal analogies, but did not satisfy that need. Part II (Chapters 4–6) retained the distinctions among action, mobilization, and trajectories, but lined up pairs of complex episodes for identification of similar mechanisms and processes.

By the end of Part II the arbitrariness of distinctions among actors/action, mobilization, and trajectories had become vividly clear, the value of searching for explanatory mechanisms and processes manifest. At that stage, the analysis achieved a measure of dynamism and a capacity to deal with more than one action at a time by emphasizing relational mechanisms, though still acknowledging the importance of cognitive and environmental mechanisms.

Part III (Chapters 7–9) then abandoned the distinctions among action, mobilization, and trajectories in favor of comparisons among contrasting episodes involving revolution, nationalism, and democratization. Those chapters did not seek to produce new general models of those phenomena or to offer complete explanations of the episodes under examination. Instead, they showed that similar mechanisms and processes play significant parts in quite disparate episodes, but produce varying overall outcomes depending on their sequence, combination, and context.

We have covered a lot of ground to this point, but we still have a distance to go. In this chapter, we hope to do four things. First, we summarize the central conclusions from the previous chapters and spell out their practical implications. Second, we sketch three additional robust processes to illustrate the sorts of explanatory frameworks that follow from our alternative program. Third, we revisit the general issue of scope conditions, to speculate on how broadly applicable our approach might be. Finally, we point out limitations of our approach, enumerating challenges that still lie before us and other students of contentious politics.

Our Claims

What have we accomplished? First, we have sketched partial explanations for some puzzling recurrences in contentious politics. Take, for example, the frequency with which long-continued action suddenly changes direction in the course of a sustained contentious episode: a regime collapses, a guerrilla group comes to power, a set of activists shift from terror to collaboration. In standard accounts of contentious politics, such reversals usually result from one or both of two situations. First, on the analogy of a steam boiler that gradually builds up pressure and then explodes when it reaches an intolerable limit, stress of some kind accumulates until it passes a critical threshold. Second, participants in some collective cause undergo a cognitive conversion and act accordingly, perhaps because some visible event crystallizes slowly forming understandings, perhaps because a new leader articulates a different vision.

We have not denied that both situations sometimes arise in contention. Instead, we have claimed that the threshold effect occurs rarely and that the cognitive conversion characteristically depends in part on relational and environmental changes. More important, a number of our episodes show us shifts of direction resulting from the activation of relational mechanisms and processes, such as brokerage, certification, and crossclass coalition formation. Thus, the decertification of the Somoza regime by the governments of Costa Rica, Venezuela, Panama, Mexico, and the United States in the late 1970s boosted defections from that regime as well as promoting support for the Sandinista opposition. Similarly, brokerage, certification, and crossclass coalition formation all played significant parts in the escalation of the 1954 Hindu–Muslim confrontation described by Beth Roy. One need not deny accumulations of grievances or alterations in consciousness to recognize the centrality of relational mechanisms and processes in these rapid mutations.

Our second contribution is the introduction of a more dynamic relational analysis into a field often weighed down by static individualistic accounts. To be more exact, analysts of contentious politics have long described dynamic processes and changes in social relations. But they have done so largely in asides and descriptive narratives rather than in their major explanatory schemes. Predominant models have remained static, concentrating on following one actor at a time, and reconstructing the self-propulsion of that actor. We are, of course, partly to blame; our own earlier models provided much better specifications of static boxes than of the dynamic arrows connecting those boxes. They also worked better in accounting for the actions of a single actor – individual or collective – at a time.

Explicit identification of relational mechanisms and processes promotes a more dynamic analysis of contention. Compare our analyses of trajectories in Chapters 2 and 6. In the section of Chapter 2 that discussed the Italian postwar experience in light of available models of movement careers and protest cycles, it became clear that matching this complex episode as a whole with such models obscured the contingencies of its path, provided little guidance in identifying critical junctures, forced a focus on one actor at a time, and offered little or no space to strategic interaction. By the comparison in Chapter 6 of America antislavery mobilization and Spanish exit from the Franco regime, we tried to remedy these deficiencies. In that comparison, we called attention to identity shifts, brokerage, polarization, and convergence as crucial causes of changing trajectories within both episodes.

Here is our third major claim: to have breached barriers among ostensibly different varieties of contention. We began with complaints about segmentation among studies of war, revolution, social movements, and other forms of contentious politics. We replied to our own complaints by searching deliberately for similar causal mechanisms and processes in distinctive forms of politics. Brokerage, for example, figured prominently in all six episodes of Part II: Mau Mau and the Philippines' Yellow revolution, South Asian Hindu–Muslim conflict and South African transition from the apartheid regime, American struggles over slavery and the end of the Franco regime in Spain. Across these same episodes, we frequently encountered processes variously combining identity shift, object shift, certification, and social appropriation, for example, in the formation of a connected opposition to Ferdinand Marcos' regime. If such processes turn out to be as robust as we think they are, and in so many nominally different types of contention, they should guide future researchers in comparing the dynamics of contention across these types of contention.

Methodological Implications

We have given little explicit attention to methodology in these chapters, but our analyses have important methodological implications. Let us single out four of them: (1) simultaneous downgrading and upgrading of contentious episodes as objects of study; (2) reorientation of explanations from episodes to mechanisms and processes; (3) better operational specification and integration of cognitive, relational, and environmental mechanisms; (4) reconciliation of contingency with explanation.

Simultaneous downgrading and upgrading of contentious episodes as objects of study. The downgrading consists of denying *sui generis* reality to such episodes. As conventional or arbitrary entities, events we call revolutions, social movements, wars, and even strikes take shape as retrospective constructions by observers, participants, and analysts. They do not have essences, natural histories, or self-motivating logics. Moreover, they intersect with more routine processes – even more reason to avoid segmenting their study. Had we, for example, focused only on the Abolitionist movement in American antislavery, we would have ignored the crucial buildup of tensions among constituted political actors and the resulting formation of the Congressional coalition that destroyed intersectional compromise and brought to fruition abolition's long-frustrated goal.

Episodes also require upgrading, however. Once we recognize that we have snipped them from their historical and social contexts, we must make explicit the procedures and criteria that mark their beginning, ends, boundaries, and participants. That calls for the development of expertise in delineating comparable events. There are two distinct challenges here.

- The first is to distinguish episodes of contention – whether *contained* or *transgressive* – from more routine or *prescribed politics*. We have focused on transgressive ones in this book, but without providing anything like an operational kit bag for demarcating contentious episodes. This remains one of the key challenges awaiting anyone who adopts our program. We return to the challenge later in this chapter
- The second challenge centers on coming to better understand the process by which conventional designations of form get applied to particular episodes. The process by which a given episode acquires the standing of revolution, social movement, war, strike, or something else has political weight and consequence. Such designations affect not only how subsequent analysts explain them, but also how participants behave and how third parties react to them. Thus social processes that label and bound episodes belong on our agenda

Reorientation of explanations from episodes to mechanisms and processes. Although our analyses point to retention of comparable episodes as units of observation, they also recommend abandonment of efforts to explain all salient features of whole episodes. They thereby rule out the common procedure of matching episodes to general models in order to demonstrate that the model does not fit some salient feature of the episode, then modifying the general model to increase the fit. Our analyses do not offer much hope of gaining explanatory leverage by matching whole episodes with invariant models of social movements, wars, strikes, revolutions, or other recurrent forms of contention, much less with invariant models of contention in all its permuatations.

Instead, we recommend concentrating explanations on selected features of episodes (for example, why rapid shifts in identity occur across a range of otherwise disparate episodes) or on recurrent processes in families of episodes (for example, how and why crossclass alliance formation frequently creates or expands revolutionary situations). In either mode, explanation consists of identifying crucial mechanisms and their combination into transforming processes. Our analysis of Mexican democratization, for example, by no means provides a comprehensive account of political conflicts in Mexico from 1980 to 2000, but it does show how brokerage produced significant realignments that other observers have often attributed to shifts in mentalities or effects of external pressures.

Specification and integration of cognitive, relational, and environmental mechanisms. Proceeding from the view that theorists of contentious politics have slighted relational dynamics, we have deliberately emphasized relational mechanisms. Nevertheless, our concrete analyses have repeatedly invoked combinations of relational with cognitive and/or environmental mechanisms. The mechanism we have called "suddenly imposed grievances," for instance, involves both changed relations among actors and altered cognition on the part of at least one actor. In disasters and war, the same mechanism also commonly involves a shift in the connections of actors to their environments.

In such circumstances, it is not clear in principle whether we are observing two or three distinct mechanisms that frequently conjoin, or have discovered a sufficiently invariant combination of cognitive, relational, and environmental changes to justify treating the complex as a single robust process. Nor can we decide in general and in advance how the elements interact – whether, for example, cognitive shifts always precede relational changes – or vice versa. Interaction among cognitive, relational, and environmental mechanisms presents urgent problems for theory and research on contentious politics.

Whether relational, cognitive, or environmental, a more basic challenge we have generally skirted in this book is the operational specification of the various mechanisms that we have deployed in our analyses. As with the concept of episode, we have offered only general analytic definitions of our mechanisms, leaving the details of operationalization to later studies. Comfortable as we are with that decision, we cannot emphasize enough how important this methodological challenge is to the ultimate viability of our program. Absent clear and consensual empirical markers for any given mechanism, the program risks degenerating into the same kind of exercise in plausible, post hoc storytelling that has too often afflicted the analysis of contention. We will have more to say regarding this key challenge later in the chapter.

Contingency and mechanisms. Finally, contingency dogs our analytical path, as it does that of any scholar who rejects deterministic structural, cultural, or individualist accounts of contention. More than once we have concluded that *x* would not have happened had *y* actors not done what they did at time *z*. Remember the role of the Managua earthquake in the runup to the Nicaraguan revolution or the catalytic effect of Hu Yaobang's death on events in China? Such events cannot be predicted, but they can be understood as they work through our mechanisms, for example through attribution of threat and opportunity. Managua's earthquake was simultaneously interpreted by Somoza as an opportunity for expanded state graft and, in response to the regime's action, as a threat to the interests of important sectors of the Nicaraguan bourgeoisie. Hu's funeral offered the students an opportunity to innovate around a familiar form of collective action and draw upon culturally legitimated scripts for criticism of the regime.

Contingency also operates through the intersection of our mechanisms in ways that cannot be predicted in advance. Recall the role of radicalization in the Spanish and antebellum episodes analyzed in Chapter 6: The radicalization of the Basque nationalist movement as Franco's death approached threatened repression and militarization, a threat that combined with brokerage and coalition formation to produce a convergence between moderates in government and opposition, which led them to fashion a pacted transition to democracy. Conversely, development of the antislavery controversy in America led to radicalization as it combined with the shift of land-seeking northerners to the West and the brokerage of a new coalition of northern and western politicians in the new Republican party. Two cases of radicalization: One led to convergence and the other to civil war. The contingent outcomes of the interaction of different mechanisms of contention remain a major item on the agenda of our program.

A New Research Program for Contentious Politics

What sort of research program do we therefore recommend to students of contentious politics? The program has a negative and a positive side. In order not to get lost in details, let us lay out the program schematically.

Negative

- Abandon efforts to prove that rationalism, culturalism, or structuralism explain particular episodes.
- Abandon explanation of events by matching them with the classic social movement model or any other invariant general model; for example, move from the invariant model of protest cycles touched on in Chapter 2 to the identification of mechanisms and processes that under specified conditions generate cycle-shaped trajectories; compare them to those that generate differently shaped trajectories; compare the correlates and the critical junctures found in each.
- Abandon critiques of standard models that add elements or simply modify their major features; for example, forget about adding variables to existing general models of revolution in order to accommodate new cases.
- Abandon efforts to specify necessary and/or sufficient conditions for whole classes of episodes through yes/no comparison or correlational analysis; for example, shift studies of strike waves away from identifying general conditions under which they occur to an explanation of their dynamics.
- Use those same methods sparingly, and chiefly to specify what must be explained; for example, having demonstrated through regression or other correlation-based analyses that mobilization typically occurs in established social settings, intervene with different methods to determine what dynamic, interactive mechanisms typically shape the mobilization process.

Positive

- Across a range of cases, identify and test for the presence of specified operational markers for particular mechanisms; for example, formulate proxies for elite defection and test for their presence across a range of revolutionary situations.
- Identify, study, and compare common processes – frequently recurring sequences and combinations of mechanisms; for example, theorize and explain polarization as a common process by close study of its recurrence in a variety of contentious episodes.
- Specify how particular mechanisms work, examining evidence from multiple episodes; for example, criticize and improve the account of

identity shift in this volume by confronting our formulations with new, well documented instances.

- When attempting to explain whole episodes, specify what is distinctive about them and therefore requires explanation, identify mechanisms and processes that caused those distinctive features, then solidify that identification by comparison with at least one other episode that differs with respect to that distinctive feature; for example, extend our own comparison of democratization in Switzerland and Mexico to new episodes, not in the expectation that those episodes will greatly resemble either case, but on the hypothesis that mechanisms affecting interfaces between public politics and trust networks will significantly affect democratization or its absence.
- Take a category of episodes that people have thought *sui generis*, identify what is problematic about the episodes, then specify the mechanisms and processes that caused those problematic features; for example, apply the sort of analysis we have offered for revolutions, nationalism, and democratization to episodes of interstate war, civil war, industrial conflict, or social movement.

Three Robust Processes

So much for a schematic representation of our program. The challenge to this chapter lies in moving beyond schematic statements to demonstrate the utility of the approach our book has crafted. Recall that in Part II we proceeded case-by-case to discover mechanisms that recurred in wide varieties of cases. We moved, in Part III to discussions of very broad macro-historical processes – revolution, nationalism, and democratization – finding the presence of many of our mechanisms within them. But these familiar forms of contention do not illuminate our position on the crucial issue of case-specific versus more general explanations. The key to balancing the demands of both is the elucidation of robust processes in which the same or similar sets of mechanisms combine.

We began this book with a caution: Readers in search of general covering laws of contentious politics should look elsewhere. Should our program be understood as proposing that each such episode is made up of a unique set of mechanisms and processes that shape it? Have we only rediscovered narrative history and applied to it a new, scientistic vocabulary? We think not. While convinced of the futility of deducing general covering laws of contention, we think our program – if it succeeds – will uncover recurring sets of mechanisms that combine into robust processes which, in turn, recur over a surprising number and broad range of episodes. If we can validate that claim, we will have suggested a new path to the analysis of contentious politics: neither through the stamping of the same general laws onto all the world's contention, nor through the description of different cases on a case-wise basis, but through the comparison of episodes of contention in light of the processes that animate their dynamics.

The origins of contention have earned so much scholarly attention over the years that we could confidently use mobilization in Chapter 2 to hazard a provisional sketch of our procedure. Mobilization, we argued there, can best be seen as a composite of attribution of opportunity and threat, social appropriation of existing sites, identities, and organizations, plus innovation around familiar forms of contention. The studies in Parts II and III did not lead us to revise fundamentally our image of how mobilization works. But contentious politics (as we have said over and over) does not begin and end with mobilization and demobilization. It is not limited to the origins of contention. In the intervening chapters, episode by episode, we worked toward the discovery of a broader set of robust processes through a case-by-case focus on mechanisms. Our goal was to interrogate a broad range of episodes to learn whether they concatenate in recurring combinations of mechanisms – robust processes – that are consequential across a significant number of cases.

These analyses were frankly exploratory, but the fifteen cases reviewed in our book do point to a number of such processes. In this concluding chapter, we take up three crucial processes that recur in roughly the same form in a wide variety of episodes of contention:

- *constitution of new political actors and identities* within contentious episodes
- *polarization* of political groups within such episodes
- *scale shift* in political contention from local to translocal (even transnational) arenas and changes in the actors and the character of their interaction that this involves

We began our quest in Chapter 2 with three "touchstone" cases: American civil rights, French revolution, and Italian student contention. Let us return to all three for a demonstration that our program can unveil new aspects of even familiar cases. In the exploratory spirit of our book we also

Table 10.1. *Three Robust Processes and Six Illustrative Cases*

Robust Process:	Illustrative Cases: Touchstone	Illustrative Cases: New
Actor Constitution	American Civil Rights	Chinese Cultural Revolution
Polarization	French Revolution	Maluku War, 1999
Scale Shift	French/Italian Student Movements	Rwandan Genocide, 1994

point forward by briefly applying these processes to three new episodes from the world of contentious politics. Though we make no claim to interrogate these cases as thoroughly as we did the previous fifteen, we nonetheless find strong evidence of the same processes, comprised of the same linked mechanisms that we will explore in our touchstone cases.

Table 10.1 sketches the three robust processes and the six cases we will use to illustrate them.

Actor Constitution

Throughout this volume we have emphasized the distinction between contained and transgressive contention. Contained contention is waged by constituted (that is, self-defined and publicly recognized) political actors. By contrast, transgressive contention commonly introduces previously unorganized or apolitical actors into public conflict processes. How do these new actors get constituted? New political actors can emerge in several different ways, some of them highly institutionalized. Many electoral systems, for example, include standard routines for the creation of new political parties. Over wide sweeps of history, new military entities have formed through well-established procedures for raising armed forces. Here, however, we concentrate on what appears to be another robust process by which segments of civilian population acquire names and public political standing. Figure 10.1 sketches this process of actor constitution.

The first two linked mechanisms in the figure will be familiar to the reader from Chapter 2. These mechanisms – social appropriation and innovative action – define the final dynamic links in the mobilization process sketched there. Appropriation paves the way for innovative action by reorienting an existing group to a new conception of its collective purpose. But for the initial mobilization process to be fully realized, this disposition to act must be translated into innovative collective action. Once this occurs we can say that the group in question is acting contentiously. It is important to note that such action does *not* necessarily entail a shift in the group's collective identity. In the episodes we have examined, social appropriation and innovative action often activate two additional mechanisms that result in the public constitution of new actors and related collective identities. These two additional, and by now familiar, mechanisms are:

- certification: validation of actors, their performances, and their claims by external parties, especially authorities, and its obverse, de-certification
- category formation: creation of a set of sites sharing a boundary distinguishing all of them and relating all of them to at least one set of sites visibly excluded by the boundary

The causal link between innovative action and certification/decertification is straightforward. Having violated the behavioral expectations of other parties to a developing conflict, insurgent groups typically provoke intense interpretive efforts by affected others who aim at restoring intelligibility to an environment rendered less certain and predictable by the innovative action. These efforts often touch on a number of issues, but typically center on attempts to assert publicly the legitimacy (certification) or illegitimacy (decertification) of the imputed identity of the insurgent actor and, by extension, the claims advanced by the actor. For its part, the latter group is hardly passive in the face of these certifying and decertifying attempts. On the contrary, the emerging group is simultaneously involved in its own public (and internal) efforts to reconstitute group identity and purpose, in part through attempts to redefine its relationship to other actors in its environment. The typical result of this process is the formation of a new actor category, identity shift on the part of the insurgent group, and a significant reconstitution of relationships among a broader set of actors comprising an emergent field of political contention.

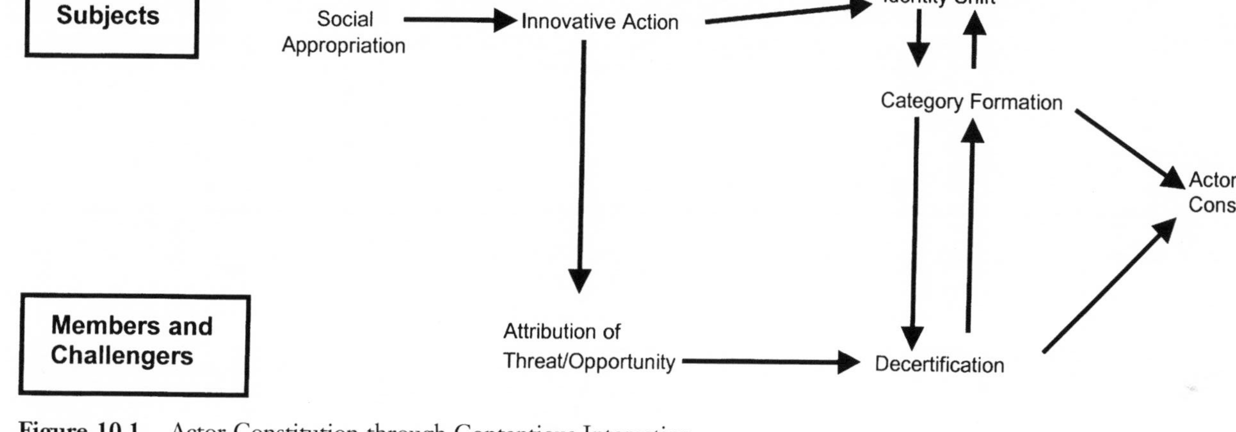

Figure 10.1. Actor Constitution through Contentious Interaction

Civil Rights in the United States

In Chapter 2 we offered a brief reinterpretation of the emergence of the postwar American civil rights conflict. Here, we focus on a crucial turning point in the struggle: the Montgomery bus boycott, which set the transgressive phase of the episode in motion and introduced an important new actor – the civil rights movement – on to the American political scene.

The decision to continue the boycott beyond what was initially conceived as a one-day action plunged the city into divisive conflict and initiated a period of intense local contestation over the meaning of the boycott and identity of its principal combatants. Given sympathetic coverage by the national media, this debate quickly spread beyond Montgomery. The key adversarial representations of the combatants emerged early in the episode.

Letters published in the *Montgomery Advertiser* articulated the prosegregationist view of the struggle. On January 9, 1956, the paper printed a letter from Mrs. George Foster asserting that "fear," not dissatisfaction with the racial status quo, lay behind the decision of local blacks to stay off the buses. "There are," Foster claimed, "many Negroes . . . that want to ride the busses but are afraid to. *Where* are these people getting this fear and *who* is putting this fear into them?" (quoted in Burns 1997: 118). Another white writer sketched the widely held answer to Mrs. Foster's question; Montgomery's black population was simply a cowed "bunch that is controlled by that Communist front, the NAACP." (Burns 1997: 116). Not willing to believe that local blacks – "our Negroes" to quote a phrase repeated often in the letters – were motivated to, or capable of, mounting such a campaign on their own, the boycott was attributed to shadowy outside forces, quite often associated with a Communist dominated NAACP. For their part, southern political leaders were but dutiful and courageous protectors of "the southern way of life" and victims of subversive "outside agitation."

But in letters to northern newspapers and national editorial commentary on the boycott, there quickly emerged an alternative account of the campaign and its chief adversaries. In contrast to the segregationist point of view, this liberal alternative held that the boycott and broader movement was a courageous grassroots effort by Montgomery's black community to redress decades of oppressive treatment. Writing in 1956, Eleanor Roosevelt argued that "the bus protest . . . has been one of the most remarkable achievements of people fighting for their own rights . . . that we have ever witnessed in this country" (quoted in Burns 1997: 314).

Liberal clergyman Harry Emerson Fosdick, concurred, saying that "Montgomery, Alabama, has become one of the most significant places in the world. . . . Racial prejudice and discrimination are a fundamental denial of the Christian gospel. . . . The dignified, resolute and peaceable protest of the Montgomery Negroes against such inequality and injustice is a godsend to our country, and a lesson that, North as well as South, we need to learn" (quoted in Burns 1997: 315–16). Fosdick invoked the same general enemy – Communism – as segregationists did, only this time charging that it was the defenders of "the southern way of life" who were aiding and abetting the Communists, if only inadvertently.

These two diametrically opposed attempts to certify (northern liberals) and decertify (southern segregationists) the antisegregation campaign came to dominate public debate on the boycott. But participants in the boycott were hardly passive in the face of this broad definitional struggle. Figures associated with the campaign – most notably Martin Luther King, Jr. – were engaged in "signifying work" or their own. Much of this work is what Jane Jenson (1998) has termed "group naming"; we prefer to call it category formation. Having constituted themselves as an ongoing campaign, how were the Montgomery insurgents to be known? Their actions had rendered the conventional identities – members of this or that congregation, "our Negroes," etc. – inadequate as collective descriptors of the emerging group. In March of 1956, King, in a widely quoted statement, asserted a new definition of Montgomery's "Negroes." Said King:

> Our non-violent protest in Montgomery is important because it is demonstrating to the Negro, North and South, that many of the stereotypes he has held about himself and other Negroes are not valid. . . . In Montgomery we walk in a new way. We hold our heads in a new way. Even the Negro reporters who converged on Montgomery have a new attitude. One tired reporter, asked at a luncheon in Birmingham to say a few words about Montgomery, stood up, thought for a moment, and uttered one sentence: "Montgomery has made me proud to be a Negro" (quoted in Burns 1997: 244).

This image of a "new Negro" was invoked in countless statements issued by movement leaders throughout the period of the boycott and beyond. The implication was clear: The movement was more than an instrumental effort to change the bus seating laws in Montgomery, it was an expression of a new collective identity among southern blacks more generally. Thus, besides illustrating the crucial mechanism of category formation, these statements also afford a clear and highly consequential example of "identity shift" as a function of contentious interaction.

African-Americans were hardly unaware of their shared racial identity prior to the movement, but the nature of that awareness was often complicated by other identities (class, region, gender, darkness of skin) that tended to divide rather than unify the population. For many, the onset of the movement effectively reordered these identities, placing shared racial identity in the foreground and muting, though not eliminating, divisions within the black community. A strong and enduring racial consciousness has been among the most important and consequential legacies of the movement and the Montgomery campaign that helped set it in motion.

We can discern the same general process of actor constitution in some of our other cases: for example, in the Mau Mau rebellion, which set in motion category formation and certification struggles by parties in both Kenya and England. But whereas Montgomery spawned two resonant, and opposed, public narrative accounts of the movement, Mau Mau produced only one, the official one. So while a new actor, Mau Mau, was constituted through the fashioning and dissemination of this narrative, the demonized nature of the characterization effectively decertified the movement, dooming it from the start. A more demanding test is to see whether the sketch of actor constitution we have sketched for U.S. civil rights activists applies to other cases.

The Cultural Revolution

In his fascinating account of the onset of the 1966 Cultural Revolution in Beijing, Andrew Walder (2000) offers another clear instance of the process of actor constitution. Consistent with events in Montgomery, Walder argues that shifts in identity did not so much motivate action in Beijing as develop as a logical consequence of contentious interaction in a highly risky and uncertain political context. It is worth quoting Walder at length on this point:

> Structural explanations of Red Guard factionalism during China's Cultural Revolution of 1966–68 presume that the interests and identities that motivated collective action were formed prior to the onset of the movement. The sequence of events through which student factions emerged in Beijing during the last half of 1966, however, is inconsistent with structural explanations. . . . Factions did not

form until after participants took initial actions under ambiguous political circumstances that varied widely across schools. These individual choices split preexisting status groups and local political networks, and in turn imposed new political identities that had potentially severe consequences for the movement activists who would lead opposed factions. These identities constrained choice, sharply defined interests for the first time, and subsequently served as a basis for group formation and conflict. [Walder 2000: 1]

Walder's account dovetails with the process sketched in Figure 10.1. The initial actions taken by dissidents at Beijing University in May 1966 were clearly interpreted as threatening by the University's party organization, which responded to them as an "unprincipled factional attack" on legitimate party authority. But, when on June 2 the wall poster that had launched the dissident attack was printed with editorial praise in the *People's Daily*, it became clear that higher placed officials, including Mao himself, viewed the attack as an opportunity to review the revolutionary commitments of the party's nominal university leaders. This elite certification of the Beijing University dissidents set in motion similar efforts at a host of other universities and high schools in the city, in turn triggering the mix of mechanisms shown in Figure 10.1.

In all affected institutions fierce certification/decertification struggles raged, pitting dissidents against party officials, with various outside "review committees," and other party/state elites joining the fray on occasion. The intensity of these episodes and the often life and death stakes involved compelled highly consequential shifts in identity and interests as emergent factions fought to defend themselves against the characterizations of their similarly emergent factional foes. Social psychologists use the term "altercast" to capture the process by which others seek to shape behavior by depicting a given alter in a certain way. Like many instances of contention, the Cultural Revolution turned on these competitive altercasting conflicts. Out of them emerged new collective identities and a host of new constituted political actors.

We close our discussion of this process with a specific prediction drawn from our comparative consideration of all of the cases reviewed here. While we think the process of actor constitution is likely to occur across a fairly wide range of contentious episodes, following Walder, we hypothesize that it will be most likely and consequential in cases where the risks associated with the conflict and the uncertainty of its outcome are both very high. We will see that the same is true of our second process, polarization.

Polarization

By polarization we mean widening of political and social space between claimants in a contentious episode and the gravitation of previously uncommitted or moderate actors toward one, the other, or both extremes. When it occurs, polarization is an important accompaniment to contentious episodes because it vacates the moderate center, impedes the recomposition of previous coalitions, produces new channels for future ones, fills even the most concrete of policy issues with ideological content which can block their solution, and can lead to repression, armed conflict, and civil war.

In the course of these chapters we have encountered a variety of examples of polarization processes. Polarization figured most explicitly in Chapter 6, where it destroyed the Whig party, separated proponents and opponents of slavery into armed camps, and led to civil war. But in the form of a radical flank effect, it had a positive outcome for Spanish democratization: It brought together opponents and supporters of the regime in consensual democratization for fear of a military coup. Polarization also appeared prominently in Nicaragua, in Mau Mau, in the Philippines, in Switzerland, and elsewhere.

Polarization combines mechanisms of opportunity/threat spirals, competition, category formation, and the omnipresent brokerage. Take the case of Switzerland between 1830 and 1848. As of 1830, communal and cantonal identities formed the stuff of public politics, with national identity rarely providing answers to the question "Who are you?", even when it came to relations with foreign powers. Yet from the Catholic Sonderbund's formation in 1845, divisions between conservative Catholics and a liberal alliance deepened to the point of civil war. That polarization created a new boundary, across which the constitution-makers of 1848 had to negotiate. It did not for a moment erase all difference among constituted actors on either side of the boundary. But its combination of competition and opportunity/threat spirals, leading to category formation and brokerage – once again absolutely critical on both sides – polarized the Swiss polity to the point of lethal conflict in 1847.

In this section, we return to our second benchmark case, revolutionary France, to illustrate the strength of our program and compare it briefly to a totally different one (1999's Maluku civil strife in Indonesia) to show how widely polarization is found in contentious politics. Despite wide differences in scope, scale, actors, and outcomes, the same mechanisms appear in each.

A Revolution Devours its Children

The most celebrated case of polarization in western history – and one that provided many authors with a virtual template for future models of revolution – was the split between the Jacobins of the "Mountain" in the 1792–1793 Convention and their former comrades, the "Girondins." After

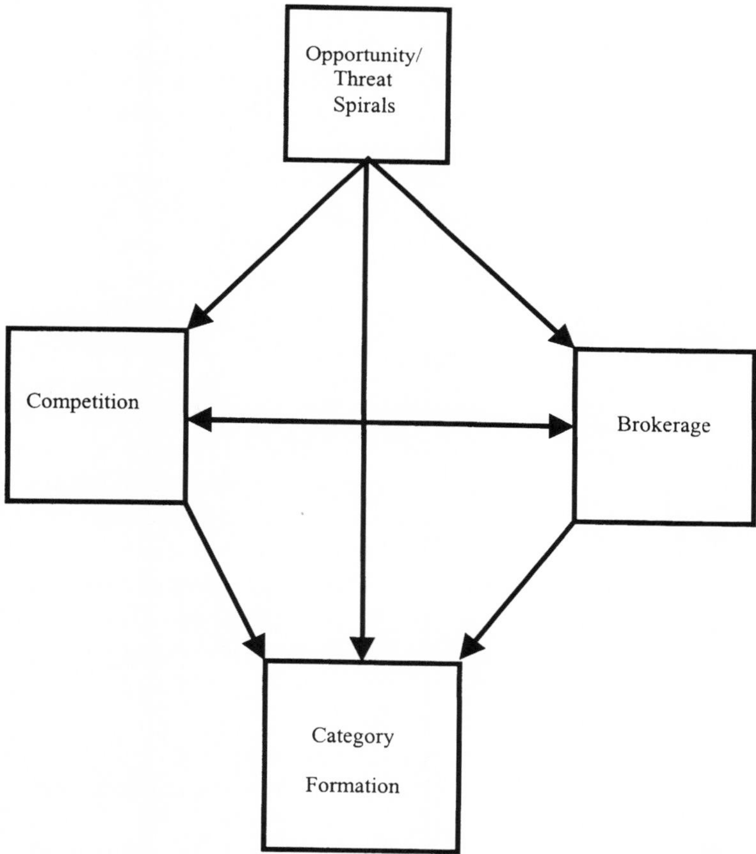

Figure 10.2. Polarization

the fact participants and generations of historians have reified these divisions and in some cases found in them the source of enduring cleavages in French politics (see the review in Sydenham 1961: ch. 1). They sometimes forgot that the two groups had united only a year earlier against the monarchy and the *feuillants* who supported it, and that each emerged from a split within the Jacobin clubs only in August–September 1992 (Higonnet 1998: 35). In other words, polarization was not written in the stars of French political culture; it was a *process* that resulted from the interactive politics of the revolution.

In that episode, left and right in the convention competed for support from the waffling and uncertain Plain. Categories were formed as each faction crystallized around a set of leaders and themes. Opportunity spirals fed by street actors raised tensions between the two hardening groups of deputies, and brokerage produced the coalition that enabled the victorious Jacobins to liquidate their Girondin enemies. We return to that process to illustrate the workings of the conjoined mechanisms we see operating in polarization.

The first point to establish is that the Girondins were not as inherently moderate as their later defenders constructed them (Lamartine 1848; Tierchant 1993). More adventurous in warmaking than hesitant Robespierre, they were just as willing as their future enemies to use sans-culotte violence against the King and as a springboard to power. The threat of the leftist, sans-culotte-dominated Paris Commune produced the Girondins' desire to protect the revolution's conquests by stopping its drift to the left.

The breach that opened in August over the monarchy widened in September, with the Parisian massacre of 1,400 prisoners (Schama 1989: 630–37). Robespierre calmly interpreted that event as "a popular movement and not a seditious riot as has been ridiculously supposed" (quoted in Higonnet 1998: 38). The split became irrevocable with the arrest, condemnation, and execution of the King, over Girondin objections, in December and January (Patrick 1972: 39, ch. 4). Though they agreed the King was guilty, many Girondins doubted that the Convention had the power to try him, two-thirds supporting an "appeal to the people" to decide on his sentence; and 70 percent voting for mercy, against the 95 percent of the Mountain who called for execution (for precise voting figures, see Patrick 1972: 78, 93, 96).

Girondin arguments in favor of a referendum and against execution were constitutionally founded and politically prudent. But amid mounting tension in the provinces, military defeats and defections, and a near-breakdown of grain supplies to the cities, Girondin calls for legality and restraint could be framed by their opponents as defeatist, if not actually treasonous. In a Paris that was buzzing with street corner agitators and gutter journalists, their claims "had very limited access to the revolutionary enthusiasm from which the Republic had to get its driving power if it were to survive" (Patrick 1972: 72). Polarization developed out of contrasting interpretations of the events revolutionary France experienced.

The driving power of revolutionary enthusiasm was increasingly harnessed to the Jacobins' policy: missions to put down provincial revolts; radical economic measures to control prices and provision the cities; and (as war on the frontiers went from bad to worse) shrill denunciation of aristocrats and traitors. That party was at first hesitant about making war on France's neighbors; it also started out economically liberal. But as the military situation became desperate and the economy faltered, Robespierre and his colleagues became increasingly militant. Pressure from the front incited a *levée en masse* and punitive measures against reluctant officers. Rebellions in the provinces stirred savage repression and suspicion of federalism. Economic distress, finally, inspired measures of control over prices and supply that required a strong state apparatus and repression against speculators and hoarders. War, rebellion, and economic duress led to conflating opponents with foreigners, traitors, speculators, and hoarders.

Jacobin policies found a mass base in an assertive and aggressive group of Parisian Section assemblies. A tiny minority at the best of times, when goaded by adequate propaganda and supported by allies within the Convention, these sections were capable of mobilizing entire neighborhoods – especially in the poor northern and eastern *quartiers* of the city. In August, they had brought thousands into the streets to bring down the monarchy. In January and February 1793, they focussed their rage on the King's execution. In March came widespread struggles over food and attacks on Girondin presses. These conflicts produced a return to a controlled grain market and a shift in the Jacobins' economic views toward those of the radical *enragés* who animated the sections.

As spring moved into summer, the sections became more militant (Higonnet 1998: 55). By the end of May, they felt strong enough to take over the Commune, and on June 2, they surrounded the Convention and demanded the expulsion and arrest of the Girondin leaders. After some hesitation, the frightened deputies of the Plain joined the Mountain in expelling twenty-nine Girondin leaders. Some escaped, to foment rebellion in the already restive provinces; still others were placed under house arrest; most were executed a few months later. They were the first victims of the system of organized terror that would become the effective government of France in the next year.

What is striking about this entire bloody episode is how much interaction constructed actors who would later be understood as if they had been present from the beginning. Guenniffey writes:

> In reality, Jacobinism was never a party or even a faction; it formed a space where parties and factions struggled to claim the legitimacy that space embodied and, legitimated, to pursue their own particular and diverse purposes. Jacobinism was not one piece among others on the revolutionary chessboard; it was the chessboard itself, the stage on which the drama of the revolution played until 1794. [Guenniffey 2000: 220]

Although the term *Montagne* was launched in October 1791, "the Montagnards only became significant when facing the Gironde and its attacks in the autumn of 1792" (Soboul 1980: 7). It then "forged its coherence in the implacable resolution to try, condemn, and execute the king" (Lewis-Beck, et al. 1988: 531), becoming steadily more radical over the next six months. Never more than a minority in the Convention, the Mountain's radicalism grew in response to the Girondins' moderate reaction to the arrest of the King, the desperate situation on the frontiers and in the provinces, and the demands of the increasingly strident sections. Their ultimate success did not stem from control of terror's instruments – that had to await the defeat of their enemies. It depended on their ability to convince, convert, and coerce a sufficient number of uncommitted deputies of the Plain – and not always the same ones by any means – to vote with them (Lewis-Beck, et al. 1988: 530). Polarization emerged from category formation, brokerage, and competition. Those mechanisms responded in turn to a spiral of opportunity and threat driven by dearth, defection, and foreign invasion.

What of the Girondins? If the Montagnards' identity crystallized in response to the foreign and provincial conjuncture and to the moves of the crowd in early 1793, it is not clear that the Girondins ever had one at all until they became the Revolution's victims. That the ultimate victims voted together on many issues is certainly true, but this cohesion was far from ironclad. On six major recorded votes (four of them relating to the

King's sentence) less than 70 percent of the supposed Girondists fell into the category of the "consistent" Right, only 10 percent higher than members of the Plain (Lewis-Beck, et al. 1988: 531). It was only as the Girondins' fate approached – in the votes on Marat's impeachment in April and on the reinstatement of the Committee of Forty in May – that near unanimous moderate votes emerged from the Girondist category (Lewis-Beck, et al. 1988: 534). "The group," concluded Sydenham, "became an entity only in the hour of its downfall" (Sydenham 1961: 176).

Even as they sat in jail or escaped to the provinces, polarization proceeded, for persecution paid political dividends to the now dominant Jacobins. The Jacobin run Committee on Public Safety at first sought a face-saving compromise (Sydenham 1961: 21). But as the military situation continued to degenerate and revolt rose in the provinces, the Committee's accusations hardened and the number of accused expanded. Seventy-five more deputies were placed under arrest, and the original twenty-one were put to death at the end of October (Sydenham 1961: 28).

Montagnard/Girondin polarization resulted from a number of mechanisms in concatenation:

- competition, as they and their opponents outbid each other for allies amongst the uncommitted deputies of the Plain
- opportunity/threat spirals arising from the combination of proffered support to the Jacobins from the sections and the threats of sedition from the provinces and attack from abroad
- category formation, as the Montagnards shaped the categorical identity Republican around their own beliefs and excluded those of their enemies
- brokerage, as the Jacobins mediated between the hesitant members of the Plain, on the one hand, and the savage onslaught from the streets that might have caught them up if they failed to take its leadership

These mechanisms came together on June 2, 1793, when, surrounded by Section militants bristling with weapons and followed by a Plain that was terrified of the consequences if they failed to convict them, the Jacobins called for expulsion and extermination of their opponents. The polarization of 1792–1773 resulted, not from French temperamental divisions or from the very nature of Revolution, but from the dynamics of contention.

Communal Contenders in Maluku

Oceanic Indonesia at the turn of our century may seem a poor partner for hexagonal France at the end of the eighteenth century, and so it is. First brought to western attention through the lucrative spice trade, Indonesia as we know it today was created by the Dutch around Java, Maluku[1] and South and West Sumatra between 1850 and 1910. An indigenous nationalist movement dates only from the 1930s, when Sukarno became its generally recognized leader. Japanese occupation in World War II increased nationalist sentiment as well as Sukarno's prestige (Kahin 1952). At war's end, the country emerged as an extreme version of a heterogeneous colonialism-made new state, made up, literally, of thousands of islands, with a broad spectrum of languages and a split between various versions of Islam, animist enclaves in the countryside, and a 15 percent Christian minority. Despite this, no serious separatist movements developed until late in the Suharto era, except in the Christian Moluccas.

As president, Sukarno held the country together by his charisma, international prestige in the Third World and a delicate balancing act. Part of that balancing act consisted in keeping the military at arm's length; another part in keeping the powerful Communist Party (PKI) in play, a strategy that gained Soviet and Chinese support but enraged the military and frightened both Muslim leaders within and the western powers without. These pressures converged on Sukarno in the military coup and mass massacres of 1965, in which hundreds of thousands were killed under cover of religious purification from Communism, and the "New Order" regime of General Suharto was established (Anderson 1966).

Suharto's kleptocratic regime lasted for over three decades. Fueled by its oil and natural gas revenues, by the entrepreneurial energy of the Chinese minority within and by the patronage of western powers without, it rested on the power of the military, on a Potemkin-village ruling party, Golkar, and on the expanding world market for cheaply produced Southeast Asian goods and increasingly lucrative oil (Sidel 1998: 160). In the process, the regime became famously corrupt and dangerously inefficient. By the 1990s, the army that had seized power in the 1960s had degenerated into a business empire, its martial energy sapped by its occupation of East Timor. Each military command had its own businesses and extortion

[1] We are grateful to Gerry Van Klinken, on whose unpublished article, "The Maluku Wars of 1999" we have drawn heavily in this brief discussion.

rackets (Kammen 1999). Suharto's power came partly from international trade, partly from local monopolies, and partly from commissions on virtually all foreign investments. His reign ended abruptly in the Asian financial crisis of the mid-1990s (Sidel 1998: 162–5).

That crisis was severe throughout Asia, but it hit Indonesia especially hard because it coincided with a political one. In the event, it brought down numerous businesses, triggered uncontrolled riots in the streets of Jakarta, and sparked communal strife in many of the country's far-flung provinces. The violence began in Jakarta itself, spreading from the students to the "massa" and rapidly taking aim at Chinese businesses and institutions (Siegel 1998). From there it spread across the archipelago (Robinson 1998; Rutherford 1999; Van Klinken forthcoming), stoking smoldering fires – like the twenty-five-year insurgency in East Timor – and sparking new ones, as in Maluku. From late 1998 until early 2000, waves of fighting broke out between Christians and Muslims on this band of islands, with the best estimates that 3,000–4,000 people were killed and between 123,000 and 370,000 displaced by violence, fear and intimidation (Van Klinken forthcoming: 3).

Much of the Malukan violence was carried out by bands of young men, both in Ambon, the capital of the province, and in its hinterland. But Jakarta-based and local elites were also accused of being protagonists of the conflicts, taking advantage of the power vacuum in the capital to seek local advantage and defending their respective religious groups from what were claimed to be attacks by the other. External actors included Islamic fighters who were seen coming from Java to help their coreligionists and Christian thugs who had lost a turf battle against Muslim competitors in Jakarta and came home to provide gun power for their brethren. But gangs of Christian thugs were responsible for much of the worst violence and even units of the military sent to restore order became involved, "as the armed forces reproduced the factionalism evident within society" (Van Klinken forthcoming: 33).

It was easy to find sources of the conflict in high unemployment and social disintegration, center-periphery and ethnic conflicts, communal tensions, and intervillage rivalry. Urban Maluku had an exceptionally high proportion of young people in the late 1990s, joined with a very high rate of unemployment. Center-periphery conflicts inherited from the New Order were exacerbated by the breakdown of the Golkar patronage system when Suharto fell. A high rate of in-migration of Muslims and their invasion of the profitable civil service sector threatened the once-privileged position of the region's Christians. A credible case can be mounted for the argument that the Maluku conflict represented "a resurgence of a . . . political pattern that predates the arrival of the centralised modern state, one characterized by many small centers of power with very local bases" (Van Klinken forthcoming: 18).

Readers who have followed us this far will guess that rather than seek the structural causes of contention, we look instead for the mechanisms and processes that triggered the outbreak, created the objects of contention, formed the alignments, and polarized the contenders. In a region in which most social institutions are church related, the process of mobilization was aided by many of our by now familiar mechanisms. For example, consider social appropriation, one of the earliest mechanisms we outlined. Religious community organizations were the only ones not thoroughly corporatized under the New Order, and became havens for articulation of every kind of interest, economic, ethnic, and so on. This is why they became centers of mobilization when the regime collapsed.

We focus here on the process of polarization, supported – as in revolutionary France – by opportunity/threat spirals, competition, category formation, and brokerage:

Opportunity/threat spirals: When, in October, 1998, fighting broke out between Christians and Muslims in Jakarta, there was an almost immediate reaction in far-off Maluku. Christian youths sympathizing with the victims of the Jakarta rioting attacked mosques and shops, but also constructed their attacks as defense against Muslim "newcomers." Ex-Golkar politicians soon seized the opportunities offered by the breakdown of authority to rally supporters on communal grounds.

The Muslim threat was embodied in the feeling among Christians that Muslim governor Saleh Latuconsina was filling posts in the predominantly Christian civil service with Muslims. In October 1998, just before the fighting broke out, an anonymous pamphlet claimed that the governor planned to replace all thirty-eight top civil servants with Muslims (Van Klinken forthcoming: 22). Many think this was the trigger for the entire violent episode.

Competition: Electoral competition was a trigger for the fighting. Maluku had been a Golkar preserve under the New Order, regularly winning majorities of up to 70 percent of the electorate. Suharto's fall in 1998 threw the local political elite into disarray, leading them to look around desperately for local sources of support. Thus began a spiral of political competition that, in the absence of legitimate cleavages, soon turned to religion as a source of electoral alignments (Van Klinken forthcoming: 26).

Category formation: Christians and Muslims in Maluku entered the period divided into sharply defined categories. While North Maluku is two-thirds Muslim, Ambon city, the capital, is three-fifths Protestant (cited by Van Klinken from the 1971 census: 15). Some villages are so segregated that even the wells are designated Christian or Muslim. Categorical inequality is most marked in the professions, with settlements that are heavily Protestant well installed in the civil service and those that are heavily Muslim concentrated in the private sector. Categorical lines were deepened as the conflict spread and Christians and Muslims were ejected or frightened out of their areas of residence. By January 2000, writes Van Klinken, "the entire island of Ambon was . . . segregated into white (Muslim) and red (Christian) areas, while heavily armed soldiers guarded the cross-over points." Fighters from each side wore colored strips of cloth identifying them as Muslim or Christian, more reminiscent of political party colors than of the religions.

Brokerage: Religious and indigenous groups, contenders for bureaucratic jobs, unemployed youth, village notables, Christian thugs from Jakarta and Muslim militants from elsewhere on Java. These were assembled in an amazingly short time into loose coalitions by political operators, some of them with ties to the underworld, under the frame of religion. Once the conflict became militarized and the competing groups separated by troops, even Christians and Muslims who had lived cheek-by-jowl were physically separated and forced to reshape their lives along communal lines. As in revolutionary France, polarization in the Maluku wars of 1999 was the product of opportunity/threat spirals, category formation, competition, and brokerage.

Scale Shift

The final process we take up is that of *scale shift*. By scale shift we mean a change in the number and level of coordinated contentious actions leading to broader contention involving a wider range of actors and bridging their claims and identities. (Here we neglect downward scale shift, by which widely coordinated contentious action fragments; it involves similar mechanisms in different concatenations.) The vast majority of contentious action never outgrows the local, categorical, or institutional context in which it first emerges. But in major episodes of contentious politics, almost by definition, at least some degree of scale shift must occur. In all of our cases, we see new incidents following the outbreak of contention; new actors latching onto forms of conflict hazarded by their predecessors; broader claims and identities crystallizing out of the interactions among contestants.

Consider these two examples, chosen at random from our panoply of episodes: the "great fear" among broad sectors of the French provincial population following the July 1789 events in Paris – widespread panics featuring stories of approaching marauders – and the adoption and spread of radical oathing as a tool of commitment and mobilization during Kenya's Mau Mau revolt. Our challenge is to examine how the mechanisms and processes that characterize contention at one scale shift it to another and whether, for example, the same kinds of mechanisms that govern scale shift from the local to the national level will be found in transnational contention.

Many of our mechanisms bridge different levels. Tactical innovation takes place at a local scale but when it catches on it is followed by diffusion to broader scales. Certification sometimes produces changes in small groups as well as in whole countries. Democratization, in contrast, depends by definition on the presence of government and polity, thus belonging to scales from community to world region. While nationalist writers can hatch their ideologies in their heads, as a movement, nationalism requires a wider scale.

Not only do major episodes of contention spread conflict from one site to another; as the scale of contention shifts and the range of actors expands its meaning to participants, opponents and third parties changes. Remember the Solidarity movement in Poland in 1981? Beginning as a strike at the Lenin shipyard in Gdansk, it spread to plants all along the Baltic coast and as it spread, the solidarity between factory groups of workers became both the symbol and the key to the success of the movement. Scale shift not only spreads conflict; it creates new frames around which the conflict is organized and raises the stakes of the game.

We see scale shift as a robust process consisting of two sometimes-linked pathways: what we call the diffusion/emulation pathway and a brokerage/coalition formation pathway. The two pathways both lead to scale shift through a common mechanism that we call attribution of similarity. Figure 10.3 portrays the two processes together.

Diffusion involves the transfer of information along established lines of interaction while *brokerage* entails the linking of two or more currently unconnected social sites. Both mechanisms operate in a number of our cases. So, for example, both diffusion and brokerage were evident in the spread of Mau Mau in Kenya. Here, however, we call attention to a significant difference in the pattern and spread of contention depending on whether diffusion or brokerage tend to predominate as the mediating mechanism. Contention that spreads primarily through diffusion will almost always remain narrower in its geographic and/or institutional scale than contention that spreads through brokerage. Why? Because it will not

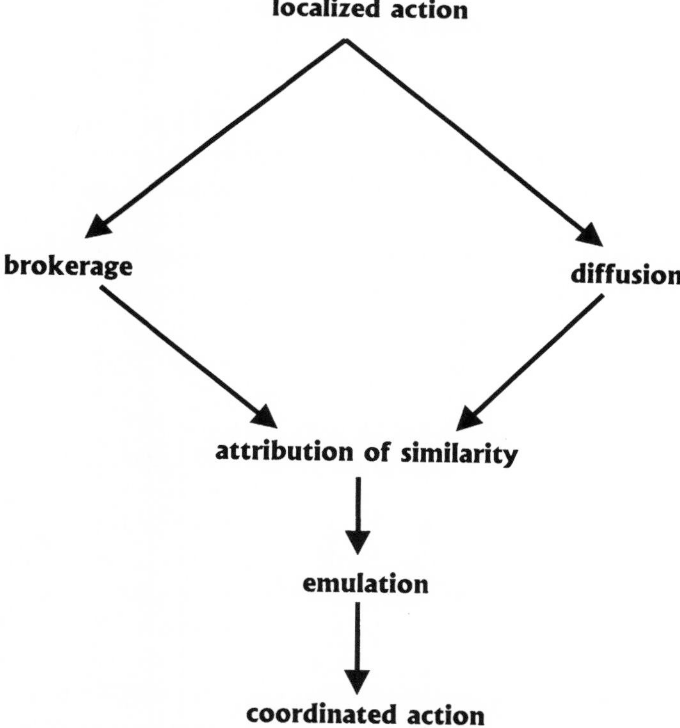

Figure 10.3. Scale Shift

transcend the typically segmented lines of interaction which characterize social life. So, for example, the initial instance of radical oathing in Olenguruone and its immediate environs appeared to have spread through diffusion, the broader campaign of radical oathing which preceded the State of Emergency involved brokerage as well as diffusion. Brokerage and coalition formation drew previously segmented actors together in an expanding conflict.

While diffusion and brokerage are distinct mechanisms, both work through the two additional mechanisms shown in Figure 10.3. The first of these, *attribution of similarity*, we define as "the mutual identification of actors in different sites as being sufficiently similar to justify common action." This mechanism is one that scholars of diffusion have long stressed as mediating between information and adoption (Strang and Meyer 1993; McAdam and Rucht 1993). The idea is simple enough. Information alone will not lead someone to adopt a new idea, cultural object, or behavioral practice. This, in turn, depends on at least a minimal identification between innovator and adopter.

What factors make such identification more likely? It results, first, from deliberate attempts of would-be brokers to frame the claims and identities of different actors as sufficiently similar to each other to justify coalition formation. We see such deliberate brokerage attempts all the time in contentious politics: the formation of a clerical-monarchist-regionalist coalition against Paris in France's 1793 Vendée revolt, the Free Men-Free Soil-Fremont electoral campaign of 1856 by Republicans in antebellum America, the invention of the composite category "people of color" to link African–Americans with Latino(a)s in the United States. Movement entrepreneurs who wish to increase their appeal to either previously connected or disparate groups work constantly to draw parallels between the group they represent and the targets of their influence attempts.

Attribution of similarity need not be a purposive, strategic process. A second factor encouraging identification among different actors is Strang and Meyer's (1993) concept of "institutional equivalence." These authors highlight the tendency of policy makers within particular institutional domains (e.g., urban planning) to identify with their counterparts in other countries, thus facilitating the spread of policy innovations. In the history of contentious politics, we see institutional equivalence in the channeling effect of mass production on industrial action; workers in mass production units with similar relations to management will find it easier to join their struggles to others in similar situations than, say, to handicraft workers in isolated workshops. Another factor in attribution of similarity is the revelation of similar claims that often occurs through the performance of distinct collective actions. Institutional equivalence and revealed similarity came together in the rapid diffusion of collective action across the similarly constituted Eastern European state socialist regimes in 1989.

The final mechanism mediating scale shift is *emulation*: "collective action modeled on the actions of others." While straightforward as a mechanism, its inclusion in Figure 10.3 underscores an important point. Awareness of prior action and even a strong identification with the actor does not guarantee emulative action on the part of the observing group. Groups sometimes learn of and strongly identify with a contentious action by another group, yet refrain from emulative action out of fear or a sensible desire to monitor the reaction of authorities before acting themselves. Emulative action is a significant accomplishment in its own right and therefore properly modeled as a mechanism distinct from the others.

Although diffusion and brokerage often combine in major episodes, there are significant differences in the character of scale shift depending on which of the two predominates as the triggering mechanism. Contention that spreads primarily through diffusion may be violent and powerful (like the 1960s ghetto riots in the United States), but it will almost always remain narrower in its reach and generality than contention that spreads through brokerage. Why? Because the diffusion pathway will not easily transcend the typically segmented lines of interaction that characterize social life. Brokerage by definition brings together different actors with frames and forms of action that cross these segmented lines.

By the same line of reasoning, diffusion will be far more common than brokerage in the spread of contention. More common because actors who are connected through established lines of interaction are already likely to attribute similarity to themselves; and also more common because diffusion requires a much lower investment in time, entrepreneurship and frame transformation than brokerage. It follows that brokerage, though less common than diffusion, is likely to be far more consequential in its impact on episodes of contention. To the extent that brokered ties help previously disconnected groups see themselves as similar to one another, contention can quickly spread beyond narrow geographic, institutional, and/or categorical boundaries and produce new identities that are more durable than the incidents that give rise to them.

To take but a single well-known case of this, by brokering a series of ties between the southern civil rights movement and northern white college campuses, the 1964 Freedom Summer project set in motion a significant "revolution beyond race" by encouraging many seemingly disparate groups (e.g., white college students, women, Hispanics – ultimately gays and lesbians, etc.) to identify with and draw lessons from black America.

Student Scale Shift

The diffusion and brokerage pathways came together electrically but imperfectly in the process of scale shift in the student movements of the late 1960s. That there were diffusion and emulation is obvious from the near simultaneity of the movement in many universities and countries and in the use of similar symbols and forms of action; but there was brokerage as well.

We saw in Chapter 2 how the Italian student movement was organized through a series of local faculty occupations in the winter and spring of 1967–1968. Localism was no barrier to the spread of the movement; it occurred almost simultaneously in Milan and Trento, Pisa and Florence, Rome and Naples. When the occupations ended, enthusiastic veterans went home on vacation and spread their message to younger brothers and sisters, who imitated their elders in the high schools. Brokerage was not only vertical. When the academic year ended, groups of students who had organized voting groups in occupation assemblies reached out to link up with kindred spirits in other universities and bring their movement to other sectors – for example to the slums of the urban periphery. What began as networks of local groups within the universities turned into a panoply of national extraparliamentary organizations, each with its own statutes, local branches, newspapers, characteristic forms of action, and *servizi d'ordine* (paramilitary corps of parade marshals).

As students began to organize nationally, the movement's framing shifted from the local issue of reforming of the university to general challenges to university authorities, to challenging the consumer society, to attacks on the political regime. Nowhere was this shift more marked than in the France of May 1968, when, thanks to the heavy-handed French police, a local dispute among students and administrators at the new university of Nanterre electrified students across the country and triggered a working class strike that paralyzed the economy. The crisis produced a general challenge to the regime.

Scale shift was also transnational. Young Germans who had studied in the United States brought back exciting news of the Columbia and Berkeley student revolts to their country (McAdam and Rucht 1993). Young French communists who had been to Italy tried to stir up the stolid PCF with reforms that were simultaneously enlivening its sister party. Italians who studied in Frankfurt came home bursting with messages from Adorno and Marcuse. These would-be brokers never succeeded in building a transnational student coalition, but they did diffuse the energy and the tactics of the American student movement to Western Europe and, within Europe, helped to construct a new student political identity.

Scale shift is frequently impeded from occurring between countries by the impermeability of boundaries, the resistance of governments, and the diffidence between people from different cultures. But in today's world, this may be changing as diffusion/emulation and brokerage/coalition formation combine in the formation of transnational social movements. Global television as well as increased immigration and cheaper transportation assure that movements that erupt in one part of the world are rapidly perceived and often emulated elsewhere. New kinds of alliances in the areas of human rights, the environment, and women's causes are being deliberately constructed by "transnational activist networks" (Keck and Sikkink 1998). Both diffusion and coalition formation frequently occur against increasingly powerful international institutions like the European Union, the World Bank, and the World Trade Organizations, which offer not only targets for transnational contention but arenas in which brokerage can take place (Tarrow 2001).

Rwandan Genocide

Scale shift often plays a significant part in collective violence. Isolated attacks on individuals and property escalate into widespread, and at least partly coordinated, destruction at a regional or national scale. The Rwandan genocide of 1994 provides a chilling example (Des Forges, et al. 1999; Grimshaw 1999; Jones 1995; Mamdani 2001; Newbury and Newbury 2000; Uvin 1998). In July 1973, Rwanda's senior military officer, General Juvénal Habyarimana, had seized power in a relatively bloodless coup. Soon he was establishing a one-party regime that lasted for two decades. Habyarimana, a Hutu from the northwest, faced opposition from Tutsi-based military forces in Uganda and along Rwanda's northern border as well as from Hutu political leaders based in the south.

After a number of earlier forays across the frontier, the Tutsi-based Rwanda Patriotic Front launched an invasion from the north late in 1990, failed, but renewed its effort a year later. The RPF offensive drove (mainly Hutu) refugees before it as it occupied Rwandan territory. In response, the Habyarimana regime increasingly backed a previously rejected program of Hutu Power. Outside areas of RPF control, massacres of Tutsi and of Hutu accused of collaboration with the RPF began in 1990. Government paramilitary forces and more autonomous Hutu Power death squads did the killing.

On April 6, 1994, President Habyarimana's aircraft was approaching its landing at the Rwandan capital, Kigali, when someone using sophisticated missiles shot it down. In that crash, not only the president but also Rwanda's army chief of staff General Nsabimana, Burundian president Cyprien Ntaryamira, and several others died. Habyarimana and Ntaryamira were returning from a meeting of African heads of state in Dar es Salaam, Tanzania, where participants had discussed (and perhaps agreed upon) installation of a broad-based transitional Rwandan government. Both inside and outside Rwanda, a number of power-holders had reasons to oppose such a settlement.

With Habyarimana's killing, within a day, one of the twentieth century's greatest single massacres had begun. From the start, military men and Hutu Power activists targeted not only members of the Tutsi minority but also prominent rivals among the Hutu. Scale shift occurred, however, as participation in killing expanded from well established specialists to a large numbers of civilians who had never killed before. "At first," in the words of Alison Des Forges, the

> assailants generally operated in small bands and killed their victims where they found them, in their homes, on the streets, at the barriers. But, as early as the evening of April 7, larger groups seized the opportunity for more intensive slaughter as frightened Tutsi – and some Hutu – fled to churches, schools, hospitals, and government offices that had offered refuge in the past. In the northwestern prefecture of Gisenyi, militia killed some fifty people at the Nyundo seminary, forty-three at the church of Busogo, and some 150 at the parish of Bursasamana. [Des Forges, et al. 1999: 209]

Massacres continued in that fashion, with Interahamwe (members of a Huti militia originally formed by the dead president Habyarimana) especially active in tracking down and killing their presumed enemies. Eventually hundreds of thousands of Rwandan civilians took part in massacres of Tutsi and of Hutu accused of siding with Tutsi. Within ten days after Habyarimana's death, attacks on Tutsi had escalated from occasional and localized killings to a national bloodbath. Scale shift occurred rapidly, and with devastating results.

Rwanda's scale shift connected the work of committed killers and fearful members of the general population. Although previously connected militias and Hutu Power activists provided crucial links among sites of killing:

> Hundreds of thousands of others chose to participate in the genocide reluctantly, some only under duress or in fear of their own lives. Unlike the zealots who never questioned their original choice, these people had to decide repeatedly whether or not to participate, each time weighing the kind of action planned, the identity of the proposed victim, the rewards of participating and the likely costs of not participating. Because attacks were incited or ordered by supposedly legitimate authorities, those with misgivings found it easier to commit crimes and to believe or pretend to believe they had done no wrong. [Des Forges, et al. 1999: 1–2]

In producing this result, diffusion and brokerage worked together. Word of Habyarimana's death and of early retaliation against presumed conspirators spread through interpersonal networks and mass media – notably the Hutu Power radio station Mille Collines. Alerted, local self-defense units the Habyarimana regime had formed for resistance to the RPF advance moved into action. So did already connected networks of Hutu Power activists. More than anyone else, however, the Interahamwe militia supplied brokers that connected localities with each other and with the killing apparatus as a whole. Those brokers reinforced definitions of the RPF and their supporters as a common threat, of ordinary Hutu patriots as a threatened population, of massacre as an acceptable and even necessary response, of the government as a supporter of death for traitors and for those who failed to kill traitors. Thus both diffusion and brokerage promoted attribution of similarity on both sides of the conflict, which in turn promoted coordinated action. The result was genocide.

Scale shift is a moderately complex process within which the relative salience of diffusion and brokerage varies, but passage through attribution of similarity and emulation regularly produces a transition from localized to large-scale coordination of action. Like actor constitution and polarization, scale shift operates across the whole range of contentious politics in similar ways, yet in conjunction with other mechanisms and processes produces anything from strike waves to mass murder. In that sense, actor constitution, polarization, and scale shift all qualify as robust processes.

Revisiting Scope Conditions

Let us reiterate the explanatory status we attach to these processes. They do not constitute a general model of contention. Nor should they be viewed as determinant models even of the more narrow features of contention to which they apply. Rather they define common dynamic pathways shaping particular features of contention. So Figure 10.1 delineates a common dynamic path to the constitution of new actors through contentious interaction, Figure 10.2 the exacerbation of cleavages within a contentious trajectory; and Figure 10.3 a set of linked mechanisms that very often mediate the spread of contention; and so on.

This leaves an important question unanswered. What scope do we attribute to these partial frameworks? While we have touted the breadth of our cases, our selection of episodes actually maximized variation on only two dimensions of contention while holding several others constant. We aimed to maximize breadth in the geographic distribution of our cases and the nominal form of the episode (e.g., social movement, revolution, or democratization). In at least three other respects, however, we sought to hold important features of contention more or less constant. Overwhelmingly our cases have been *national* episodes of *transgressive contention* located squarely within the *institutional realm* of politics. The decision to reduce variation on these dimensions was pragmatic and, given the already ambitious scope of our enterprise, entirely sensible in our view. But it leaves the effective scope of our analysis up in the air. In this section, we discuss each of the scope conditions with an eye to clarifying our explanatory claims. Our claim: Our program has far broader scope than even our cases suggest.

Scale: Our cases have generally been national in scale, involving conflicts whose resolution would affect social, political, and economic relations over the territorial breadth of the nation in question (even, as in the case of Italian unification, when the scope of national authority was at the heart of matter). This obviously does not mean that the conflict was equally intense in all regions of the affected nation. Though it had critically important implications for the entire Philippine nation, the Yellow Revolution was confined overwhelmingly to the capital and its environs. The same could be said for the 1989 Chinese student movement. While there were student-led protests in many other Chinese cities during and immediately following the occupation of Tiananmen Square, Beijing remained the site of the most significant and consequential action during the course of the episode.

These examples actually underscore the point we want to make regarding scale: the notion of a distinctly *national* scale of contention is illusory. National contention can be overwhelmingly local in its locus of action (e.g., as in Tiananmen). Even when the action is more geographically dispersed, national contention consists of an aggregation of local conflicts. What marks a conflict as national, then, is not its locus of action, but the broader social/political implications of the struggle. But since ours is a program for studying contentious action, or more precisely, interaction, it should apply wherever that action takes place. We are betting that our approach is just as applicable in the case of a conflict in which the stakes are exclusively local as to the kinds of nationally significant episodes highlighted in the book.

Transgressive versus contained contention: Besides being "national" in scale, all of our cases were of the transgressive rather than contained variety. That is, they all involved significant participation by newly constituted political actors and innovative forms of action. But, as defined in Chapter 2, the general designation "contentious politics" applies to both transgressive and contained contention. So why concentrate only on the former? In a sense, the question is poorly framed. Most of our cases began with episodes of contained contention that eventually evolved into broader transgressive episodes. So we have not really ignored the dynamics of contained contention in our selection of cases. It is true, however, that our sample includes no instances of exclusively contained contention. The question is: Would our approach have worked as well when applied to such a case? We are convinced that it would.

Take the period of contained contention that preceded and helped set the later transgressive phase of the American civil rights struggle in motion. If we confine our attention to the ten-year period following World War II, it is clear that a significant episode of contention is underway, but that all of the key combatants are constituted political actors using well established means of contention. Our explanatory approach should apply just as well to this period of more contained contention.

The onset of the Cold War constituted the key social change process that helped set in the episode in motion. For their part, established civil rights organizations clearly recognized the strategic opportunity that the Cold War afforded them. By drawing a stark parallel between Jim Crow policies in the United States and the suppression of freedom in the Soviet bloc, established leaders sought to prod a reluctant federal establishment into action by framing civil rights reform as a tool in America's struggle against communism. This rhetorical effort was joined to a stepped up legal assault on segregation, with the NAACP taking the lead in identifying and following through on cases designed to erode incrementally the legal foundations of Jim Crow.

In this context, government officials began to treat domestic racism as a threat to American foreign relations, civil rights organizations reinforced the theme, southern politicians reacted to the threat with mobilization on behalf of states' rights, and the U.S. Supreme Court began to strike down laws that supported segregation. Almost all these by now familiar forms of interaction took place in the zone of contained contention before the civil rights movement shifted into the more transgressive mode we analyzed in Chapter 2.

Even this stylized reading of the origins of the civil rights conflict of the postwar years should serve to make the point. The process of mobilization sketched in Chapter 2 fits the case very well. Broad social change processes – most notably the Cold War – destabilized America's system of racial politics, triggering innovative interpretive processes and action by the three sets of constituted actors touched on here. In turn, each new action reinforced the shared sense of uncertainty that sustains contention and in turn inspired responsive actions by the other parties to the conflict. The iterative, interactive process of contention had begun, and well before Montgomery thrust Martin Luther King, Jr., into the national spotlight.

Institutional locus of contention: The final limiting condition reflected in our cases concerns the institutional locus of contention. All of the episodes have been set within an expressly political context, that is, one defined in Chapter 2 as featuring "at least one government . . . [as] claimant, an object of claims, or a party to the claims." But are instances of contention involving non-state actors beyond the scope of our approach? Our hunch is that the framework can be readily adapted to the analysis of contention within any system of formal institutionalized power. This might be a firm, an industry, a local voluntary association, a church, or an entire denomination. The generic model only requires that the analyst be able to identify at least one member and one challenger actively engaged in contestation over the shape of a given organizational or institutional field. Indeed, there already exists a significant body of empirical studies that appear to attest to the salience of the same kind of dynamic processes and mechanisms in the development of contention in a host of such organizational/institutional settings.

In his book, *The Transformation of Corporate Control*, Neil Fligstein (1990) offers a historical account of the rise of the "finance strategy" within American firms that closely accords with the mobilization process sketched in Chapter 2. Fligstein sees various destabilizing change processes – including key court decisions – triggering interpretive processes within firms that lead to innovative collective action by finance and marketing challengers intent on wresting control from the traditionally dominant manufacturing elite. Other analysts have identified contentious processes in the health services industry and elsewhere (e.g., Rao, Morrill and Zald 2001).

These empirical examples could be multiplied many times over. When joined with the increasing theoretical calls for more dynamic, cultural, and relational approaches to the study of organizational/institutional change and conflict, the implication should be clear (Brint and Karabell 1991; Davis and McAdam 2001; DiMaggio 1988, 1991; DiMaggio and Powell 1991; Fligstein 1996; Friedland and Alford 1991; Hirsch 1986; Katzenstein 1998; Kurzman 1998; Morrill 1996; Rao, Morrill and Zald 2000; Zald and Berger 1978). Contention is not something peculiar to the realm of politics. It is a generic phenomenon inextricably linked to the establishment of institutionalized power relations. Whether that power is wielded for formal political purposes or other institutional aims – economic, cultural, or religious – contention is inevitable. Accordingly, we see no reason ultimately to restrict the application of our approach to the political realm, narrowly defined.

What Next?

The previous two sections should make the agenda clearer. The robust processes sketched above provide ample illustration of the kind of partial analytic frameworks we are betting on. Our discussion of relaxed scope conditions reveals the broad comparisons to which we aspire. Are we there yet? Far from it. Surely our arguments and program will prove wrong in many ways. So much the better: We are hoping to promote new knowledge, not to codify old information. As others will no doubt do, we intend to engage some of the many challenges identified but not solved by the preliminary formulation offered here. Let us concentrate on four of them.

The devil, architects say, is in the details; in this case, the methodological details. Our analyses turn on the plausible, but as yet nonsystematic, deployment of various explanatory mechanisms. Nowhere have we demonstrated the empirical reality of any of these mechanisms. A formidable challenge therefore lies in the operationalization and systematic empirical interrogation of these, and other, candidate mechanisms.

There is a second operational challenge that we have skirted to this point. Though we have granted central importance to the concept of "contentious episode," we have failed to delineate its empirical features. How are we as analysts to bound such episodes? Should we rely on the shared perceptions of the combatants? Or intervene as analysts and define them on the basis of features derived from our theories? We pose the questions, not to answer them, but to highlight the important challenge at their heart. If we are to make episodes the fundamental unit of observation in the study of contention, we had better be able to fashion a reliable way of identifying such episodes.

A third major challenge, of a more conceptual sort, faces anyone who heeds our call. Without denying the efficacy of cognitive or environmental mechanisms, our proposed explanations of contention have stressed relational mechanisms. Analysts of both the phenomenological and rationalist persuasion have, in contrast, generally emphasized cognitive mechanisms, treating relational and environmental circumstances as constraints and/or resources. Other analysts have concentrated on environmental mechanisms; extreme versions of resource mobilization theory and organizational ecology fall into this category. Notwithstanding our emphasis on relational mechanisms, any adequate theory of contention will have to integrate environmental, cognitive, *and* relational mechanisms far more firmly than this volume has. Even those who accept our program will have to revisit the conundrums with which this book began, notably how and to what extent cognitive mechanisms mediate environmental and relational effects.

One last challenge, and not the least. When we began working on this book, we imagined that we would organize the entire enterprise around a well-developed analysis of variation in governments, regimes, and polities. We soon recognized that to do so would make the analysis unbearably complex. Traces of speculation regarding differences between democratic and undemocratic, strong states and weak states, and various forms of governmental repression, toleration, and facilitation appear here and there in our cases, but for the most part standard analysis of political structure has absconded from the book. As a result, the polity model we adopted as a heuristic frame at the outset remains unmodified by the dynamic, relational analysis central to the enterprise. Governments have appeared repeatedly in the analysis as powerful actors, but not as the dynamic, contested, continuously recreated entities we know them to be. A full realization of our perspective then, will require a more satisfactory rendering of state actors in these more dynamic, relational terms.

History, Culture, and Local Knowledge

In closing, let us make explicit a problem that confronts scholars more concerned with the interpretation of individual episodes, countries, and periods of history than with general patterns of contention. Consider the profound challenge that comes with trying to reconcile circumstances and features of any particular social episode with the desire to fashion more general understandings of social life. This is a daunting challenge, one that translates into the following stark question: Can particularities in history, culture, and local knowledge be reconciled with a more general focus on cognitive, relational, and environmental mechanisms? For all the difficulties inherent in this act of analytic reconciliation, we end this book as we began it: in confidence that our program is as relevant to the interpretation of specific social processes as it is to the general mechanisms and processes on which the book has focused. Analysts who seek to explain particular episodes actually do so by identifying explanatory principles that extend beyond these episodes. We propose mechanisms and processes as just such principles.

What about culture's particularities? If we consider culture as shared understandings and their representations in symbols, objects, and practices, our empirical accounts of contentious episodes reek with culture. In the case of Mau Mau, for example, the effectiveness of brokerage depended on the longstanding cultural resonance of oathing as both belief and practice; that was a particular embodiment of a general process. In the development of the U.S. protest cycle of the 1960s, the ideological ties forged by the Freedom Summer project facilitated brokerage as well – but in ways that drew on the routines and relationships of American culture. The understandings and practices that facilitated brokerage in the two cases could not have been more different, but the general concept of brokerage helps to interpret their embodiments in each case.

The point bears underscoring: We are betting that *particular* cultural understandings and practices can produce quite *general* effects through our intervening mechanisms and processes and that analysis of the latter facilitates understanding of how culture imbricates within contentious episodes.

Furthermore, the historical and cultural particulars of a given episode actually encourage, rather than discourage, more general understanding of contentious dynamics and understandings. When seen in a comparative light, cultural understandings are rarely particular. Two examples of this relationship will make our case. The first concerns the reification of various contentious forms – social movements, revolutions, nationalism, democratization, and the like. We have criticized this reification in scholarshop, but the forms in question have achieved a cultural standing that make them potent models for real world actors.

Actors who engage in contentious claims making have available to them models of previous episodes, with attendant stories about these models. In 1848, European revolutionaries already knew about the French Revolution of 1789–1799, and (as Karl Marx commented sardonically in his *Eighteenth Brumaire of Louis Bonaparte*) could even try to reenact 1789, 1792, or 1795. For actors to describe their action as revolution, war, democratization, or a social movement focuses their attention, and that of other actors, on certain models while diminishing the relevance of other models that could, in principle, serve the same function. Historical precedents matter, but it does not surpass our capacities to try to understand how and with what effects those precedents constrain the mechanisms and processes of contention.

We go further: A number of mechanisms that have proven important to our explanations actually depend on the existence of models, stories, and practices associated with previous episodes within a family. Certification and decertification offer the most obvious examples: certifying agencies always operate from previously established conceptions of valid political actors. The United Nations' certification of a new nation (e.g., East Timor) as an independent entity has this character, but so do other international agencies' designation of regimes as democratic, stable, economically sound, respectful of human rights, or failures in any of these regards.

Other mechanisms involve invocation of previously existing models, stories, and beliefs that tip contentious action in one direction of the other. Suddenly imposed grievances, for example, do not appear out of thin air in response to some kind of external intervention. People map such events into available cultural templates, modifying those templates as they do so. Certain kinds of cultural frames – "master frames" in Snow and Benford's (1992) formulation – achieve broad resonance across many instances of contention. To embrace the idea of robust mechanisms and processes across contentious episodes, countries, and periods of history is not to reject the idea that culture and local knowledge shape contention but to propose a strategy for their reconciliation in between the celebration of particularism and the laying down of general laws. By embedding our analytical categories in the historical and cultural particulars of each episode we study, we are betting that analysts can discern the more general, dynamic processes that typically fuel contention.

Our work provides a starting place, but no more than that.

References

Adell Argilés, Ramon (1989): *La Transición Politica en la Calle. Manifestaciones Politicas de Grupos y Masas. Madrid 1976–1987.* Madrid: Universidad Complutense.

(1998): "El estudio de la movilización, como indicador de participación sociopolitica: parametros analíticos y significado," unpublished paper presented to the Sixth Spanish Congress of Sociology.

Aguilar Fernández, Paloma (1995): *La memoria histórica de la guerra civil española (1936–1939): Un proceso de aprendizaje politico.* Madrid: Centro de Estudios Avanzados en Ciencias Sociales.

(1997): "Collective Memory of the Spanish Civil War: The Case of the Political Amnesty in the Spanish Transition to Democracy," *Democratization* 4: 88–109.

Alberoni, Francesco (1968): *Statu nascenti.* Bologna: Il Mulino.

Anderson, Benedict (1966): "The 1965 Coup in Indonesia: A Preliminary Analysis of the October 1, 1965, Coup in Indonesia." Unpublished research monograph, Cornell University.

(1991): *Imagined Communities. Reflections on the Origin and Spread of Nationalism.* London: VERSO. Rev. edn.

(1998): *The Spectre of Comparisons.* New York and London: Monthly Review Press.

Anderson, Bo, and James D. Cockroft (1972): "Control and Co-optation in Mexican Politics," in J.D. Cockroft, A.G. Frank, and D.L. Johnson, eds. *Dependence and Underdevelopment: Latin America's Political Economy.* New York: Doubleday.

APSR (American Political Science Review) (1995): "Review Symposium: The Qualitative-Quantitative Disputation: Gary King, Robert O. Keohane, and Sidney Verba's "*Designing Social Inquiry*," *American Political Science Review* 89: 454–481.

Atkin, Muriel (1997): "Thwarted Democratization in Tajikistan," in Karen Dawisha and Bruce Parrott, eds. *Conflict, Cleavage, and Change in Central Asia and the Caucasus.* Democratization and Authoritarianism in Postcommunist Societies: 4. Cambridge: Cambridge University Press.

Atkins, G. Pope (1977): *Latin America in the International Political System*. New York: Free Press.

Azurmendi, Mikel (1998): *La Herida patriotica: La cultura del nacionalismo vasco*. Madrid: Taurus.

Baer, Marc (1992): *Theatre and Disorder in Late Georgian London*. Oxford: Oxford University Press.

Balibar, Etienne (1991): "The Nation Form: History and Ideology," in Etienne Balibar and Immanuel Wallerstein, eds. *Race, Nation, Class: Ambiguous Identities*. London: Verso.

Barnes, Gilbert Hobbs (1957): *The Antislavery Impulse, 1830–1844*. Gloucester, MA: Peter Smith.

Barnett, Donald L., and Karari Njama (1966): *Mau Mau from Within*. New York: Monthly Review Press.

Barrington, Lowell (1995): "The Domestic and International Consequences of Citizenship in the Soviet Successor States," *Europe-Asia Studies* 47: 731–763.

Bates, Robert H., Avner Grief, Margaret Levi, Jean-Laurent Rosenthal, and Barry R. Weingast (1997): *Analytic Narratives*. Princeton, NJ: Princeton University Press.

Bearman, Peter S. (1991): "Desertion as Localism: Army Unit Solidarity and Group Norms in the U.S. Civil War," *Social Forces* 70: 321–342.

(1993): *Relations into Rhetorics. Local Elite Social Structure in Norfolk, England, 1540–1640*. New Brunswick: Rutgers University Press.

Beissinger, Mark (1995): "The Persisting Ambiguity of Empire," *Post-Soviet Affairs* 11: 149–184.

(1996): "How Nationalisms Spread: Eastern Europe Adrift the Tides and Cycles of Nationalist Contention," *Social Research* 63: 97–146.

(1998): "Event Analysis in Transitional Societies: Protest Mobilization in the Former Soviet Union," in Dieter Rucht, Ruud Koopmans and Friedhelm Neidhardt, eds. *Acts of Dissent. New Developments in the Study of Protest*. Berlin: Sigma.

(forthcoming): *The Tides of Nationalism: Order, Event, and the Collapse of the Soviet State*. Unpublished ms.: University of Wisconsin-Madison.

Bensel, Richard (1990): *Yankee Leviathan: The Origins of Central State Authority in America, 1859–1877*. New York: Cambridge University Press.

Berman, Bruce, and John Lonsdale (1992): *Unhappy Valley: Conflict in Kenya and Africa*. London: James Curry.

Bermeo, Nancy (1997): "Myths of Moderation: Confrontation and Conflict during Democratic Transitions," *Comparative Politics* 27: 305–322.

(1997): "The Power of the People," Madrid: working paper 1997/97, Instituto Juan March de Estudios e Investigaciones.

Bier, Alice Gail (1980): *Crecimiento urbano y participación vecinal*. Madrid: Centro de Investigaciones Sociologicas.

Black, George (1981): *Triumph of the People: The Sandinista Revolution in Nicaragua*. London: Zed Press.

Black, George, and Robin Munro (1993): *Black Hands of Beijing*. New York: John Wiley and Sons, Inc.

References

Blyth, Stuart (1999): "Spain 1974–77; Democratic Opposition, Neighbourhood Associations and Civil Society," unpublished paper, University of Wolverhampton School of Languages and European Studies.

Booth, John A. (1982): *The End and the Beginning: The Nicaraguan Revolution.* Boulder, CO: Westview Press.

Bose, Sugata, and Ayesha Jalal (1998): *Modern South Asia. History, Culture, Political Economy.* London: Routledge.

Boudreau, Vincent (forthcoming): *At the Margins of the Movement: Grassroots and Cadre in Philippine Protest.* Manila: Ateneode Manila University Press.

Brass, Paul R. (1994): *The Politics of India Since Independence.* Cambridge: Cambridge University Press. The New Cambridge History of India, IV-1. 2d edn.

(1996): ed. *Riots and Pogroms.* New York: New York University Press.

(1997): *Theft of an Idol. Text and Context in the Representation of Collective Violence.* Princeton: Princeton University Press.

Braun, Rudolf (1960): *Industrialisierung und Volksleben.* Zurich: Rentsch.

(1965): *Sozialer und kultureller Wandel in einem ländlichen Industriegebiet.* Zurich: Rentsch.

Brewer, John (1979–80): "Theater and Counter-Theater in Georgian Politics: The Mock Elections at Garrat," *Radical History Review* 22: 7–40.

Brint, Steven, and Jerome Karabell (1991): "Institutional Origins and Transformations: The Case of American Community Colleges," pp. 337–60 in Walter W. Powell and Paul DiMaggio, eds. *The New Institutionalism in Organizational Analysis.* Chicago: University of Chicago Press.

Brinton, Crane (1938): *The Anatomy of a Revolution.* New York: Norton.

Brook, Timothy (1998): *Quelling the People.* Stanford: Stanford University Press.

Buijtenhuijs, Rob (1982): *Essays on Mau Mau.* Leiden: African Studies Centre.

Bunce, Valerie (1981): *Do New Leaders Make a Difference? Executive Succession and Public Policy under Capitalism and Socialism.* Princeton: Princeton University Press.

(1999): *Subversive Institutions. The Design and the Destruction of Socialism and the State.* Cambridge: Cambridge University Press.

Burns, Stewart, ed. (1997): *Daybreak of Freedom.* Durham: University of North Carolina Press.

Burt, Ronald S. (1992): *Structural Holes. The Social Structure of Competition.* Cambridge: Harvard University Press.

Burt, Ronald S., and Marc Knez (1995): "Kinds of Third-Party Effects on Trust," *Rationality and Society* 7: 255–292.

Butsch, Richard (1995): "American Theater Riots and Class Relations, 1754–1849," *Theatre Annual* 48: 41–59.

(2000): *The Making of American Audiences: From Stage to Television, 1750–1990.* Cambridge: Cambridge University Press.

Buxo i Rey, Maria Jesus (1995): "El imaginario etnico en Cataluña," *Antropológico* No. 18: 119–132.

Cadena-Roa, Jorge (1999): "State Pacts, Elites, and Social Movements in Mexico's Transition to Democracy," unpublished paper; UNAM.

Calhoun, Craig (1994): *Neither Gods nor Emperors: Students and the Struggle for Democracy in China*. Berkeley: University of California Press.

(1995): "'New Social Movements' of the Early Nineteenth Century," in Mark Traugott, ed, *Repertoires and Cycles of Collective Action*. Durham, NC: Duke University Press.

Carr, Raymond (1980): *Modern Spain, 1875–1980*. Oxford: Oxford University Press.

Carson, Clayborne (1981): *In Struggle: SNCC and the Black Awakening of the 1960s*. Cambridge: Harvard University Press.

Cerulo, Karen A. (1997): "Identity Construction: New Issues, New Directions," *Annual Review of Sociology* 23: 385–409.

Charney, Craig (1999): "Civil Society, Political Violence, and Democratic Transitions: Business and the Peace Process in South Africa 1990 to 1994," *Comparative Studies in Society and History* 41: 182–206.

Chaturvedi, Jayati, and Gyaneshwar Chaturvedi (1996): "*Dharma Yudh*: Communal Violence, Riots, and Public Space in Ayodhya and Agra City: 1990 and 1992," in Paul R. Brass., ed. *Riots and Pogroms*. New York: New York University Press.

Christian, Shirley (1986): *Revolution in the Family*. New York: Vintage Books.

Chubb, Judith (1982): *Politics, Power and Poverty in Southern Italy: A Tale of Two Cities*. New York: Cambridge University Press.

Collier, David, and Steven Levitsky (1997): "Democracy with Adjectives: Conceptual Innovation in Comparative Research," *World Politics* 49: 430–451.

Congressional Research Service (1979): "Human Rights and United States Foreign Assistance: Experiences and Issues in Policy Implementation." Report to the Committee on Foreign Relations, U.S. Senate. Washington, DC: Government Printing Office.

Connor, Walker (1994): *Ethnonationalism. The Quest for Understanding*. Princeton: Princeton University Press.

Cook, Maria Lorena, Kevin J. Middlebrook, and Juan Molinar Horcasitas, eds. (1994): *The Politics of Economic Restructuring: State-Society Relations and Regime Change in Mexico*. La Jolla, CA: Center for U.S.-Mexican Studies.

Cooper, Frederick (1996): *Decolonization and African Society*. Cambridge, UK: Cambridge University Press.

Copland, Ian (1998): "The Further Shores of Partition: Ethnic Cleansing in Rajasthan 1947," *Past and Present* 160: 203–239.

Cornelius, Wayne, Todd A. Eisenstadt, and Jane Hindley, eds. (1999): *Subnational Politics and Democratization in Mexico*. La Jolla: Center for U.S.-Mexican Studies.

Cornell, Stephen, and Douglas Hartmann (1998): *Ethnicity and Race. Making Identities in a Changing World*. Thousand Oaks, CA: Pine Forge.

Cosio Villegas, Daniel (1973): *La Constitución de 1857 y sus criticos*. Mexico City: S.E.P.

Crofts, Daniel W. (1989): *Reluctant Confederates: Upper South Unionists in the Secession Crisis*. Chapel Hill: University of North Carolina Press.

Crouch, Colin, and Alessandro Pizzorno (1978): *The Resurgence of Class Conflict in Western Europe after 1968*, 2 vols. London: Macmillan.

References

Cruz, Rafael, ed. (1997): *El anticlericalismo*. Madrid: Marcial Pons.

CSCE [Commission on Security and Cooperation in Europe] (1998): *Political Reform and Human Rights in Uzbekistan, Kyrgyzstan and Kazakhstan*. Washington, DC: CSCE.

Daniel, E. Valentine (1996): *Charred Lullabies. Chapters in an Anthropography of Violence*. Princeton: Princeton University Press.

Davis, David Brion (1969): *The Slave Power Conspiracy and the Paranoid Style in American Politics*. Baton Rouge: Louisiana State University Press.

Davis, Gerald F., and Doug McAdam (2001): "Corporations, Classes, and Social Movements after Managerialism," *Research in Organization Behavior* 22: 195–238.

Davis, Natalie Zemon (1975): *Society and Culture in Early Modern France*. Berkeley: University of California Press.

Davis, Richard H. (1996): "The Iconography of Rama's Chariot," in David Ludden, ed. *Contesting the Nation: Religion, Community, and the Politics of Democracy in India*. Philadelphia: University of Pennsylvania Press.

Dawisha, Karen (1997): "Democratization and Political Participation: Research Concepts and Methodologies" in Karen Dawisha and Bruce Parrott, eds. *The Consolidation of Democracy in East-Central Europe*. Authoritarianism and Democratization in Postcommunist Societies, vol. 1. Cambridge: Cambridge University Press.

de Capitani, François (1983): "Vie et mort de l'Ancien Régime," in Jean-Claude Fayez, ed. *Nouvelle Histoire de la Suisse et des Suisses*, vol. 2. Lausanne: Payot.

de Miguel, Amando (1976): "Spanish Political Attitudes 1970," in Stanley G. Payne, ed. *Politics and Society in Twentieth-Century Spain*. New York: New Viewpoints.

della Porta, Donatella (1990): *Il terrorismo di sinistra*. Bologna: Il Mulino.

(1998): "Police Knowledge and Protest Policing: Some Reflections on the Italian Case," in Donatella della Porta and Herbert Reiter, eds. *Policing Protest. The Control of Mass Demonstrations in Western Democracies*. Minneapolis: University of Minnesota Press.

Deneckere, Gita (1997): *Sire, het volk mort. Sociaal protest in België (1831–1918)*. Antwerp: Baarn; Ghent: Amsab.

Des Forges, Alison, et al. (1999): *Leave None to Tell the Story. Genocide in Rwanda*. New York: Human Rights Watch.

de Tocqueville, Alexis (1983): *Correspondance d'Alexis de Tocqueville et de François de Corcelle*. Paris: Gallimard. Oeuvres Complètes, t. XV.

Deutsch, Karl (1976): *Die Schweiz als ein paradigmatischer Fall politischer Integration*. Bern: Haupt.

DiMaggio, Paul (1988): "Interest and Agency in Institutional Theory," pp. 3–21 in Lynn G. Zucker, ed. *Institutional Patterns and Organizations: Culture and Environment*. Cambridge, MA: Ballinger.

DiMaggio, Paul, and Walter W. Powell (1991): "Introduction," pp. 1–37 in Walter W. Powell and Paul DiMaggio, eds. *The New Institutionalism in Organizational Analysis*. Chicago: University of Chicago Press.

di Palma, Giuseppe (1990): *To Craft Democracies: An Essay on Democratic Transitions*. Berkeley: University of California Press.

Dix, Robert H. (1984): "Why Revolutions Succeed and Fail." *Polity* 16: 423–446.

Duara, Prasenjit (1996): "Historicizing National Identity, or Who Imagines What and When," in Geoff Eley and Ronald Grigor Suny, eds. *Becoming National: A Reader.* New York: Oxford University Press.

Durán Muñoz, Rafael (1997): "Acciones colectivas y transiciones a la democracia: España y Portugal. 1974–1977," Doctoral thesis, Universidad Autonoma de Madrid (to be published as *Contención y transgresión. Las movilizaciones sociales y el Estado en las transiciones española y portuguesa.* Madrid: Centro de Estudios Constitucionales.

Edgerton, Robert B. (1989): *Mau Mau: An African Crucible.* New York: The Free Press.

Edles, Laura Desfor (1998): *Symbol and Ritual in the New Spain: The Transition to Democracy in the New Spain.* Cambridge: Cambridge University Press.

Eisinger, Peter (1973): "The Conditions of Protest Behavior in American Cities," *American Political Science Review* 67: 11–28.

Elias, Norbert, and John L. Scotson (1994): *The Established and the Outsiders: A Sociological Enquiry into Community Problems.* London: Sage. 2d edn.

Eley, Geoff, and Ronald Grigor Suny eds. (1996): *Becoming National: A Reader.* New York: Oxford University Press.

Elster, Jon (1989): *Nuts and Bolts for the Social Sciences.* Cambridge: Cambridge University Press.

Fane, Daria (1996): "Ethnicity and Regionalism in Uzbekistan. Maintaining Stability through Authoritarian Control," in Leokadia Drobizheva, Rose Gottemoeller, Catherine McArdle Kelleher and Lee Walker, eds. *Ethnic Conflict in the Post-Soviet World. Case Studies and Analysis.* Armonk, New York: M.E. Sharpe.

Farhi, Farideh (1990): *States and Urban-Based Revolutions: Iran and Nicaragua.* Urbana: University of Illinois Press.

Feige, Edgar (1998): "Underground Activity and Institutional Change: Productive, Protective, and Predatory Behavior in Transition Economies," in Joan M. Nelson, Charles Tilly and Lee Walker, eds. *Transforming Post-Communist Political Economies.* Washington: National Academy Press.

Fellman, Michael (1979): "Rehearsal for the Civil War: Antislavery and Proslavery at the Fighting Point in Kansas, 1854–1856," in Lewis Perry and Michael Fellman, eds. *Antislavery Reconsidered: New Perspectives on the Abolitionists.* Baton Rouge: Louisiana State University Press.

Fierman, William (1997): "Political Development in Uzbekistan: Democratization?" in Karen Dawisha and Bruce Parrott, eds. *Conflict, Cleavage, and Change in Central Asia and the Caucasus.* Democratization and Authoritarianism in Postcommunist Societies: 4. Cambridge: Cambridge University Press.

Finer, Samuel E. (1997): *The History of Government from the Earliest Times.* 3 vols. Oxford: Oxford University Press.

Fishman, Robert M. (1990): *Working-Class Organization and the Return to Democracy in Spain.* Ithaca: Cornell University Press.

References

Fligstein, Neil (1990): *The Transformation of Corporate Control.* Cambridge: Harvard University Press.

(1996): "Markets as Politics: A Political Cultural Approach to Market Institutions," *American Sociological Review* 61: 656–673.

Foner, Eric (1995): *Free Soil, Free Labor, Free Men: The Ideology of the Republican Party Before the Civil War.* Oxford: Oxford University Press.

Foran, John (1990): "A Theory of Third World Social Revolution," Paper presented at the meetings of the International Sociological Association, Madrid, Spain, July 1990.

(1993): "Theories of Revolution Revisited: Toward a Fourth Generation?" *Sociological Theory* 11: 1–20.

(1997): "The Future of Revolutions at the *fin-de-siècle*," *Third World Quarterly* 18: 791–820.

Fox, Jonathan (1994): "The Difficult Transition from Clientelism to Citizenship: Lessons from Mexico," *World Politics* 46: 151–184.

(1995): "Governance and Rural Development in Mexico: State Intervention and Public Accountability," *Journal of Development Studies* 32: 1–30.

Fox, Jonathan, and Josefina Aranda (1996): *Community Participation in Oaxaca's Municipal Funds Program.* La Jolla: Center for U.S.-Mexican Studies, University of California, San Diego, Monograph Series no. 42.

Franzosi, Roberto (1995): *The Puzzle of Strikes. Class and State Strategies in Postwar Italy.* Cambridge: Cambridge University Press.

Fredrickson, George M. (1971): *The Black Image in the White Mind.* Middletown Ct: Wesleyan University Press.

(1981): *White Supremacy. A Comparative Study in American and South African History.* Oxford: Oxford University Press.

Freitag, Sandria B. (1996): "Contesting in Public: Colonial Legacies and Contemporary Communalism," in David Ludden, ed. *Contesting the Nation. Religion, Community, and the Politics of Democracy in India.* Philadelphia: University of Pennsylvania Press.

Friedland, Roger, and Robert R. Alford (1991): "Bringing Society Back In: Symbols, Practices, and Institutional Contradictions," pp. 232–62 in Walter W. Powell and Paul DiMaggio, eds., *The New Institutionalism in Organizational Analysis.* Chicago: University of Chicago Press.

Fundación FOESSA (1970): *Informe sociologico sobre la situación social de España.* Madrid: Editorial Euramerica.

Furedi, Frank (1973): "The African Crown in Nairobi: Popular Movements and Elite Politics," *Journal of African History* 14 (No. 1).

(1974a): "Olenguruone in Mau Mau Historiography," paper presented at the One-Day Conference on the Mau Mau Rebellion, Institute of Commonwealth Studies, March 29, 1974.

(1974b): "The Social Composition of the Mau Mau Movement in the White Highlands," *Journal of Peasant Studies* 1 (No. 4).

Gambetta, Diego (1988): "Can We Trust Trust?" in Diego Gambetta, ed. *Trust. Making and Breaking Cooperative Relations.* Oxford: Blackwell.

(1993): *The Sicilian Mafia. The Business of Private Protection*. Cambridge: Harvard University Press.
(1998): "Concatenations of Mechanisms," in Peter Hedström and Richard Swedberg, eds. *Social Mechanisms. An Analytical Approach to Social Theory*. Cambridge: Cambridge University Press.
Gamson, William A. (1989): *Power and Discontent*. Homewood: Dorsey. Rev. edn.
(1990): *The Strategy of Social Protest*. Belmont, California: Wadsworth. 2d edn.
(1992): *Talking Politics*. Cambridge: Cambridge University Press.
Gamson, William A., Bruce Fireman, and Steven Rytina (1982): *Encounters with Unjust Authority*. Homewood, Ill: Dorsey.
Garmendia, José A., Francisco Parra Luna, and Alfonso Pérez-Agote (1982): *Abertzales y vascos: Identificación vascista y nacionalista en el País Vasco*. Madrid: Akal.
Geddes, Barbara (1990): "How the Cases You Choose Affect the Answers You Get: Selection Bias in Comparative Politics," in James A. Stimson, ed. *Political Analysis* 2. Ann Arbor: University of Michigan Press.
Genovese, Eugene (1969): *The World the Slaveholders Made: Two Essays in Interpretation*. New York: Random House.
(1992): *The Slaveholders' Dilemma: Freedom and Progess in Southern Conservative Thought, 1820–1860*. Columbia: University of South Carolina Press.
Gerth, Hans H., and C. Wright Mills (1946): *From Max Weber: Essays in Sociology*. New York: Oxford University Press.
Ghosh, Amitav (1992): *In an Antique Land. History in the Guise of a Traveler's Tale*. New York: Vintage.
Gienapp, William E. (1987): *Origins of the Republican Party*. New York: Oxford University Press.
Ginsborg, Paul (1989): *Storia d'Italia dal dopoguerra a oggi. Società e politica 1943–1988*. Turin: Einaudi, 2 vols.
Giugni, Marco, and Florence Passy (1997): *Histoires de mobilisation politique en Suisse. De la contestation à l'intégration*. Paris: L'Harmattan.
Godechot, Jacques (1965): *La prise de la Bastille*. Paris: Gallimard.
Goldstone, Jack (1980): "Theories of Revolution: The Third Generation," *World Politics* 32: 425–453.
(1980): "The Weakness of Organization," *American Journal of Sociology* 85: 1017–1042.
(1991): *Revolution and Rebellion in the Early Modern World*. Berkeley: University of California Press.
(1998): "Social Movements or Revolutions? On the Evolution and Outcomes of Collective Action," in Marco Guigni, Doug McAdam, and Charles Tilly, eds. *From Contention to Democracy*. Boulder, CO: Rowman and Littlefield.
Goodwin, Jeff (1994): "Old Regimes and Revolutions in the Second and Third Worlds: A Comparative Perspective," *Social Science History* 18: 575–604.
(1994): "Toward a New Sociology of Revolutions," *Theory and Society* 23: 731–766.
Goodwin, Jeff, James Jasper, Charles Tilly, et al. (1999): "Mini-Symposium on Social Movements," *Sociological Forum* 14: 27–136.

References

Gossman, Lionel (2000): *Basel in the Age of Burkhardt. A Study in Unseasonable Ideas.* Chicago: University of Chicago Press.

Gould, Roger V. (1995): *Insurgent Identities.* Chicago: University of Chicago Press.

(1998): "Political Networks and the Local/National Boundary in the Whiskey Rebellion," in Michael P. Hanagan, Leslie Page Moch and Wayne te Brake, eds. *Challenging Authority. The Historical Study of Contentious Politics.* Minneapolis: University of Minnesota Press.

(1999): "Collective Violence and Group Solidarity: Evidence from a Feuding Society," *American Sociological Review* 64: 356–380.

Granovetter, Mark (1973): "The Strength of Weak Ties," *American Journal of Sociology* 78: 1360–1380.

Granovetter, Mark, and Charles Tilly (1988): "Inequality and Labor Processes," in Neil J. Smelser, ed. *Handbook of Sociology.* Newbury Park, CA: Sage.

Greif, Avner (1994): "Cultural Beliefs and the Organization of Society: A Historical and Theoretical Reflection on Collectivist and Individualist Societies," *Journal of Political Economy* 102: 912–950.

Greif, Avner, Paul Milgrom, and Barry R. Weingast (1994): "Coordination, Commitment, and Enforcement: The Case of the Merchant Guild," *Journal of Political Economy* 102: 745–775.

Grew, Raymond (1996): "The Paradoxes of Italy's Nineteenth-Century Political Culture," in Isser Woloch, ed. *Revolution and the Meanings of Freedom in the Nineteenth Century.* Stanford, CA: Stanford University Press.

Grimshaw, Allen D. (1999): "Genocide and Democide," *Encyclopedia of Violence, Peace, and Conflict* 2: 53–74. San Diego: Academic Press.

Gruner, Erich (1968): *Die Arbeiter in der Schweiz im 19. Jahrhundert.* Bern: Francke.

Gschwind, Franz (1977): *Bevölkerungsentwicklung und Wirtschaftsstruktur der Landschaft Basel im 18. Jahrhundert.* Liestal: Kantonale Drucksachen- und Materialzentrale.

Guenniffey, Patrice (2000): *La politique de la Terreur. Essai sur la violence révolutionnaire, 1789–1794.* Paris: Fayard.

Gumperz, John J. (1982): *Discourse Strategies.* Cambridge: Cambridge University Press.

Gunther, Richard (1992): "Spain: The Very Model of the Modern Elite Settlement," in John Higley and Richard Gunther, eds. *Elites and Democratic Consolidation in Latin America and Southern Europe.* New York: Cambridge University Press.

Gunther, Richard, Giacomo Sani and Goldie Shabad (1986): *Spain After Franco: The Making of a Competitive Party System.* Berkeley: University of California Press.

Gurr, Ted Robert, and Barbara Harff (1994): *Ethnic Conflict in World Politics.* Boulder, CO: Westview.

Gwertzman, Bernard, and Michael T. Kaufman eds. (1991): *The Collapse of Communism.* Revised edn. New York: Random House.

Haas, Ernst B. (1986): "What is Nationalism and Why Should We Study It?" *International Organization* 40: 707–744.

(1997): *Nationalism, Liberalism, and Progress.* Ithaca: Cornell University Press.

Hall, Peter (1986): *Governing the Economy: The Politics of State Intervention in Britain and France*. New York: Oxford University Press.

Hayes, Carleton (1966): *Essays on Nationalism*. New York: Macmillan.

Head, Randolph C. (1995): *Early Modern Democracy in the Grisons. Social Order and Political Language in a Swiss Mountain Canton, 1470–1620*. Cambridge: Cambridge University Press.

Hechter, Michael, and Satoshi Kanazawa (1997): "Sociological Rational Choice Theory," *Annual Review of Sociology* 23: 191–214.

Hedman, Eva-Lotta Elisabet (1998): *In the Name of Civil Society: Contesting Free Elections in the Post-Colonial Philippines*. Ph.D. diss. Department of Government. Cornell University.

Hedström, Peter, Rickard Sandel, and Charlotta Stern (2000): "Mesolevel Networks and the Diffusion of Social Movements: The Case of the Swedish Social Democratic Party," *American Journal of Sociology* 106: 145–172.

Hedström, Peter, and Richard Swedberg, eds. (1998): *Social Mechanisms. An Analytical Approach to Social Theory*. Cambridge: Cambridge University Press.

Hellman, Judith Adler (1983): *Mexico in Crisis*. New York: Holmes and Meier.

(1994a): *Mexican Lives*. New York: The New Press.

(1994b): "Mexican Popular Movements, Clientelism and the Process of Democratization," *Latin American Perspectives* 21: 124–142.

(1999): "Real and Virtual Chiapas: Magic Realism and the Left," in Leo Panitch and Colin Leys, eds. *Necessary and Unnecessary Utopias: Socialist Register 2000*. Rendlesham: Merlin.

Heredia Rubió, Blanca (1997). "Clientelism in Flux: Democratization and Interest Intermediation in Contemporary Mexico," Documentos de Trabajo del Centro de Investigación y Docencia Economicas, No. 31.

Higonnet, Patrice (1985): "The Social and Cultural Antecedents of Revolutionary Discontinuity: Montagnards and Girondins," *English Historical Review* C/396: 513–544.

(1998): *Goodness Beyond Virtue: Jacobins During the French Revolution*. Cambridge: Harvard University Press.

Hirsch, Paul M. (1986): "From Ambushes to Golden Parachutes: Corporate Takeovers as an Instance of Cultural Framing and Institutional Regeneration," *American Journal of Sociology* 91: 801–937.

Hobsbawm, Eric J. (1990): *Nations and Nationalism since 1789. Programme, Myth, Reality*. Cambridge: Cambridge University Press.

Hroch, Miroslav (1985): *Social Preconditions of National Revival in Europe: A Comparative Analysis of the Social Composition of Patriotic Groups among the Smaller European Nations*. Cambridge and New York: Cambridge University Press.

Hunt, Lynn (1984): *Politics, Culture, and Class in the French Revolution*. Berkeley: University of California Press.

(1992): *The Family Romance of the French Revolution*. Berkeley: University of California Press.

Huskey, Eugene (1997): "Kyrgyzstan: The Fate of Political Liberalization," in Karen Dawisha and Bruce Parrott, eds. *Conflict, Cleavage, and Change in*

Central Asia and the Caucasus. Democratization and Authoritarianism in Post-communist Societies: 4. Cambridge: Cambridge University Press.

Ingwerson, Marshall (1997): "Into the Steppe of Genghis Khan Ride the Conquerors of a Sea's Oil Bounty," *Christian Science Monitor*, electronic edition, August 18, 1997.

Jarman, Neil (1997): *Material Conflicts. Parades and Visual Displays in Northern Ireland*. Oxford: Berg.

Jenson, Jane (1998): "Social Movement Naming Practices and the Political Opportunity Structure," Working Paper 1998/114, Instituto Juan March de Estudios e Investigaciones, Madrid.

Johnson, Charles S. (1941): *Growing Up in the Black Belt*. Washington, DC: American Council on Education.

Johnston, Hank (1991): *Tales of Nationalism: Catalonia 1939–1979*. New Brunswick, NJ: Rutgers University Press.

Jones, Bruce (1995): "Intervention Without Borders: Humanitarian Intervention in Rwanda, 1990–1994," *Millennium. Journal of International Affairs* 24: 225–249.

Joris, Elisabeth (1994): "Auswirkungen der Industrialisierung auf Alltag und Lebenszusammenhänge von Frauen im Zürcher Oberland (1820–1940)," in Joseba Agirreazkuenaga and Mikel Urquijo (1994): eds. *Historias Regionales – Historia Nacional: La Confederación Helvetica*. Bilbao: Servicio Editorial, Universidad del País Vasco.

Joris, Elisabeth, and Heidi Witzig (1992): *Brave Frauen, Aufmüpfige Weiber. Wie sich die Industrialisierung auf Alltag und Lebenszusammenhänge von Frauen auswirkte (1820–1940)*. Zurich: Chronos.

Juraeva, Gavhar, and Nancy Lubin (1996): "Ethnic Conflict in Tajikistan," in Leokadia Drobizheva, Rose Gottemoeller, Catherine McArdle Kelleher and Lee Walker, eds. *Ethnic Conflict in the Post-Soviet World. Case Studies and Analysis*. Armonk, NY: M.E. Sharpe.

Kahin, George McT. (1952): *Nationalism and Revolution in Indonesia*. Ithaca, NY: Cornell University Press.

Kakar, Sudhir (1996): *The Colors of Violence. Cultural Identities, Religion, and Conflict*. Chicago: University of Chicago Press.

Kammen, Douglas (1999): "Notes on the Transformation of the East Timor Military Command and its Implications for Indonesia," *Indonesia* 67: 61–76.

Karl, Terry Lynn (1990): "Dilemmas of Democratization in Latin America," *Comparative Politics* 23: 1–23.

Kattenburg, Paul (1980): *The Vietnam Trauma in American Foreign Policy, 1945–1975*. New Brunswick, NJ: Transaction.

Katzenstein, Mary Fainsod (1998): *Faithful and Fearless: Moving Feminism into the Church and the Military*. Princeton: Princeton University Press.

Katzenstein, Peter J. (1984): *Corporatism and Change: Austria, Switzerland, and the Politics of Industry*. Ithaca, NY: Cornell University Press.

Keck, Margaret, and Kathryn Sikkink (1998): *Activists Beyond Borders: Transnational Activist Networks in International Politics*. Ithaca, NY: Cornell University Press.

Keddie, Nikki R., ed. (1995): *Debating Revolutions*. New York: New York University Press.

Khazanov, Anatoly M. (1995): *After the USSR. Ethnicity, Nationalism, and Politics in the Commonwealth of Independent States*. Madison: University of Wisconsin Press.

King, Martin Luther Jr. (1963): *Why We Can't Wait*. New York: Harper and Row.

King, Gary, Robert O. Keohane, and Sidney Verba (1994): *Designing Social Inquiry: Scientific Inference in Qualitative Research*. Princeton: Princeton University Press.

Klandermans, Bert (1994): "Transient Identities: How Activists Changed During the Life Cycle of the Dutch Peace Movement," in Laraña, Enrique, Hank Johnston, and Joseph R. Gusfield, eds. *New Social Movements: From Ideology to Identity*. Philadelphia: Temple University Press.

Knight, Alan (1992): "Mexico's Elite Settlement: Conjuncture and Consequences," in John Higley and Richard Gunther, eds. *Elites and Democratic Consolidation in Latin America*. Cambridge: Cambridge University Press.

(1993): "State Power and Political Stability in Mexico," in Neil Harvey, ed. *Mexico: Dilemmas of Transition*. London and New York: Institute of Latin American Studies and British Academic Press.

Kohn, Hans (1955): *Nationalism: Its Meaning and History*. Princeton: Princeton University Press.

(1956): *Nationalism and Liberty. The Swiss Example*. London: George Allen and Unwin.

Krauze, Enrique (1998): *Mexico: Biography of Power; A History of Modern Mexico, 1810–1996*. New York: Harper.

Kriesi, Hanspeter, Ruud Koopmans, Jan Willem Duyvendak, and Marco Giugni (1995): *New Social Movements in Western Europe. A Comparative Analysis*. Minneapolis: University of Minnesota Press.

Kriesi, Hanspeter, René Levy, Gilbert Ganguillet, and Heinz Zwicky (1981): *Politische Aktivierung in der Schweiz, 1945–1978*. Diessenhofen: Verlag Rüegger.

Kurzman, Charles (1998): "Organizational Opportunity and Social Movement Mobilization: A Comparative Analysis of Four Religious Movements," *Mobilization* 3: 23–49.

Laitin, David (1992): *Language Repertoires and State Construction in Africa*. New York: Cambridge University Press.

(1998): *Identity in Formation. The Russian-Speaking Populations in the Near Abroad*. Ithaca: Cornell University Press.

(1999): "The Cultural Elements of Ethnically Mixed States: Nationality Re-formation in the Soviet Successor States," in George Steinmetz, ed. *State/Culture. State Formation after the Cultural Turn*. Ithaca: Cornell University Press.

(2000): "Language Conflict and Violence: Or the Straw That Strengthened the Camel's Back," in Paul C. Stern and Daniel Druckman, eds., *International Conflict Resolution After the Cold War*. Washington, DC: National Academy Press.

Lamartine, Alphonse de (1848): *Histoire des Girondins*. 5 vols. Paris: Furne.

Lande, Carl H. (1986): "The Political Crisis," in John Bresnan, ed., *Crisis in the Philippines: The Marcos Era and Beyond*. Princeton: Princeton University Press.

(1987): "Introduction: Retrospect and Prospect," in Carl H. Lande ed. *Rebuilding a Nation*. Washington, DC: Washington Institute Press.

Lawson, Steven F. (1976): *Black Ballots: Voting Rights in the South 1944–1969*. New York: Columbia University Press.

Lewis-Beck, Michael S., Anne Hildreth, and Alan B. Spitzer (1988): "Was There a Girondist Faction in the National Assembly?" *French Historical Studies* 15: 519–536.

Lichbach, Mark Irving (1987): "Deterrence or Escalation? The Puzzle of Aggregate Studies of Repression and Dissent," *Journal of Conflict Resolution* 31: 266–297.

(1995): *The Rebel's Dilemma*. Ann Arbor: University of Michigan Press.

(1998): "Contending Theories of Contentious Politics and the Structure-Action Problem of Social Order," *Annual Review of Political Science* 1: 401–424.

Lichbach, Mark Irving and Alan S. Zuckerman, eds. (1997): *Comparative Politics. Rationality, Culture, and Structure*. Cambridge: Cambridge University Press.

Lindenberger, Thomas (1995): *Strassenpolitik. Zur Sozialgeschichte der öffentlichen Ordnung in Berlin 1900 bis 1914*. Bonn: Dietz.

Linz, Juan (1967): "The Party System of Spain: Past and Future," in Seymour Martin Lipset and Stein Rokkan, eds. *Party Systems and Voter Alignments: Cross-National Perspectives*. New York: The Free Press.

(1970): "An Authoritarian Regime: Spain," in Eric Allardt and Stein Rokkan. eds. *Mass Politics*. New York: the Free Press.

(1973): "Opposition In and Under an Authoritarian Regime: The Case of Spain," in Robert Dahl, ed. *Regimes and Oppositions*. New Haven: Yale University Press.

(1979): "From Great Hopes to Civil War," in Juan Linz and Alfred Stepan, eds. *The Breakdown of Democratic Regimes: Europe*. Baltimore: Johns Hopkins University Press.

Linz, Juan, and José Ramón Montero (1999): "The Party Systems of Spain: Old Cleavages and New Challenges," Estudio/Working Paper 1999/138. Madrid: Instituto Juan March de Estudios e Investigaciones.

Linz, Juan, and Alfred Stepan, eds. (1979): *The Breakdown of Democracy*. Baltimore: Johns Hopkins Press.

(1996): *Problems of Democratic Transition and Consolidation: Southern Europe, South America, and Post-Communist Europe*. Baltimore: Johns Hopkins University Press.

Lipset, Seymour Martin (1960): *Political Man: The Social Bases of Politics*. New York: Doubleday.

Lonsdale, John (2000): "Kenyatta's Trials: Breaking and Making an African Nationalist," in Peter Coss, ed. *The Moral World of the Law*. Cambridge: Cambridge University Press.

Lowi, Theodore (1971): *The Politics of Disorder*. New York: Norton.

Ludden, David, ed. (1996): *Contesting the Nation. Religion, Community, and the Politics of Democracy in India*. Philadelphia: University of Pennsylvania Press.

Lumley, Robert (1990): *States of Emergency: Cultures of Revolt in Italy from 1968 to 1970*. New York: Verso.

Lyttleton, Adrian (1991): "The Middle Classes in Liberal Italy," in John A. Davis and Paul Ginsborg, eds. *Society and Politics in the Age of the Risorgimento*. Cambridge: Cambridge University Press,

Mack Smith, Denis (1954): *Cavour and Garibaldi 1860: A Study in Political Conflict*. Cambridge: Cambridge University Press.

(1968): ed. *The Making of Italy, 1796–1870*. New York: Walker and Co.

(1969): *Italy, A Modern History*, rev. ed. Ann Arbor: University of Michigan Press.

(1985): *Cavour*. New York: Knopf.

Madan, T.N. (1997): "Religion, Ethnicity, and Nationalism in India," in Martin E. Marty and R. Scott Appleby, eds. *Religion, Ethnicity, and Self-Identity. Nations in Turmoil*. Hanover, NH: University Press of New England/Salzburg Seminar.

Malefakis, Edward E. (1970): *Agrarian Reform and Peasant Revolution in Spain: Origins of the Civil War*. New Haven: Yale University Press.

(1982): "Spain and its Francoist Heritage," in John W. Herz, ed. *From Dictatorship to Democracy*. Westport, CT: Greenwood.

Mamdani, Mahmood (1996): *Citizen and Subject. Contemporary Africa and the Legacy of Late Colonialism*. Princeton: Princeton University Press.

(2001): *When Victims Turn Killers: Colonialism, Nativism, and the Genocide in Rwanda*. Princeton: Princeton University Press.

Maravall, José Maria (1978): *Dictatorship and Political Dissent: Workers and Students in Franco's Spain*. New York: St. Martin's.

Marks, Gary T., ed. (1971): *Racial Conflict*. Little, Brown.

Marks, Michael P. (1993): "The Formation of European Policy in Post-Franco Spain: Ideas, Interests, and the International Transmission of Knowledge," Unpublished Ph.D. dissertation, Cornell University, Ithaca, New York.

Marx, Anthony W. (1998): *Making Race and Nation. A Comparison of the United States, South Africa, and Brazil*. Cambridge: Cambridge University Press.

Marx, Karl (1973): "The Eighteenth Brumaire of Louis Bonaparte," in David Fernbach, ed. *Surveys from Exile*. London: Allen Lane and New Left Review.

Maxwell, Kenneth, ed. (1983): *The Press and the Rebirth of Iberian Democracy*. Westport, CT: Greenwood.

Mays, Benjamin, and Joseph W. Nicholson (1969): *The Negro's Church*. New York: Arno Press and the New York Times.

McAdam, Doug (1982): *Political Process and the Development of Black Insurgency 1930–1970*. Chicago: University of Chicago Press.

(1983): "Tactical Innovation and the Pace of Insurgency," *American Sociological Review* 48: 735–754.

(1999): *Political Process and the Development of Black Insurgenc, 1930–1970*, rev. edn. Chicago: University of Chicago Press.

McAdam, Doug, and Dieter Rucht (1993): "The Cross-National Diffusion of Movement Ideas," *The Annals* 528: 56–74.

McAdam, Doug, and William H. Sewell, Jr. (2001): "It's About Time: Temporality in the Study of Contentious Politics," in Ronald Aminzade et al., *Silence and*

Voice in the Study of Contentious Politics. Cambridge: Cambridge University Press.

McAdam, Doug, and Sidney Tarrow (2001): "Charles Tilly: Big Structures, Large Processes, Enormous Headaches," *Journal of Complex Triangulations* 14: 1995–2000.

McAdam, Doug, Sidney Tarrow, and Charles Tilly (1997): "Toward an Integrated Perspective on Social Movements and Revolutions," in Mark Irving Lichbach and Alan S. Zuckerman, eds. *Comparative Politics*. Cambridge: Cambridge University Press.

McCarthy, John, and Mayer N. Zald (1973): *The Trend of Social Movements in America: Professionalization and Resource Mobilization*. Morristown, NJ: General Learning Corporation.

(1977): "Resource Mobilization and Social Movements: A Partial Theory," *American Journal of Sociology* 82: 1212–1241.

(1987): ed. *Social Movements in an Organizational Society*. New Brunswick and Oxford: Transaction Press.

McTeam, Dugney (2000): "Improbable but Fruitful Collaborations," *Review of Social Anomalies* 14: 237–261.

Meier, August, and Elliott Rudwick (1973): *CORE*. New York: Oxford University Press.

Merton, Robert K. (1968): "The Self-Fulfilling Prophecy," in *Social Theory and Social Structure*. New York: The Free Press.

Michels, Robert (1962): *Political Parties. A Sociological Study of the Oligarchical Tendencies of Modern Democracy*. New York: The Free Press.

Minnaar, Anthony (1992): *Patterns of Conflict. Case Studies of Conflict in Natal*. Pretoria: Human Sciences Research Council.

Montero, José Ramón (1997): "Secularization and Cleavage Decline: Religiosity, Electoral Behaviour, and Generational Change in Spain," presented to the ECPR Joint Sessions, Bern.

Moore, Barrington Jr. (1966): *Social Origins of Dictatorship and Democracy*. Boston: Beacon Press.

Morlino, Leonardo (1998): *Democracy Between Consolidation and Crisis: Parties, Groups, and Citizens in Southern Europe*. Oxford: Oxford University Press.

Morrill, Calvin (1996): *The Executive Way*. Chicago: University of Chicago Press.

Morris, Aldon (1984): *The Origins of the Civil Rights Movement: Black Communities Organizing for Change*. New York: Free Press.

Myers, Daniel J. (2000): "The Diffusion of Collective Violence: Infectiousness, Susceptibility, and Mass Media Networks," *American Journal of Sociology* 106: 173–208.

Nahaylo, Bohdan, and Victor Swoboda (1990): *Soviet Disunion. A History of the Nationalities Problem in the USSR*. New York: Free Press.

Newbury, David, and Catharine Newbury (2000): "Bringing the Peasants Back In: Agrarian Themes in the Construction and Corrosion of Statist Historiography in Rwanda," *American Historical Review* 105: 832–877.

Nirenberg, David (1996): *Communities of Violence. Persecution of Minorities in the Middle Ages*. Princeton: Princeton University Press.

O'Donnell, Guillermo, and Philippe C. Schmitter (1986): *Transitions from Authoritarian Rule: Tentative Conclusions about Uncertain Democracies.* Baltimore: Johns Hopkins University Press.

Oi, Jean C. (1991): *State and Peasant in Contemporary China: The Political Economy of Village Government.* Berkeley: University of California Press.

Olcott, Martha Brill (1997): "Democratization and the Growth of Political Participation in Kazakhstan," in Karen Dawisha and Bruce Parrott, eds. *Conflict, Cleavage, and Change in Central Asia and the Caucasus.* Democratization and Authoritarianism in Postcommunist Societies: 4. Cambridge: Cambridge University Press.

Oliver, Pamela (1989): "Bringing the Crowd Back In: The Nonorganizational Elements of Social Movements," in *Research in Social Movements, Conflict and Change* 11: 1–30, Greenwich, CT: JAI, 1–30.

Oliver, Pamela E., and Daniel J. Myers (1999): "How Events Enter the Public Sphere: Conflict, Location and Sponsorship in Local Newspaper Coverage of Public Events," *American Journal of Sociology* 105: 38–87.

Olson, Mancur, Jr. (1965): *The Logic of Collective Action.* Cambridge, Mass.: Harvard University Press.

(1982): *The Rise and Decline of Nations. Economic Growth, Stagflation, and Social Rigidities.* New Haven: Yale University Press.

Ozouf, Mona (1988): *Festivals and the French Revolution.* Cambridge, MA: Harvard University Press.

Paige, Jeffery M. (1997): *Coffee and Power.* Cambridge, MA: Harvard University Press.

Parsa, Misagh (1995): "Conversion or Coalition: Ideology in the Iranian and Nicaraguan Revolutions," *Political Power and Social Theory* 9: 23–60.

(2000): *States, Ideologies & Social Revolutions. A Comparative Analysis of Iran, Nicaragua, and the Philippines.* Cambridge: Cambridge University Press.

Patrick, Alison (1972): *The Men of the First French Republic: Policial Alignments in the National Convention of 1792.* Baltimore: Johns Hopkins University Press.

Payne, Charles M. (1995): *I've Got the Light of Freedom. The Organizing Tradition and the Mississippi Freedom Struggle.* Berkeley: University of California Press.

Payne, Stanley G. (1987): *The Franco Regime, 1936–1975.* Madison: University of Wisconsin Press.

Pérez Díaz, Victor (1990): "The Emergence of Democratic Spain and the 'Invention' of a Democratic Tradition," *Estudios/Working Papers 1990/1*, Madrid: Instituto Juan March de Estudios e Investigaciones.

(1993): *The Return of Civil Society: The Emergence of Democratic Spain.* Cambridge: Harvard University Press.

Pérez-Agote, Alfonso (1987): *El nacionalismo vasco a la salida del franquismo.* Madrid: Centro de Investigaciones Sociologicas.

Piven, Frances Fox, and Richard Cloward (1977): *Poor People's Movements: Why They Succeed, How They Fail.* New York: Vintage Books.

Plotz, John M. (2000): *The Crowd: British Literature and Public Politics.* Berkeley: University of California Press.

Poole, Jonathan, and Howard Rosenthal (1997): *Congress: A Political-Economic History of Roll Call Voting*. New York: Oxford University Press.

Prak, Maarten (1998): "Burghers into Citizens: Urban and National Citizenship in the Netherlands during the Revolutionary Era (c. 1800)," in Michael P. Hanagan and Charles Tilly, eds. *Expanding Citizenship, Reconfiguring States*. Lanham, MD: Rowman and Littlefield.

Preston, Paul (1986): *The Triumph of Democracy in Spain*. New York: Methuen.

Przeworski, Adam (1986): "Some Problems in the Study of the Transition to Democracy," in Guillermo O'Donnell, Philippe C. Schmitter and Laurence Whitehead, eds. *Transitions from Authoritarian Rule: Comparative Perspectives*. Baltimore: Johns Hopkins University Press.

Ragin, Charles C. (1987): *The Comparative Method. Moving Beyond Qualitative and Quantitative Strategies*. Berkeley: University of California Press.

(1994): *Constructing Social Research. The Unity and Diversity of Method*. Thousand Oaks, California: Pine Forge.

(2000): *Fuzzy-Set Social Science*. Chicago: University of Chicago Press.

Raines, Howell (1983): *My Soul is Rested: Movement Days in the Deep South Remembered*. New York: Penguin Books.

Rao, Hayagreeva, Calvin Morrill, and Mayer Zald (2001): "Power Plays: Social Movements, Collective Action and New Organizational Forms," *Research in Organization Behavior*. Forthcoming.

Rancière, Jacques (1992): *Les mots de l'histoire. Essai de poétique du savoir*. Paris: Seuil.

Ransom, Roger L. (1989): *Conflict and Compromise: The Political Economy of Slavery, Emancipation and the American Civil War*. New York: Cambridge University Press.

Reinares, Fernando (1987): "The Dynamics of Terrorism During the Transition to Democracy in Spain," in Paul Wilkinson and Alasdair M. Stewart, eds. *Contemporary Research on Terrorism*. Aberdeen: Aberdeen University Press.

Riall, Lucy (1998). *Sicily and the Unification of Italy: Liberal Policy and Local Power, 1859–1866*. Oxford: Oxford University Press.

Riker, William (1982): *Liberalism Against Populism*. San Francisco: Freeman.

Ringmar, Erik (1996): *Identity, Interest and Action. A Cultural Explanation of Sweden's Intervention in the Thirty Years War*. Cambridge: Cambridge University Press.

Robinson, Geoffrey (1998): "*Rawan* is as *Rawan* Does: The Origins of Disorder in New Order Aceh," *Indonesia* 66: 128–155.

Romeo, Rosario (1950): *Il Risorgimento in Sicilia*. Bari: Laterza.

(1963a): *Mezzogiorno e Sicilia nel Risorgimento* (Naples: Edizioni Scientifiche Italiane).

(1963b): *Risorgimento e capitalismo*. Bari: Laterza.

Rosberg, Carl G., Jr., and John Nottingham 1966. *The Myth of "Mau Mau": Nationalism in Kenya*. New York: Praeger.

Rosenband, Leonard N. (1999): "Social Capital in the Early Industrial Revolution," *Journal of Interdisciplinary History* 29: 435–458.

Rosenthal, Naomi B., and Michael Schwartz (1990): "Spontaneity and Democracy in Social Movements," in Bert Klandermans, ed. *Organizing for Change: Social*

Movement Organizations in Europe and the United States. International Social Movement Research 2. Greenwich, CT: JAI.
Roy, Beth (1994): *Some Trouble with Cows. Making Sense of Social Conflict*. Berkeley: University of California Press.
Rubin, Jeffrey W. (1997): *Decentering the Regime: Ethnicity, Radicalism, and Democracy*. Durham, NC: Duke University Press.
Russell, Diana (1974): *Rebellion, Revolution and Armed Force*. New York: Academic Press.
Rutherford, Danilyn (1999): "Waiting for the End in Biak: Violence, Order, and a Flag Raising," *Indonesia* 67: 40–59.
Rutten, Roseanne (1991): "Class and Kin: Conflicting Loyalties on a Philippine Hacienda," in Frans Husken and Jeremy Kemp , eds. *Cognation and Social Organization in Southeast Asia*. Leiden: KITLV Press.
(1994): "Courting the Workers' Vote in a Hacienda Region: Rhetoric and Response in the 1992 Philippine Elections," *Pilipinas* 22: 1–34.
(1996): "Popular Support for the Revolutionary Movement CPP-NPA: Experiences in a Hacienda in Negros Occidental 1978–1995," in Patricio N. Abinales, ed. *The Revolution Falters: The Left in Philippine Politics After 1986*. Ithaca: Cornell University Southeast Asia Program Publications.
Salvati, Michele (1981): "May 1968 and the Hot Autumn of 1969: The Responses of Two Ruling Classes," in Suzanne Berger, ed. *Organizing Interests in Western Europe*. New York: Cambridge University Press.
Salvemini, Gaetano (1955): *Scritti sulla questione meridionale, 1896–1955*. Turin: Einaudi.
Sanderson, Susan R. Walsh (1984): *Land Reform in Mexico: 1910–1980*. Orlando, FL: Academic Press.
Saul, John S. (1994): "Globalism, Socialism and Democracy in the South African Transition," *Socialist Register 1994*: 171–202.
Schama, Simon (1989): *Citizens: A Chronicle of the French Revolution*. New York: Knopf.
Schneider, Jane C., and Peter T. Schneider (forthcoming): *Reversible Destiny: Mafia, Antimafia, and the Struggle for Palermo*. Berkeley and Los Angeles: University of California Press.
Seidman, Gay W. (1993): "'No Freedom without the Women': Mobilization and Gender in South Africa 1970–1992," *Signs* 18: 291–320.
(1994): *Manufacturing Militance. Workers' Movements in Brazil and South Africa 1970–1985*. Berkeley: University of California Press.
(1999): "Gendered Citizenship. South Africa's Democratic Transition and the Construction of a Gendered State," *Gender and Society* 13: 287–307.
(2000): "Blurred Lines: Nonviolence in South Africa," *PS. Political Science & Politics* 33: 161–168.
Selbin, Eric (1993): *Modern Latin American Revolutions*. Boulder, CO: Westview Press.
Sewell, Richard H. (1976): *Ballots for Freedom: Antislavery Politics in the United States; 1837–1860*. New York: W.W. Norton.

References

Sewell, William H., Jr. (1985): "Ideologies and Social Revolutions: Reflections on the French Case," *Journal of Modern History* 57: 57–85.

(1994): *A Rhetoric of Bourgeois Revolution: The Abbé Sieyès and "What is the Third Estate."* Durham, NC: Duke University Press.

(1996): "Historical Events as Transformations of Structures: Inventing Revolution at the Bastille," *Theory and Society* 25: 841–881.

Share, Donald (1986): *The Making of Spanish Democracy.* New York: Praeger.

Sidel, John T. (1998): "*Macet Total:* Logics of Circulation and Accumulation in the Demise of Indonesia's New Order," *Indonesia* 66: 160–194.

Siegel, James T. (1998): "Early Thoughts on the Violence of May 13 and 14, 1998 in Jakarta," *Indonesia* 66: 76–06.

Silbey, Joel (1967): *The Transformation of American Politics, 1840–1860.* Englewood Cliffs, NJ: Prentice-Hall.

(1985): *The Partisan Imperative: The Dynamics of American Politics Before the Civil War.* Englewood Cliffs, NJ: Prentice-Hall.

Skocpol, Theda (1979): *States and Social Revolutions.* Princeton: Princeton University Press.

Smith, Anthony D. (1990): "The Supersession of Nationalism?" *International Journal of Comparative Sociology* 31: 1–31.

(1996): "The Origins of Nations," in Geoff Eley and Ronald Grigor Suny, eds. *Becoming National: A Reader.* New York: Oxford University Press.

Smith, Graham, Vivien Law, Andrew Wilson, Annette Bohr, and Edward Allworth (1998): *Nation-building in the Post-Soviet Borderlands. The Politics of National Identity.* Cambridge: Cambridge University Press.

Snow, David, and Robert Benford (1988): "Ideology, Frame Resonance, and Participant Mobilization," in Bert Klandermans, Hanspeter Kriesi, and Sidney Tarrow, eds. *From Structure to Action: Social Movement Participation Across Cultures.* Greenwich, CT: JAI.

(1992): "Master Frames and Cycles of Protest," in Aldon Morris and Carol McC. Mueller, eds. *Frontiers in Social Movement Theory.* New Haven : Yale University Press.

Snow, David A., E. Burke Rochford, Jr., Steven K. Worden, and Robert D. Benford (1986): "Frame Alignment Processes, Micromobilization, and Movement Participation," *American Sociological Review* 51: 464–481.

Snyder, Richard (1999): "After the State Withdraws: Neoliberalism and Subnational Authoritarian Regimes in Mexico," in Wayne A. Cornelius, Todd A. Eisenstadt and Jane Hindley, eds. *Subnational Politics and Democratization in Mexico.* La Jolla, CA: Center for U.S.-Mexican Studies.

Soboul, Albert (1980): "Introduction," *Actes du Colloque: Girondins et Montagnards.* Paris: Société des Etudes Robespierres.

Solnick, Steven L. (1998): *Stealing the State: Control and Collapse in Soviet Institutions.* Cambridge: Harvard University Press.

Spencer, John (1975): "KAU and 'Mau Mau': Some Connections," Unpublished Paper.

(1977): *The Kenya African Union 1944–1953: A Party in Search of a Constituency.* Ph.D. Study, Columbia University.

(1983): *James Beauttah, Freedom Fighter.* Nairobi: Stellascope Publishing Co.

Steinberg, Jonathan (1996): *Why Switzerland?* 2d edn. Cambridge: Cambridge University Press.

Steinberg, Marc W. (1999): *Fighting Words. Working-Class Formation, Collective Action, and Discourse in Early Nineteenth-Century England.* Ithaca: Cornell University Press.

Stinchcombe, Arthur L. (1991): "The Conditions of Fruitfulness of Theorizing About Mechanisms in Social Science," *Philosophy of the Social Sciences* 21: 367–388.

(1998): "Monopolistic Competition as a Mechanism: Corporations, Universities and Nation-States in Competitive Fields," in Peter Hedström and Richard Swedberg, eds. *Social Mechanisms. An Analytical Approach to Social Theory.* Cambridge: Cambridge University Press.

(1999): "Ending Revolutions and Building New Governments," *Annual Review of Political Science* 2: 49–74.

Strang, David, and John W. Meyer (1993): "Institutional Conditions for Diffusion," *Theory and Society* 47: 242–243.

Suny, Ronald Grigor (1993): *The Revenge of the Past. Nationalism, Revolution, and the Collapse of the Soviet Union.* Stanford: Stanford University Press.

(1995): "Ambiguous Categories: States, Empires, and Nations," *Post-Soviet Affairs* 11: 185–196.

Sydenham, Michael J. (1961): *The Girondins.* London: The University of London, Athlone Press.

(1974): *The First French Republic; 1792–1804.* Berkeley: University of California Press.

Tambiah, Stanley J. (1996): *Leveling Crowds. Ethnonationalist Conflicts and Collective Violence in South Asia.* Berkeley: University of California Press.

(1997): "Friends, Neighbors, Enemies, Strangers: Aggressor and Victim in Civilian Ethnic Riots," *Social Science and Medicine* 45: 1177–1188.

Tanner, Albert (1982): *Spulen – Weben – Sticken. Die Industrialisierung in Appenzell Ausserrhoden.* Zurich: Juris Druck.

Tarrow, Sidney (1989): *Democracy and Disorder: Protest and Politics in Italy 1965–1974.* Oxford: Oxford University Press.

(1998): *Power in Movement.* 2nd edn. Cambridge: Cambridge University Press.

(2001): "Transnational Politics," *Annual Review of Political Science*, 4, forthcoming.

Tierchant, Hélène (1993): *Hommes de la Gironde ou la Liberté eclairée.* Bordeaux: Dossiers d'Aquitaine.

Tilly, Charles (1964): *The Vendée.* Cambridge: Harvard University Press.

(1978): *From Mobilization to Revolution.* Reading, MA: Addison-Wesley.

(1993): *European Revolutions, 1492–1992.* Oxford: Blackwell.

(1995): "State-Incited Violence 1900–1999," *Political Power and Social Theory* 9: 161–179.

(1997): "Parliamentarization of Popular Contention in Great Britain, 1758–1834," *Theory and Society* 26: 245–273.

(2000): "Processes and Mechanisms of Democratization," *Sociological Theory* 18: 1–16.

(2001): "Mechanisms in Political Processes," *Annual Review of Political Science* 4, forthcoming.

Tomasi di Lampedusa, Giuseppe (1960): *Il gattopardo.* Milan: Feltrinelli.

Traugott, Mark, ed. (1995): *Repertoires and Cycles of Collective Action.* Durham, NC: Duke University Press.

Trechsel, Alexander (2000): *Feuerwerk Volksrechte. Die Volksabtimmungen in den schweizerischen Kantonen 1970–1996.* Basel: Helbing and Lichtenhahn.

Turner, Victor (1982): *From Ritual to Theatre: The Human Seriousness of Play.* New York: Performing Arts Journal Publications.

United Nations (1995): *Kazakhstan. The Challenge of Transition. Human Development Report 1995.* www.undp.org/undp/rbec/nhdr/Kazakhstan.

Uvin, Peter (1998): *Aiding Violence. The Development Enterprise in Rwanda.* West Hartford, CT: Kumarian Press.

van Klinken. Gerry (2001): "The Maluku Wars of 1999: Bringing Society Back In," *Indonesia*, forthcoming.

Vilas, Carlos. (1986): *The Sandinista Revolution: National Liberation and Social Transformation in Central America.* New York: Monthly Review Press.

Viola, Lynne (1996): *Peasant Rebels under Stalin. Collectivization and the Culture of Peasant Resistance.* New York: Oxford University Press.

Volkov, Vadim (1999): "Violent Entrepreneurship in Post-Communist Russia," *Europe-Asia Studies* 51: 741–754.

Walder, Andrew G. (1986): *Communist Neo-Traditionalism: Work and Authority in Chinese Industry.* Berkeley: University of California Press.

(2000): "Identities and Interests in the Beijing Red Guard Movement: Structural Explanation Reconsidered," Unpublished paper, Department of Sociology, Stanford University.

Walder, Andrew, Bobai Li, and Donald J. Treiman (2001): "Politics and Life Chances in State Socialist Regimes: Dual Career Path into Urban Chinese Elite, 1949–1996," *American Sociological Review*, forthcoming.

Waldron, Arthur N. (1985): "Theories of Nationalism and Historical Explanation," *World Politics* 37: 416–433.

Walton, John (1984): *Primitive Rebels: Comparative Studies of Revolution and Underdevelopment.* New York: Columbia University Press.

Wasserstrom, Jeffrey N. (1995): "Bringing Culture Back In and other Caveats: A Critique of Jack Goldstone's Recent Essays on Revolution," in Nikki R. Keddie ed. *Debating Revolutions.* New York: New York University Press.

(1991): *Student Protests in Twentieth-Century China: The View from Shanghai.* Stanford: Stanford University Press.

Weekley, Kathleen (1996): "From Vanguard to Rearguard: The Theoretical Roots of the Crisis of the Communist Party of the Philippines," in Patricio N. Abinales, ed., *The Revolution Falters: The Left in Philippine Politics After 1986.* Ithaca: Cornell University Southeast Asia Program Publications.

Weingast, Barry (1999): "Political Stability and Civil War: Institutions, Commitment, and American Democracy," in Robert Bates, et al., *Analytic Narratives*. Princeton: Princeton University Press.

Whitehead, Laurence (1995): "An Elusive Transition: The Slow Motion Demise of Authoritarian Dominant Party Rule in Mexico," *Democratization* 2: 246–269.

Wickham-Crowley, Timothy (1989): "Winners and Losers and Also-Rans: Toward a Comparative Sociology of Latin American Guerrilla Movements," in Susan Eckstein, ed. *Power and Popular Protest: Latin American Social Movements*. Berkeley: University of California Press.

(1992): *Guerrillas and Revolution in Latin America: A Comparative Study of Insurgents and Regimes since 1956*. Princeton: Princeton University Press.

(1994): "Elites, Elite Settlements, and Revolutionary Movements in Latin America 1950–1980," *Social Science History* 18: 543–574.

Willerton, John P. (1992): *Patronage and Politics in the USSR*. Cambridge: Cambridge University Press.

Youngblood, Robert L. (1982): "Structural Imperialism: An Analysis of the Catholic Bishops' Conference of the Philippines," *Comparative Political Studies* 15: 29–56.

(1987): "Church and State in the Philippines: Some Implications for United States Policy," in Carl H. Lande, ed., *Rebuilding a Nation*. Washington, DC: Washington Institute Press.

(1990): *Marcos Against the Church: Economic Development and Political Repression in the Philippines*. Ithaca: Cornell University Press.

Zald, Mayer N., and Michael A. Berger (1978): "Social Movements in Organizations: Coup d'Etat, Insurgency, and Mass Movements," *American Journal of Sociology* 83: 823–861.

Zhao, Dingxin (1997): "Decline of Political Control in Chinese Universities and the Rise of the 1989 Chinese Student Movement," *Sociological Perspectives* 40: 159–182.

(1998): "Ecologies of Social Movements: Student Mobilization during the 1989 Prodemocracy Movement in Beijing," *American Journal of Sociology* 103: 1493–1529.

(2000): *The Power of Tiananmen*. Chicago: University of Chicago Press.

Zolberg, Aristide R. (1972): "Moments of Madness," *Politics and Society* 2: 183–207.

Index

Index

Index

Made in United States
Orlando, FL
08 May 2024

46645283R00248